IMAGES of COLOR, IMAGES of CRIME

Readings

Coramae Richey Mann
Indiana University

Marjorie S. Zatz
Arizona State University

Roxbury Publishing Company
Los Angeles, California

Library of Congress Cataloging-in-Publication Data

Images of color, images of crime:readings/Coramae Richey Mann and
  Marjorie S. Zatz
  p. cm.
  Includes bibliographical references.
  ISBN 0-935732-97-7
  1.Crime—United States. 2. United States—Race relations.
  I. Mann, Coramae Richey, 1931-   . II. Zatz, Marjorie Sue, 1955-
HV6791.I48 1998
364.1'089'00973—dc21   97-23659
                                                             CIP

**Images of Color, Images of Crime:
Readings**

Publisher and Editor: Claude Teweles
Copy Editor: Helen Greenberg
Assistant Editor: Sacha Howells
Production Editors: C. Max-Ryan, Renée Burkhammer
Production Assistants: James Ballinger, David Massengill
Typography: Synergistic Data Systems
Cover Design: Marnie Deacon Kenney

Printed on acid-free paper in the United States of America. This paper meets the standards for recycling of the Environmental Protection Agency.

ISBN: 0-935732-97-7

Roxbury Publishing Company
P.O. Box 491044
Los Angeles, California 90049-9044
Tel: (213) 653-1068 • Fax: (213) 653-4140
Email: roxbury@crl.com

For all my students everywhere
CRM

For Rick, Richie, Patrick, and Cameron
MSZ

And for all oppressed people of color
CRM & MSZ

Table of Contents

Foreword
The Perils of Racial Prophecy

Derrick Bell

I envy the Old Testament prophets. Although greatly abused, the prophets were convinced that they held divine credentials, that quite literally they spoke for God. I have received no instructions from on high. Rather, I try to exact some small wisdom from 40 years of experience in every kind of civil rights work. Even so, I continue to learn from those I am trying to teach.

Take, for example, a discussion period following a public lecture when I was trying to respond to a question about the value of racism to this country. Quickly summarizing how beliefs in white superiority enabled the exploitation of blacks and the acceptance by so many whites of their relatively poor economic and social status, I contended that racism was a stabilizing force, the reason so many accepted our economic system despite its enrichment of a few and disadvantaging of so many. Racism, I concluded, was a value on so many levels that if black people had not existed, America would have invented us. In quick response, one old black guy whose wit and insight raised a serious question as to which of us deserved to be behind the podium, quickly responded:

"Professor, they did invent us."

Had Ursula Le Guin, the famous science fiction writer, been in the audience, she might have added: "They had to invent us." Every society has its scapegoat people whose presence provide the majority with a target for their frustrations, insecurities, and hate. Without them, internecine fighting would be endemic and anarchy an ever-threatening possibility.

Ms. Le Guin made her point in a memorable fable titled "The Ones Who Walked Away from Omelas." In it she portrays Omelas, an idyllic community where the citizens are prosperous and happy and much given to carnivals, parades, and festivals of all kinds. There is neither crime nor want in Omelas. Its leaders are wise and free of corruption. In a word, the people of Omelas live in an idyllic land. There is, though, a problem, one that forces some who learn of it—and some who have known of it for a long time—to conclude that they cannot remain and they leave Omelas. They leave and never look back, never return.

Having set the stage, she then explains that in a cellar of one of the beautiful buildings, a small child is held and forced to live in dank squalor. When visitors come to look at the child, they act cruelly, leave a small portion of bread and water, and then depart, ignoring the child's pathetic cries to be released, its heartfelt promises to be good.

While it is hidden away from public view, all the people of Omelas know the child is there, know that somehow its presence, its suffering, is the necessary ingredient in the success of their land, its prosperity, its peace, its beauty. Most know and accept the situation, but there are some who know and cannot accept. It is these who leave Omelas, never to return.

Omelas' open secret has scary connotations for African Americans and for all people of color in this country. Whether or not intended as such, the Omelas story is a marvelous metaphor for this country's racism. It suggests that in addition to providing a comforting sop to the poor and a convenient scapegoat for policymakers, racism connects all whites in a knowing but unspoken alliance. The writer bell hooks is right when she says that whites bond on the basis of race, whether that bonding is conscious or not. "And," she adds, "as paradoxical as it seems, viewing racism as an amalgam of guilt, responsibility, and power—all of which are generally known but never acknowledged—may explain why educational programs are destined to fail."

More important, the onus of this open but unmentionable secret about racism marks the critical difference between those able to claim whiteness as an identity and those who cannot. Here is the unbreachable barrier, the essence of why those not deemed white can never be deemed the orthodox, the standard, the conventional. Indeed, the fact that as victims we suffer racism's harm, but as a people, cannot share the responsibility for that harm may be the crucial component in a definition of what it is to be white in America.

This phenomenon is as old as this society. Because race, more specifically "whiteness," continues to serve as a connector spanning the gargantuan gap between those whites at the top of the economic ladder and most of the rest scattered far below, and because politicians and others can so easily deflect attention from what they are not doing for all of us to what whites fear blacks might do to them, I have concluded, sadly but with great certainty, that racism in America is a permanent phenomenon. Nothing in this book of essays does other than strengthen this conclusion.

Many view this prediction as despairing, not defiant. It is rejected out of hand by civil rights professionals, and those who pursue—despite all—the dream that "We Shall Overcome." Oh, I understand the conviction that "we must keep the faith." But just as we learn from the Book of James that faith without works is dead standing alone, just so, faith alone, serving as a sole shield against disaster, is fashionable foolishness.

We might wish it otherwise, but the daily reality will not permit us to deny that racism is alive and flourishing in this transitional period from one century to another. The civil rights gains, so hard won, are being steadily eroded. Despite undeniable progress for many, no persons of color are insulated from incidents of racial discrimination. Our careers, even our lives, are threatened because of our color. And even the most successful of us are haunted by the plight of our less fortunate brethren who struggle for existence in what some social scientists call the "underclass." Burdened with lifelong poverty and soul-devastating despair, they live beyond the pale of the American Dream.

Crime is that conduct a society finds threatening, and when that conduct is that of persons of color, it is—as the essays in this book make painfully clear—particularly threatening, the actor becoming a greater danger than the deed. The authors here, like a bevy of prophets, seek to provide details about aspects of life in America that, at some level, everyone already knows. In one way or another, the writers call for acknowledgment that might be the foundation of repentance. They do so with full knowledge of the usual fate of prophets. About the least dire fate for a prophet is that they preach, and no one listens; that they risk all to speak the truth, and nobody cares. ✦

Acknowledgments

We wish first to thank our students, who inspired this book. As professors teaching race and crime courses, we were frustrated by the lack of a book such as this one. We decided to undertake this project largely because of our sense that our students, and students elsewhere, needed to better understand the relationship between stereotypic images of color and images and realities of crime and punishment.

Many friends and colleagues encouraged us and provided valuable suggestions throughout the project. In particular, we thank Susan Caringella-MacDonald, Julius Debro, Drew Humphries, Nancy Jurik, and Dorothy Taylor. We also thank one another, as this was a truly collaborative effort and we both contributed equally. We extend our thanks to the Department of Criminal Justice at Indiana University and the School of Justice Studies at Arizona State University, as well as to our colleagues and students for their support and for providing an atmosphere conducive to this type of interdisciplinary, multiethnic project.

We thank Shelby Lunning, Cheryl Hanley-Muñoz, and Edwardo Portillos, all of Arizona State University, for their excellent research assistance in preparing the book. We also thank Mary Fran Draisker and Janet Soper of the College of Public Programs, Arizona State University, for their willingness to revise the manuscript continually as we wrestled with changes in terminology and layout. Mary Fran's valuable suggestions and skills in formatting and copy editing the manuscript were a tremendous help. Somehow, she remained cheerful throughout the project. We are grateful to Claude Teweles of Roxbury Publishing Company for inviting us to edit this book, for his patience with unexpected delays, and for his helpful suggestions throughout the process of developing and completing this project. We thank our copy editors at Roxbury for their capable assistance. We also gratefully acknowledge the constructive and insightful suggestions offered by the anonymous reviewers who commented on the manuscript.

We want to applaud publicly the scholars and activists who wrote chapters for us. All of the chapters are original contributions written specifically for this book. Unlike most readers, the way that we organized this book required the authors to adhere to strict guidelines about content so that it could come together as a seamless whole, and without undue repetition.

Finally, for their continuing support and encouragement, and for the love they have given us and the extra chores they have done while we worked, we thank our families and friends. It saddens us that Coramae's father, Edward Richey, is no longer with us to share her pride in this effort. But Rick, Richie, Patrick, and Cameron, you won't have to wait "just another moment" any longer—the book is done. ✦

About the Editors

Coramae Richey Mann, Professor Emerita at the Indiana University Department of Criminal of Justice and Professor Emerita at the Florida State University School of Criminology, received undergraduate and graduate degrees in clinical psychology from Roosevelt University in Chicago and her Ph.D. in sociology (criminology) from the University of Illinois, Chicago Circle. She received an American Sociological Association fellowship for graduate study and was also later awarded a postdoctoral Ford Research Fellowship.

Professor Mann's research has been directed toward those oppressed by the juvenile and criminal justice systems: youths, women, and racial/ethnic minorities. She is the author of over 30 scholarly articles and chapters on these topics and three books: *Female Crime and Delinquency* (University of Alabama Press, 1984), *Unequal Justice: A Question of Color* (Indiana University Press, 1993), and *When Women Kill* (SUNY Press, 1996).

In 1994 Professor Mann was appointed to the National Criminal Justice Commission with the goal of producing an independent critical assessment of the U.S. justice system that will lead to performance and equity improvements in that system. The final report of the Commission, *The Real War on Crime*, was released in February 1996 (HarperCollins). As a member of the American Society of Criminology Policy Task Force, Professor Mann recently advised U.S. Attorney General Janet Reno on drugs and the community.

Dr. Mann was the recipient of both the Bruce Smith, Sr., Award of the Academy of Criminal Justice Sciences and the Distinguished Scholar Award of the American Society of Criminology Division of Women and Crime in 1995. She was also the 1996 Fellow of the Academy of Criminal Justice Sciences and was awarded the 1998 Wayne G. Basler Chair of Excellence at East Tennessee State University.

* * *

Marjorie S. Zatz is Professor of Justice Studies at Arizona State University. She received her B.A. in sociology with a minor in Latin American studies from the University of Massachusetts and her M.A. and Ph.D. in sociology with a minor in Latin American studies from Indiana University.

Professor Zatz's research focuses on racial, ethnic, and gender-based discrimination in court processing and sanctioning; Chicano and Chicana gangs and the larger communities of which they form a part; the impact of juvenile and criminal justice policies on Chicano/a youths; gender and the legal profession; and social and legal change in Cuba and Nicaragua. She is the author of over 25 scholarly articles and book chapters, the author of *Producing Legality: Law and Socialism in Cuba*, published by Routledge in 1994, and the editor (with William Chambliss) of *Making Law: The State, the Law, and Structural Contradictions*, published by Indiana University Press in 1993.

Professor Zatz served as a member of the National Criminal Justice Commission from 1994 to 1996, when the Commission's final report, *The Real War on Crime*, was released by HarperCollins. In 1997, she received the Herbert Block Award of the American Society of Criminology. ◆

About the Contributors

Derrick Bell is an educator, writer, lawyer, and activist. He is a visiting professor at New York University Law School. He was previously a member of the Harvard Law School faculty—where he was that school's first black, tenured law professor—and the dean of the University of Oregon Law School. Bell's early career included work with the Civil Rights Division of the Justice Department and the legal team at the NAACP Legal Defense Fund. His scholarly writings have placed him in the forefront of Critical Race Theory, a new jurisprudence that explores the influences of society's racism and sexism on the law's policies and precedents. He is the author of *Race, Racism and American Law* (Little, Brown and Company, 1973), the third edition of which was published in 1992; *And We Are Not Saved: The Elusive Quest for Racial Justice* (Basic Books, 1987); *Faces at the Bottom of the Well: The Permanence of Racism* (Basic Books, 1992); *Confronting Authority: Reflections of an Ardent Protester* (Beacon Press, 1994); *Gospel Choirs: Psalms of Survival in an Alien Land Called Home* (Basic Books, 1996); and *Constitutional Conflicts* (Anderson Press, 1997). Bell's writings also have appeared in legal journals published by Harvard, Yale, and Berkeley, among others, and in the *New York Times Sunday Magazine*, *The Boston Globe*, the *Los Angeles Times*, and other respected news outlets.

Diego O. Castro is a doctoral student in the School of Justice Studies at Arizona State University. He holds a B.A. in political science from Washington University (St. Louis, Missouri) and an M.A. in policy studies from the University of Chicago. His areas of interest include contemporary critical theory, and power and oppression in higher education.

Donald R. Culverson is a Visiting Research Scholar in the African American Studies Program and Department of Political Science at the University of Houston. His primary research interests are African American politics and social/political movements. His current research concerns the relationship between social-economic structural change and the construction of race as a policy problem in American society. His published works are included in *Sage Race Relations Abstract*, *TransAfrica Forum*, and *Political Science Quarterly*. He has taught at Macalester College, the University of Wisconsin, and Syracuse University.

Laura T. Fishman, an Associate Professor of Sociology at the University of Vermont, holds an M.A. in sociology from the University of Chicago and a Ph.D. in sociology from McGill University. She has taught at Brooklyn College, City University of New York, and the New York University School of Social Work. After she completed her M.A., she worked as a researcher in several low-income areas of Chicago and New York City. Her research activities have culminated in the acquisition of streetwise familiarity with crime, drug distribution, and the administration of justice. Her major research interests include the criminalization of African Americans, drugs and American society, women and crime, domestic violence, and families of prisoners. She has published numerous articles in the field of criminology, and a book, *Women at the Wall: A Study of Prisoners' Wives Doing Time on the Outside* (Albany: State University of New York Press, 1990). Currently she is working on a manuscript that addresses the reactions of African American and Latino convicted offenders and their significant women to AIDS, imprisonment, and reentry.

Mark S. Hamm is Professor of Criminology at Indiana State University. He is the author of *American Skinheads: The Criminology and Control of Hate Crime, The Abandoned Ones: The Imprisonment and Uprising of the Mariel Boat People,* and *Apocalypse in Oklahoma: Waco and Ruby Ridge Revenged.* He is also the recipient of the 1993 Frederic Milton Thrasher Award for Outstanding Gang Scholarship, the 1995 Research/Creativity Award from Indiana State, and the 1996 Critical Criminologist of the Year Award from the American Society of Criminology. He is currently at work on a book about the dangers of conducting field research.

Suzan Shown Harjo (Cheyenne and Hodulgee Muscogee) is President of The Morning Star Institute, a Washington, D.C.-based national organization for Native Peoples' cultural and traditional advocacy and arts promotion. A poet, writer, curator, lecturer, and policy analyst, she has developed Native religious freedom, repatriation, sacred lands protection, and other federal Indian law and policy for more than 20 years and has helped Native Nations to recover more than one million acres of Native lands. Founding Co-Chair of The Howard Simons Fund for Indian Journalists and a Founding Trustee of the National Museum of the American Indian (1990-96), she also has served as News Director of the American Indian Press Association, as Executive Director of the National Congress of American Indians, and as a Carter Administration Special Assistant for Indian Legislation and Liaison. She is the mother of two grown children.

Taiping Ho is an Assistant Professor of Criminal Justice and Criminology at Ball State University. He earned his doctoral and masters degrees from Florida State University and worked as a police officer in Taiwan for several years. His current research interests include mentally retarded criminal defendants, the criminal justice system on the Cherokee Indian Reservation, police recruitment and testing processes, and Asian-organized crimes.

Bong Hwan Kim is currently on leave from the Korean Youth and Community Center (KYCC), a nonprofit organization based in Los Angeles, where he serves as Executive Director. Mr. Kim has played a major role in addressing the community-based development needs of Korean American and other disenfranchised minority communities throughout California for over 15 years. He has also been actively pursuing the private support of joint business ventures for job creation and economic development. Mr. Kim was a senate appointee to the California State Advisory Board on Drug and Alcohol Programs. He is a board member of Rebuild Los Angeles (RLA). He has served on numerous government and corporate advisory bodies including those of Pacific Bell, the Department of Health and Human Services, and Union Bank of California. Mr. Kim has also been Co-Chair of the Black-Korean Alliance and President of the Asian Pacific Planning Council.

Karen Joe Laidler teaches sociology and criminology at the University of Hawaii and at Hong Kong University. She has been involved in criminal justice research for over 14 years and has worked on projects in areas ranging from juvenile detention risk assessment and juvenile court intervention effectiveness to felony sentencing reform and prison crowding. For the last five years, her research has focused on drug use among women and Asian Americans, youth gangs, and the transnational character of crime in Hong Kong.

Peter Levin is a Ph.D. candidate in sociology at Northwestern University. His areas of interest are race and gender, with an emphasis on masculinity. He is particularly interested in the ways race, class, and gender intersect and interact in popular culture.

Carol Chiago Lujan, a member of the Diné (Navajo) Nation, is an Associate Professor at Arizona State University in the School of Justice Studies. She holds a Ph.D. in sociology from the University of New Mexico. Dr. Lujan is actively involved in American Indian issues and policy. She has worked directly with numerous Indian Nations across the country, including Native Nations located in the Southwest, the northern plains and the northwestern coast. During a two-year leave of absence from ASU, she worked with the Bureau of Indian Affairs as Director of the Office of Alcohol and Substance Abuse Prevention. While in this position, she gained considerable knowledge about and insight into the political structure and was able to directly observe politicians as they relate to and work with American Indian issues and governments.

Alberto G. Mata Jr. is Associate Professor of Human Relations at the University of Oklahoma and Visiting Research Scientist at the University of Texas San Antonio's Hispanic Research Center. He holds a Ph.D. from the University of Notre Dame. His research focuses on Mexican-American youth involvement with gangs and drugs, border health issues, and national and state policies for promoting community-based demonstration and applied research studies. He is currently completing a study of gangs, drugs, and violence involving South Texas youth, funded by the National Institute on Drug Abuse. Dr. Mata has served on a wide variety of national, state, and local advisory boards and planning groups, including the Presidential Commission on the HIV Epidemic.

Peggy McIntosh is Associate Director of the Wellesley College Center for Research on Women. She is founder and co-director of the National SEED Project on Inclusive Curriculum (Seeking Educational Equity and Diversity). She consults widely throughout the United States and the world with college and school faculty who are creating gender-fair and multicultural curricula. She is the author of many influential articles on curriculum change, women's studies, and systems of unearned privilege. McIntosh has taught at the Brearley School, Harvard University, Trinity College (Washington, D.C.), the University of Denver, the University of Durham (England), and Wellesley College. She is Co-Founder of the Rocky Mountain Women's Institute and consulting editor to *Sage: A Scholarly Journal on Black Women*. In addition to having two honorary degrees, she recently received the Klingenstein Award for Distinguished Educational Leadership from Columbia Teachers College.

Ada Pecos Melton is a member of the Pueblo of Jemez in New Mexico and Executive Director of American Indian Development Associates (AIDA). Her work includes conducting training sessions in various areas of the Indian justice system for tribes and organizations throughout the country and providing technical assistance in program development, public policy development, research and design of tribal justice and social services systems, and, in particular, incorporating the use of indigenous methods, traditions, practices, conflict resolution, and counseling to respond to issues of crime, violence, and victimization. She served as the Principal Investigator for a national American Indian and Alaskan Natives child abuse and neglect study funded by the Indian Health Service. Furthermore, as a member of the New Mexico Children's Code Task Force Subcommittee, she helped draft provisions for the current New Mexico Children's Code regarding Indian children in adoption cases and juvenile delinquency, child abuse and neglect, family-in-need-of-care, and mental health proceedings. Ms. Melton's public service experience includes work as a juvenile and adult probation officer; her administrative experience includes work as court administrator and director of juvenile programs for the Pueblo of Laguna and the Pueblo of Jemez, and most recently as Director of the American Indian and Alaskan Native Desk in the U.S. Department of Justice, Office of Justice Programs. She received both her bachelor of arts degree in criminal justice and her masters in public administration from the University of New Mexico.

Jerome Miller is the founder and Executive Director of the National Center on Institutions and Alternatives. He holds a doctoral degree in social work and has taught at The Ohio State University. He has directed juvenile justice detention systems in Massachusetts and Illinois. Most recently, he has served as General Receiver of the Washington, D.C., child welfare system. He is the author of *Search and Destroy: African-American Males in the Criminal Justice System* (Cambridge University Press, 1996) and *Last One Over the Wall* (The Ohio State University Press, 1991).

Jody Miller is an Assistant Professor of Criminology and Criminal Justice at the University of Missouri-St. Louis. Her research interests are race, gender, juvenile delinquency, and justice. She is currently working on a book about young women's involvement in gangs.

Thomas K. Nakayama is Associate Professor of Communication at Arizona State University. He writes in the areas of cultural studies and critical communication studies, focusing particularly on popular texts. His research deals with racial and sexual politics in contemporary cultural discourses.

William Oliver is currently Assistant Professor of Criminal Justice at Indiana University, Bloomington. He is a criminologist with research interests in the causes, dynamics, and prevention of interpersonal violence among African Americans. His most recent book is *The Violent Social World of Black Men* (Lexington Books, 1994), which examines the interpersonal dynamics of violent confrontations that occurred in bars and various street-corner settings. He is currently designing a research project that will focus on the interpersonal dynamics of violent confrontations involving female combatants. Professor Oliver is a graduate of Tuskegee Institute and received his M.A. and Ph.D. in criminal justice from the State University of New York at Albany.

Leon E. Pettiway is an Associate Professor in the Department of Criminal Justice at Indiana University, Bloomington. His research interests include urban crime patterns, environmental criminology, and race and crime, as well as the relationship between drug use and criminal activities. He has published articles in the *Journal of Quantitative Criminology, Criminology, Justice Quarterly, Urban Affairs Quarterly,* and the *Journal of Environmental Systems.* He is the author of *Honey, Honey, Miss Thang: Being Black, Gay, and on the Streets* and *Workin' It: Women Living Through Drugs and Crime,* both published by Temple University Press.

Edwardo L. Portillos is a doctoral student in the interdisciplinary Justices Studies Program at Arizona State University. His recent publications have focused on Chicano gangs, youth, and the criminal justice system. Mr. Portillos' research interests include issues of gender, race, ethnicity, and crime. He holds a B.A. in sociology/criminology from the University of Colorado at Boulder and an M.S. in justice studies from Arizona State University.

James Riding In is a Pawnee and Assistant Professor of Justice Studies at Arizona State University. He is a historian by training. His research focuses on the relationship between Indians and whites, particularly in the areas of repatriation, federal policy, and cultural survival. He teaches courses about social and Indian (in)justice.

Luis Rodríguez is a founder of Youth Struggling for Survival and the Increase the Peace Network in Chicago. He also directs Tia Chucha Press, a poetry publishing house, and is a founder of Los Angeles's Rock-A-Mole! Music, which produces innovative musical works from the city's most neglected communities.

Dennis M. Rome is an Assistant Professor in the Department of Afro-American Studies at Indiana University, Bloomington. He holds a doctorate in sociology from Washington State University, Pullman. His areas of interests include crime, race relations, and mass communications. He is currently writing an investigation of the media's presentation of African American males as criminals. ✦

A Point of Departure

In any anthology such as this, authors, editors, and readers must wrestle with the question of how best to refer to members of different racial and ethnic groups. Any selection of terms is a political decision, and preferences change over time and from one region of the country to another. While some of our contributors demonstrate such variation in their chapters, we have chosen to follow the terminology preferred by most of our authors as they write about themselves and other members of their racial/ethnic group in our intitial and concluding chapters, and in the introductions to the five major parts. These terms are "American Indian," "African American," "Latino and Latina," "Asian American," and "European." Please note further that hyphens are not used in this book, with the exception of Euro-Americans.

Throughout this book, we suggest a series of discussion questions. We ask that you begin by addressing the question: *What do you think each group should be called, and why?*

—The Editors

Chapter 1

The Power of Images

*Marjorie S. Zatz and
Coramae Richey Mann*

*I'm white inside
But that don't help my case
Cause I can't hide
What is in my face.*

("Black and Blue." Razaf,
Brooks, and Waller, 1929)

In the late 1920s the three African American musical geniuses listed above, one of whom was the renowned "Fats" Waller, wrote a haunting song called "Black and Blue." Among many other equally gifted African American vocalists over the years, Louis "Satchmo" Armstrong and Dinah Washington, "Queen of the Blues," recorded their renditions of the melody, each plaintively wailing, *"My only sin is in my skin. What did I do to be so black and blue?"*

The identical cry, "What did I do?", could be made by millions of other men and women in this nation as they, too, face exploitation, marginalization, powerlessness, and other forms of oppression simply because of the color of their skin. Because they look "different" from Americans of European descent and, in some cases, speak languages other than English, millions of people are stigmatized, stereotyped, and victimized by our social institutions—in particular, the juvenile and criminal justice systems and the police. This book tells their stories.

Images of Color, Images of Crime is designed to help readers recognize how popular perceptions of crime and criminality are racialized. By linking images of color with images of crime, the stereotypes underlying media reporting on crime and criminality become more apparent. The ways in which politicians have capitalized on the "race card" are also exposed. Once these linkages are understood, readers will be better equipped to recognize how racism permeates our society and its institutions.

With very few exceptions, books on race and crime usually focus on only one or two racial/ethnic groups. Even those authors who *do* include information about several groups tend to center most of their attention on African Americans. There are several reasons for this emphasis. First, in many regions of the country when people—and perhaps especially Euro-Americans—think about race, they think of African Americans. Second, a consequence of this focus on African Americans has been the practice by the U.S. Census Bureau and local police departments and courts, until very recently, to record ethnicity as white-nonwhite or black-white-other. As a result, quantitative data on the experiences members of other groups have had with the criminal justice system are very difficult to obtain. This leads to a third reason why books about race and crime tend to focus on African Americans—because there have been far more empirical studies of African Americans' experiences with crime and criminal injustice than those of any other group, and so there is more information available upon which authors can draw. In contrast, we devote equal attention to American Indians, African Americans, Latinos/as, Asian Americans, and Euro-Americans.

We use the word "color" quite purposefully in this book. We have found that when we and our students start thinking about skin hues, we immediately recognize the diversity within ethnic groups. Persons of Chinese, Japanese, Korean, or Samoan heritage, for example, are all Asian Americans, but there are profound differences among them based on culture and language, in addition to differences attributable to gender, income, age, sexual orientation, and physical abilities. Attention to color also reminds us of how fluid racial and ethnic boundaries are. For instance, the terms "Latinos" and "Latinas" refer to men and women from all parts of Latin America, whether from the Caribbean, Mexico, Central America, or South America. So how do we classify a black Cuban, or a black Puerto Rican? As an African American or as a Latino or Latina? What about a Cuban boy whose great-grandparents moved to Cuba from China and whose parents brought him to the U.S. as a young boy? Is he Asian American or Latino? Or how about the daughter of a Tarahumara Indian from Mexico whose parents moved to the United States before she was born? Is she American Indian or Chicana? We are all multiethnic if we go back far enough in our lineages. Thus, the key questions become "How do we view ourselves?" (self-identity) and, of at least equal importance when we have encounters with social control agents, "How do others view us?"

Race and Racism as Social Constructions

It is generally recognized today that race is a *social construction*. This means that (1) race is not a fixed identity—it is socially decided rather than biologically determined; (2) racial categories and the meanings attached to race make

sense only in their historical contexts and in light of specific social relations (e.g., slave-master, maid-employer, doctor-patient); and (3) racial dynamics are flexible, fluid, and *always* political (see further Omi and Winant, 1986; Frankenberg, 1993; Guillaumin, 1995). In some contexts, attributions of race can change overnight. Marvin Harris wrote in 1964 that Brazilians recognized 40 different racial types. In Brazil, and to a lesser extent in other parts of Latin America, one's "color" is based more on one's wealth and social status than on skin hue. In Harris' (1964, p. 59) words:

> In Brazil one can pass to another racial category regardless of how dark one may be without changing one's residence. The passing is accomplished by achieving economic success or high educational status. Brazilians say "Money whitens," meaning that the richer a dark man gets the lighter will be the racial category to which he will be assigned by his friends, relatives and business associates. Similarly, light-skinned individuals who rank extremely low in terms of educational and occupational criteria are frequently regarded as actually being darker in color than they really are.

Although some members of racial or ethnic minorities in the U.S. can "pass" as white, it is not uncommon for light-skinned African Americans to find that people who previously had acted friendly withdraw upon learning they are black. Also, education and wealth offer little protection from abuse by law enforcement agents. Physicians of color with M.D. emblems on their cars are pulled over routinely by police, as are minority lawyers, university professors, and other professionals. Sometimes they are stopped precisely because they are driving "fancy" cars (which could mean anything that isn't ready for the junk yard), the implication being that they must have stolen the car because a person of color could not possibly afford it.

Like race, racism is socially constructed. Whether we are talking about racist structures or racist ideologies, racism is all about power. Because conditions of dominance and subordination, and of control and resistance, differ across social and historical contexts, racism, too, must be multifaceted and flexible. That is, the ways in which racism displays itself—what we might call its form—change as social conditions change (Zatz, 1987a; Mann, 1993). For instance, it is hard to imagine a juvenile court judge today saying publicly what Judge Chargin of Santa Clara, California, told a Chicano boy in 1969: "You ought to commit suicide. That's what I think of people of this kind. You are lower than animals and haven't the right to live in organized society—just miserable, lousy, rotten people. . . . Maybe Hitler was right" (in Hernández, Haug, and Wagner, 1976, pp. 62–63). Although such overtly racist statements in courts of law are unusual today, stories of police beatings of young African American and Latino men are not. Rodney King's beating galvanized the nation because it was irrefutably visible on videotape, not because it was rare. The police departments of many major cities today face formal charges or citizen complaints of excessive force in subduing persons of color.

Race relations in our country are very complex, however, and we cannot assume that the same stance will be taken by all social control agents. Perhaps one of the most striking aspects of Judge Chargin's tirade is that it came from a member of the judiciary. While it is undeniable that some judges operate on the basis of racial prejudices, such overtly racial statements are rare today. More common are judges who simply follow the law because that is their responsibility, regardless of any personal concern that the law's effects may be racially biased. And yet, several Euro-American state and federal judges and the U.S. Sentencing Commission have taken public stands against the harsher penalties for possession of crack than powder cocaine because they view these statutes as racially discriminatory in their impacts, whether or not that was the intent of the legislators. In addition, the Minnesota Supreme Court in 1991 formally ruled that differing sentences for possession of crack and powder cocaine were racially discriminatory (Tonry, 1995; Donziger, 1996; Miller, 1996)

Defining Racism

This brings us to a very important point—the definition of racism. At its most general, "racism" can be defined as "social practices which (explicitly or implicitly) attribute merits or allocate values to members of racially categorized groups solely because of their 'race' " (Omi and Winant, 1986, p. 145). Although there are many positive aspects of our nation's history, it is also undeniable that our national economy was based initially on a system of slave labor, on the theft of land from American Indians, and on the conquest of massive territories from Mexico. As Cornel West (1994, p. 156) said of "this democratic experiment we call America,"

[it] began by taking for granted the ugly conquest of Amerindians and Mexicans, the exclusion of women, the subordination of European working-class men and the closeting of homosexuals. . . . What made America distinctly American for [European-Americans] was not simply the presence of unprecedented opportunities, but the struggle for seizing these opportunities in a new land in which black slavery and racial caste served as the floor upon which white class, ethnic, and gen-

der struggles could be diffused and diverted.

Accordingly, we must consider the ways in which economic, political, and social relations reinforce and perpetuate racial inequalities.

This perspective is in marked contrast to the view of those who would define racism simply as behavior that results from the prejudicial attitude of an individual. Like most social scientists, we think this narrow definition is seriously flawed. Everyone, regardless of skin color, has certain prejudices. However, not everyone has the *power* to act on the basis of them. So long as Euro-Americans continue to control the major political, economic, and social institutions in this country, including the criminal justice system, they have the institutional resources to discriminate, whereas people of color do not.

Racism has at least three guises: (1) *personal prejudice*, which, as we have discussed, is the most limiting view of racism and serves simply to disguise and defend racial privileges; (2) *ideological*, in which culture and biology are invoked to rationalize and justify the superior social, economic, and political position of Euro-Americans; and (3) *institutional*, in which the policies and practices of societal institutions operate in a way that produces systematic and persistent differences between racial groups (see further Wellman, 1977, p. 39; Omi and Winant, 1986; Goldberg, 1990). It is the *outcome* that matters most when we look at institutional racism. It does not matter whether those persons creating the policies and continuing the practices consciously intend to discriminate or not. As Daniel Georges-Abeyie (1990, p. 28) has noted, "the key issue is *result, not intent*. Institutional racism is often the legacy of overt racism, of *de facto* practices that often get codified by *de jure* mechanisms."

Another aspect of institutionalized racism is what Georges-Abeyie (1989, pp. 46-47) has called "petit apartheid realities." These are the everyday activities that contribute to poor relations between the police and persons of color, such as routine stop-and-question or stop-and-frisk law enforcement practices.

African Americans have been the victims of a particularly virulent form of racism because of their early status as slaves and because their continued economic plight has resulted in substantial media attention to segregated urban communities characterized by poverty, single-parent families, poor schools, and very visible street crimes. Nevertheless, American Indians, Asian Americans, and Latinos and Latinas have also suffered from arbitrary and legally sanctioned exclusion and from other forms of discrimination (see, among others, Takaki, 1979; Deloria and Lytle, 1983; Mirandé, 1987; Ringer and Lawless, 1989). And, as a number of the chapters in this book remind us, many of the red and brown people in this country were the only residents who did *not* immigrate here. "America" was their land initially.

One consequence of racism that echoes and exacerbates the deep schisms between American citizens is racial segregation in housing and jobs (for further discussions of how segregated housing and jobs have resulted in large part from racist real estate and lending policies and from economic restructuring at the regional, national, and global levels, see Moore and Pinderhughes, 1993; Hacker, 1995; Oliver and Shapiro, 1995). The proliferation of African American rural and inner-city ghettos, Latino barrios, and Chinatowns, and the shameful theft of land from Indians that left them on small, isolated reservations, reflect the imposed segregation that is "more entrenched in American cities today than ever imagined" (Steele, 1990, p. 79). This social isolation creates many deleterious effects, both structural (e.g., systematic differences in opportunities to acquire disposable income and to generate wealth) and psychological (e.g., being unable to understand what life is like for members of other groups).

As Peterson and Harrell (1992, p. 1) suggest, there are many ways to look at isolation:

> The concept of isolation has multiple dimensions. There is literal, physical separation such as the distancing of inner-city residents from the suburban locations where jobs are being created and the racial isolation imposed by segregated housing patterns. There is social isolation resulting from class homogeneity of contacts, and according to some authors, weak participation of inner-city residents in social organizations. There is the isolation imposed by high rates of crime and drug activity, as well as the habits of inner-city street life, where acceptance of neighborhood behavioral norms can progressively cut off access to mainstream society. . . . These dimensions of isolation overlap with one another and profoundly affect opportunity patterns.

The renowned African American sociologist William Julius Wilson made us intensely aware of the social isolation of inner-city African Americans in his classic work, *The Truly Disadvantaged*, in which he also introduced the controversial notion of the black "underclass."[1] Wilson described this underclass as "socially isolated," or lacking contact or "sustained interaction with the individuals or institutions that represent mainstream society" (1987, p. 60). Mainstream society, in this instance, was epitomized by gainfully employed people who lived in stable areas free from blight, who were not on public welfare rolls, and who could provide conventional role models (see further Fernández and Harris, 1992).

Racial Formation

Another term we must introduce here is "racial formation," the process by which we attach meaning and importance to racial categories (see Omi and Winant, 1986, p. 61). What it means to be African American in the United States at this time, for instance, is determined by social, economic, and political factors such as the globalization of the economy, the decline of the middle class, the political decision to wage a "war" on drugs and drug users, the assault on affirmative-action policies, and so forth. The meaning and material consequences attached to being black are thus different now from what they were at the apex of the Civil Rights Movement or under slavery.

At the individual level, racial formation is part of the process by which people formulate their identities; at the societal level racial formation is structural, based on social relations between groups. When we think about racial formation this way, it becomes clear that race plays a central role in social relations and cannot be reduced to something else, such as socioeconomic class or nationality. Thus, although a poor Euro-American person and a poor African American person will both face some of the same difficulties, such as an inability to pay the necessary bail to get out of jail until their trial date, their situations will not be identical. To the extent that these differences are structured in such a way that most African Americans have one set of experiences and most Euro-Americans another, the differences can be said to be racialized. More formally, "racialization" is "the extension of racial meaning to a previously racially unclassified relationship, social practice, or group" (Omi and Winant, 1986, p. 64). Racialization is an ideological process, and it is necessarily historically specific.

Race and gender as interlocking systems of oppression. Thus far we have been speaking only in terms of race; however, our relations with others and our societal institutions are simultaneously constructed along *gender* lines. Race, ethnicity, and gender intersect in multifaceted and interlocking ways. Sometimes, race or ethnicity is most salient; at other times, gender is most salient. But most of the time, race, ethnicity and gender cannot be separated. To try to do so risks splitting a person in two. Kimberlé Crenshaw (1991, 1992) refers to this as the "intersectionality" of race and gender. An African American woman is never just black, she is also always a woman; and she is never just a woman, she is also always black.

Failure to recognize this intersectionality has been the bane of the women's movement and of movements based on ethnicity. Many women of color have described feeling subordinated and oppressed in these contexts by the Euro-American women who felt that they could speak for every woman and by the men of color who felt that they could speak for everyone of color.[2] For instance, within the white women's movement a central concern has been the "public-private" split. This split reflects the invisibility and exclusion of Euro-American women from the public arena of the workplace and the state's reluctance to interfere in the private sphere of the home, where the women are to be found, because this is the jurisdiction, or "castle," of the man who lives there. Yet this split ignores the reality of many African American women's lives which are spent not only in the paid labor force but physically in the homes of wealthier Euro-American women, caring for their babies, scrubbing their floors, and cleaning their toilets.

The conflicts are not just between women, and they are not based solely on race, ethnicity, or class. There are also serious conflicts between men and women of the same race or ethnicity, as well as between straight and gay, liberal and conservative, and rich and poor women or men of the same race. As Toni Morrison (1992, p. xxx) states in the book she edited, appropriately entitled *Race-ing Justice, En-gendering Power:*

> It is clear to the most reductionist intellect that black people think differently from one another; it is also clear that the time for undiscriminating racial unity has passed. A conversation, a serious exchange between black men and women, has begun in a new arena, and the contestants defy the mold. Nor is it as easy as it used to be to split along racial lines, as the alliances and coalitions between white and black women, and the conflicts among black women, and among black men, during the intense debates regarding Anita Hill's testimony against Clarence Thomas's appointment prove.

If "intersectionality" describes how each person simultaneously experiences racial and gender oppression at the individual level, at the societal level we can speak of how race, gender, and class—the three fundamental and interrelated axes of our social structure—create interlocking systems of domination and oppression. As Margaret Anderson and Patricia Hill Collins point out, the patterns of race, class, and gender relations that are formed and reformed from this matrix affect individual consciousness, interactions between and within social groups, and group access to institutional power and privileges (Anderson and Collins, 1995,

p. xi; see also Frankenberg, 1993; Oboler, 1995).

The essays in this volume demonstrate that racial and ethnic stereotypes are very much gendered. Consider, for example, the centrality of gender to stereotypes of African American welfare queens, drunken American Indian men, and Latino drug-dealing gangbangers. Consider, too, Aunt Jemima of pancake batter and syrup fame; the evil Fu Manchu and the sexy Susie Wong; and Pocahantas and her Mexican counterpart, la Malinche, who fell in love with white conquerors and are depicted alternatively as race traitors and mothers of "new" races. Gender is very much a part of each of these racist depictions.

One of our aims in this book is to help unravel the ways in which these stereotypes reflect our *simultaneously racialized and gendered* social relations, institutions, and ideologies. We also want to help readers see that gender isn't just about women and race isn't just about people of color. *Everyone's* experiences are shaped by the interrelationships among race, gender, and class.

The faces of oppression and the power of stereotypes. When we begin to think about race and gender simultaneously and as inextricably interwoven, we also come to see what Iris Young (1990, pp. 48–65) has called the "faces of oppression." She identifies five such faces: exploitation, marginalization, powerlessness, violence, and cultural imperialism.

Exploitation is the process whereby the work performed by one group benefits a different group. Slavery is the starkest example of this form of oppression, but exploitation can also be seen in other contexts, such as when garment workers in the Third World and in U.S. slums are paid very low wages for their work and then the clothes they produce are sold for tremendous profits.

Young (1990, p. 53) suggests that today *marginalization* is a more common form of social oppression than exploitation. "Marginals," she suggests, "are people the system of labor cannot or will not use." Among other social categories, the marginalized may be old people, young African Americans and Latinos who are unable to secure jobs, single mothers, the physically disabled, or American Indians living on reservations.

Powerlessness refers to the daily situation of those who have little or no control over their working conditions. They can make few if any decisions in the workplace and are not allowed any creativity in designing the work product or even in deciding how best to do their work. No one reports to them, but they are constantly reporting to and being judged by others. Think of the clerk at a drug store, or a food server at McDonald's, or a factory worker on an assembly line and you will realize how little say any of these people have over their work conditions. They are powerless.

Hate crimes exemplify yet another face of oppression—systemic *violence.* Random, unprovoked attacks on persons or their property that have no purpose other than to damage, humiliate, or destroy the person and that occur *because* the person is a member of a given social group are oppressive. Consider, for example, the string of church burnings throughout the South in recent years—31 incidents since 1989 (Klanwatch Intelligence Report, May 1996, p. 12). These churches were set on fire solely because most members of their congregations were African American. Consider too the practice of "gay bashing," in which groups of straight young men go looking for gay men to beat up; the looting of Korean groceries; the painting of swastikas on synagogues; and the old practice of giving "gifts" of smallpox-infested blankets to American Indians.

The final face of oppression identified by Young is *cultural imperialism.* This occurs when members of one group, which has power over another group, assume that their way of doing something is the only way. The dominant group's experiences, values, goals, and achievements are taken as normal, as the way things are. And thus it becomes surprising when members of a subordinated group do things differently, whether we are speaking of styles of dress, religious practices, ways of conducting business, or any other category.

Stereotyping is an important part of cultural imperialism. Typically, stereotypes connect something about the "nature" of subordinated groups to an undeniable and often visible aspect of their bodies. Young (1990, p. 59) states:

> These stereotypes so permeate the society that they are not noticed as contestable. Just as everyone knows that the earth goes around the sun, so everyone knows that gay people are promiscuous, that Indians are alcoholics, and that women are good with children. White males, on the other hand, insofar as they escape group marking, can be individuals.

Ironically, it is the very invisibility of race when we are talking about Euro-Americans, and of gender when we are talking about men, that should signal to us that we are dealing with a social construction. Members of certain groups—Euro-Americans, men, heterosexuals, the able-bodied, the wealthy—often do not even recognize their own privilege. They simply take it for granted as "normal." The danger, of course, is that anyone different becomes "not normal," or "the Other."

The media play very important roles in portraying members of some groups as normal and others as Other. In particular, films and television programs use the power of visual images to create and reinforce stereotypic images of Others as scary and different. As Michael Omi and Howard Winant (1986, p. 63) suggest, these media "have been notorious in disseminating images of racial minorities which establish for audiences what people from these groups look like, how they behave, and 'who they are.' The power of the media lies not in their ability to reflect the dominant racial ideology, but in their capacity to shape that ideology in the first place." They note further that efforts to reach a large and diverse television audience have led "to the perpetuation of racial caricatures, as racial stereotypes serve as shorthand for scriptwriters, directors and actors."

Organization of the Book

We have called this book *Images of Color, Images of Crime* because we hope to help readers recognize that the myriad images confronting them daily are racialized and gendered. Except in old movies, images are not black and white; they come in a multitude of hues and tones. Generally speaking, the darker the color, the greater the evil associated with it and the more dehumanizing the stereotypes (Steele, 1990, p. 43). When *Time* magazine altered O.J. Simpson's skin color, making him appear darker than he is, many African Americans were furious because the news weekly appeared to recognize that a darker skin tone would cause people to react negatively to Simpson and because *Time* used this artistic trick to attract readers. It appeared, then, that *Time* was making money by playing into racist stereotypes of violent African American men.

Attention to "color" also reminds us that not all people of that "color" identify as a group. We tend to think of all Asian Americans as "Orientals," lumping together Japanese Americans and Chinese Americans, for example. Yet their cultures and languages are very different, and historically there has been great antipathy between the Japanese and Chinese peoples. We could take this reasoning a step further. When we think of people from China, we tend to think of members of the dominant Chinese ethnic group, ignoring other groups indigenous to China that were conquered by the Han. It is only when "yellow" people are made the Other that we forget their tremendous heterogeneity.

We know of no other book that devotes equal attention to all of the major racial/ethnic groups in the U.S. To draw attention to the heterogeneity of racial and ethnic groups, not only in terms of gender, wealth, sexual orientation, and physical abilities but also and fundamentally in terms of skin coloration, we toy with the word "color." The sections of this book are organized in terms of the colors red, black, brown, yellow, and white. Although there are many pinkish skin tones called "white," white is not a color in the same way as the others are. It is, as we discussed above, the very invisibility of white skin to Euro-Americans, the fact that Euro-Americans do not notice when someone else is white, but only when they are *not* white, that accords Euro-Americans racial privilege in our society.

Thinking in terms of gender may make this point more apparent. Everyone and everything is gendered, but it is the presence of women in certain settings that reminds us that we have taken the presence of men and the invisibility of women for granted. Parents of young children today often must remind their preschoolers that because many members of the police force are women, we call all of them police *officers* rather than police*men*. Use of the gendered terms police*men*, fire*men*, garbage*men*, and so forth evokes images of men, even though many of the persons in these occupations are women. This is also why we purposely use the terms "Latinos and Latinas" or "Latinos/as" instead of subsuming Latinas under the term "Latino." From our perspective, "Latinos" doesn't include women any more than does "mankind." Both terms make men the norm and make women invisible. Throughout this book, we try to jolt readers out of such complacency.

The chapters in this book offer numerous examples of the ways in which American Indian, African American, Latino/a, and Asian American men and women experience oppression and domination. Although our primary emphasis is on racial oppression, our identities, social relations, and institutions are not solely racialized; they are also gendered. In some circumstances, the ways in which social structures and ideologies are racialized are clearly apparent. In others, the ways in which they are gendered are readily visible, but they are always and simultaneously *both* racialized and gendered.

Each section begins with a chapter written in a narrative, storytelling format. This genre of writing, which is often associated with Critical Race Theory, merges autobiographical material with theoretical and historical insights to jar readers out of their comfortable assumptions. The personal narratives help readers to understand better how it feels to be treated in particular ways because of one's skin color, primary language, and culture, thereby debunking some of the popular stereotypes about people of that color. The second and third chapters in each section address stereotyping by the media and by politicians, respectively. These chapters focus attention on how and why particular stereotypes were generated, the role of the media and politicians in creating or perpetuating these stereotypes, and the effects of the stereotypes on the racial/ethnic group and on society more generally. As we have mentioned above and as the authors of these chapters demonstrate artfully, the film and television media (and to a lesser extent the print media) are very powerful conveyers of racist ideology. Given the importance of media images to electoral politics today, it is perhaps not surprising that politicians have very effectively used what has come to be called the "race card" in their campaigns. The final chapter in each section builds upon its predecessors to show how these racialized images relate to issues of crime and punishment. The contributors unravel the types of discrimination faced by members of that racial or ethnic group when they come into contact with social control agents, helping readers to understand better the ways in which their experiences with the criminal and juvenile justice systems, as well as their experiences as victims of crime, are racialized and gendered. Following the major five sections of the book, we conclude with a discussion of some of the policy recommendations raised by the contributors and our own reflections about the political and social implications of linking images of crime with images of color.

This book seeks to help readers understand better the complex and multifaceted relations between color and crime. In particular, it seeks to clarify the linkages between (1) social structures that institutionalize racism by reinforcing dominant/subordinate group relations; (2) stereotypic perceptions of members of different racial and ethnic groups and the complicity of the media and politicians in maintaining these stereotypes; (3) racialized images of crime and criminology; and (4) vari-

ation in how the criminal and juvenile justice systems respond to people of different colors.

Finally, readers have a right to know who we, the editors and authors, are, particularly given the unique and personal approach taken in this book. We, the editors, are two women, one black, the other white. The authors of the chapters in each section are all persons of that "color." Some are men, some are women. Some are gay, some are straight. Some are younger, some are older; a few are graduate students, others are established academics, and still others are political activists. The academic authors represent a wide range of disciplines including sociology, political science, history, communication, criminology, and women's studies. As a group, then, we are very diverse. Our hope is that you, the readers, will come to better recognize and value that diversity of perspectives—not only in the chapters of this book, but in all aspects of your lives.

Notes

1. For a critique of the concept of the underclass as it applies to Latinos/as, see Moore and Pinderhughes (1993).
2. See, for instance, the following collections of writings by women of color: *This Bridge Called My Back: Writings by Radical Women of Color*, edited by Cherríe Moraga and Gloria Anzaldúa(1983); *All the Women Are White, All the Blacks Are Men, But Some of Us Are Brave: Black Women's Studies*, edited by Gloria Hull (1981); *Making Face, Making Soul: Haciendo Caras: Creative and Critical Perspectives by Women of Color*, edited by Gloria Anzaldúa (1990); and *Building with Our Hands: New Directions in Chicana Studies*, edited by Adele de la Torre and Beatríz Pesquera (1993).

References

Anderson, Margaret L., and Collins, Patricia Hill (Eds.). (1995). *Race, class, and gender: An anthology.* 2nd ed. Belmont, CA: Wadsworth Publishing Co.

Anzaldúa, Gloria (Ed.). (1990). *Making face, making soul: Haciendo caras: Creative and critical perspectives by women of color.* San Francisco: Aunt Lute Foundation.

Crenshaw, Kimberlé. (1992). "A black feminist critique of antidiscrimination law." In David Kairys (Ed.), *The politics of law: A progressive critique.* Rev. ed. New York: Pantheon Books, 195–218.

———. (1991). "Mapping the margins: Intersectionality, identity politics, and violence against women of color." *Stanford Law Review, 43,* 1241–1299.

de la Torre, Adela, and Pesquera, Beatríz M. (Eds.). (1993). *Building with our hands: New directions in Chicana studies.* Berkeley: University of California Press.

Deloria, Vine, Jr., and Lytle, Clifford M. (1983). *American Indians, American justice.* Austin: University of Texas Press.

Donziger, Steven A. (Ed.). (1996). *The real war on crime: The report of the National Criminal Justice Commission.* New York: Harper Perennial.

Fernández, Roberto M., and Harris, David. (1992). "Social isolation and the underclass." In Adele V. Harrell and George E. Peterson (Eds.), *Drugs, crime, and social isolation: Barriers to urban opportunity.* Washington, DC: Urban Institute Press.

Frankenberg, Ruth. (1993). *White women, race matters: The social construction of whiteness.* Minneapolis: University of Minnesota Press.

Georges-Abeyie, Daniel E. (1990). "Criminal processing of non-white minorities." In Brian D. MacLean and Dragan Milovanovic (Eds.), *Racism, empiricism and criminal justice.* Vancouver: Collective Press.

———. (1989). "Race, ethnicity, and the spacial dynamic: Toward a realistic study of black crime, crime victimization, and criminal justice processing of blacks." *Social Justice, 16* (4), 35–54.

Goldberg, David Theo (Ed.). (1990). *Anatomy of racism.* Minneapolis: University of Minnesota Press.

Guillaumin, Colette. (1995). *Racism, sexism, power and ideology.* New York: Routledge.

Hacker, Andrew. (1995). *Two nations: Black and white, separate, hostile, unequal.* New York: Ballantine Books.

Harris, Marvin. (1964). *Patterns of race in the Americas.* New York: W.W. Norton and Company.

Hernández, C.A., Haug, M.J., and Wagner, N.N. (1976). *Chicanos: Social and psychological perspectives.* St. Louis: C.V. Mosby.

Hull, Gloria T. (Ed.). (1981). *All the women are white, all the blacks are men, but some of us are brave: Black women's studies.* Old Westbury, NY: The Feminist Press.

Klanwatcher Intelligence Report. (1996, May). Southern Poverty Law Center, 12.

Mann, Coramae Richey. (1993). *Unequal justice: A question of color.* Bloomington: Indiana University Press.

Miller, Jerome G. (1996). *Search and destroy: African-American males in the criminal justice system.* Cambridge: Cambridge University Press.

Mirandé, Alfredo. (1987). *Gringo justice.* Notre Dame, IN: University of Notre Dame Press.

Moore, Joan W., and Pinderhughes, Raquel (Eds.). (1993). *In the barrios: Latinos and the underclass debate.* New York: Russell Sage Foundation.

Moraga, Cherríe, and Anzaldúa, Gloria (Eds.). (1983). *This bridge called my back: Writings by radical women of color.* New York: Kitchen Table, Women of Color Press.

Morrison, Toni (Ed.). (1992). *Race-ing, justice, en-gendering power: Essays on Anita Hill, Clarence Thomas, and the construction of social reality.* New York: Pantheon Books.

Oboler, Suzanne. (1995). *Ethnic labels, Latino lives: Identity and the politics of (re)presentation in the United States.* Minneapolis: University of Minnesota Press.

Oliver, Melvin L., and Shapiro, Thomas M. (1995). *Black wealth/white wealth: A new perspective on racial inequality.* New York: Routledge.

Omi, Michael, and Winant, Howard. (1986). *Racial formation in the United States: From the 1960s to the 1980s.* New York: Routledge and Kegan Paul.

Peterson, George E., and Harrell, Adele V. (1992). "Introduction: Inner-city isolation and opportunity." In Adele V. Harrell and George E. Peterson (Eds.), *Drugs, crime, and social isolation: Barriers to urban opportunity*. Washington, DC: The Urban Institute Press.

Ringer, Benjamin B., and Lawless, Elinor R. (1989). *Race-ethnicity and society*. New York: Routledge.

Steele, Shelby. (1990). *The content of our character*. New York: St. Martin's Press.

Takaki, Ronald T. (1979). *Iron cages: Race and culture in nineteenth-century America*. New York: Alfred A. Knopf.

Tonry, Michael. (1995). *Malign neglect: Race, crime, and punishment in America*. New York: Oxford University Press.

Wellman, David T. (1977). *Portraits of white racism*. New York: Cambridge University Press.

West, Cornel. (1994). *Race matters*. New York: Vintage Books.

Wilson, William Julius. (1987). *The truly disadvantaged: The inner city, the underclass, and public policy*. Chicago: University of Chicago Press.

Young, Iris Marion. (1990). *Justice and the politics of difference*. Princeton NJ: Princeton University Press.

Zatz, Marjorie S. (1987a). "The changing forms of racial/ethnic biases in sentenc-ing." *Journal of Research in Crime and Delinquency, 24* (1), 69–92.

———. (1987b). "Chicano youth gangs and crime: The creation of a moral panic." *Contemporary Crisis, 11*, 129–158.

Discussion Questions

1. How do images of crime and criminology emerge in the course of dominant/subordinate group relations?

2. How are our society's institutions, ideologies, and images racialized and gendered? Provide at least one gendered and one racialized image that is not mentioned in the chapter.

3. What do we mean when we say that race is a "social construction?" Provide an example illustrating this concept.

4. Why is attention to stereotypes so important?

5. Discuss at least three of the five faces of oppression identified by Iris Young. Provide an example to illustrate each. ✦

Part I

The Color Red

In recent years, non-Indians have become increasingly interested in American Indian cultures. American Indian art and jewelry are now very fashionable, and people come from all over the United States to watch powwows and other cultural events open to the general public. Non-Indian children are still told that they are acting "like wild Indians" when they are unruly and are warned that if they continue to misbehave, their parents might "sell them to the Indians." Horrific images of flying tomahawks are tempered a bit, however, by popular culture's depictions of some Indians as "noble savages."

The government of the United States recognizes 557 distinct American Indian and Alaska Native nations.[1] The tremendous diversity that exists among them in terms of language, customs, gender relations, and control over natural resources and other sources of wealth, among other factors, is also visible in their diverse governmental structures and judicial systems. Because each of these sovereign nations has separate relations with the federal government and with state and local governments, making sense of all of these intertwined governmental and juridical structures and relationships can be-

come exceedingly complex. These complexities are perhaps especially apparent when crimes occur on Indian reservations as, depending on the offense and the circumstances, multiple jurisdictions may become involved.

In many respects, little has changed since Robert Berkhofer discussed the ways in which stereotypic images have been used as political instruments against American Indian sovereignty, culture, and land holdings in his 1978 book, *The White Man's Indian*. Our history books still tell us very little about the relations between the European colonizers and settlers and the American Indian peoples after the Pilgrims' first Thanksgiving dinner, and the sovereign status of American Indian governments is still not well understood by the general public. For these reasons, the authors in this section have included background information to help non-Indians better understand these historical and contemporary relations and their ramifications.

These authors bring us a sense of the strength and perseverance of American Indian communities, even after centuries of physical and cultural genocide, theft of American Indian lands, and other institutionalized forms of racism.

They also highlight some of the negative stereotypes that have caused the most damage to American Indian people and their respective governments. The stereotype of the drunken Indian has been one of the most pernicious, with most crimes involving American Indians associated in some way with perceptions of widespread alcoholism.

In the last few years, a few tribes have established casinos. The casinos provide jobs for previously unemployed persons, both Indian and non-Indian. They contribute to tourism in ways that are approved by tribal leaders, and the revenues from gambling have been used to improve living conditions for these communities. Casinos also benefit the regional economy through the growth of hotels and fast-food restaurants. Efforts by local and state governments to restrict development of casinos on tribal land are often couched in terms of a fear that organized crime will follow the casinos onto the reservations. Yet from the perspective of tribal leaders, this fear reflects perceptions of ignorant savages who would squander their new found wealth and be incapable of countering efforts by "the Mafia" to muscle their way into the casinos. After all, if Indians sold Manhattan for a few strings of colored beads, how can they control the gambling industry?

Tribal leaders, however, are more concerned about the effects of poverty on their people than they are about the risk that organized crime will try to take over their casinos. As the authors in this section demonstrate, poverty, not gambling or alcohol, is the primary cause of crime and delinquency on American Indian lands. Specifically, they relate poverty and lack of opportunity to the growing allure of gangs for poor American Indian teenagers.

Note

1. Many American Indians and the federal government use the term "American Indian and Alaska Native" to include the Aleut and Inuit peoples living in what is now the state of Alaska because the designation "American Indian" often refers only to those persons and nations within the contiguous borders of the continental United States.

References

Berkhofer, Robert F., Jr. (1978). *The white man's Indian: Images of the American Indian from Columbus to the present.* New York: Vintage Books. ◆

Chapter 2

Images of American Indians

American Indians in Popular Culture: A Pawnee's Experiences and Views

James Riding In

Being native in contemporary U.S. society offers us Indians both comfort and conflict. Rich cultural heritages continue to shape our world views, customs, and values in an often hostile and complex world that demands conformity in thought, action, and deed. Our traditions on the North American continent preceded the first arrival of European colonizers in the late 1400s by millennia. Despite repetitive efforts by the newcomers to strip us of our customary life ways, our ancestors found means to maintain their political and social identity. Native ceremonies, kinship systems, names, social gatherings, humor, food, and oral traditions provide us a sense of identity, pride, and self-respect. We have also incorporated new ideas gained through contact with others into our traditional ways of life. We are not a vanishing race.

U.S. society has a long legacy of concocting stereotypes to define Indians and using them as powerful ideological

and political devices to rationalize acts of aggression and hostility. Imagery frequently provides basic assumptions about the moral character and worth of a people, and changes over time. Legal thinkers, scholars, and others have drawn upon the beliefs and imagery found in popular culture. As the United States grew to its current size and Indian nations lost their ability to offer military challenges, the stereotypes have undergone revision. Non-Indians have presented Indians as either demonic or untainted children of nature. Often these images coexist, depending on the racial attitudes, issues, and conditions. Many have relegated us to the lowly status of objects of amusement, scorn, and ridicule, whereas others have elevated us to the plank of environmental purists. Still others have viewed us as unworthy recipients of unlimited federal largess. Words that deny us humanity include "squaw," "buck," "savage," "redskin," "heathen," "loafer," and "drunk."

Understanding the evolution and uses of stereotypes of Indians requires an examination of the interrelationship between historical processes and popular culture. This chapter seeks to uncover and explore some of the social, economic, and political factors that have contributed to the development, transformation, and ramification of stereotypes of Indians held by white America. I begin by discussing a few of my experiences with negative imagery and then examine factors that contributed to the development and changes of stereotypes about Indians.

Personal Experiences

Over the years, words and phrases such as "incompetent", "unworthy beneficiary of affirmative action," "backwards," "stupid," "superstitious," and "lazy" have been hurled in my direction. I have heard the terms "squaw" and "buck" used as synonyms for "woman" and "man." Although I have experienced numerous racial incidents and stereotypes at different times and places, I will discuss three encounters that perhaps best reflect the impact of stereotypes on my life.

One evening during the early 1980s I overheard the owner of a Gallup, New Mexico, pizza establishment spew racist venom. Speaking to white patrons seated near her in the bar about the failure of a Diné (Navajo) employee to report to work, she declared, "Goddamn these Indians and the government that feeds them. I hope they all starve to death." Her promotion of genocide as a solution to a mere act of absenteeism reflects a deep-seated hatred of Indians. Moreover, her views of Indians thriving on generous federal handouts is one of many disparaging stereotypes that have hampered people's understanding of reality. The average American citizen probably benefits more from federal programs than most Indians. In fact, poverty, health afflictions, and social problems among Indians stem from the disruptive effects of U.S. territorial expansion and federal policies.

Next, my son came home from kindergarten one day this past year and asked why Indians always lost. His query came as a surprise but not a shock. It presents an important question about how extensively negative imagery of Indians continues to influence school curricula, television programming, and popular culture. Virtually everywhere I go, I meet people who profess an understanding of Indian history and culture. Generally, however, their views have been tainted by the old stereotypes found in written history, films, cartoons, and other forms. Similarly, most students, Indians and non-Indians alike, who enter my courses have to unlearn the stereotypes, errone-

ous history, and misconceptions they carry. Many of them are willing and eager to explore and discover more truthful accounts, but others remain committed to maintaining the old views.

Finally, watching Hollywood movies can be an exasperating experience, cspccially for a Pawnee. Generally, the popular genre of the western that dominated Hollywood throughout much of this century offered the viewing public an image of Indians that was popularized in the eighteenth and nineteenth centuries. In films such as *Stagecoach*, scriptwriters and producers presented Indians as savage barriers to western expansion. Beginning in the late 1960s, Hollywood, influenced by the war in Vietnam, countercultural movements, and critical examinations of the U.S. historical experience, made several attempts to portray Indians in a more sympathetic fashion. *Soldier Blue*, *Billy Jack*, and *Tell Them Willie Boy Was Here* are examples of this change in perception. Somehow, however, film makers exempted my people. Movies such as *Little Big Man*, *Dances With Wolves*, and *Cheyenne Warrior* romanticized the Sioux and Cheyenne as noble savages while willfully denigrating the Pawnees.

Historical Development of Stereotypes

Stereotyping of Indians is inextricably linked to the land and to the cultural conflicts that began in the late 1400s and continue to this day. Since the time of Columbus, the English, Spaniards, French, and other Europeans have labeled Indians with a host of self-serving stereotypes that cast us as noble or ignoble. Colonial ambitions for territory to settle, resources to exploit, people to enslave, and souls to proselytize ensured that people characterized one day as kind, noble, and trustworthy would be denigrated and warred against the next day. When Europeans needed Indians as guides, military allies, and trading partners, they saw us as honest, friendly, and loyal. When they sought souls to convert to Christianity, missionaries projected us as tender, kind, and loving. But driven by a compulsion to grab new lands to control, occupy, and exploit, settlers deemed us bloodthirsty savages who had to be removed or exterminated.

Although the images differed in many ways, each reinforced the Europeans' sense of being the intellectual, biological, and cultural superiors. In their eyes, the struggle for the continent pitted civilization against savagery. Providence had given them a right to acquire land by whatever means necessary. With the conflict presented in this manner, there could be no compromise. Indian culture and resistance had to be squashed by whatever means possible.

Europeans invented the concept of the Indian as a monolithic entity. In actuality, at the time of contact in the late 1400s, the Western Hemisphere was very diverse. California alone was more linguistically diverse than Europe. Millions of natives lived in thousands of separate nations, or tribes. Some lived in empires under powerful rulers, whereas many others resided in decentralized settings with less formal political and religious mechanisms. Although sharing numerous commonalities, our ancestors followed values, philosophies, ceremonies, and customs distinct to their respective cultures. Each nation had a name for itself, but the Europeans usually called them something else.

The development of the printing press played an important role in the dissemination of mental images of Indians throughout Europe. Slanted reports of contacts with Indians written by European explorers and colonizers gave readers biased and fantasized descriptions of Indian behavior and culture. In a widely disseminated account written in the late 1400s and first published in 1503, Amerigo Vespucci, an imaginative Italian explorer, gave a gruesome picture of Indian cannibalism:

> I met a man who told me that he had eaten more than three hundred human bodies. And I spent twenty-seven days in a town where I saw cured human flesh hung up in the houses as we hang up hams in ours (Honour 1975, p. 8).

The cannibal image was eventually discarded, but other stereotypes painted pictures of Indians as human monsters.

Reproductions of woodcuts, engravings, drawings, and paintings in the publications gave the public visual imagery of Indians that usually reflected distortions found in the written and spoken words as well. Symbols of Indians in artwork included bows and arrows, instruments representative of death and destruction; feathers, denoting natives living in nature; and nudity, signifying promiscuity. Other pictures depicted them as childlike, living without morality, and bestial.

Under Columbus' reign of terror as Spanish viceroy and governor of the island of Hispaniola from 1493 to 1500, more than half a million natives died from harsh treatment, execution, warfare, or diseases. Spanish colonizers, who as a class avoided work at all costs, not only severed the hands of persons who did not furnish them with a certain amount of gold, but also tracked down and killed those who sought sanctuary from their brutality in the mountains. In addition, they enslaved thousands of others, subjecting them to an existence characterized by constant hunger, back-breaking work, cruel punishment, deadly pestilence, and premature death.

Indians lacked biological immunity to most of the diseases brought from Europe, including smallpox, measles, influenza, whooping cough, and the common cold. After about 50 years of colonization, Spanish brutality, aided by recurring pandemics, resulted in the virtual disappearance of the indigenous population of Hispaniola. Other islands and regions of the Western Hemisphere suffered a similar fate. Yet, many nations possessed the resilience to resist European encroachments.

The genocide in the Americas had far-reaching ramifications. Seeking a more durable supply of laborers, the Spanish turned to Africa as its major source for slaves. English colonists subsequently followed this practice. The ensuing quest for cheap labor ultimately resulted in the largest involuntary migration of humans.

Even as the brutality ensued, Spanish intellectuals, religious leaders, and rulers debated the humanity of Indians. Most felt that the natives were so low on the chain of being that they could not be Christianized and had no title to the land. Others felt that Europeans had a right to enter Indian land only for the purpose of proselytism. Individuals such as Bartolomé de Las Casas, a priest who had worked in the Caribbean and witnessed the tyranny and genocide, condemned the slaughter and enslavement of Indians. Overall, however, few expressed compassion over the tragic consequences of expansion for the Indians.

Columbus' policies set the tone for English colonization enterprises. English settlers who crossed the Atlantic and occupied the northeastern coast of North America held the same basic stereotypes of Indians and assumptions about their own superiority. Nonetheless, they found themselves at the mercy of the natives. In general, Indians treated the newcomers respectfully, providing them food and aid. Indians

eventually outlived their usefulness, and when the English settlers learned to survive without native assistance, the stereotypes underwent a dramatic transformation. From being handsome, generous, and friendly people, the natives became dirty brutes, barbarians, bloody infidels, and savages. Proclaiming their moral superiority, the English felt no constraints to keep treaties, truces, and promises, no matter how solemnly made. They showed little remorse when they killed innocent people in "just" wars over land and resources.

Labeling a people savage was tantamount to issuing them a death sentence. As the English pushed deeper into the continent, a series of bloody wars erupted in Virginia, Massachusetts, Connecticut, the Carolinas, and other places. Indians initially held their own, winning some battles, but they eventually lost more and more. Attrition, diseases, and hunger forced them to seek peace. But the English showed them no mercy. Those not killed in battle, executed while in captivity, or sold into slavery in the West Indies often spent the rest of their days as servants or slaves.

Not all colonists held such disparaging views of Indians, however. Some advocated that the English should follow fair and honorable practices in their dealings with the natives. In addition, many captives and individuals who had run away from the colonies to join Indian communities refused to return home and to accept the superior-race myth. Benjamin Franklin noted that "when white persons of either sex have been taken prisoners by the Indians and lived a while among them, tho' ransomed by their friends, and treated with all imaginable tenderness . . . yet in a short time they become disgusted with our manner of life, and take the first opportunity of escaping again into the woods, from hence there is no reclaiming them" (Koning, 1993, p. 61). Franklin should not be seen as a friend of the Indians; in fact, he advocated their extermination. Yet, he felt that the divided American colonies should adopt a political system that resembled that of the Iroquois confederacy.

After the United States gained its independence from England, the conjoined issues of territorial expansion and the "Indian problem" presented something of a moral dilemma for the new nation. Although the political rhetoric arising from the revolutionary fervor avowed such egalitarian principles as truth and justice, Indians, along with blacks, white women, and others, were systematically excluded from fair and equal treatment, in part, at least, because of their alleged inferiority.

Like the Spanish and English colonizers, white Americans, following the Revolutionary War, often used the stereotypes as a convenient rationalization for pursuing a ruthless territorial acquisition program. In doing so, they denied Indians humanity while simultaneously placing themselves on a lofty pedestal. Writing and speaking in self-righteous terms, newspaper editors, journalists, scholars, and government officials repeatedly lauded the growth of their country in religious, economic, and political terms. They not only claimed that Indians were barriers to progress but also asserted that the natives did not use the land as God had intended.

Nineteenth-century U.S. society offered Indians two choices: perish or give way. Settlers moving to the frontier tended to espouse the first solution. When Indians offered armed resistance to preserve their homeland, their families, and their cultures, the settlers, overland travelers, and military officers virtually always blamed the natives for instigating the conflict and cast themselves as innocent victims of uncon-

trollable Indian rage. An article appearing in the *Omaha Daily Republican* in 1873 illustrates how some Nebraskans used stereotypes, lies, and distortions for this purpose. "The plains are a cemetery from Omaha to San Francisco, of tortured, murdered victims, killed by useless savages. . . . There is but one way to deal with the Indians, and that is with brute force." People holding this perspective praised Colonel John Chivington, a Methodist minister and Colorado militia officer, for massacring friendly Cheyenne and Arapaho Indians at Sand Creek in 1864. They called for taking drastic measures to punish the Sioux, Cheyenne, and Arapahoes who had defeated Lt. Colonel George Armstrong Custer in 1876. In California following the gold rush, armed homesteaders routinely formed groups for the purpose of finding and killing Indians.

Reformers and humanitarians from eastern states where Indians previously had been removed, decimated, and pacified usually advocated the second solution. While condemning the slaughter and brutal treatment of Indians, they viewed assimilation as preferable to genocide. They wanted Indians transformed into mirror images of white farmers, whether Indians wanted to change or not. Thus, reservations became places where the resocialization of Indians was to occur.

Although reformers demanded the extension of U.S. laws and codes of punishment to include Indians as a vital step forward in the assimilation process, racial attitudes, often expressed in stereotypical terms, denied Indians fair treatment. Two Nebraska incidents epitomize the relationship between race and justice. In 1865, two settlers killed an elderly Pawnee merely to test the firepower of a recently purchased pistol. Although local citizens knew the identity of the murderers, the authorities refused to press charges. But four years later, when settlers suspected that some Pawnees had killed a homesteader, they used coercive measures to force the Pawnee chiefs to hand over some individuals to try for the crime. The subsequent legal proceedings involving four Indian defendants were so biased that a local newspaper called the whole affair a mockery of justice. With only highly circumstantial evidence and perjured testimony to offer the court, prosecutors resorted to race baiting, negative imagery, and fear to gain convictions. In the closing arguments, one of them told the jury that "prejudice towards their [the defendants'] race is deserved because of their actions toward white people." Another prosecutor asked rhetorically, "Why should these filthy savages receive any more sympathy than white men?" (National Archives). After five hours of deliberation, an all-white jury convicted each of the defendants.

Such incidents were not confined to the Great Plains. Nationally, each of the three branches of the federal government responded in coordinated ways to give a sense of legality and morality to flagrant acts of aggression, deception, and hostility. Congress enacted a number of bills aimed at appropriating vast tracts of native land and assimilating the Indians. To prevent Indians from falling under the corrupting influences of white society and to open millions of acres for non-Indian settlement, it passed the *Removal Act of 1830*, which had a devastating impact on the affected nations. They faced the trauma of leaving behind the graves of their loved ones, the sites where they worshiped, and the places of their birth. Thousands of relocated Indians died as a result of starvation, diseases, and other hardships experienced along the way. Because they suffered the loss of about a third of their population, the Cherokees called their forced removal from Geor-

gia to the Indian Territory "The Trail of Tears."

Viewing customary modes of punishment as backward and as retarding assimilation, Congress attached a rider to the 1885 *Indian Appropriation Act*. Known as the *Major Crimes Act*, this action extended federal jurisdiction to crimes including murder, arson, rape, and assault that occurred on Indian land. On reservations, Courts of Indian Offenses imposed white American penalties on Indians accused of other transgressions.

Seeking to "save Indians from themselves" through integration into U.S. culture as lowly farmers, Congress enacted the *General Allotment Act*, or *Dawes Act*, in 1887. This piece of legislation sought to supplant traditional Indian values, beliefs, and behaviors with those of white society by making Indians individual landholders, farmers, and U.S. citizens. Implementation required breaking Indian reservations into small tracts of land ranging in size from 40- to 160-acre plots and opening the "surplus land" to non-Indian settlers. The allotment process ultimately left many Indians landless and trapped in a cycle of poverty, ill health, and despair.

Presidents not only enforced the laws of Congress, but also participated fully in the campaign to subdue and transform "savagery." As Commanders-in-Chief, presidents allowed the U.S. military to conduct brutal operations to subjugate uncooperative Indians and drive them onto reservations. In treaty negotiations, they let their representatives use whatever tactics were deemed necessary to acquire coveted land, including fraud, coercion, deception, and bribery. A saying among Indians is that the U.S. entered into 371 treaties with Indian nations and subsequently violated each of them. Nevertheless, many Indian nations managed to retain reduced tracts of lands called "reservations," along with hunting and fishing rights. Rejecting assimilation, multitudes of families struggled to carry on their customary ways of life, including religious worship.

The Bureau of Indian Affairs (BIA), an agency initially placed within the Department of War and then within the Department of the Interior, employed repressive measures to detribalize Indian society. BIA agents often attempted to gain absolute authority over uncooperative inhabitants by extralegal methods including withholding provisions and rations guaranteed by treaty. In times of destitution, which occurred more frequently on many reservations as the nineteenth century progressed, coercive actions of this nature gave agents powerful leverage over Indian leaders and their people. A set of BIA regulations adopted during the 1890s, called the *Code of Indian Offenses*, provided criminal punishment for Indians who participated in most religious and healing ceremonies. Missionaries supported the outlawing of rituals they saw as expressions of devil worship, savagery, and heathenism.

The abuse did not end there. Federal agents, following a policy that sought to "kill the Indian but save the man," literally ripped apart thousands of Indian families, placing children in distant boarding schools. In keeping with this philosophy, school policies subjected the captive children to involuntary hair shearing, to hours of uncompensated labor each day, and to harsh military regimens. Compulsory courses in reading and arithmetic sought to inculcate in the students the arts and habits of "civilization," and history courses aimed to replace traditional understandings of history with those held by white Americans. Those youths who dared to speak in their own language were punished by physical beatings, mouth washings with soap, and solitary confinement.

Finally, the U.S. Supreme Court provided a legal foundation for subjugating Indian nations under U.S. domination. During the 1820s and 1830s, Chief Justice John Marshall handed down a series of landmark cases concerning Indians that demonstrated an acceptance by the federal judiciary of insulting language, condescending attitudes, and stereotypical views. In *Macintosh v. Johnson* (1823), Marshall applied a version of the doctrine of discovery to federal Indian policy, holding that Indians merely had occupancy rights to the land until the U.S. wanted it. In making a case to support the dispossession of Indian nations by just wars and acts of conquest, Marshall declared that Indians were "warlike" and nomadic.

Other court decisions were equally derisive, contemptuous, and arrogant. In *U.S. v. Sandoval* (1913, p. 39), the high court ruled that the Pueblos of New Mexico should be legally classified as Indian because

> [t]he people of the Pueblos, although sedentary rather than nomadic in their inclinations and disposed to peace and industry, are nevertheless Indians in race, customs, and domestic government, always living in separate and isolated communities, adhering to primitive modes of life, largely influenced by superstition and fetishism, and chiefly governed according to the crude customs inherited from their ancestors. They are essentially a simple, uninformed, and inferior people.

Viewing territorial expansion as essential for the nation's future, few U.S. citizens questioned the "manifest destiny" that purportedly guided their country across the continent into lands inhabited by undeserving and depraved peoples. Intellectuals and other trained minds of the era gave an ethnocentric expression to the national experience. Without critical analysis of the causes of conflict resulting from U.S. encroachments, historians apparently reveled with delight in depicting Indians as murderous villains, brutal savages, and barriers to progress. In a classic expression of blaming the victim for the crimes of the aggressor, the historian Francis Parkman, writing during the mid-1840s after traveling along the Oregon Trail, declared that "by a thousand acts of pillage and murder, [the Pawnees] have deserved chastisement at the hands of government" (Parkman, 1950, p. 54).

A decade before Parkman penned those words, science had embarked on a campaign to validate the intellectual superiority of Anglo-Saxons. Proving the alleged inferiority of Indians would in effect confirm the negative stereotypes of people considered inferior and sanction taking land from people who lacked the intelligence to use it properly. Given the popularity of such views, researchers skewed their data to obtain the desired results. To amass collections of remains for study, craniologists paid frontier settlers and soldiers to loot native burial grounds. In the 1860s, the U.S. army became involved in this type of research. Following orders issued by the U.S. Surgeon General, military medical personnel stole bodies from native graves and decapitated hundreds of Indians killed in battle. While the mutilations and "body snatching" proceeded unimpeded, promoters of territorial expansion continued to present Indians as cruel, heartless butchers.

Most credible scholars eventually discredited craniometrics, but the abuse against dead Indians committed in the name of science continued unabated. Subsequent generations of anthropologists, archaeologists, museum curators, and others eagerly embarked on careers that relied heavily on looting Indian graves and storing and studying the remains. Racist attitudes that cast Indians as an inferior, childlike, and vanishing race guided the development of scientific research well into the twentieth century. Through practices sanctioned in the name of scientific curiosity, hundreds of thousands of Indian burial sites were disrupted. Viewing the remains as specimens rather than as representing human life, curators placed them on public display, in storage cabinets, and on shelves. In most parts of the country, the public could satisfy its ghoulish curiosity by visiting local museums and Indian burial sites turned into tourist attractions. It should also be noted that pot hunters, usually ordinary citizens who peddled native burial objects and human remains, contributed significantly to the desecration of cemeteries.

Stereotypes in Popular Culture

Writings carried similar themes throughout much of American history. During the colonial period, captivity narratives, a popular genre, gave readers vivid illustrations of alleged Indian brutality and savagery. Women and children in particular, according to the writers, suffered unspeakable atrocities at the hands of their Indian captors.

Nineteenth-century literary figures such as James Fenimore Cooper portrayed Indians of different nations in a dichotomous light. Cooper's Indians in his *Leatherstocking Tales*, written between 1821 and 1841, possessed keen senses and stamina. His "good" Indians manifested loyalty and faithfulness, and were true to the white Americans with whom they associated. Conversely, his "bad" Indians delighted in repetitive acts of torture, gratuitous murder, and generally barbarous behavior.

Other forms of popular culture emerged as important promoters of myths and stereotypes. Surfacing during the latter part of the nineteenth century, wild west shows organized by such men as William "Buffalo Bill" Cody and Gordon "Pawnee Bill" Lillie traveled extensively across the United States, Canada, and Europe, thrilling audiences with extravagant performances featuring mounted warriors attacking innocent settlers and travelers. It should not come as a surprise that by the end of each show, virtuous white frontiersmen always triumphed over the "warlike" Indians. Dime novels gave readers an equally fanciful view of adventurous Westerners outwitting, outfighting, and ultimately slaughtering scores of bloodthirsty "red fiends." A novel entitled *Young Wild West Running the Gauntlet; or, The Pawnee Chief's Last Shot* (Le Blant, n.d.) offers a common view of Indians as presented in the dime-novel genre. "The awful deeds of the Indians in those days," the author claimed, "could but make one's blood run cold to hear about them, and that is why we have not described in detail what took place at that massacre when Young Wild West arrived on the scene just in time to be captured by the fiends" (n.d., p. 42).

The motion picture industry surfaced early in the twentieth century as a powerful conveyer of images. Westerns quickly emerged as a staple of the movie industry. Some films attempted to present a sympathetic version of history, but most scriptwriters and producers presented the distorted themes and images of Indians found in novels, wild west shows, and written history. Children and adults could watch heroic matinee idols save innocent settlements and wagon trains from hordes of swarming savages. Cartoons, an important element of movie theaters, often reified the stereotype of Indians as the "bad" guys. They presented Indians as brutish people dressed in feathers who constantly engaged in acts of violence and destruction.

Shifting of Attitudes

As movies glorified the alleged triumph of U.S. society over savagery, attitudes toward natives began to change, in some quarters at least. With the Indian wars now over and white society stretching across the North American continent, the twentieth century witnessed a gradual decline in overt racism. The growth of multiculturalism and more truthful interpretations of U.S. history and culture surfaced nearly simultaneously. Some bold writers even dared to depict Indians as victims of U.S. expansion. Seeking to see justice done, Helen Hunt Jackson's *A Century of Dishonor: The Early Crusade for Indian Reform*, published in 1881, exposed much of the hatred that underlined the treatment Indians suffered at the hands of white settlers, military officers, and government officials. Angie Debo (1940, reprinted 1989) revealed the graft, corruption, and abuse perpetrated in Oklahoma by white citizens who had been assigned as the legal guardians of Indians. Rather than acting in the best interest of their wards, guardians often embezzled or stole their money. Even worse, some committed murder to gain ownership of Indian assets. With old prejudices thriving, authorities prosecuted only a few of the criminals.

As notions of pluralism and cultural relativity grew, academic and popular thought began to challenge the civilization-over-savagery theme. Some romantic artists, writers, and scholars expressed admiration for the collectivism that characterized daily native life and the spirituality that united people and the environment in a harmonious web. They viewed federal missions of assimilation and capitalism as misguided, exploitive, and destructive. Growing sympathy encouraged outbursts of support for the Pueblo Indians of New Mexico in their successful effort to stop Congress from enacting the *Bursum Bill,* a measure that sought to bestow title to millions of acres of land on non-Indian squatters.

The Great Depression, which shook public faith in the country's values of individualism, capitalism, democracy, and assimilation, provided an impetus for other changes in attitude and practice. Reformers seized the opportunity to alter the course of federal Indian policy. In 1934, Congress, responding to growing concern about the deleterious impact of federal policy on native life, enacted the *Indian Reorganization Act* (IRA). In addition to ending allotments, the IRA encouraged Indian nations to adopt constitutional forms of government, to apply for funds from a revolving credit account, and to engage in some customary forms of worship without fear of arrest. It promised the dawning of a new era for Indian people.

Yet old attitudes that cast Indians as backward, incompetent, inferior, and incapable of making it on their own continued to permeate decision-making bodies and the wider society. The IRA sought to impose a form of government on Indians that more closely resembled white America's structures than it did customary ones. It also subjected the actions of tribal councils to the scrutiny of the Secretary of the Interior, who had the power to veto council decisions. Some Indian nations resisted, preferring to keep their existing government structure, but others accepted IRA governments. In addition, assimilation remained the overwhelming thrust of federal, state, and parochial schools that served Indian children. Congress, led by representatives from western states with many constituents who loathed Indians, refused to appropriate adequate funds for native nations to repurchase lost lands.

Resurgence of Old Attitudes

The post-World War II era saw the renewal of massive outpourings of negative imagery as the country emerged victorious in the struggle against fascism. Popular opinion once again demanded conformity from all of its citizens. Although thousands of Indians had served with distinction in the war and many had died fighting for their country, western congressmen and senators advocated the elimination of Indian nations and reservations. Others, denying that racism existed, demanded the absorption of Indians into U.S. society. They couched their arguments in terms of getting government off the backs of Indians and used stereotypes that cast natives as lazy and backward, but a desire for more Indian lands and resources underscored the assimilation drive.

Inspired by the political climate, Congress embarked on two programs, called "termination" and "relocation," designed to integrate Indians into mainstream America. During the 1950s and 1960s, Congress terminated several hundred Indian nations by severing the federal trust relationship with those nations. As a result, the terminated governments could no longer receive federal assistance, including education, health, and social services. Citizens of terminated nations faced new difficulties with the loss of their land and federal services. Nonterminated tribes faced further erosion of their sovereignty and customs. In 1953, Congress enacted Public Law 280, turning criminal and civil jurisdiction of Indian lands over to state governments in six states.

The relocation program removed thousands of Indian families from reservations and rural areas to such cities as Los Angeles, Chicago, Phoenix,

Cleveland, Minneapolis, Oklahoma City, and Seattle. Some program participants eventually thrived, but many others did not. The latter frequently returned home because they faced resentment from their neighbors, lacked educational and job skills, and could not adjust to city life.

Stereotypes during this era of cultural repression worked in other ways against Indians. From the 1950s to the 1970s, social workers, doctors, nurses, attorneys, and others took thousands of children from reservation families and placed them on the black market for adoption. In addition to kidnaping, they used high-pressure tactics, including threats, shame, and intimidation, to convince impoverished parents that their children would have a better chance in life if they were adopted by affluent white families. In other instances, children falling into the hands of state child protective workers were stripped from their families by legal means. Whether acting legally or illegally, the perpetrators and their accomplices saw themselves as saving the children from the harsh cycle of poverty and the hardships of reservation life. Having little understanding of or respect for Indian life, they judged Indian culture by their own standards. Of course, with the imagery presented in history and popular culture looming large, Indian society was deemed inferior. Indian government officials and families were virtually powerless to stop the transgressions because U.S. government authorities either looked away or sanctioned the snatching of Indian children.

The impact of the thefts on individuals, families, and nations was tremendous. Some children experienced physical, psychological, and sexual abuse, but others found comfortable lives. Whatever their experiences, the "Lost Birds," as they have been called, generally could not retain their language, ceremonies,

and traditions. Native parents often remained hopeful of finding their lost children. Some lucky ones eventually reestablished contact, but sealed or nonexistent records prevented most others from doing so.

Medical personnel committed another form of genocide on Indian people. During the 1960s, 1970s, and 1980s, U.S. Public Health Service doctors working for Indian Health Service hospitals and contract physicians sterilized perhaps as many as several thousand unwitting women. In many instances, women discovered that surgical procedures performed on them after childbirth had left them incapable of bearing any more children. As a result, doctors not only shattered the dreams, hopes, and aspirations of many families, but they also acted to check the growth of the Indian population.

Although bigotry influenced the kidnaping of children and the involuntary sterilization of women, cultural and socioeconomic differences between the perpetrators and the victims also came into play. Doctors, social workers, and attorneys who participated in the genocide tended to come from affluent backgrounds. Viewing a nonmaterialistic culture as wanting, they formed self-righteous judgments based on their class and personal values, which, when it came to Indians, were mean-spirited, ethnocentric, and damaging.

Indian Resistance and Struggles for Respect and Dignity

As active historical participants, Indians have long understood the significance and ramifications of negative stereotypes. Over the years, they responded to them in a variety of ways. Some, who had succumbed to the indoctrination of the boarding, parochial, and public schools, accepted the stereotypes as reality. Feeling stigmatized and impaired, they sought relief by denying their Indian heritage, dissociating themselves from other natives, and refusing to carry on traditional values, customs, and beliefs. Others, suffering from poor self-esteem, turned to alcohol, drugs, or quicker methods of suicide.

Fortunately, many Indians opted to challenge the legacy of the stereotypes and mistreatment. They advocated religious freedom, sought access to sacred sites on lands that had been taken from them, and demanded a lasting burial for their ancestors. Others challenged discrimination in prisons against native spirituality. Still others mobilized to halt the theft of Indian children and the involuntary sterilizations.

In many communities, traditionalists continued to speak Indian languages in family, religious, and social settings. Operating in secrecy to avoid arrest, they sponsored, attended, or participated in banned ceremonies. The Native American Church used state courts to challenge laws that interfered with their use of peyote as a holy sacrament. Many tribal leaders who refused to accept BIA paternalism continued fighting for tribal autonomy, economic self-sufficiency, and dignity. Terminated nations, usually reduced by federal policy to conditions of poverty and landlessness, sought to restore their status as federally recognized tribes. In December 1971, Taos Pueblo of New Mexico won a lengthy struggle for the return of its sacred Blue Lake and surrounding traditional lands, which had been taken from them by President Teddy Roosevelt in 1906 and placed under the jurisdiction of the U.S. Forest Service.

Facing opposition, stonewalling, and ignorance, native protesters often resorted to militant tactics. The climate created by the anti-Vietnam War, civil rights, and countercultural movements probably helped spur Indian activism, but Indian goals and objectives differed dramatically from those of other social critics. In the 1960s and 1970s, Pacific Northwest and Great Lakes region natives resisted state attempts to deny them the right to hunt and fish "in usual and customary places" guaranteed by treaty. The American Indian Movement (AIM) formed in the late 1960s to fight for treaty rights, sovereignty, and cultural survival. As the 1970s progressed, however, Federal Bureau of Investigation agents attempted to disrupt and destroy the Indian movement. Many native leaders were killed and incarcerated, but the movement had inspired Indian people to fight for justice and political rights.

By presenting accurate historical facts and debunking stereotypes in a widespread drive to reeducate the public, Indian activism achieved some significant accomplishments. Beginning in the 1970s, courts began granting Indian inmates the right to wear their hair long, to conduct sweat ceremonies, and to participate in other forms of religious worship. Protests forced Indian Health Service officials to stop the practice of involuntary sterilization. Congress responded with significant pieces of legislation. The *Indian Self-Determination Act* of 1975 allowed Indian nations and groups to contract with facilities that offered educational, health, and other services to Indian people. The *Indian Child Welfare Act* of 1978 ended the kidnaping of native youths by medical personnel and social workers, enabling Indian courts to have a say in the disposition of native children. In the same year, the *American Indian Religious Freedom Act* professed to extend religious freedom to American Indians, but the measure lacked enforcement mechanisms. The *Native Graves Protection and Repatriation Act of 1990* enabled Indian nations to reclaim lost ancestral remains and burial objects for proper reburial. It also established a legal avenue for Indian governments to repatriate lost sacred objects and objects of cultural patrimony.

Ongoing Problems With Old Stereotypes

More than ever before, Indians began to use the written word and film to espouse native themes, challenge stereotypes, and issue calls for justice. Some of their writings sought to shape public consciousness concerning ongoing problems, and others offered insider perspectives on native experiences.[1] Despite the rise of Indian writers and filmmakers, however, non-Indian authors, professors, filmmakers, and others continued to function as the primary molders of perceptions of Indians. With the rise of social history in the 1970s, some historians became more receptive to flushing out the old ethnocentric views and stereotypes that had tainted so many works in the field. Dee Brown's *Bury My Heart at Wounded Knee* (1971), a best-seller for many months, offered readers a shocking view of the long legacy of broken treaties, government abuse, massacres, racism, and native resistance that characterized Indian-white relations. Unfortunately, many of these individuals have had minimal, if any, contact with living Indians.

Despite some accomplishments in battling negative stereotypes, Indians still face many challenges. Old images continue to permeate public consciousness, and changing times have given rise to new problems of imagery and injustice. The result is that stereotypes often promote acts of disrespect, ridicule, misunderstandings, and insensitivity. Compounding matters is widespread ignorance about Indian history and culture.

Sports logos constitute an important area of long-standing concern. During the twentieth century it became popular for professional, collegiate, and public school sports teams to adopt Indian logos and team names. In professional football, the Kansas City Chiefs and Washington Redskins are two examples. In baseball, it's the Atlanta Braves and Cleveland Indians. At sporting events, many fans depreciate Indian culture by making hand movements called the "tomahawk chop" and donning "native clothing," complete with chicken feathers dyed to resemble eagle feathers. Although native protesters have sought to have the offending teams change their names, the owners have refused to budge. Representatives of the Washington football team, for instance, have even gone so far as to make the ridiculous and preposterous declaration that the term "redskin" actually honors Indian people. Historically, "redskin" was used synonymously with "savage," "red devil," and other negative terms. Conversely, some colleges and universities have voluntarily renamed their teams out of respect for native concerns. Nevertheless, popular organizations such as the Boy Scouts and the YMCA still actively promote programs with stereotypical Indian themes. Youths playing "Indian" roles act out the part of the noble savage without understanding the cultural and historical processes, keeping alive the American stream of consciousness through cultural imperialism.

Problems of religious freedom and tribal economic development remain constant. As I mentioned above, during the 1970s and 1980s, Indian inmates filed numerous lawsuits, winning the right to wear their hair long in accordance with custom and to hold sweat ceremonies and other forms of traditional worship in prison. But during the 1990s, state and county officials took steps to limit religious opportunities for Indian inmates. Although gaming has enabled some Indian nations to obtain a level of economic self-sufficiency and to improve the quality of life for their members, powerful forces, perhaps fearful of native empowerment and economic competition, oppose the development of casinos. Newspaper editorialists—joined by elected officials—have called for abolishing or strictly regulating native gambling operations while simultaneously encouraging new non-Indian gambling boats on our rivers and lakes. Their strategies appeal to public fears that tribal gaming will promote the cancerous growth in society of corruption, violence, prostitution, and compulsive addictions. Essentially, these stereotypes have the dual effect of presenting white Americans as morally superior and Indians as being vulnerable to greed, ineptness, and criminal behavior. Despite the rhetoric and the brandishing of old stereotypes in new forms, many non-Indians remain supportive of Indian gaming. Funds generated by the casinos have enabled Indian nations to fund reservation health, education, and social programs.

On the opposite end of the spectrum stand the romanticists. Often called "New Agers," these individuals find so much value and inspiration in Indian beliefs that they seek to uncover its mysteries for personal guidance, health, pleasure, or profit. After reading ethnographic studies, attending a ceremony, or receiving instructions, usually from Indians of dubious authority who willingly exploit their religion for gain, New Agers seek a meaningful religious experience. Some seek an Indian identity, name, title, or connection so that they can reap potentially huge profits from individuals willing to pay to participate in a ceremony. Others, professing to have been endowed with the spiritual powers of a "shaman," charge gullible people for a "healing" ceremony. Of course, many Indians disapprove strongly of these individuals appropri-

ating and mimicking Indian traditions, viewing the behavior of New Agers and other exploiters as sacrilege.

Conclusion

Negative stereotypes not only constitute a major barrier to interracial harmony, they also promote injustice, disrespect, oppression, unequal treatment, and genocide. They keep people from understanding differences, similarities, problems, and potential solutions. Although many non-Indians truly care about the welfare of Indians and have deep, abiding admiration for native culture, many others are ambivalent, if not callous and resentful. Still others are exploitive. For these reasons, Indian struggles for acceptance as equals in the family of humankind have not ended.

The key factor behind the development and continuance of the stereotypes is the simple fact that Indians occupied American soil that the incoming Europeans coveted. To rationalize their territorial expansion, European settlers and their progeny devised a series of stereotypes to soothe their collective conscience and sanction a host of aggressive actions—conduct that included dispossession, enslavement, removal, genocide, political subjugation, and coercive assimilation.

White America must come to grips with its treatment of its natives. Denial of responsibility and historical amnesia merely prolong the problems rooted so deeply in this country's history. Studying the significance of stereotypes in the history of this country offers a means to understand the past and present. Significant changes in consciousness have occurred during the present century, but we still have a long way to go. Acquiring a more accurate view of the past should facilitate the emergence of an environment where we can celebrate the diversity and the rich ethnic mix of our nation.

Note

1. In the 1930s, Black Elk, a Lakota holy man, told John G. Neihardt of the visions he had experienced, the holy circle, and the Wounded Knee massacre. Scholars such as Beatrice Medicine (Sioux), Anna Walters (Pawnee/Otoe), Vine Deloria, Jr. (Sioux), Duane Champaign (Chippewa), Carol Chiago Lujan (Diné/Pima), Donald Fixico (Sac, Fox, Shawnee, and Seminole), and Devon Mihesuah (Choctaw) presented views of Indian history, cultural survival, and philosophy. In the 1980s, a small but growing number of Indian filmmakers, including Ava Hamilton (Arapaho), Victor Masayesva (Hopi), and Arlene Bowman (Diné), began producing quality works dealing with native topics. In 1995, Russell Means, a Lakota and former AIM leader turned actor, produced *Where White Men Fear to Tread*, an autobiography detailing many aspects of twentieth-century life experiences and AIM activities. Leslie Marmon Silko, a Laguna, Simon Ortiz, an Acoma, and Dinés Laura Tohe and Lucy Tapahanso employed literary techniques to reflect Indian life in contemporary settings.

References

Brown, Dee. (1971). *Bury my heart at Wounded Knee: An Indian history of the American west.* New York: Holt, Rinehart, and Winston.

Cooper, James Fenimore. *The pioneers* (1823), *The last of the Mohicans* (1826), *The prairie* (1827), *The pathfinder* (1840), *The deerslayer* (1841). In *Leatherstocking Tales.* 2 vols. New York: Literary Classics of the United States, 1985.

Debo, Angie. (1989). *And still the waters run: The betrayal of the five civilized tribes.* 1940. Reprinted. Norman and London: University of Oklahoma Press.

Jackson, Helen Hunt. (1881a). *A century of dishonor: A sketch of the United States government's dealings with some of the Indian tribes.* New York: Harper and Brothers.

——. (1881b). *A century of dishonor: The early crusade for Indian reform.* Edited by Andrew F. Rolle. NY: Harper and Row, 1965.

Johnson v. McIntosh. (1823). 21 U.S. (8 Wheat.) 53.

Koning, Hans. (1993). *The conquest of America: How the Indian nations lost their continent.* New York: Monthly Review Press.

Le Blant, Edward T. (Ed.). (n.d.). *Young Wild West running the gauntlet or, The Pawnee Chief's last shot.* Derby, CT: Goldstar Books.

National Archives, Microcopy 234, Office of Indian Affairs, Letters Received, Pawnee Agency, Reel 660, Samuel M. Janney to Ely S. Parker, 15 November 1869.

Means, Russell. (1995). *Where white men fear to tread: The autobiography of Russell Means.* New York: St. Martin's Press.

Parkman, Francis. (1950). *The Oregon Trail.* New York: The American Library, Inc., a Signet Classic.

United States v. Sandoval. (1913). 231 U.S. 28.

Discussion Questions

1. What social, economic, and political factors have contributed to the development, transformation, and ramifications of stereotypes of Indians held by white Americans?

2. Think about your own views of what you have been taught about Indians. Did this reading prompt you to reconsider any views you have held about Indians? If so, how?

3. How does popular culture reinforce and otherwise influence stereotypes? Please give specific examples from the reading.

4. Discuss in detail the impact of the three branches of the U.S. government (executive, legislative, and judicial) on Indians. According to the author, how has the government not only allowed but actively participated in the "assimilation" of Indians?

5. What are some of the factors that led to a change in attitude toward Indians? Was the change lasting or substantial? Explain. ✦

Chapter 3

Stereotyping by the Media

Redskins, Savages, and Other Indian Enemies: An Historical Overview of American Media Coverage of Native Peoples

Suzan Shown Harjo

Savage and Sexy—Columbus and Other Early Reporters on Native Peoples

The first print reporters on Native Peoples in this hemisphere were the European sailors and priests who thought they were spreading the news about surviving their westward ocean voyage to India. Their ship-to-shore news reports, of course, were about the "Indians." Even in later reports on the "New World," they continued writing about the "Indians." Admittedly lost, they were sure they had gotten the rest of the story right. Columbus sailed back to Spain in 1493 with living proof—six Native captives—that he had landed in a new world, reporting a "Paradise on Earth" with gold aplenty.

Europeans did not know if "Indians" were human beings. The Catholic Church decided that they were, with gold and land that could be divided between church and state and with souls that could be converted for Christendom or killed in the name of God. The Church devised "The Requiremento"—the first Miranda rights. Upon hearing the Word—in an unfamiliar language—the captives could accept it and deliver gold or be dispatched to heaven. Or they could reject it, be killed, and go to hell. By 1537, Pope Paul III proclaimed that Indians were "truly men." It was settled then, and widely reported at home and abroad, that the Indians, although savages, were humans.

These early reporters used a lot of ink on the appearance and sexuality of Native men and women. Columbus reasoned that they were "uncivilized" because they "go naked" (cited in Honour, 1975, p. 5). Amerigo Vespucci, in the 1504–1505 *Mundus Novas*, reported that the "very lustful" and "very libidinous" women "cause the private parts of their husbands to swell up to such a huge size that they appear deformed and disgusting; and this is accomplished by a certain device of theirs, the biting of certain poisonous animals." He wrote that the women "have bodies that are tolerably beautiful and cleanly. Nor are they plump, their ugliness is less apparent" (cited in Honour, 1975, pp. 8, 10).

As the press was developing in the American colonies, Native Peoples were reported as Indians or "noble savages" if they made treaties and joined the colonists in warfare against others but as "savages" or "savage Indians" if they were enemies. The term "Indian savages" was used in the Declaration of Independence and "Indians" in the U.S. Constitution. During the colonial period, Native Peoples also began to be called "redskins" and "squaws." "Redskins" derived from the bounty hunters' custom of delivering skins and scalps—rather than the cumbersome practice of hauling wagon loads and gunny sacks of whole bodies and skulls—for "Indian kill" payments. "Squaw" was taken from an Algonquian word for vagina, which also was used by the English and French trappers to mean "wife" or to refer to any Native woman.

From the earliest writings and engravings to the lithographs, paintings, and photographs of the 1800s, Native women rarely were depicted as fully clothed or named individuals. Typically portrayed as scenery, they seldom were recognized for their governmental or family leadership in matrilineal and egalitarian societies. These portrayals became prototypes for Native women in popular culture that continue in the modern era as cartoons—the most obvious examples being the "Land o' Lakes" Indian butter maiden and the animated-movie character Pocahontas.

For the most part, Native women were named, recorded, and reported only in connection with white men. The most notable examples of this are Pocahontas (Powhatan) and Sacajawea (Shoshone). Pocahontas is famous for saving one white man and marrying another in the early 1600s. It is less well known that she went to England, where she was paraded and displayed, caught smallpox, and died on the ship home. Sacajawea is remembered as the faithful Indian who guided Meriwether Lewis and William Clark from St. Louis, Missouri, to the Pacific Ocean in the early 1800s. She is not well known for her heroism and extraordinary feat—blazing the Trail, usually ahead of Lewis and Clark, and saving the records of the expedition—all while pregnant or carrying her baby on her back.

Native men usually were portrayed either as magnificent chiefs and diplomats or as brutal creatures lusting after white women. Thomas Jefferson, who helped write Indian and treaty rights into the U.S. Constitution, thought that the "savage" was incapable of love for women or society. In *Notes on the State of Virginia*, Jefferson wrote that the "savage is feeble, and has small organs of generation; he has neither hair nor beard, and no ardor whatever for his female . . . and consequently they have no love for their fellow man; not knowing this strongest and most tender of all affections, their other feelings are also cold and languid. . . . Nature, by refusing him the power of love, has treated him worse and lowered him deeper than any animal" (Jefferson, 1975, pp. 93-94).

The views about savages and Indians came to a head in the early 1800s, when Native Nations split loyalties in U.S. fights with European countries. As more immigrants arrived daily, avaricious Americans clamored for westward expansion. Finally, gold was discovered in Georgia. When the Indian fighter Stonewall Jackson became President Andrew Jackson, he immediately signed the 1830 *Indian Removal Act*. He and former military aides in Congress had crafted the legislation when he was a senator. He used the law, over the objections of the Supreme Court, to force-march the Cherokee, Chickasaw, Choctaw, Muscogee (Creek), and Seminole Nations to the Indian Territory. Reports that tens of thousands were killed on the "Trails of Tears" generated some sympathy, but the newspapers sided with Jackson.

The American Press Helped Settle the West, Too

As gold fever, land grabs, and the taste for blood spread across the hemisphere, the European-American newspapers, periodicals, and other published reports, with few exceptions, took the U.S. Army accounts of encounters with the "hostiles" as gospel, applauding and encouraging even the most heinous atrocities against Native Peoples. When faced with conflicting "official military reports," newspapers often took the one that showed the American side to best advantage. The *Rocky Mountain News*, for example, celebrated the Sand Creek "Battle" of November 29, 1864, proclaiming that the Colorado Volunteers' "Bloody Thirdsters" had "covered themselves with glory," while Army officers on site characterized the events there as the Sand Creek "Massacre" and the soldiers as "barbaric" and "covered with gore." The Sand Creek Massacre began with a dawn attack on a peaceful, sleeping village of Cheyenne and Arapaho old men, women, and children. Most who did not escape were murdered and mutilated, and babies were ripped from their mothers' wombs. In a public meeting shortly before the Massacre, the head of the Colorado Volunteers was asked if children of the "hostile Cheyennes" should be killed, too. "Yes," he said. "Nits make lice."

In 1867, an important report was released by the prestigious Doolittle Committee, which found that white aggression was the cause of most armed confrontations with Indians. The report was noted in newspapers but dismissed in most editorials. The Committee's work did little to sway public opinion, stop the aggression, or temper the press coverage. Twenty years after the Sand Creek Massacre, the August 8, 1887, *Chicago Tribune* ran a retrospective on the "Battle" with the subheads "Wholesale Slaughter of Indians on the Plains, An Account of the Bloody Fight by Col. William M. Chivington, the Leader of the White Forces—About Eight Hundred Redskins Killed in the Engagement—Savage Atrocities Which Provoked the Fearful Retribution." During the Indian Wars, newspapers used the terms "Indians" and "good Indians" for those who were not resisting encroachment on their lands. "Good Indian" was dropped in the late

1860s after General Philip H. Sheridan spawned the phrase, "The only good Indian is a dead one."

On November 27, 1868, Lt. Colonel George Armstrong Custer and the Seventh Cavalry attacked the Washita camp of the elderly Cheyenne Chief Black Kettle, who had escaped from Sand Creek four years earlier. As at Sand Creek, the attack came at dawn, killing most of the people, plundering or burning all their possessions, slaughtering their ponies, and raping the women and children captives. Sheridan gave Custer a hero's welcome home and later reported a great triumph over the "savage butchers" and "cruel marauders." On December 22, *The New York Times* declared "The End of the Indian War and Ring," editorializing that "The truth is, that Gen. Custer, in defeating and killing Black Kettle, put an end to one of the most troublesome and dangerous characters on the Plains. . . . [I]t was a fortunate stroke which ended his career and put the others to flight."

When it came to actual battles where Native Peoples were victorious, the American press proclaimed them massacres, vastly inflating the number of "redskins" and "hostiles." The most notable example of this was the Battle of the Little Big Horn on June 25, 1876, which was widely reported as the "Custer Massacre." The *Denver Post* headlined one of its stories on Captain Benteen, "Major's Men Were Lured into Ambush by Fleeing Redskins/Force of 5,000 Hostiles Surrounded Pursuing Troopers Who Galloped into Huge Village; Desperate Retreat Prevented Annihilation."

The Wounded Knee Massacre of December 29, 1890, continues to this day to be referred to in print and broadcast reports as the "Wounded Knee Battle" and the "last battle of the Indian Wars." It was not a battle, and it was not the last battle with or massacre of Native Peoples. At Wounded Knee Creek on the Pine Ridge Sioux Reservation, the aged Chief Big

Foot—the half-brother of Chief Sitting Bull, who had been killed that month after the brothers were targeted as "fomenters of dissent"—was dying of pneumonia. He and the other Lakota people had turned in their weapons to the Seventh Cavalry, who surrounded them. The soldiers—drunk, hung over, and talking of vengeance for the "Custer Massacre"—opened fire with Gatling and Hotchkiss guns, killing some of their own men as they annihilated some 400 of the "hostiles." The *Rocky Mountain News* of December 30 carried its story under such headlines as "Redskins Are Being Shot Down . . . Without Mercy/Squaws and Bucks Treated Alike/No Quarter Being Shown to Any Hostiles."

The *Times* of London ran a Reuters report on January 1, 1891, under the headline "Latest Intelligence: The American Indian Difficulty." Their report differed from the U.S. press in both tone and perspective. "The latest accounts of the battle . . . describe vividly the fury, inspired by racial hatred, with which the combatants on both sides fought. . . . The Indians seemed possessed with demoniacal courage and, indeed, both sides forgot everything except the loading and discharging of guns. . . . It was a war of extermination with the troopers, and the firing was kept up until not a live Indian remained in sight."

American Press, 'A Careful Propaganda,' and 'Civilizing' Indians

Most of the American publishing world gained its wealth from the theft of Native lands and gold. The fortunes of the newspaper families were integrally tied to the railroads, to "settling" the West, and to "civilizing" the Indians. The Hearst publishing empire, for example, was built with Black Hills gold

stolen from the Lakota, Cheyenne, Arapaho, and other Native Nations. Its "us-and-them" reporting reflected the economic, political, and racial self-interest of the white newspaper owners, as well as that of their readership and government.

As interesting as what and how the press reported on Native Peoples was what they did not report. They did not report on the Army Surgeon General's "Indian Crania Study," which began in 1862 and continued into the new century (see Chapter 2 of this volume). Nor did the press report on the related Army Medical Museum-Smithsonian Institution Indian collection agreement of 1868, under which the Army received human remains and the Smithsonian received burial and cultural materials. The agreement also initiated collections of human remains, funerary items, and sacred objects at the American Museum of Natural History in New York, the Field Museum of Natural History in Chicago, the Peabody Museum at Harvard University in Cambridge, Massachusetts, and the Physiological Institute in Berlin.

At the turn of the century, the Army and the Euro-American scientists abandoned their study of heads as invalid after scientific measurements "proved" that the French were less intelligent than Cro-Magnon man. The Army transferred thousands of skulls to the Smithsonian in 1898 and 1904. The crania collection was counted at 4,500 in the late 1980s, when Native Peoples found evidence of the study among records of the Smithsonian's holdings of 20,000 Indian human remains. Only then did the American media report the story. Yet, there is no question that the American newspapers and journals were well aware at the time of the collecting directive, the agreement, and the decapitating and grave-robbing practices. The Army and the Smithsonian advertised in the publications for years, calling for "collectors" to gather Indian artifacts and skulls.

Occasionally, a newspaper would carry an article about an Indian skull decorating a local establishment. A typical example was one in the November 16, 1890, *Rocky Mountain News* under multiple headlines: "A Bad Ute's Skull/An Indian's Brain Pan in a Denver Gun Store/Tab-we-ap Was a Redskin of the Worst Type/His Career of Deviltry Was Brought to an End by the Avenging Bullet of a White Man."

The press also failed to cover the "Civilization Regulations" of the Secretary of the Interior. These rules—issued in 1880, 1884, 1894, and 1904 and in force until the mid-1930s—banned all Native traditional religious activities, ceremonies, and dancing and imposed stiff incarceration sentences, starvation, and, in some cases, open-ended penalties on those found guilty of the detailed "Indian offenses." They outlawed the "usual practices" of a "so-called 'medicine man' [who] operates as a hindrance to the civilization of the tribes," who "resorts to any artifice or device to keep the Indians under his influence," or who "shall use any of the arts of a conjurer to prevent the Indians from abandoning their heathenish rites and customs."

Federal agents were directed "to impress upon the minds of their Indians the urgent necessity for a strict compliance with these instructions, and warn them that without this protection they are liable to be looked upon and treated as hostile Indians." Characterization as a "hostile" was tantamount to a death sentence. Periodically, in the late 1800s and early 1900s, lists of "hostiles," "fomenters of dissent," and "ringleaders" were circulated among the Army and the Indian Police. They justified, for example, murders of Dakota Chiefs Sitting Bull and Big Foot; massacres at Sand Creek, Washita, and Wounded Knee; and imprisonment of Chief Geronimo and his Chiricahua and Warm Springs Apache people as prisoners of war for more than a quarter-century into the 1900s.

The Civilization Regulations outlawed the Sun Dance "and all other similar dances and so-called religious ceremonies." Commissioner's Circulars were posted prominently on reservations until 1934. It was not the case that reporters did not travel to the remote locations and could not have known about the Circulars. Numerous stories about the dances and ceremonies were filed from the reservations, and most were written in what one circular promoted as a "careful propaganda" to "educate public opinion against the dance."

The press did not report on the hostage-students who were taken from their families to federal boarding schools during this period for the Christian-only/English-only education mandated by the Civilization Regulations. The hostage-students were taken to the first federal boarding school, the Carlisle Indian Industrial School in Carlisle, Pennsylvania, between 1879 and 1913. They were usually the sons and daughters of famous chiefs and strong families the Army wanted to keep in line on the reservations. The Carlisle motto, as articulated by its founder, Captain Richard H. Pratt, was "Kill the Savage, Kill the Indian, Save the Man."

Press accounts of the hostage-students were cheery and upbeat local features that might have been stories about family picnics. The June 26, 1886, *Cheyenne Transporter* of Darlington (Oklahoma Indian Territory on the Cheyenne and Arapaho Reservation) wrote of Cheyenne Peace Chief Bull Bear's son Thunder Bird attending Carlisle. The article noted that Thunder Bird was taking a five-year course in printing and had adopted a white man's name, "Richard Davis." Bull Bear and other Cheyenne and Arapaho chiefs were lauded for "willingly giving up their children to be educated." In Bull Bear's and Thunder Bird's family history, the "giving up" is known as a "time of wrenching, sorrow and fear that the promise of life would be broken."

The Carlisle School received more positive press attention when the student sports hero Jim Thorpe (Sac and Fox) put it on the football map. When he won four 1912 Olympic gold medals, Carlisle was reported as a model for all Indian schools and applauded for having produced Indians with "warrior-like athletic prowess." In 1913, Thorpe was stripped of his medals for having received *de minimus* payment for playing "professional" baseball. Carlisle was closed that same year. Unreported were the religious icons, cultural items, clothes, and shoes that were confiscated from Indians at Carlisle and other schools and on the reservations in the name of civilization. Many of these materials made their way into public and private collections, including some of those still held today by the great newspaper families. Native Peoples were forbidden to travel to traditional places of worship, and these sacred sites became public lands and, in some cases, the private property of wealthy newspaper families.

The Vanishing American, Modern Warriors, and Citizenship, 1900s–1930s

By the turn of the century, the Native population had dwindled to 250,000, according to the 1900 census. News reports, popular writing, and still photography—and the new technology of cylinder sound recordings and moving pictures of the 1890s and early 1900s—focused on Native Peoples as the "Vanishing American." For the most part, they did not report on the reasons or the ways that Indians were disappearing. They simply recorded what they thought were the last tribe, ceremony, and Indian, documenting the vanishing points. The best-known Indian of the time, "Ishi," was called the last California Yahi and was emblematic of a dying Indian population. Many press features during this period focused on dead Indians and anniversaries of battles. The May 28, 1936, *Lusk Herald* of Wyoming reprinted a 33-year-old *Denver Daily News* report—"Story of Battle on Lightning Creek in 1903 . . . Eagle Feather's Skull Found and Now Preserved"—next to a photo of a local man holding the purported Sioux man's skull. Once in a while, newspapers ran articles in the form of bounty notices on a current "uprising."

A February 5, 1922, *Rocky Mountain News* article filed in Phoenix reported "a reward of $25" for those who defeated "efforts to sign the roads into the Navajo reservation. . . . The redskins are said to tear out or carry away all signboards. . . . On this account scores of parties were lost on the Painted Desert or wound up at trading posts many miles from their objective."

Throughout this century, the American and world media have "discovered" Indians roughly every 20 years. Following the "Vanishing American" period of 1900 to 1920 came the "Indian Citizen/Hero" cycle of reporting. From 1920 to 1940, many of the stories were about the Choctaw Code Talkers and other Indian soldiers in the U.S. military services who had distinguished themselves in battle during World War I. Early articles about the "warrior exploits" often were accompanied by editorials calling for Indians to be rewarded with American citizenship, noting that Indians who fought for America deserved voting and other U.S. citizen privileges. In 1919, a special law was enacted that accorded U.S. citizenship to any Indian veterans of World War I who requested it. In 1924, the *Indian Citizenship Act* accorded U.S. citizenship to all "Indians born within the territorial limits of the United States." This law recognized all Natives as dual citizens—first, of their Native Nations and second, of the U.S.

A major news story about oil-rich Indians also appeared during this period. Of some 40 Indian Nations in Oklahoma, only the Osage Tribe was making any money of note from the black-gold boom, but all Native Peoples were depicted as wealthy, if unwise about money. This image helped draw many white men to Oklahoma in search of rich Indian women, and dozens of them married and murdered Osage women for the mineral rights. This story—the only one of the time to focus on Native women—was given significant play nationally.

War Heroes and Mainstream Americans, 1940s–1950s

During the 1940s and 1950s, Indian soldiers were featured in articles and broadcasts about their valor in World War II and in Korea. Two Medal of Honor recipients, Ernest Childers (Creek) and Jack Montgomery (Cherokee), also were covered broadly for their heroism in Europe with other Indian soldiers in the 45th Infantry's "Thunderbird" Division, which liberated Dachau. Ira Hayes (Pima) was depicted with fellow Marines in one of the most famous wartime photographs raising the American flag at Iwo Jima in 1945. Hayes and Jim Thorpe were the subjects of subsequent movies about their achievements and battles with alcohol. These movies—and the fact that Natives have maintained the highest rate of al-

coholism nationally throughout this century—have made the "drunken Indian" an inevitable and indelible image in popular culture.

Reports of the day often emphasized individual Native achievements as indicators that Indians were moving into the melting pot and becoming "mainstream Americans." The Indian men made news in battle, sports, and music. "Big Chief" Russell Moore (Pima), "Big Chief" Shunatona (Otoe-Missouri and Pawnee), and other "chiefs" were accomplished musicians with their own big bands. Indian women made news in the Miss America and other beauty contests and as the wives of prominent white men. Dancer Maria Tallchief (Osage) emerged as an important figure in American and European ballet. The boarding schools promoted band music, dance, and art on the walls.

As Indian students were being deculturalized, Congress and the Truman and Eisenhower administrations were mainstreaming Indians by stripping away tangible resources—a huge story the media missed. The federal government took Indian lands for such war-effort and Cold War purposes as atomic (and, later, nuclear) weapons building, testing, and disposal, and for massive water and power projects. The federal "termination" policy (see Chapter 2 of this volume) cashed out certain "assimilated" tribes and Indians, resulting in the redistribution of tribal lands and resources among the federal and state governments and among white bankers, lawyers, and private property owners. Termination was supported by the "progressive" Indians—others were not asked—and by the media in the affected local areas.

The press supported the federal initiatives by ignoring the known land grabs. The weapons buildup and disposal on Indian lands and tests affecting

Native Peoples were conducted secretly and not reported. Some newspapers favorably reported and editorialized the termination programs. They picked up the terminology of the policy crafters, who hinted darkly that the breakup of the tribes' collective holdings and power was part of the war on communism and socialism. Termination was cast as the "Americanization of the Indian" and as freeing Indians from the "domination" of the "reservation system." Indians were sailing down the mainstream.

Bullets, Bloodshed, and Justice, 1960s–1970s

Media coverage of Native Peoples in the 1960s and 1970s followed the bullets, bloodshed, and leg irons of Indian activism, the resultant legal trials, and other quests for justice in the courts and Congress. Indian activism increased as termination and other federal policies worsened conditions in Indian Country and for Indians in the cities, and as more treaties were broken and Indians were maimed and murdered. The tone of many of the stories mirrored that of the period 1860 to 1890. Activists generally were referred to as "militants" and the events were the news, initially to the exclusion of the conditions that produced them. Land grabs, poverty, and other disastrous conditions in Indian Country were the subjects of demonstrations in Oklahoma, the Northeast, and the Southwest during the 1960s. They went largely unreported until the end of the decade. Similarly, the 1960s fishing rights struggle in the Pacific Northwest did not become news until blood was shed and until Marlon Brando and Jane Fonda visited the sites of the "fish wars."

In 1969, Indians of All Tribes began their 19-month occupation of Alcatraz Island. Congress completed a study started by Senator Robert F. Kennedy, "Indian Education: A National Tragedy—A National Challenge." N. Scott Momaday (Kiowa) won the Pulitzer Prize for his 1968 best-selling novel about a modern Indian warrior, *House Made of Dawn. Custer Died for Your Sins* by Vine Deloria, Jr. (Standing Rock Sioux), was a popular book, explaining what was wrong, who was at fault, and what could be done about it. From that point—and continuing through the 1972 six-day takeover of the Bureau of Indian Affairs building in Washington, D.C., the 1973 three-month occupation of Wounded Knee, and dozens of other armed confrontations—the world learned the "Indian story" from television and news photo images of young warriors and elders, with "militant leaders" and government officials trading point-counterpoint sound bites.

The image was predominantly male and the news was usually about the monolithic Indian. The only Indian women activists who received significant media attention were LaNada Means Boyer (Shoshone-Bannock) at Alcatraz and Anna Mae Aguash (Micmac). The press covered Aguash only after she was murdered in the violent aftermath of the Wounded Knee occupation and her body was found in 1976 on the Pine Ridge Reservation. Even in the better papers and broadcasts, news leads were of a type consigned today to some sports and entertainment coverage: "Chiefs and Feds Pow-Wow Today" and "Braves Still on Warpath."

Coverage of serious tribal lawsuits and legislation was not exempt from Indian stereotyping in the media. The most widely covered of these were the 1974 federal district court decision reaffirming the 1790 *Indian Trade and Intercourse Act* and Indians' right to recover land in the East, *American Indian Religious Freedom Act of 1978*, and the 1979

Supreme Court ruling upholding an 1854 Treaty and Native Peoples' rights to fish in the Northwest. When white men burned federal judges in effigy, they were reported as citizen protesters, whereas tribes seeking redress through orderly legal processes were cast as war parties. The campaigns to recover Native sacred lands and to reverse termination acts were covered in more straightforward reporting style once they involved federal actions. Prior to their resolution, they also were treated stereotypically, with the weight of local editorial opinion against Native efforts to regain traditional holy lands. The most prominent examples of this during the early 1970s were the return of the sacred Blue Lake to the Taos Pueblo by Congress in 1970, the *Menominee Restoration Act of 1971*, and the 1972 Executive Order returning the sacred Mount Adams to the Yakama Nation, all of which were signed by President Richard M. Nixon.

Many good print journalists looked behind the gore score and ammo count, producing hundreds of stories about the situations that led to the dramatic events. Others, however, got lost in the long, complex tribal histories and mostly got those wrong, too. As Wounded Knee became a metaphor for Vietnam, the media rarely reported on Native soldiers in Vietnam, despite the fact that they served in disproportionately high numbers. Indian Vietnam veterans ordinarily were identified as such only when they were featured as "militants" at "uprisings" of the 1960s and 1970s.

Reporters generally searched for "the Indian spokesman," and many seemed confused to learn that there was at least one other "Indian side" to an issue. As they then looked for two spokesmen, more than a few were daunted by the discovery of numerous and disparate Indian voices and perspectives. As Indian activism was on the rise, the

Nixon Administration offered up spokesmen—some well-heeled tribal leaders, "Republican Indians for Nixon," and the federally funded National Tribal Chairmen's Association—to denounce the activities and views of the "militants". Much of the coverage of activities then became press-release journalism pitting the two sides' statements against each other, leaving the federal statements as the reasonable middle ground and last word.

The proliferation of Native newspapers and radio programs and stations throughout the 1970s also produced and promoted coverage of health, education, housing, child welfare, land recovery, and environmental protection. The reports from Indian Country provided valuable insights into Native Peoples' values and world views, perspectives on national issues, and the local stories that the mainstream press missed.

The longest-running Indian media story began in 1975 with the shootout on the Pine Ridge Reservation between American Indian Movement (AIM) activists and Federal Bureau of Investigation (FBI) agents. Three men were killed, but most of the news accounts concentrated on the two dead white men and many neglected to mention that an Indian man also was killed. The story continued throughout the prosecutions and acquittals of two Indian men and the trials, conviction, appeals, and continuing imprisonment of a third, Leonard Peltier (Lakota/Ojibwe). Peltier has been the subject of thousands of articles and radio and televisions pieces; a Peter Matthiessen book, *In the Spirit of Crazy Horse*; investigative pieces by "60 Minutes" and other news shows; a half-dozen film documentaries, including one by Robert Redford; and numerous letters from dozens of members of Congress to three presidents, petitioning for his release. Peltier, who has served more than 20 years of two consecutive life sentences, was convicted on circumstantial evidence, some of which was proven false and all of which was called into question by more than 35,000 FBI documents released after his legal remedies were exhausted.

The major story that most reporters missed or ignored was the widespread federal surveillance of Native Peoples and the high level of government disruption and agent provocateurism in Indian communities. Investigative pieces in this area of Indian life nationwide were exceedingly rare. When a smoking-gun government document was found, as several were in the 1970s, it became a one-day-wonder story, when picked up at all. For example, a mid-1970s FBI communication alleged that thousands of "Sioux Dog Soldiers" were training in military operations in Nevada. The document, elaborately detailed and devoid of fact, was distributed broadly to myriad federal law enforcement agencies, most likely for the purpose of tightening security and increasing surveillance in Indian Country in the face of some common enemy. The story behind the story was not pursued.

Increased Coverage and More Diversity, 1980s–1990s

During the 1980s and 1990s, media stories regarding Native Peoples increased in quantity and diversity. There was extensive and detailed coverage of the Eastern Indian land cases, particularly the largest one—the claim of the Passamaquoddy Tribe, Penobscot Nation, and Maliseet Tribe to two-thirds of Maine. They won their initial lawsuit against the Nixon Administration, forcing an investigation of the claim. The Ford Administration found it valid and, in 1976, filed suit against Maine on behalf of the Indians, and the bond market

stopped approving transactions in the claim area. President Jimmy Carter was personally involved in resolving the Eastern land claims. Shortly after taking office he approved the Narragansett Tribe's settlement with Rhode Island, and the 1980 *Maine Indian Land Claims Settlement Act* was one of the last measures he signed into law.

The Maine settlement involved nearly $90 million and 300,000 acres. Unlike the intensive reporting on the Maine and other claims involving substantial sums of money and land, the Mashantucket Pequot Tribe's claim to lands in Connecticut and the $900,000 settlement a few years later was considered small change in Congress and barely reported. Its passage in the House as the *Mashantucket "Paraquat"* bill went unnoticed in Congress and in the media. The 300-member Pequot Tribe made major news later, however, when they turned the small settlement into a few acres of federal Indian trust land and opened the largest casino in the U.S. on it in 1992. They became the richest Native Americans, with assets in the neighborhood of $4 billion. Today the individual Pequots are multimillionaires, and the Tribe is an important American financial benefactor and force that is followed closely by business and political reporters.

Gaming in Indian Country has commanded the greatest sustained media attention since the late 1980s, with every news outlet covering the legal battles in Congress and the courts but mostly just following the money. Much of the reporting and nearly all of the entertainment-media coverage of Indian gaming—prior to and since the *Indian Gaming Regulatory Act of 1988*—has been tinged with an envious, resentful, and racist tone reminiscent of the coverage early in this century of oil-rich Indians in Oklahoma as making foolish financial decisions and driving "Geronimo's

Cadillacs." The high-powered opponents of tribal gaming and the skewed coverage of it have created the public impression that all Indians are gaming rich, even though only 100 of the more than 500 Native Nations in the country have any gambling operations and despite the fact that Indians remain the most economically impoverished U.S. population.

President Ronald Reagan made news with a 1988 speech in Russia, where he told students at Moscow University, "Perhaps America should not have humored Indians by putting them on reservations back then." This and other remarks about Native Americans and federal Indian policy made headlines worldwide and were the butt of jokes in editorials and cartoons. The talk-show hosts had a field day. "Humoring the Indians," said one. "What's next? Kidding the homeless?" Numerous media outlets made space and time available for Native writers, politicians, and lawyers to comment on Reagan's remarks and explain in detail what was off-base about them. His gratuitous swipe spotlighted the essence of the Reagan Administration's policy, which was to cut one-third of the federal Indian budget, to turn over control of tribal programs to the states, and to place nuclear waste dumps on Indian lands. Those stories, which had been covered in considerable detail for six years, were given new legs by the Moscow remarks and slowed down the budget-cutting attempts—but not the state control or dumping ground efforts—in the remaining Reagan months.

In the late 1980s, the Senate Special Committee on Investigations spent millions of dollars and three years to examine and improve federal management of Indian resources. What Indians and the public got was a propaganda machine exposing and publicizing crimes and misdeeds by tribal leaders, employees, and contractors, as well as a self-serving 1989 report with little new or useful information. The exposés were covered extensively in media reports, almost exclusively from the committee's leaks and perspective. The major news was that Navajo Nation Chairman Peter MacDonald was captured alive in the cookie jar. He was twice convicted, first in the public eye and later, in 1990, in the tribal and federal justice systems. As head of the Navajo Nation—which has more land than any other reservation and is about the size of West Virginia—MacDonald was a leading "spokesman" in media Indian reports during the 1970s and 1980s. He was a high roller on a modest tribal chairman's salary. His finances and political clout in Washington—where he often dined at pricey restaurants with politicos, including then-Senator Dennis DeConcini of Arizona, chairman of the investigative committee, who had his own Savings and Loan scandal problems—had gone unexamined until he was caught on tape making deals for hundreds of thousands of "golf balls," his code for dollars.

The combination of the smoking-gun evidence and a known personality was irresistible and reporters ran with the story, never questioning why the committee did nothing else. The story that the committee failed in its main mission was quashed or poorly and scantily reported. Although the committee did generate a fair amount of press on the issue of widespread sexual abuse of Indian children in federal boarding schools, it clutched when it came to getting the goods on losses of Native Peoples' resources and money at the hands of federal agencies, mineral companies, and other developers.

While the attention of the committee, the public, and the media was occupied elsewhere, it was religious freedom and the cultural agenda that topped the list of priorities in Indian Country. In 1987, Northwest Natives received an apology from nine Christian denominations for their role in destroying traditional religious ceremonies and places. Afterward, religious groups nationwide joined a broad-based coalition for American Indian religious freedom, and Native Peoples began negotiating with the Smithsonian and other museums for the return of dead Indians and sacred objects. By 1989, editorial opinion was clearly on the side of Native Peoples' right to recover their relatives and cultural property from museums. It was estimated that there might be more dead Indians in museums and other collections than the two million live ones in the U.S. The Smithsonian alone held some 20,000 Native human remains and many times that number of religious objects.

Meanwhile, the Museum of the American Indian—a private trust in New York with the world's largest collection of Indian materials—was broke and looking for a new home. Its collection of more than one million art and cultural objects was deteriorating and poorly housed. The story was given play only in New York and as a local story, but the local paper was *The New York Times,* so the story was picked up and noted nationally. The Smithsonian was salivating over the prospect of gaining the collection—the highest quality and quantity of any collection ever on the block. Few in Congress knew or cared enough about the situation to commit the necessary public funds. Then, the Texas billionaire H. Ross Perot made headlines by bidding $85 million to build a world-class museum in Dallas for the collection. Politicians in New York and Washington closed ranks against the move. They mobilized to nationalize the collection, transfer it to the Smithsonian, and form a public/private funding partnership for exhibit space in New York City, a research center in the Washington area, and a museum on the National Mall.

The congressional effort was led by Senator Daniel K. Inouye of Hawaii, the first nonwhite (a Japanese American) to chair the Senate Committee on Indian Affairs. As the final museum deal was struck, Inouye and then-Representative Ben Nighthorse Campbell of Colorado—the only Native American (a Cheyenne) in Congress—held up the legislation to give Native Peoples time and leverage to reach an accord with the Smithsonian for the return of human remains and cultural property. By the end of the year, Congress passed and President George Bush approved the *National Museum of the American Indian (NMAI) Act of 1989,* which contained the historic repatriation policy provision for Smithsonian holdings. Eleven months later, the *Native American Graves Protection and Repatriation Act of 1990* was signed into law (see also Chapter 2 of this volume). One year later, in 1991, the NMAI Trustees' Repatriation Policy was issued.

Each step of the repatriation issues and policies was well covered and analyzed in print and in broadcasts. High-volume coverage of the NMAI has focused on its $10 million donation from the Pequots and its official opening gala and exhibits in New York, both in 1994. At the end of 1991, a new law authorized a memorial to the Cheyenne, Sioux, and other Indian Nations' heroes of the 1876 Battle of the Little Big Horn, settling a long-standing issue in Indian Country. The popular aspect, and the story that was picked up everywhere, was the part of the law that dropped the name of Custer from the area's official designation, renaming it as the Little Bighorn Battlefield National Monument.

Ongoing efforts begun in the late 1980s to provide legal protections for Native Peoples' sacred lands and ceremonies have been covered sporadically and superficially in print and on radio but rarely on television. Native Americans are the only segment of American society whose churches cannot be defended with the First Amendment. The Supreme Court ruled in 1988—in a case that pitted a federal logging road against a Native sacred site in Northern California—that the First Amendment did not provide a cause of action for protection of Native sacred lands, leaving Indians locked out of the American courthouses.

An Executive Order on Indian Sacred Sites was signed by President Bill Clinton in 1996. It expressly did not provide the needed cause of action and did little more than restate the 18-year-old policy and review process of the *American Indian Religious Freedom Act*. Even though the order merely kept the issue alive, it was seen as so politically risky that the White House ensured limited news coverage and low visibility by releasing it on the Friday afternoon of the Memorial Day weekend and naming a sole press contact in the Interior Department, who did not respond to press calls for two weeks. Clinton had signed an earlier bill in 1994 codifying an existing exemption to a drug regulation, allowing the use of peyote in ceremonies of the Native American Church, and the White House had played it way down with a dead-of-night release.

High on good words and symbolic gestures, the Clinton Administration held a meeting with tribal leaders on the White House grounds in 1994. Acting on wildly faulty information from advisors, the president wrongly claimed that the event was the first presidential meeting with tribal leaders to occur in the White House in U.S. history. The event was covered widely, and nearly all stories used the "first" and "historic" angle as their lead-ins. In fact, more presidents than not have met with tribal leaders, and most of the meetings have taken place in the White House since its construction. Before then, most of the

meetings took place in the various Capitol locations. Beginning with President George Washington, several heads of state also went to Indian Country to meet with Indian Nations' chiefs.

In the 1980s, the plans for the 1992 Columbus Quincentenary and the enormous popularity of Tony Hillerman's best-selling novels about a Navajo police officer generated phenomenal interest in things Indian. They provided the impetus for a plethora of books, documentaries, and movies about Indians and the greatest Native employment boom in Hollywood since the days of the cowboy-and-Indian oaters. Most, however, portrayed Native Peoples in the past tense. For example, even though Kevin Costner's 1990 award-winning *Dances with Wolves* featured scores of Lakota actors, it ended with an epilogue pronouncing the Sioux Nation dead at the end of the last century.

The Columbus craze and Hillerman's series also created a demand for works by Native authors, especially the literary superstar couple Michael Dorris (Modoc) and Louise Erdrich (Turtle Mountain Chippewa). Each of their books—before and after their 1991 coauthored novel, *The Crown of Columbus*—was highly critiqued, awarded, and sold. They and their works received more press attention than any Native literary figures ever did. Dorris' suicide in 1997 and the tragic circumstances surrounding it were followed in the media, the literary community, and Indian Country with intense interest.

Beginning in the late 1980s, Native Peoples throughout the hemisphere declared that October 12, 1992, would be a Day of Mourning and the 500th Anniversary of the Invasion. Whereas the governments of the U.S., Spain, and Italy committed millions of dollars to promote the Columbus Quincentenary in the U.S., a handful of private foundations and individuals funded efforts, most prominently The 1992 Alliance, to provide Native voices on the occasion of the Quincentenary. Initially, only the Quincentenary celebrants' take on the "discovery" was reported: Indians were at fault, too, because they resisted civilization and would not share their plentiful resources. Most Indians died of diseases, but the Europeans could not be blamed for that, and Indians spread the sexual diseases to the sailors. Indians did not own the land and were just the first inhabitants, having come across the Siberian land bridge from Asia.

Native Peoples responded: It was not a discovery but an invasion. It was the "civilization" of forced delivery of land and gold, assaults on their families, and imposed European mores that Natives resisted. Syphilis originated in Europe and was brought here—along with pneumonia, plagues, tuberculosis, influenza, and the common cold—and smallpox and measles were used as weapons and deliberately spread to Indians. Also, the land bridge went both ways, and most Natives originated in this hemisphere.

In 1990, The 1992 Alliance and the Traditional Circle of Elders and Youth declared 1992 as the Year of the Indigenous Peoples and called on the "entertainment and news industries, the sports and advertising worlds and all those with influence in shaping popular culture to forego the use of dehumanizing, stereotyping, cartooning images and information regarding our peoples, and to recognize their responsibility for the emotional violence their fields have perpetuated against our children." Native voices and views were amplified by reporters and editors, and by teachers in classrooms. Traditional Native perspectives were spotlighted in virtually all coverage of the Quincentenary, which was a high-profile story from 1990 to 1992. This coverage led to myriad stories about all aspects of Native life,

opening a forum for Native writers in most American publications. It was a career boom time for Native journalists, as well as for Natives in the arts and humanities, whose work was in great demand internationally. A 1991 law declared 1992 the Year of the American Indian. The United Nations declared it the Year of the Indigenous People and the 1990s as the Decade of the Indigenous People. Rigoberta Menchu, a Quiche activist, was honored with a 1992 Nobel Peace Prize. All these stories were reported in a straightforward manner and given wide coverage.

Protests against Native-related sports names and mascots reemerged as a popular news story in the 1980s and 1990s. As increasing numbers of colleges and high schools dropped their "Indians" and "Redskins" labels and images, the issue was covered with greater seriousness than it had been in the 1960s and 1970s, with notable changes in editorial opinion and policy. In a 1988 column for *The Washington Post Magazine*, Richard Cohen called on Washington's professional football team to drop the name "Redskins." In what could have been a commentary on portrayals of Native Peoples in popular culture generally, he wrote, "It hardly enhances the self-esteem of an Indian youth to always see his people—himself—represented as a cartoon character. And, always, the caricature is suggestive of battle, of violence—of the Indian warrior, the brave, the chief, the warpath, the beating of tom-toms. For the young Indian—for the Indian of any age—none of this has anything to do with the present, but only with the Indians' futile fight to hold on to what was once *theirs*." In 1992, *The Washington Post* editorialized that the team should change its name. Andy Rooney of "60 Minutes" took the opposite view. Calling protests "silly," he said, "American Indians have more important problems to worry about than sports teams calling themselves by Indian nicknames. . . . The real problem is we took the country away from the American Indians, they want it back and we're not going to give it to them. We feel guilty and we'll do what we can for them within reason, but they can't have their country back. Next question." IIis commentary was vast in its reach and ignorance. The "impact of their culture on the world has been slight," he said. "There are no great American Indian novels, no poetry . . . no memorable music . . . no American Indian art." He concluded with an echo of Reagan in Moscow: "If Indians are truly offended by these names and symbols we use for fun, we'll drop them, but someone should tell the Indians living on reservations that the United States isn't a bad country to be part of."

Seven Native Americans petitioned the U.S. Patent and Trademark Office in 1992 to cancel the federal licenses held by Pro Football, Inc., to the name and associated logos of the "Washington Redskins." The petitioners in this widely covered suit asked the federal government to withdraw the exclusive right to make money off the name because it is the most demeaning term in English for Native Peoples. In 1994, at the first national conference of journalists of color, Unity '94, the Native American Journalists Association and other Native reporters and editors called on the wire services and all editors to follow the lead of the Minneapolis *Star Tribune* and *The Oregonian* to decline to use any racist, demeaning sports team names or symbols.

Senator Ben Nighthorse Campbell made big news in 1995 when he switched political parties and became a Republican. The story was played straight in the media as a political shocker. Reporters resisted all possible Indian puns and allusions, and most even avoided mentioning that Campbell

is Cheyenne or reported it simply as one fact about him. It was that fact that proved problematic for conservative pundit Rush Limbaugh as he attempted to explain the story to his television audience. "He's not the far-left radical liberal that people think that he is," gushed Limbaugh, "simply because he's a Democrat and a member of the Indian—African—whatever—trying to be politically—he's an Indian, ok? A lot of them think he's Native American, an Indian, and he'd be far left and so forth—he's not really." Two years later, in 1997, Campbell became the first Native person to chair the Senate Committee on Indian Affairs in its 177-year history. The story went virtually unreported.

The biggest story of early 1997 also involved Cheyennes—the $107,000 campaign contribution to the Democratic National Committee (DNC) by two of the poorest tribes in the country, the Cheyenne and Arapaho of Oklahoma. They expected President Clinton to issue an executive order returning the Tribes' Fort Reno lands, which have been wrongly held by federal agencies for a century. As soon as *The Washington Post* began asking questions, tribal advisors alerted Washington politicos. The DNC, which had failed to report the contribution, quickly filed the legally required reports of the donations with the Federal Election Commission before the story broke. Although the fact of the late filing was mentioned in a few stories, this aspect went largely unreported, and no reporters connected the dots. The story was given play everywhere. It was one story among the myriad campaign flaps, scandals, and investigations that anyone could understand. And it was somehow worse than the other stories because the donors had both limited means and naive expectations. The reporting, for the most part, was stereotype-free. In Oklahoma, however, the articles and cartoons were as anti-Indian as those at any time in the history of the state's newspapers, most of which were built on the fortunes from stolen Indian lands.

Conclusions: 'Non-Indians Still Regard You as the Enemy'

"America is missing the Indian story." That was Howard Simons' assessment of news coverage of Native issues in a 1986 speech to the National Congress of American Indians (NCAI) Annual Convention (September 27, Phoenix, Arizona). Then-curator of Harvard's Nieman Foundation for Journalism, Simons had been managing editor of *The Washington Post* from 1971 to 1984. "There are very few experts on papers who know or care about American Indians," he said. "And, worse, there are very few Indians on American newspapers. Things won't change appreciably until we can capture more Indians into all phases of journalism, not just the newsroom, but circulation and the business side."[1]

During his 13 years at the *Post*, Simons tried to "scratch people's minds where they don't know they itch" but could interest only three reporters in covering Native issues in any "intelligent, sustained way." He also said that uninterest at the bully pulpit can have a greater effect on an issue than even a constituency's lack of political clout. "The president is a powerful voice in setting not just the national agenda for the press. This president [Reagan] either doesn't like Indians or doesn't care about them, or both."

Simons conducted a survey of editors on coverage of Indian issues in their papers. He recalled that one editor drew an analogy between avoiding driving through a black ghetto and an Indian reservation. He quoted the editor as saying, "If you never see them, you never have to bother about them. Even let them rip off the white man with bingo as long as you don't prick the white man's conscience. If they are not visible, you don't have to cover them and, unlike any other problem in our society, this won't change." He recounted another editor as responding, "There is no circulation for us on the reservation. There's no economically compelling need for newspapers to circulate because there's low readership. It's difficult to distribute over vast distances and there's no advertising. And, as newspapers are profit-making machines in this capitalist society, they have to distribute their papers pro bono, which they won't do."

Simons quoted another editor, who likened covering Indians to covering Appalachia: "The press discovered poverty, television discovered poverty. They filmed it, they wrote about it. It was front page for a long while. It won Emmy Awards on television. But poverty is still unchanged in Appalachia. The only difference is, it's no longer a story."

"Yours is a tiny voice among other minorities," Simons told the gathering. "You have very little political clout, and a lot of the non-Indians still regard you as the enemy."

Note

1. This and later quotes from Simons are from his speech to the National Congress of American Indians on September 27, 1986. The speech was taped and transcribed by the author. It was later published in the Winter 1986 *NCAI Sentinel/Bulletin*.

References

Honour, Hugh. (1975). *The new golden land: European images of America from the discoveries to the present time*. New York: Pantheon Books.

Jefferson, Thomas. (1975). "Note on the State of Virginia." In M. D. Peterson (Ed.), *The portable Thomas Jefferson*. New York: Penguin Books, 23–232.

Discussion Questions

1. Describe how the early reporters portrayed Native men and women, including the appearance, sexuality, and prototype of each.

2. What were the federal "civilization" and "termination" policies? Elaborate on the implications of these policies.

3. How were stereotypes incorporated into the media's coverage of tribal lawsuits and legislation?

4. Why were the reporters not able to locate a single "Indian spokesman?" Examine the various voices that were discovered.

5. Describe three stories regarding Native people covered by the media during the late 1980s and early 1990s. Discuss the stereotypes that these stories reinforce, and their implications, or the absence of stereotypes and the implications for this type of reporting. ◆

Chapter 4

Stereotyping by Politicians

Or, 'The Only Real Indian Is the Stereotyped Indian'

Carol Chiago Lujan

Public records are replete with comments regarding American Indians. Statements such as "The only good Indian is a dead Indian" and "Indians are the very dregs of the earth" were common among early Euro-American politicians, writers, and Christian leaders. Throughout U.S. history, numerous politicians helped to perpetuate these negative stereotypes of American Indian nations and American Indian people to the general public. Currently, misconceptions of American Indians persist. Whether it is intentional or not, public officials continue to contribute to the erroneous images of American Indian nations and the American Indian people. Unfortunately, these inaccurate stereotypes are not limited to local politicians but extend to the highest political officials in our country.

This chapter is designed to examine politicians' stereotyping of American Indian nations and American Indian people. It begins with a general description of American Indians and presents the problems of stereotyping. It continues with a brief overview of how and why stereotypes emerge and persist. A major portion of the chapter concentrates on how politicians perpetuate negative images of American Indians. Basic information about American Indian nations and people is also presented to give the reader a more accurate image of American Indians. This is followed by a discussion of the effects of the stereotypes on American Indians. The conclusion examines possible policy recommendations.

The American Indian population is one of the fastest-growing and youngest populations in the United States. According to the 1990 U.S. Census report, almost two million people identified themselves as American Indian. This is a population increase of 37.9 percent over the 1980 recorded total. Furthermore, 39 percent of the American Indian population was under 20 years old, compared to 29 percent of the nation's total population. Women comprised slightly more than half (52 percent) of the total American Indian population. Almost half (46 percent) of the American Indian women were under age 25 (U.S. Census Bureau, 1993, p. WE-5).

Why Do People Stereotype?

According to social science literature, "stereotypes play an important part in the development and maintenance of prejudice. Where intergroup conflict exists, they are used to justify feelings of hostility on both sides. Once formed, stereotypes are highly resistant to change. By repeating a stereotype, people strengthen their belief in its accuracy" (DeFleur, D'Antonio, and DeFleur, 1976, p. 267). Social scientists contend that people "invent" prejudices to gain and/or maintain economic or political dominance. Eventually, "prejudices tend to become institutionalized as a part of the general culture and begin to play a part in the socialization of the next generation" (ibid., 1976, p. 265).

The stereotypes of American Indians have ranged from "noble savage" to "ignoble savage," including everything in between. Some common stereotypes include the "drunken Indian" or the poverty-stricken reservation Indian. More recent stereotypes include the "wise, nature-loving, new-age" Indian (identified by their long black hair and abundant turquoise jewelry) and/or the "casino-rich Indian." Although the more recent stereotypes appear less pejorative, they are equally absurd and damaging because they perpetuate a distorted image of the American Indian.

Several factors help explain the development of stereotypes of American Indians. For example, in an attempt to understand how American Indian society compared with European society, early European philosophers such as Montaigne and Rousseau developed an idealized view of the American Indian and helped to perpetuate the image of the noble savage (Bordewich, 1996). Conversely, military personnel and early colonists villainized the American Indians and portrayed them as bloodthirsty savages.

Throughout the history of Indian and Euro-American relations, the more threatening the Indian was perceived to be, the more negative the stereotype became. Politicians also relied on the racist philosophy of "manifest destiny" to justify the methodical colonization and destruction of American Indian nations and American Indian people. Euro-Americans who believed in manifest destiny maintained that through "divine ordination and the natural superiority of the white race" they had the right to seize and occupy all of North America (Morris, 1992). In 1846, Senator Thomas Hart Benton stated that Euro-Americans "had alone received the divine command to subdue and replenish the earth," and indigenous people had no right to the land or the Americas because this land had been created for use "by the white races . . . according to the intentions of the Creator" (ibid., 1992, p. 67).

Stereotyping American Indian Nations and American Indian People

The stereotyping of American Indians is not only directed at the individual, but also extends to American Indian nations and their sovereign governments. Just as individual negative characteristics of American Indian people are exaggerated into stereotypes, so are the characteristics of Indian nations. American Indian governments are often portrayed by the media and politicians alike as unsophisticated, corrupt, and/or inept. Such stereotypes diminish the importance of the sovereign nations. American Indian nations are no more or less important and/or corrupt than any other government, whether it is local, state, federal, or international. However, until recently, American Indian governments were not taken seriously by local, state, and federal officials. Both politicians and the media have contributed significantly to the negative imagery by emphasizing scandals and minimizing the progressive actions of American Indian governments.

The Role of Politicians in Creating Stereotypes

The following are a few recent examples of negative comments and/or legislation made by top United States officials, including a president of the U.S., a U.S. senator, members of the U.S. House of Representatives, and U.S. Supreme Court justices.

U.S. President. In 1988, a Russian student asked U.S. President Ronald Reagan, who was visiting Moscow, about American Indians living on reservations (see also Chapter three of this volume). Reagan said that the federal government should not have "humored" the Indians by allowing them to live on reservations and instead should have said, "Come, join us . . . and be part of our society" (Frontline, 1988). People familiar with the history of American Indians were angered at Reagan's ignorant and cavalier statements regarding American Indian nations and U.S. policy.

If President Reagan had been knowledgeable about American Indian issues, he would have known that over 550 American Indian nations survived the European invasion, as well as the land theft, forced removal, and genocidal acts sanctioned by the U.S. government. Furthermore, American Indians did not "choose" to live on reservations but were forced onto restricted areas of land that were a fraction of the size of the area they previously had occupied. These parcels of land were referred to as "Indian reservations" and were considered unproductive and worthless by the U.S. government. A number of American Indian nations were able to remain in their traditional areas such as the Pueblo and the Diné (Navajo) in Arizona, New Mexico, and Utah. However, many other Native Nations were forced to leave their original homelands.

The most dramatic forced removal was that of the Native Nations from the eastern part of the United States, including the Choctaw, Chickasaw, Creek, Cherokee, and Seminole. These Indian nations were forced to move to the Oklahoma Territory. Historians often refer to this U.S. policy as the "Trail of Tears." During the forced removal, "tens of thousands of Indians perished on forced marches that were often conducted in the dead of winter. As many as one-third of their tribal members, especially the very young and the very old, died before they reached the new Indian Territory" (Champagne, 1994, p. 238).

In retrospect, it seems incredible that a U.S. President would be so naive and uninformed about basic American history as it relates to American Indian Nations. Unfortunately, Reagan's reckless comments are not uncommon. And because his statement received international media coverage, it not only reinforced inaccurate images of American Indians in the United States but also extended the stereotypes to the rest of the world.

U.S. Senate. The belief that American Indians cannot tolerate alcohol is a persistent myth. This stereotype is difficult to change due to the perpetuation of exaggerated statistics about American Indians that were presented in 1994 with the introduction of legislation concerning "fetal alcohol syndrome" (FAS) and "fetal alcohol effects" (FAE), medical terms used to describe birth defects caused by women who drink during pregnancy. The statement that "one in four" babies on a South Dakota reservation is affected with FAS/FAE has been used extensively to support the FAS/FAE legislation (Anquoe, 1994). However, although this figure has been used liberally, it has no scientific basis. May (1992), a sociologist who has done extensive research in this area, maintains that "much of the newspaper and conference coverage of FAS [among the American Indian communities] has been highly dramatic and quite distorted. The figures quoted of 'one in three' or 'one of four' Indian babies having FAS have no support at all in screening or epidemiologic studies." Sensationalizing FAS/FAE among American Indian populations perpetuates the image of the "drunken Indian," one of the most pervasive and damaging stereotypes of native people. Until very recently, this negative image was generally accepted by the nonnative population and, in some cases, by the American Indians themselves.

Unlike other areas of research on American Indians there is an abundance of articles on American Indians and alcohol. May (1989) contends that no "other group in America, or possibly the world, has been stigmatized more by alcohol-related behavior than American Indians. . . . At least the tragic history of the effects of alcohol usage on a group of people has never been so abundantly documented elsewhere. . . . Whether the stereotype is, or ever was, warranted is, however, another question" (pp. 95–96).

Part of the stigmatization may be due to the early alcohol legislation prohibiting the sale of alcohol to American Indians both on and off the reservation. In 1832 Congress passed laws officially prohibiting the sale of alcoholic beverages to Indians. Although the law was repealed in 1953, many American Indian governments maintain the prohibition on reservations. According to May (1989), the overall effect of alcohol prohibition may have been substantial and negative. "As documented in a number of other cultures around the world, prohibition may produce drinking patterns which are abusive and undesirable. . . . Thus, a specific reaction to prohibition may have eventually become normative" (p. 99).

Because of the negative stereotyping of American Indians as alcoholics, both Indian and non-Indian people may have distorted and negative views regarding alcohol. A common assumption is that American Indians are biologically predisposed to alcoholism. However, research to date does not show that American Indians are different from other people regarding the physiology of alcohol metabolism (Bennion and Li, 1976; Schaefer, 1981).

U.S. House of Representatives. The recent publicity regarding the tremendous success of a handful of Indian nations in the gaming industry, such as the Mashantucket Pequot Tribe of Connecticut and the Shakopee-Mdewakanton Dakota in Minnesota, has created yet another inaccurate stereotype—that of the casino-rich Indian. During the recent efforts to balance the federal budget, a few members of Congress suggested that the federal government terminate its responsibilities to the American Indians. Evidently, they felt that Indian nations were now capable of financing their own governments with profits from their casinos. Furthermore, the House members reasoned, wealthy Indian nations could support the native nations that do not have gambling casinos. What they failed to consider, in attempting to balance the budget, is that only one-fifth of the over 550 Indian nations have gambling income and only five are making money from the casinos. Moreover, as Harjo (1996, p. A15), a longtime Indian rights activist, states, "federal Indian funding is not welfare—much of it runs the health, education and other programs that the U.S. promised in exchange for a country over which to govern."

Politicians appear to have difficulty understanding and recognizing the sovereign status of American Indian nations. Numerous Supreme Court decisions and legislative acts attest to this unfortunate state of affairs. This is evident in the decisions of the late 1990s. The U.S. House of Representatives overwhelmingly supported the passage of the *Adoption Promotion and Stability Act of 1996,* which gives state governments precedent over Indian nations in deciding adoption cases involving American Indian children (Melmer, 1996a). American Indian people view this adoption act as another example of U.S. politicians' unfamiliarity with or total disregard for the sovereign status of American Indian governments.

U.S. Supreme Court. Another encroachment on the sovereignty of Indian nations occurred in 1996 when the U.S. Supreme Court, in a 5-4 decision, ruled in favor of states' rights over the rights of Indian nations. The Supreme Court ruled that the U.S. Congress exceeded its authority in allowing Indian nations to file lawsuits against states. The Supreme Court decision resulted from a case in which the Seminole Nation of Florida filed suit in federal court against the governor of Florida and the state for failing to negotiate a gaming agreement (referred to as a "gaming compact") (Melmer, 1996b).

Historically, state and federal governments have viewed American Indians and their existing governments in a paternalistic and ethnocentric manner. As the cases presented here and those discussed in Chapters 2 and 3 of this volume reveal, this perspective is also reflected in numerous government policies directed at American Indians. Although the various laws differ in their intent, the common theme is the disregard for American Indian sovereignty and Indian nations' special status as distinct and unique governments.

State Politicians

The most well-publicized struggle between state governments and Indian nations focuses on casino enterprises owned and operated by American Indian governments. Ironically, the issue of gambling has done more to educate the general public about Indian nations and their unique sovereign status vis-à-vis the U.S. government than any other issue to date.

Since the establishment of the United States, Indian nations and state governments have clashed over various concerns including land, water, and mineral and fishing rights. Recently, taxation and criminal jurisdictional issues have moved to the forefront of the debate between states and Indian nations. The often precarious relationship between Indian nations and states is likely to continue and to remain fragile because of the *Indian Gaming Regulatory Act* (IGRA).

According to the IGRA, Indian nations may operate casinos only if gambling is legal in their state. Furthermore, Indian nations must negotiate compacts with the state prior to establishing gaming enterprises. As a result, friction between states and Indian governments has intensified. Some state governors have negotiated in good faith, whereas others have not. In Arizona, the governor refused to sign additional agreements with Indian nations, thus stalling any further negotiations between the state and tribal governments. Conversely, the governor of New Mexico signed gaming compacts (agreements) with tribal governments before realizing that gambling was illegal in New Mexico. Consequently, the New Mexico Indian nations that recently invested millions of dollars to build and operate their casinos are placed in precarious financial and legal positions.

Rather than call for a special session to settle the legality of this complex issue, the New Mexico state legislators preferred to wait for a decision from the federal district court judge. The decision hinges on many critical factors including knowledge of Indian law, the interpretation of the IGRA, and the unique sovereign status of American Indian nations. The public's general lack of knowledge about American Indian history and law makes it highly unlikely that American Indian governments can receive justice within the U.S. judicial system.

Dispelling the Stereotypes: A General Overview of the American Indian Nations and Their Citizens

The American Indian population is extremely diverse culturally, physically, and economically. Each of the more than 550 Indian nations in America has its own culture, language, and lifestyle. In addition to their social and cultural diversity, American Indian nations have their own styles of government that reflect their particular customs and laws. However, the unique political status vis-à-vis the U.S. federal government that Indian nations share and their common history of relations with Euro-Americans help to bind the diverse Indian nations together. Furthermore, their sovereign status legally separates American Indian nations from any other racial or ethnic group within the United States.

Sovereign Nations

The unique legal status of the American Indian nations is founded on the premise that American Indian governments were in existence before the establishment of the U.S. government. As part of the treaty relationship, Indian nations gave up external sovereignty, such as the right to ally themselves with foreign nations in wars against the United States, in return for the "protection" of the United States.

In late 1996 there were 557 federally recognized American Indian nations in the United States, including over 200 Indian, Aleut, Eskimo (Yupik and Inuit), Athapaskan, Tlingit, and Haida communities in Alaska. "Federal recognition" means that these Indian nations have a special legal relationship with the federal government. Legally, the status of American Indian nations in the United States is that of domestic dependent nations within a nation. This status is also known as "tribal sovereignty."

Throughout the years, the U.S. Supreme Court has interpreted tribal sovereignty in a variety of ways. Consequently, American Indian law is one of the most complex areas of legal study. For example, there is often confusion about which government entity has jurisdiction over a given issue. Most American Indian nations maintain jurisdiction over civil cases that occur within the Indian nations. In criminal cases that occur on Indian reservations, members of Indian nations are subject to at least three levels of government— the American Indian nation, the state, and the federal government (Deloria and Lytle, 1983). More specifically, the federal government restricts the length of the sentence (one year maximum) and the amount of a fine ($5,000 maximum) that tribes can impose in their courts. Whereas tribes have sole sovereignty over minor crimes that occur on reservations, the federal government steps in for major crimes by Indians that occur on Indian lands. These are handled concurrently by the tribe and the federal government. If a non-Indian is involved in a crime on a reservation, either as victim or offender, jurisdiction falls to either the tribe or the federal court, depending on the type of crime and whether the state in which the reservation is located is a P.L.-280 state or not (see further Deloria and Lytle, 1983: 161–192).[1] Finally, criminal and civil cases involving Indians that occur off the reservation are subject to the jurisdiction of the local municipality.

Virtually all American Indian nations have highly sophisticated governments. Many have democratic forms of government that include the executive, legislative, and judicial branches. However, some nations continue to have theocratic governments (see also Chapter 5 in this volume). Additionally, some tribal government leaders are elected and others are appointed. Many combine the contemporary U.S. form of government with the more traditional Indian forms.

Virtually each of the 557 American Indian nations has its own codified laws and comprehensive judicial systems. Most of the judicial systems are similar to those of non-Indian courts across the country. They commonly include lower courts, higher courts, police, and correction facilities. Various cases are brought before tribal courts, including minor crimes and civil disputes. Most of the people who staff the judicial systems of the American Indian nations are highly trained American Indian attorneys with law degrees from colleges across the country, including such prestigious institutions as Harvard and Stanford. Some American Indian nations continue to use their indigenous justice systems (stressing mediation and dispute resolution) concurrently with their Euro-American–styled courts.

The Diné (Navajo) Nation Peacemaker Court is conducted in both the native language and English. The Peacemaker Court emphasizes harmony and balance and works closely with the Diné Nation's Euro-American–formatted judicial system to solve civil disputes and minor crimes. Lately, this court has received much interest and attention from the non-Indian legal community. Consequently, people from around the world have visited the Diné Nation in Window Rock, Arizona, to observe the sessions and learn more about this "innovative" approach (which the Diné have practiced for thousands of years) to resolving social problems.

Effect of Negative Stereotypes on American Indians

Distorted images of Indian nations create an atmosphere that supports exploitation, oppression, and stereotyping. The prevailing attitude among American Indians is that they have been intentionally stereotyped by Euro-Americans to justify and legitimize the exploitation and oppression of native people. Wilkinson (1974) contends that the distorted images of American Indi-

ans help to reinforce Euro-America's concept of its own superiority and at the same time works to destroy the self-concept of the American Indian. Perpetuation of these images serves to continue the prejudice against American Indians.

The consequences of negative stereotyping of American Indians are many. Three of the most damaging effects are criminalization, marginalization (when the stereotypes are accepted), and loss of language and culture.

Criminalization

Research has suggested that the perpetuation of the drunken-Indian stereotype makes Indians more vulnerable to alcohol-related arrests (Stewart, 1964). The relationship between alcohol and crime among American Indians has been discussed in a number of studies. Stratton (1973) found that alcohol-related offenses accounted for 85 to 90 percent of all arrests of Indians in Gallup, New Mexico, in 1969. Many police officers in this study held the view that all Indians who drink are drunks or that Indians are racially unable to drink moderately.

American Indians are also more likely to receive longer sentences because of negative stereotypes about reservation life. Federal and local judges are more likely to give longer sentences to American Indians convicted of crimes because they believe that life on the reservation is unstable and conducive to crime. An early article by Hall and Simkus (1975) on racism and the disparate sentencing of American Indians indicates that American Indians in Montana were significantly more likely to be incarcerated than whites who committed similar offenses. A rationale for incarcerating American Indians presented by the judges was the instability of reservation life. The more recent Bureau of Justice Statistics (BJS) survey of prison populations shows that a disproportionate number of American

Indians are imprisoned in the state of Montana. Twenty-three percent of the total female prison population in Montana and 22 percent of the total male prison population are Indian, yet the entire American Indian population in Montana represents less than 6 percent of the state's total population (U.S. Census, 1992, p. CP-1-1A).

The BJS statistics on prison populations indicate that American Indians are disproportionately represented in all states that have American Indian nations. Over 24 percent of the inmate prison population in many of these states are American Indian, yet they comprise, at most, 6 to 10 percent of the states' general populations and less than 1 percent of the total U.S. population (Lujan, 1995). These rates are extreme because the states do not have criminal jurisdiction on reservation lands where 50 percent of American Indians reside, as discussed previously (Feimer, Pommersheim, and Wise, 1990).

Preconceived ideas about American Indians play a significant role at all stages of the criminal justice system including arrest, conviction, sentencing, and prison conditions. Discrimination against incarcerated American Indians is also evident within the prisons. In some states, American Indians are not allowed to practice their own religion or to participate in sweat lodge ceremonies. Additionally, American Indians who wear their hair at traditional lengths continue to be subjected to disciplinary procedures by prison officials (Green, 1991).

Marginalization

The effects of negative stereotyping include low self-esteem and low self-concept among some American Indians. In the recent past, American Indian children dropped out of school at an alarming rate and American Indian nations experienced high unemployment rates and other social problems. In part, these problems were due to an acceptance by American Indian children of the negative stereotype.

Most American Indians resist the stereotype of the noble and stoic Indian and would rather be seen as "strong-willed" and "resisting" (Bradt, 1988). However, until recently, some American Indians who accepted the stereotype were alienated from their own culture, thus contributing to low self-esteem and marginalization. In *Pedagogy of the Oppressed*, Paulo Freire (1985, p. 150) writes about cultural invasion and its impact on the invaded. He states that "the more invasion is accentuated and those invaded are alienated from the spirit of their own culture and from themselves, the more the latter want to be like the invaders: to walk like them, dress like them, talk like them."

Recently, though, there has been a renewed interest and pride in American Indian identities and American Indian cultures. Various scholars and American Indian leaders refer to the period from the 1980s to the present as a renaissance for the American Indian nations.

Loss of Language and Culture

Most American Indian nations have experienced some degree of language and culture loss. Some Indian nations are losing their languages at an alarming rate. For example, a few Indian nations in the northwestern coastal region have only two to three native speakers remaining, and the Diné Nation (with a population of over 200,000) has had approximately a 30 percent language loss within the past 20 years. Much of the language loss can be attributed to the past racist policies of the U.S. government and various Christian missionaries.

In particular, the boarding schools discussed in Chapters 2 and 3 of this volume removed Indian children from their homes and families and systematically denied them their language and culture. These drastic attempts to assimilate American Indians into mainstream America resulted in language and culture loss among many American Indian nations. Assimilation policies such as these were based on and rationalized by the prevailing negative stereotypes of American Indians.

American Indian nations are taking important steps to restore and maintain the vitality of their language and culture. For example, the Cheyenne River Sioux Nation in South Dakota recently passed legislation to require that their native language be part of the required curriculum in the schools. Other Indian nations are actively involved in ensuring the continuation of their language and culture by stressing the importance of maintaining the language and offering classes to both children and adults.

Countering Negative Stereotyping

To reduce significantly the distorted image of American Indian nations and American Indian people, the federal government must first honor the laws and treaties that it established with American Indian nations during its formation. This means that the government must recognize American Indian governments as sovereign nations—free to govern themselves. Public policy recognition of American Indian sovereignty would set an example for other institutions to follow including schools, businesses, mass media, and state and local governments. If the U.S. government continues to ignore established laws and treaties, it is highly unlikely that necessary change will occur as we approach the twenty-first century.

Other long-term efforts to reduce negative stereotyping include establishing and supporting American Indian studies programs at both state- and privately funded educational institutions.

Additionally, books and other publications in all areas of scholarship—such as law, government, history, and the social sciences—should include a more comprehensive review of American Indian nations and American Indian people. Furthermore, American Indians must become more visible and involved in politics, law, and education, as well as other leadership positions, to promote a more accurate image of American Indians.

American Indian people are determined to maintain their distinct governments, as is evident by their 500-year resistance to oppression, genocide, and assimilation. Their resistance will continue regardless of unsophisticated and insensitive statements and actions of U.S. politicians. The following statement by the Diné (Navajo) Nation most likely represents the views of American Indian nations across the country:

> What is rightfully ours, we must protect; what is rightfully due us, we must claim. What we depend on from others, we must replace with the labor of our own hands and the skills of our own people. What we do not have, we must bring into being. We must create for ourselves. (Harvey, 1996, p. 161)

Note

1. P.L. 280 extended state jurisdiction to all crimes committed on Indian lands in California, Minnesota, Nebraska, Wisconsin, and Oregon, with a few exceptions (see Deloria and Lytle, 1983).

References

Anquoe, Bunty. (1994). "Lawmakers wage war on FAS." *Indian Country Today, 13* (33), A1–A2.

Bennion, L., and Li, T.K. (1976). "Alcohol metabolism in American Indians and whites." *New England Journal of Medicine, 284,* 9–13.

Bordewich, Fergus. (1996). *Killing the white man's Indian: Reinventing Native Ameri-*

cans at the end of the twentieth century. New York: Doubleday.

Bradt, Beth. (1988). *A gathering of spirit.* New York: Firebrand Books.

Champagne, Duane. (1994). *Native America: Portrait of the peoples.* Detroit: Visible Ink.

DeFleur, Melvin L., D'Antonio, W., and De-Fleur, L.B. (1976). *Sociology: Human society.* 2nd ed. Glenview, IL: Scott, Foresman and Company.

Deloria, Vine, Jr., and Lytle, Clifford M. (1983). *American Indians, American justice.* Austin: University of Texas Press.

Feimer, S., Pommersheim, F., and Wise, S. (1990). "Marking time: Does race make a difference? A study of disparate sentencing in South Dakota." *Journal of Crime and Justice, 13,* 86–102.

Freire, Paulo. (1985). *Pedagogy of the oppressed.* Translated by Myra Bergman Ramos. New York: Continuum.

Frontline. (1988). "Indian country." Reported by Joe Rosenblum and Mark Trahant, produced by Michael Kirk. Sponsored by the Corporation for Public Broadcasting and Public Television Stations. *Crime and Justice, 13,* 86–102.

Green, Donald. (1991). "American Indian criminality: What do we really know?" In Donald E. Green and Thomas V. Tonnesen (Eds.), *American Indians: Social justice and public policy.* Madison: University of Wisconsin System.

Hall, E., and Simkus, A.A. (1975). "Inequality in the types of sentences received by Native Americans and whites." *Criminology, 13,* 199–222.

Harjo, Suzan Shown. (1996, June 7). "Create independent agency to oversee Indian programs." *Albuquerque Journal,* A15.

Harvey, Sioux. (1996). "Two models to sovereignty: A comparative history of the Mashantucket Pequot Tribal Nation and the Navajo Nation." *American Indian Culture and Research Journal, 20* (1), 147–194.

Lujan, Carol Chiago. (1995). "Women warriors: American Indian women, crime, and alcohol." *Journal of Women and Criminal Justice,* Spring.

May, Philip A. (1992). *The epidemiology of alcohol abuse among American Indians: The mythical and real properties.* Paper presented at the University of Arizona, January.

———. (1989). "Alcohol abuse and alcoholism among American Indians: An overview." In T.D. Watts and R. Wright, Jr. (Eds.), *Alcoholism in minority populations.* Springfield, IL: Charles C. Thomas.

Melmer, D. (1996a, May 14). "Adoption bill 'guts' the ICWA." *Indian Country Today, 15* (47), 1–2.

———. (1996b, April 4). "The decision: U.S. Supreme Court rules in favor of states' rights: Impact on Indian country gaming remains uncertain." *Indian Country Today, 15* (41), 1–2.

Morris, Glenn T. (1992). "International law and politics: Toward a right to self-determination for indigenous peoples." In Annette Jaimes (Ed.), *The state of Native America: Genocide, colonization, and resistance.* Boston: South End Press.

Schaefer, J.M. (1981). "Fire water myths revisited." *Journal of Studies on Alcohol, 9,* 99–117.

Stewart, O.C. (1964). "Questions regarding American Indian criminality." *Human Organization, 23* (1), 64–76.

Stratton, J. (1973). "Cops and drunks: Police attitudes and actions in dealing with Indian drunks." *The International Journal of the Addictions, 8* (4), 613–621.

U.S. Bureau of the Census. (1993). *We the first Americans.* WE-5. Washington, DC: U.S. Government Printing Office.

———. (1992). *1990 census of population: General population characteristics, American Indian and Alaska Native areas.* CP-1–1A. Washington, DC: U.S. Government Printing Office.

Wilkinson, Gerald. (1974). "Colonialism through the media." *The Indian Historian, 7,* Summer, 29–32.

Discussion Questions

1. What makes American Indians different from other racial groups in America?

2. What are some of the results of negative stereotyping?

3. Explain American Indian sovereignty. Why is this status so important to American Indian nations?

4. What is "manifest destiny?" Why was this concept so popular among Euro-Americans during the 1800s?

5. Why do high-ranking (and supposedly well-educated) politicians continue to stereotype American Indians? ✦

Chapter 5

Images of Crime and Punishment

Traditional and Contemporary Tribal Justice

Ada Pecos Melton

Introduction

Research on American Indian crime and delinquency is complicated by the lack of current data or prior studies. The diversity of culture, language, customs, and traditions among tribes has made it difficult for systematic studies to be conducted on American Indian crime. However, tribes do share some views of crime and delinquency and some approaches to addressing these problems. Much of the scant literature that does exist focuses on issues faced by modern tribal courts following the American justice paradigm.[1] Some articles highlight the difficulties tribes have experienced in adopting the Euro-American legal system without discussing the effects of replacing indigenous systems with these foreign courts. They also tend to focus on issues involving federal Indian law rather than the indigenous laws of the American Indian and Alaska Native peoples. Many tribes have vastly different relationships with federal, state, and local governments, adding to the problem of uniformity in data collection and in attracting scholars to this area of research.

Indian Criminal Justice Issues

Reliable crime statistics are missing for several reasons: (1) there is no standardized method for collecting crime data in Indian country because data management systems differ from tribe to tribe; (2) the federal agencies involved in providing law enforcement services to tribes, such as the Bureau of Indian Affairs (BIA), Federal Bureau of Investigation (FBI), and U.S. Attorneys (USA), keep statistics only for the crimes they have investigated or prosecuted; (3) crimes on Indian lands are not reported in the Uniform Crime Report; (4) most tribes do not have computerized data management systems; and (5) crimes occurring in Alaska Native communities are not included in the statistics.[2] Although many tribes collect and maintain manual data systems, their formats cannot easily be extrapolated to establish a universe of reported crimes in Indian country or rates of victimization. Hence, much of what is known has been collected in a fragmented fashion and pieced together to form an understanding of crime, delinquency, violence, and victimization in Indian communities.

Alcohol-Related Crime Problems. Many tribes indicate that the most widespread juvenile problems are related to the misuse and abuse of alcohol and other drugs by a significant number of adults and juveniles, and the impact of these abuses on families and the community. Like other youths in America, Indian youths begin to drink in adolescence. This is a period when youths are at greatest risk for the most catastrophic consequences of drinking, such as unintentional injuries, traffic accidents, suicide, and school failure.

A decade ago Congress passed Public Law 99-570, the *Indian Alcohol and Substance Abuse Prevention and Treatment Act* (1986), 25 U.S.C.S. § 2411, based on findings indicating that

3) . . . alcoholism and alcohol and substance abuse is the most severe health and social problem facing Indian tribes and people today and nothing is more costly to Indian people than the consequences of alcohol and substance abuse measured in physical, mental, social, and economic terms;

4) alcohol and substance abuse is the leading generic risk factor among Indians, and Indians die from alcoholism at over 4 times the age-adjusted rates for the United States population and alcohol and substance misuse results in a rate of years of potential life lost nearly 5 times that of the United States;

5) four of the top ten causes of death among Indians are alcohol and drug related injuries (18% of all deaths), chronic liver disease and cirrhosis (5%), suicide (3%), and homicide (3%);

6) . . . because deaths from unintentional injuries and violence occur disproportionately among young people, the age-specific death rate for Indians is approximately double the United States rate for the 15 to 45 age group; and

7) Indians between the ages of 15 and 24 years of age are more than 2 times as likely to commit suicide as the general population and approximately 80 percent of those suicides are alcohol-related. . . .

The findings further indicated that while the BIA and the Indian Health Service have publicly acknowledged that "alcohol and substance abuse among Indians is the most serious health and social problem facing the Indian people," the lack of emphasis and priority in funding programs to deal with this problem on the part of these two federal agencies continues.

Child Abuse, Sexual Abuse, and Neglect. A national Indian Health Service (IHS)-funded study conducted by the National Indian Justice Center (NIJC) noted that child abuse and neglect are persistent problems in American Indian and Alaska Native communities and that they need more attention (Melton and Chino, 1994). The study indicated that nationwide the vast majority of offenders were parents (79 percent), which makes child maltreatment and victimization in tribal communities a family problem. Neglect cases (48.9 percent) outnumbered physical (20.8 percent) and sexual abuse (28.1 percent). Over 70 percent of the cases involved substance abuse, and almost 80 percent of all cases occurred in the child's home. Victims ranged in age from newborns to 18, with a disproportionate number (39.5 percent) under the age of 5 and a substantial number (9.6 percent) under 1 year of age.

The NIJC study noted that 67 percent of reported incidents of child sexual abuse occurred at the victim's home. The average age of the victims was nine years, and 80 percent of the victims were girls. Over 90 percent of the offenders were male, with most under 20 or over 50 years old. Biological relatives comprised 55.3 percent of offenders, and social fathers (such as the mother's boyfriend) comprised 22 percent. Only 47 percent of child sexual abuse cases involved substance abuse.

In a national IHS-funded American Indian and Alaska Native survey of nearly 14,000 adolescents conducted between 1988 and 1990, 18 percent of the youths surveyed reported that they had been sexually or physically abused or both. Females reported being victimized at much higher rates than males (e.g., 20 percent of senior-high-school females) (IHS, 1992). Child sexual abuse cases were reported to be the most difficult cases to prosecute at both the tribal and federal levels. Tribes noted problems with reporting, investigation, prosecution, and managing offenders. The lack of training for law enforcement officers and other service providers in child sexual abuse cases was reported as a major factor inhibiting provision of adequate services to victims and handling offenders.

The direct costs of child abuse and neglect are seen in law enforcement, the judicial system, foster care placement, medical care, social services, victim/offender treatment programs, and the adult and juvenile corrections systems. Indirect costs of child maltreatment include substance abuse, depression, teenage pregnancy, juvenile crime, suicide, violence, and school failure. All of these factors contribute substantially to the problems faced by American Indian and Alaska Native youths.

Indian Gang Issues. The infiltration of gangs into their communities is a growing concern among many tribes. They have reported offenses linked to gang violence and other crimes, as well as gang-influenced misconduct. These include minor status offenses such as curfew violation, truancy, delinquent offenses such as underage drinking, property damage or vandalism, breaking and entering, and theft; serious criminal offenses such as drug trafficking and possession of firearms or other types of weapons; and violent crimes such as beating, stabbing, rape, drive-by shooting, and homicide. Even though all the issues relevant to gang influence or infiltration have not been clearly identified, there are many indicators that validate the concerns of the tribes. The largest Indian tribe, the Navajo Nation, has reported the existence of more than 28 gangs in 13 of its tribal commu-

nities. An estimated 181 gangs are reported to be active nationwide in tribal communities as concluded by a 1994 Bureau of Indian Affairs (BIA) Law Enforcement Division Survey of 75 tribal and BIA law-enforcement officers in 31 states (Melton, 1997).[3]

In 1994, the BIA Division of Law Enforcement Services conducted a survey of tribal and BIA law enforcement officers to assess the extent of youth gangs in Indian country. The survey identified 181 gangs active on or near Indian country. The Phoenix area reported the most, and the Aberdeen area reported the least. The infiltration of gangs into the Indian communities appears similar to the migration of gangs from large metropolitan cities like East Los Angeles into such cities as Albuquerque and Phoenix. Although some gangs, such as Hispanic and other ethnic gangs, have existed for generations, the nature of these gangs has shifted from familial and neighborhood gangs to more criminally oriented and better-organized gangs, and growing numbers of them have become involved in violence and the drug trade.

Today's gangs have memberships that transcend territorial boundaries and focus on obtaining power through economics, violence, and intimidation. Members are recruited in schools, at home, and in rural locations such as Indian communities. Again, it is not clear how Indian youths are being recruited into existing gangs or if they are organizing themselves, but it is evident from the names they have taken on (Crips, Bloods, 98th Street, etc.) that there are ties to external gangs. Other indicators are the gang-style graffiti, the similar-colored clothing or caps being worn, and younger children (i.e., middle-school-age children) engaging in misconduct such as sniffing paint or selling marijuana reefers as part of gang initiation rites.[4]

It is suspected that some of the gang organizing is being initiated by Indian teenagers who have returned to the reservation, village, or pueblo after being raised in a city. And although their numbers are small, it has been shown in other parts of the country that only a small percentage of hard-core gang members can sustain and perpetuate gangs in their communities. In the 1960s, a number of young Indian adults and families were relocated to large cities such as Dallas, Los Angeles, San Francisco, Chicago, and Detroit for vocational and job training by the federal government. This was yet another American policy to "educate, civilize, and assimilate the American Indian" into mainstream society. Many of these families lived marginal lives in the inner cities in which they were relocated. After several years of chasing the "American dream" and not attaining it, many went home because they wanted to return to their Indian way of life. Due to the urban lifestyle, some children from these families did not develop healthy or strong Indian identities. Many do not speak their native language, understand their customs and traditions, or know the social and ceremonial dances of their tribe and are unaccustomed to village or reservation life.

As a result, many of these youths do not feel comfortable in their tribal communities. Because of this discomfort, coupled with their feelings of unacceptance by the non-Indian world in which they lived, they have begun to create alternative cultural groups—specifically, gangs—that offer them a sense of belonging. It is feared that unless tribes respond positively to youths and provide them with opportunities to participate in their Indian culture and community, more Indian youths will be enticed to join gangs. Tribes are now faced with a completely new reality and need to mobilize to design responses to interdict the growth and operations of gangs.

Although various federal and private agencies have made conferences and training sessions on gangs available to tribes, there has been little focused discussion about gang violence and victimization in the most seriously affected tribal communities. There is a need to understand the magnitude of the problem, and the current resources available to tribes for responding to it. It is also necessary to identify the gaps in services to victims, and to hold offenders accountable for their actions and dramatize their obligations to victims and the community.

National prevention programs have been used in tribal communities, but many have not demonstrated sufficient efficacy to survive in the tribal context. Therefore, it is essential that programs germane to the tribal environment be developed. Although tribes have been aware of the existence of gangs in cities and outside communities, there were no gangs or gang-related problems in Indian communities until recently. Tribes have noted some of the unique issues they face in providing safety to victims of gang violence and/or to gang members who want to get out. These include the lack of "safe houses" on the reservation where victims or ex-gang members can live until the danger they face is subdued. On most reservations, everyone knows everyone else and where they live. This lack of anonymity creates problems in providing safety and protection. Gang affiliation also threatens the makeup of extended families because it transcends familial and clan boundaries and sets up conflicting relationships by pitting family and clan members against one another. This type of intratribal violence places a burden on tribes to develop innovative responses.

From our experiences with areas of victimization (e.g., domestic violence, child physical abuse, and child sexual abuse) we know that Indian crime victims have faced difficulties in having their needs met.[5] The inadequate response to victims' needs has ranged from slow police responses to incidents, lengthy investigations, and no or poor prosecution of cases, to lack of immediate medical attention and/or shelter care, to insensitivity to the cultural needs of victims and witnesses by federal, state, and tribal service providers.

Culture significantly affects the administration of justice to Indian victims and offenders on three levels. First, state agency or program professionals and paraprofessionals need to be culturally sensitive; that is, staff should be knowledgeable about tribal languages, beliefs, practices, conflict resolution approaches, sanctions, socioeconomic issues, and other cultural nuances. Second, the Indian recipient's level of cultural competence or proficiency needs to be assessed and services provided accordingly. Finally, interventions and programs need to promote both cultural sensitivity in service provision and cultural competence in order to adequately address the needs of the Indian victim and determine the best course of action.

Tribes are the most appropriate sources for determining what is culturally appropriate for their people, and the states and federal governments need to support their efforts. This includes recognition of decisions made by modern tribal courts and the indigenous justice systems (traditional courts) existing in tribal communities.

Access issues faced by Indian people extend beyond the need for justice-related services. Although most Indian families speak at least some English, cultural differences inhibit communication, understanding, and the level of

assertiveness needed to advocate for victims in the justice and correctional systems. Justice personnel tend to focus on the offender's problem, whereas victims and their families are concerned about the victim's overall quality of life and ability to function. Misinterpretation of cultural norms, etiquette, roles, and perspectives increases the social distance between the family and service providers.

Tribal Law Enforcement. Law enforcement in Indian communities is provided by tribal, state, and federal agencies to varying degrees. On the 304 federal Indian reservations, about 60 percent of the law enforcement departments are operated by the tribes themselves through Public Law 93-638, the *Indian Self-Determination Act*, which allows tribes to contract and receive BIA funding to operate law enforcement programs.[6] The BIA Law Enforcement Division itself provides fewer than 400 uniformed BIA officers to approximately 40 locations throughout Indian country, most of whom are on the vast reservations in the West, with backup by another 97 BIA criminal investigators covering the same territory. The BIA counted at least 1,100 tribal police officers prior to the federal supplemental police hiring program under the *1994 Crime Act*.

The BIA provides training to all of its officers and the majority of tribal law enforcement officers through its Indian Police Academy, located at the Federal Law Enforcement Training Center in Artesia, New Mexico. The Academy provides the only tribal-specific basic training for law enforcement officers working in Indian communities. It has recently added specialized investigative training on child sexual abuse and on gangs. The training provided by the Academy is not sufficient to meet the needs of tribes, particularly in handling crimes related to gang violence, drugs and other substances, and guns. Most tribal law enforcement departments are small, located in rural areas, and cover large geographic areas. They generally cannot operate specialized crime units; therefore, tribal officers need continuous training in all aspects of law enforcement, ranging from standard patrolling to more specialized areas of investigation. The lack of adequate law enforcement, and how this impedes victim protection and safety, needs to be discussed by tribes to identify ways of enhancing their systems with assistance from federal law enforcement agencies.

Other Federal Law Enforcement Agencies Operating in Indian Country. As a result of the federal-tribal trust relationship, the overlapping and shared jurisdiction tribes have with the federal government, the Department of Justice plays a major role in providing law enforcement, investigation, and prosecution services to tribes throughout Indian Country. This support comes from the U.S. Attorneys and the FBI as well as from other Office of Justice programs providing funding and technical assistance to tribal governments for the enhancement of criminal justice systems. In the past, the overlapping jurisdictions in Indian country contributed to ineffective law enforcement in the following ways: (1) through lack of coordination and communication among the tribal police, BIA criminal investigators, U.S. Attorneys, and FBI agents; (2) through lack of clearly defined investigative responsibilities; (3) through inadequate training for all these agents; and (4) by inhibiting the collection of standardized nationwide statistics on crime in Indian country, which makes it difficult to identify trends in criminal and juvenile delinquent activity and victimization. Without the cooperation of the federal agencies involved, victim services are often delayed; therefore, it

is essential for good intergovernmental relationships to exist.

Detention and Corrections. Tribal justice systems and law enforcement are hampered by lack of alternatives in handling adult and juvenile offenders. The shortage of detention and correctional facilities on tribal lands also greatly hinders tribes waiting to provide immediate and certain sanctions for serious, chronic, and/or violent offenders. The BIA is the primary provider of detention services to the reservations. In 1995 the BIA reported that there were only 42 adult and juvenile detention facilities, with a combined capacity of 339 beds available nationwide for tribes to use in housing juvenile offenders. These 42 facilities include four juvenile detention centers, one juvenile holding facility, and 40 adult facilities that have some juvenile detention capacity. Another 71 contractual programs with county and other state agencies provide additional beds for adult and juvenile offenders.[7]

The lack of facilities makes it difficult for law enforcement and tribal courts to handle the more than 20,000 Indian juvenile arrests reported annually by the BIA. Therefore, it is critical for tribal officials, law enforcement officers including U.S. Marshals, juvenile justice practitioners, and service providers to discuss ways to develop community-based alternatives to provide for community safety and protection, maintain law and order, and respond immediately and effectively to adult and juvenile offenders in order to ensure victims' protection and safety and to address victims' needs for compensation and other forms of reparation.

Indigenous Concepts of Law and Justice

The oral nature of the indigenous justice paradigm[8] limits the availability of sources that discuss or describe it. In general, tribes have not rushed to document the customary law and processes they use. Native languages are predominant in these systems, and often the tribal laws, concepts, and principles cannot be translated using the legal language and precepts of Anglo-American jurisprudence. The stark contrasts between these two paradigms make it difficult for outsiders to understand how the indigenous paradigm works without concrete examples. They often cannot recognize it or are not even aware that it exists. The oral teaching and learning styles of American Indian and Alaska Native people do not predispose them to write about their institutions. In contrast, the dominant American culture greatly values the written word and has a tendency to believe that if things are not documented, they do not exist (Tso, 1989).

For many tribes, oral narration of the customary law is essential to maintain *its life* (Yazzie, 1993). Many Indian people fear that writing about the "sacred law of life" will further strain and dilute their indigenous system. Therefore, they refrain from describing it in detail to outsiders. Some fear that writing about it will open the door to exploitation and misunderstanding by outsiders. Others are concerned with protecting and strengthening what remains of a justice system that has withstood the test of time and the pressure from outside forces to replace it.[9]

Indigenous justice systems are not as visible as they once were, due mainly to the implantation of modern tribal courts styled after the Anglo-American legal system. Tribes have struggled since the time of European contact to keep their own institutions alive and, at the same time, to stay in step with changes brought on by contemporary life in America. The tribal justice system and "Indian law reflects traditional and contemporary custom which changes and adapts to accommodate the new of the dominant culture while tenaciously clinging to and deferring to the old" (Zion, 1988, p. 125). Particularly among the Pueblo communities of the Southwest, we see that traditional methods of dealing with lawbreakers are still in use today and that lawbreakers are handled differently under traditional and customary law than under modern legal systems that rely on codified laws.

Governmental Structure

To understand how contemporary American Indians exercise traditional justice, it is important to understand the historical development of their governments. For illustrative purposes, I focus particular attention in this section on the Pueblo Indians of the Southwest. Spanish, Mexican, and American Indian policies had dramatic effects on the Southwest Pueblos, but most retained their culture, language, religion, customs, and traditions. The present gubernatorial form of government was imposed on them by Spanish decree in 1620. Secular offices were established that required the annual appointment of civil officials. Several Pueblos incorporated secular offices into their traditional theocratic system and continued their religious societies, traditional officials, and methods of selecting officials. These modifications of precontact theocracy have since been referred to as "traditional pueblo governments."[10]

The theocratic leader for most New Mexico Pueblos is the *cacique*. Aided by an advisory council, the cacique annually appointed both the secular leaders and officers of the Pueblo. Secular officers were expected to cooperate with Spanish law and church officials in compelling their members to become civilized and Christianized. Because the officers were appointed by the theocratic leader, only individuals whose primary allegiance was to native ceremonial life were selected, thus helping to preserve native beliefs and practices.

A constitutional form of government was adopted by several Pueblos. This is a combination of a representative government and a modified theocracy in which secular officials, like traditional officials, are elected by tribal members rather than appointed by the theocratic leader. The secular government officials operate under a constitution; in most instances, the traditional officials rely on custom and tradition. In l863, the right of the Pueblos to self-government was recognized. Some Pueblos enacted constitutions as early as l908, preceding the 1934 *Indian Reorganization Act*,[11] but retained the government structure established under Spanish rule. These constitutions were the first instance in which the Pueblos referred to a separation of powers between church and state and the establishment of a tripartite government consisting of executive, legislative, and judicial branches. Given this history, indigenous Pueblo justice systems have had to struggle to flourish, yet they have maintained their existence.

History of Tribal Justice

Historically, Pueblos were peaceful and violent crime was rare. Conformity to tribal norms and values was instilled in all members and reinforced by one's kin. Traditional officials used informal social controls such as disapproval, whippings, ridicule, ostracism, and threats to withdraw citizenship rights to ensure that members followed the rules of acceptable behavior. When misconduct or other behavior that violated social norms did occur, the blame for this behavior was generalized to the wider kin group of the offender. This mode of social control reduced feelings of individual guilt, focusing instead on the wider sharing of shame and reparation by relatives of the accused individual.

Most crimes were considered civil in nature. Conflicts and disputes were settled through mediation and arbitration, similar to models now being revived in contemporary American justice systems. Right and wrong became more evident under Spanish rule when lawbreakers were labeled as good or bad, and their actions were determined to be either criminal or civil matters against the tribe (state). There was no evidence of early penal systems, and only the worst lawbreakers were labeled. Because they stayed in the community, families and community leaders had foremost responsibility for dealing with wrongdoers. Conflicts were resolved quickly, which made it possible for victims to receive immediate relief and provided no opportunity for offenders to minimize their behavior or escape confrontation. Handling crime problems internally provided the community with examples, thereby defining the boundaries of appropriate and inappropriate behavior and the consequences for the latter. Inappropriate actions were viewed as the result of natural human error, which required corrective intervention by elders (Maring, 1970; see also Hoebel, 1969). Customary penalties were used to help the offender make amends and to restore self-respect and dignity. The goal was to cure and cleanse the offender of the bad thoughts that caused the negative behavior. This was accomplished by apologizing and being forgiven by the victims, their relatives, and village officials present at a *gathering*.[12] Although punishment was included, the focal point of customary justice was atonement by the offender to the entire social group and restoration and healing for the victim and his or her family and relatives.

This perspective on crime continues today with some variations. Criminal and civil acts have been redefined in written law-and-order codes adopted by the Pueblos. Modern legal structures based on American models of justice and law and order were established extensively through contract with the BIA under P.L. 93-638, the *Indian Self-Determination Act of 1975.* The introduction of formalized judicial and law enforcement agencies brought about significant changes in the way cases are handled by the Pueblos.

Paradigms of Justice

In many contemporary Pueblo and tribal communities, dual justice systems exist, one based on an American paradigm of justice and the other based on an indigenous paradigm. The modern American paradigm has its origins in the world view of European foreigners and is based on a retributive justice philosophy that is vertical, adversarial, punitive, and guided by codified laws and written rules, procedures, and guidelines (Falk, 1959; Yazzie, 1993). Vertical power flows upward, with decision making limited to a few players. The retributive philosophy states that because the victim has suffered, the criminal should suffer as well. It is premised on the notion that criminals are wicked people who are responsible for their actions and deserve to be punished (Nuebauer, 1984; Travis, 1995). Punishment is used to appease the victim, to satisfy society's desire for revenge, and to reconcile the offender to the community by paying a debt to society. It does not, however, reduce future crime or offer reparations to victims.

The law is applied through an adversarial system that places two differing parties on a battlefield, the courtroom, to determine the guilt or innocence of an offender or to declare the winner or loser in a civil case. It focuses on one aspect of a problem, the act involved, which is discussed through an adversarial fact-finding process. The court provides the forum for testing the evidence, which is presented from the differing perspectives and reflects the differing objectives of the parties (Nuebauer, 1984). Interaction between the parties is minimized and remains hostile throughout the proceedings. The punitive sanctions limit the offender's accountability to the state instead of to those he or she has harmed or to the community.

In contrast, the indigenous justice paradigm is based on a holistic philosophy and the world view of the aboriginal inhabitants of North America (Tribal Justice Center, 1986; Zion, 1988; Tso, 1989; Fairbanks, 1991; Connors and Brady, 1992; Lyons et al., 1992; Yazzie, 1993; Melton, 1995). These systems are guided by the unwritten customary laws, traditions, and practices that are learned primarily by example and through the oral teachings of tribal elders. The holistic philosophy is a circle of justice that connects everyone involved with a problem or conflict on a continuum, with everyone focused on the same center. The center of the circle represents the underlying problems and issues that need to be resolved to attain peace and harmony for the individuals and the community. The continuum represents the entire process from disclosure of problems or conflicts, to discussion and resolution, to making amends and restoring relationships. The methods used are based on restorative and reparative justice concepts and the principles of healing and living in harmony with all beings and with nature (Yazzie, 1993).

"Restorative principles" refer to the mending process for renewal of damaged personal and communal relationships. The victim is the focal point, and the goal is to heal and renew the victim's physical, emotional, mental, and spiritual well-being. The process also involves deliberate acts by the wrongdoer/offender to regain dignity and trust and to return to a healthy physical, emotional, mental, and spiritual state of being. These are necessary for the offender and victim to save face and to restore personal and communal harmony.

"Reparative principles" refer to the process of making things right for oneself and those affected by the offender's harmful behavior. To repair relationships, it is essential that the offender make amends by apologizing, asking forgiveness, providing restitution, and engaging in acts that demonstrate his or her sincere desire to make things right. The communal aspect allows crime to be viewed as a natural human error requiring corrective intervention by families and elders or tribal leaders. Thus, offenders remain an integral part of the community because of their important role in defining the boundaries of appropriate and inappropriate behavior and the consequences associated with misconduct.

Keeping the Paradigm Alive

American Indian tribes face an inevitable conflict because two justice paradigms compete for existence in one community. As members of the Akwesasne community have observed, "There is a general view by many that the worst characteristics of other cultures have poisoned the attitudes of Mohawks [tribes] amongst each other, (e.g., materialism, adversarial thinking) leading to personal and legal confrontations causing confusion since *foreign jurisdictions* [emphasis added] are being used to deal with Mohawk issues" (DeKeserady, Brascoups, Ellis, Hatt, Melchin, 1991, p. 6). As shown in Table A, contradiction and conflict occur between important characteristics of the two systems.

Many Americans believe that the law is something that is applied and justice is something to be administered. In contrast, Indian people believe that law

Table A
*Differences in the Paradigms of Justice**

American Justice Paradigm	Indigenous Justice Paradigm
Vertical	**Holistic**
Communication is rehearsed	Communication is fluid
English language is used	Native/tribal language is used
Written statutory law learned from rules and procedure written record	Oral customary law learned as a way of life by example
Powers are separated	Law and justice are part of a whole
Church and state are separated	The spiritual realm is invoked in ceremonies and prayer
Adversarial and conflict oriented	Builds trusting relationships to promote resolution and healing
Argumentative	Talk and discussion is essential
Isolates behavior, freeze-frames acts	Reviews the problem in its entirety, examining contributing factors
Fragmented approach to the process and solutions	Comprehensive problem solving
Time-oriented process	No time limits on the process; long silences and patience are valued
Exclusive, and limits participants in the process and solutions	Includes all affected individuals in the process and solutions
Representation by strangers	Representation by extended family members
Focus on individual rights	Focus on victim's and communal rights
Punitive and removes offenders	Corrective; offenders are accountable and responsible for change
Prescribed penalties by and for the state	Customary sanctions used to restore the victim-offender relationship
Right of the accused, especially against self-incrimination	Obligation of the accused to verbalize accountability
Vindication to society	Reparative obligation to victims and community, apology and forgiveness

*This table represents differences noted by Judge Christine Zuni, (1993, p. 14) and re-iterated in Melton (1995, p. 128).

is a way of life and justice is part of the life process. For one paradigm to exist, it must convert people to follow it.[13] Although it may appear that tribal courts follow the Anglo-American legal system, many adhere to the traditional values of the tribal justice system. Tribes have always been wary of the ethnocentric view of the western colonizers who devalued their legal structures and wanted to replace them with an imported western system (Mohawk, Deloria, Hauptman, Berman, Grinde, Berkey, Venables, 1992). Furthermore, tribes were required to participate in the Anglo-American legal system in order to protect their lands and their people. They did so, however, without trusting or believing it. This foreign system was later imposed by the federal government through the Court of Indian Offenses in 1883.[14] Although the federal government expected Indian people to convert to this foreign legal system, it did not adequately explain the Anglo-American legal paradigm and provided no financial support for its implementation. These factors substantially undermined any efforts to convert the tribes. The continued existence of the indigenous justice paradigm attests to the U.S. government's failure to entice Indian people to relinquish their tribal beliefs for imported ones.

The resurgence of efforts by Indian people to strengthen and retraditionalize tribal justice systems stems from discontent with modern tribal courts' ability to address crime, delinquency, and other social and economic problems in tribal communities. They are joined by the dominant culture's current disillusionment with justice in this country, which is causing some to doubt the retributive justice paradigm and to move toward a more restorative framework (Umbreit, 1989; Galaway and Hudson, 1990; Van Ness, 1990; Zehr, 1990). This restorative perspective is based on the belief that "All parties should be included in the response to crime—offenders, victims, and the community. Government and local communities should play complementary roles in that response. Accountability is based on offenders understanding the harm caused by their offense, accepting responsibility for that harm, and repairing it . . . restorative justice guides professionals in the appropriate and equitable use of sanctions to ensure that offenders make amends to victims and the community" (Brazemore and Umbreit, 1994, pp. 5–6). Many supporters recognize that the restorative perspective is an ancient philosophy, although it is only since the 1970s that it has been promoted as a promising paradigm for criminal justice.

Conversion to the American justice paradigm is a difficult choice for tribes, particularly those that have a functioning indigenous justice system. For many tribes, full conversion is not possible because the indigenous justice paradigm is too powerful to abandon. The strong adversarial features of the American justice paradigm will always conflict with the communal nature of most tribes. For this reason, the inherent restorative and reparative features of the indigenous justice paradigm will continue to be more appealing to the majority of tribal people. Although the two paradigms may have common goals of justice, the specific paradigm followed will dictate the approach used to achieve these goals. Whether two paradigms can coexist in one community is a subject that requires further thought and discussion by American Indian and Alaska Native peoples.

Nonetheless, it is important for tribes to take the lead in identifying their community strengths and views on justice, law, and order. The proper role for non-Indians is to assist and support the tribes in strengthening their justice system. They must suppress the urge to take over or replace it. It is the sovereign and cultural right of Indian tribes to explain, interpret, change, enact, and apply their own law—oral and written—through whatever mechanism they choose. It is their responsibility to pass on, teach, and transfer the knowledge, skills, and abilities embedded in their indigenous paradigm to their young. American Indian and Alaska Native peoples have the clearest understanding of their indigenous law because they live by it. They must be the messengers of this law to preserve its integrity, its authority, its power, and its meaning to the people.

The many intrusions into the tribal way of life have interfered with the natural evolution of the indigenous justice paradigm. Yet, although slowed, it has never stopped. The renewed determination of tribes to strengthen and re-traditionalize their judiciaries has rejuvenated this process. While mainstream society is in the midst of a paradigm shift from a retributive justice model to a restorative one, many tribes are strengthening their indigenous paradigm. In doing so, tribes are empowering themselves to provide a justice system that has meaning to the people it serves. Tribes have the power to perpetuate the indigenous justice paradigm that was preserved by their ancestors and passed on by living elders as testimony to their commitment to the future of tribes. Contemporary American Indian and Alaska Native people are now faced with making the same commitment for the future: to preserve the indigenous justice system our elders maintained and to find ways to perpetuate it through our young.

Notes

1. The "American justice paradigm" refers to the philosophies, models, and approaches used to address crime and conflicts in mainstream America. It is based on an imported Anglo-American legal model that is guided by written laws, rules, and procedures.

2. These data management problems were identified during meetings conducted by the Youth in Federal Custody Committee of the Coordinating Council on Juvenile Justice and Delinquency Prevention in 1996.

3. Navajo Nation Department of Law Enforcement 1995, Nielson, M.O., J.W. Zion, and J.A. Hailer: *Navajo Nation Gang Formation and Intervention Initiatives.* Found in Melton, A.P., Draft Focus Group Report on Gang Violence and Victimization in Indian country. To be published by the Department of Justice, Office for Victims of Crime, Washington, D.C., 1997.

4. These are reported incidents identified by Pueblo probation officers attending a training session I conducted on juvenile justice systems in Albuquerque, New Mexico.

5. Findings referred to under P.L. 101-630, the *Indian Child Protection and Family Violence Act of 1990*, which was enacted to address the problems associated with the maltreatment of Indian children, cite underreporting, sexual abuse, and inadequate funding as areas for reform.

6. The Bureau of Indian Affairs, in the Department of Interior, was the first federal agency established to work with American Indian and Alaska Native tribes under a government-to-government relationship. It is a decentralized organization with its main office in Washington, D.C. It administers 84 agencies at the reservation level through 11 area offices: Anadarko, Aberdeen, Albuquerque, Billings, Eastern, Juneau, Minneapolis, Navajo, Phoenix, Portland, and Sacramento.

7. BIA 1995 report to a meeting of the Youth in Federal Custody Subcommittee of the Juvenile Justice Coordinating Council.

8. The "indigenous justice paradigm" refers to the shared view of tribes regarding crime and conflicts and approaches to such problems. It is based on the concepts and beliefs of the aboriginal inhabitants of North America and is

guided by unwritten customary laws, traditions, and practices.

9. Based on interviews I have conducted and discussions I have held with American Indian and Alaska Native jurists, scholars, and practitioners over the course of my career working in tribal justice systems, I can safely conclude that many people believe that tribal law ways and justice concepts should not be captured in written forms. Several factors underlie this concern.

10. For the purposes of this chapter, I refer to modified theocracies as traditional governments and distinguish the methods used by this system as *informal* methods.

11. The *Indian Reorganization Act of 1934* (IRA) permitted tribes the option of adopting a constitutional form of government. This was not mandatory and some tribes, namely the New Mexico Pueblos, retained their traditional government and forums of justice. The Act was an attempt to restore Indian self-government and to redress the adverse effects of earlier termination polices imposed by the federal government. Although tribes could formulate their own constitutions, most did not have the expertise and adopted model constitutions developed by the BIA. Under these constitutions, tribal courts were established that replaced the Court of Indian Offenses for those tribes that *reorganized.*

12. The terms "gathering" and "family gatherings" are translated words used to describe the traditional court process for conflict and dispute resolution. In this process, the first level of intervention begins with the family patriarch or another related elder designated by the family.

13. Kuhn (1970) uses the term "paradigm" to describe how prevailing scientific models, theories, and assumptions impede the ability of scientists to observe and understand new data. Scientific advances often require viewing a problem in a new light—a new paradigm. This requires individuals to convert to the new beliefs and assumptions presented by the new data. This conversion is like a complete gestalt switch in which one belief system is abandoned and replaced with a new view of the world.

14. Court of Indian Offenses, 25, C.F.R. 11.

References

Brazemore, G., and Umbreit, M. (1994). *Balanced and restorative justice: Program summary.* Office of Juvenile Justice and Delinquency Prevention, October.

Connors, J.F., and Brady, W. (1992). *Alaska native traditional dispute resolution.* Paper presented at the National Conference on Traditional Peacemaking and Modern Tribal Justice Systems in Albuquerque, NM.

DeKeserady, Walter S., Brascoups, S., Ellis, D., Hatt, K., and Melchin, K. (1991). *Documentation of the Akwasasne community peacemaking process: Observations and conclusions.* Carleton University, Inter-University Consortium on Conflict Resolutions, May.

Fairbanks, C.D. (1991). *Mediation in the tribal courts: Revitalizing traditional concepts of justice.* Paper presented at the Native American Rights Fund National Conference, "Dispute Resolution: A Reaffirmation of Indian Concepts of Justice," sponsored by the Indian Law Support Center.

Falk, R. A. (1959). "International jurisdiction: Horizontal and vertical conceptions of legal order." *Temple Law Quarterly, 32,* 295.

Galaway, B., and Hudson, J. (Eds.). *Criminal justice, restitution, and reconciliation.* Monsey, NJ: Willow Tree Press.

Hoebel, A.E. (1969). "Keresan Pueblo law." In L. Nader (Ed.), *Law in culture and society.* Chicago: Aldine.

Indian Health Service. (1992). *Adolescent health survey, The state of native American youth health.* Minneapolis: University of Minnesota Adolescent Health Program.

Kuhn, Thomas. (1970). *The structure of scientific revolutions.* Chicago: University of Chicago Press.

Lyons, O., Mohawk, J., Venables, R.W., Besman, H.R., Berkey, C.G., Grinde, Jr., D.A., Deloria, Jr., V., and Hauptman, L.M. (1992). *Exiled in the land of the free: Democracy, Indian Nations, and the U.S. Constitution.* Santa Fe, NM: Clear Light Publishers.

Maring, E.G. (1970). *The religio-political organization, customary law and values of the Acoma.* Ann Arbor, MI: University Microfilms, Xerox Co., 66–68.

Melton, A.P. (1997). *Draft focus group report on gang violence and victimization in Indian country.* Washington, DC: U.S. Department of Justice, Office for Victims of Crime.

——. (1995). "Indigenous justice systems and tribal society." *Judicature,* 79 (3), 128.

Melton, A.P., and Chino, M. (1994). *Phase III draft final report: To study the role of the Indian Health Service regarding child abuse and neglect in Indian communities.* Rockville, MD: U.S. Department of Health and Human Services, Indian Health Service, Office of Policy, Evaluation, and Legislation.

Mohawk, J.C. (Reprinted 1985). "Prologue." In P. Wallace, *The white roots of peace.* (1946). Philadelphia: University of Pennsylvania Press.

Nielson, M.O., Zion, J.W., and Hailer, J.A. (1995). *Navajo nation gang formation and intervention initiatives.* Window Rock, AZ: Navajo Nation Department of Law Enforcement.

Nuebauer, D.W. (1984). *America's courts and the criminal justice system.* 2nd ed. Monterey, CA: Brooks/Cole Publishing Company.

Travis, L.F., III. (1995). *Introduction to criminal justice.* 2nd ed. Cincinnati: Anderson Publishing Company.

Tribal Justice Center. (1986). *Indian jurisprudence and mediation the Indian way: A case review of the Saddle Lake tribal justice system.* Paper presented at the Conference on Mediation, Winnipeg, Manitoba.

Tso, T. (1989). "Decision making in tribal courts." *Arizona Law Review, 31.*

Umbreit, M. (1989). "Victims seeking fairness, not revenge: Toward restorative justice." *Federal Probation,* September.

Van Ness, D.W. (1990). "Restorative justice." In Burt Galaway and Joe Hudson (Eds.), *Criminal justice restitution, and reconciliation.* Monsey, NJ: Willow Tree Press.

Yazzie, R. (1993). "Life comes from it: Navajo justice concepts." In National Indian Justice Center, *Alternatives in dispute resolution and traditional peacemaking.* Petaluma, CA: National Indian Justice Center, Legal Education Series.

Zehr, H. (1990). *Changing lenses.* Scottsdale, PA: Herald Press.

Zion, James W. (1988). "Searching for Indian common law." In Bradford W. Morse and Gordon R. Woodman (Eds.), *Indigenous law and the state.* Dordrecht, Holland: Forus Publications.

Zuni, Christine. (1993). *Justice based on Indian concepts.* Paper presented at the Indigenous Justice Conference, Santa Fe, NM, December and re-iterated by Melton, A.P. "Indigenous Justice Systems and Tribal Society," in *Judicature,* November-December, 1995.

Discussion Questions

1. Discuss gang membership in today's Indian communities. Has this changed over time? If so, explain.

2. Why do Indian youths join gangs? Do they join for the same reasons as Euro-American, African American, Latino/a, and Asian American youths?

3. What unique factors affect law enforcement in Indian Country? Discuss at least three of these factors.

4. Discuss the historical nature of crime and its subsequent punishment within the Indian community.

5. What is meant by a dual justice system? Provide a detailed definition of both paradigms. Then compare and contrast the competing paradigms. Finally, discuss the implications of this dual justice system. ✦

Part II

The Color Black

The color black has always had a connotation of bad or evil attached to it. We speak, for example, of blackballing someone, or we put them on a black list; similarly, a black cat crossing one's path is bad luck, and black magic (e.g., voodoo) is the most feared type of witchcraft; moreover, the black market and blackmail are against the law. It can be argued that an identical history of denigration is associated with African Americans, particularly African American males, simply because they are seen as symbols of the color black, the antithesis of white.

In the almost 400 years since Africans were forcefully and brutally introduced as slaves to what were then the American colonies, African Americans have faced rape, lynching, mutilation, murder, and other forms of violence at the hands of Euro-Americans, most of whom arrived on American shores long after the slaves did. Today the proliferation of hate crimes directed at African American citizens exemplifies the racial gauntlet so frequently flung down by Euro-Americans over the decades. Until amended, even the U.S. Constitution did not recognize an African American man as a complete man, but only as three-fifths of a man. African American

women counted for even less. African American men and women continue to struggle against such overt definitions of inferiority, as well as more subtle cues. Jim Crow and other segregation laws were highly effective in maintaining an image of African Americans as evil, savage, and crazed. In sum, African American people have a long history of suffering and pain because of Euro-American fears of those who are different in color from them. As previously noted, no one could be more different than one's polar opposite. This is what makes African Americans those most feared.

Jerome Skolnick (1966) coined the term "symbolic assailant" to convey an image of certain people, often members of racial/ethnic groups, who at first sight are considered suspicious by police officers. Symbolic assailants are identified by the "way they are dressed, their language, the use of certain gestures, or their skin color, often regardless of their economic status" (Mann, 1993, p. 142). Undoubtedly one of the most poignant examples of the symbolic assailant is the African American inner-city "gang banger" who wears his gang "colors" and his supple leather jacket with pride and arrogance as he bops imperiously down his urban ghetto streets.

Closely associated with the portrayal of a symbolic assailant who is feared (and, in the case of the white police, hated) is the Euro-American conception of black savagery. From the early slave rampages against brutal oppression to the wanton destruction of property in today's urban riots (a related form of protest against current subjugation), from movies of black African savages and cannibals to today's drive-by shootings of both drug sellers and rap stars, the African American male has been consistently depicted as primitive, barbaric, and animalistic.

A closely related and widely disseminated negative image commonly attributed to African American people in the United States is one of wanton drug abuse. Heroin, cocaine, and, more recently, the odious crack cocaine are linked to African American men and women despite the fact that the majority of drug users in this country are Euro-American. Scant attention is devoted by the media or the government to the effects of drugs and the violence associated with drugs on the African American communities. Thus, there are few positive programs to stabilize communities, much less treat and rehabilitate African American addicts. Little

has been done because decades of black devaluation were permitted to occur, and such devaluation was deliberately fostered by some individuals either to attain power or to stay in power.

Despite the diversity of their topics—life stories, the media, politicians, and crime and punishment—it is striking that all of the authors in this section share a common ideological thread: the unwarranted stigmatization of African Americans, especially African American males, through the use of assumptions about urban violence (although the majority of inner-city African Americans are nonviolent) and drug involvement (although the majority of African Americans do not use drugs). They also note a closely associated untruth—the perpetual connection between drug use and violence—a myth that reinforces a nexus of African Americans, drugs, and violence in the public's mind. It is these harmful stigmata that the authors in this section independently, yet collectively, wish to dispel. ◆

References

Mann, Coramae Richey. (1993). *Unequal justice: A question of color.* Bloomington: Indiana University Press.

Skolnick, Jerome H. (1966). *Justice without trial: Law enforcement in a democratic society.* New York: Wiley.

Chapter 6

Images of African Americans
Voices of Two Black Men

Every Road Has
an End

Leon E. Pettiway

My maternal grandfather was born on that great day of emancipation, the day of the Emancipation Proclamation, and I am a product of forced segregation, born at a time when there were basic questions as to the humanity of black folks. Yes, born in a system that denied me the most basic rights and privileges accorded my white American counterparts.

I entered the light of this world in Durham, North Carolina, where red clay covered the earth and where many black men and women toiled in cotton and tobacco fields, worked as maids, took in laundry, and worked at the most menial of jobs to survive and raise families. This was done with great dignity and self-sacrifice. Durham, North Carolina, was a place where I learned of oppression and where I learned to accept the double-edged legacy of the psychology of oppression. I believe I am stronger emotionally and richer spiritually because of my experiences as a black gay man, but I also know the price I have paid because of the yokes of racism and homophobia.

Sometimes I am concerned that younger black people do not understand the great legacy of our past. For example, some would rather bury our slave past and behave as if slavery were merely a historical footnote. The dreaded Atlantic passage; the years of abject poverty, humiliation, mutilation, and strangulation of our African heritage; and the deaths of those who lifted their voices for justice are merely shrouded in history's dark past. I am afraid many young people live their lives only with the myopic view of the opportunities and the economic potentialities of their future. I fear that in their great quest for economic success, social acceptability, and integration, they fail to understand that justice and the great tradition of Enlightenment flow from the struggle of black people. I look at Jews, and I see the ways in which they remember the Holocaust. I see the ways in which they show respect for and remember the millions who lost their lives when the earth and all who lived on it were stained with blood. I think of Native Americans who did not survive their initial exposure to Europeans, and I think of those who did but were later slaughtered or forced to live out their lives on reservations, stripped of their humanity. I want my students to have hearts filled with compassion and spirits that seek justice. I want my students to remember and to believe that their humanity must bridge the darkness created by those who serve their own self-interest and the self-interest of those who are self-proclaimed as the "mighty." Today, I stand as a man who remembers because I know what it means to be labeled as different, as an outsider.

I recall at the age of five my mother dragging me to the back of the bus because even little black boys and girls could not sit at the front. I remember separate rest rooms, water fountains, and every other imaginable facility or service offered to white men and women of the South being closed to me because I was descended from Africans. I was bused from one side of the county to the other because that was where black students were required to attend high school. It did not matter that my home was only five minutes from a white high school. I remember how some black men dropped their heads as a sign of deference to whites, regardless of the white persons' demeanor, status, or age. It was "Yes, sir" and "No, sir" for whites and "Helen," "Mary," "John," or just simply "Nigger" for blacks. I remember how black mothers instructed their sons on the proper ways in which to conduct themselves in order to prevent their injury or death. I heard of awful deeds committed farther South, in Alabama, Georgia, Mississippi, and Louisiana, where sojourners of justice fell victims to Klansmen and ignorance. I remember that my first social conversations with anyone white occurred when I was twenty-two years of age and a graduate student at the University of Cincinnati.

I have never understood why some white people hate black people so much. Their hatred is so intrinsic that it reveals itself in the tightness of their jaws, the glint in their eyes, the lifting of their voices, and the movement of their bodies. It is a hatred etched deeply in their faces and spirits. So, any encounter with them simultaneously manifests feelings of terror, despair, anger, and even remorsefulness. How can I be *something* that elicits such loathing?

Just the other day, in a tile shop in Indianapolis, I witnessed a young white man serve a somewhat older black gentleman with such contempt. He was not impolite, but the tenor of his voice and his abrupt, paternal speech reminded me of my youth in North Carolina. In those days, he would have just called him "boy," "coon," or "Nigger." When he got to me and the female salesperson explained that I was interested in purchasing granite countertops to remodel my kitchen, his eyes met mine with a piercing gaze and with an equal measure of contempt.

Some of my white friends would say that black people are too sensitive and that we think that all of our experiences are conditioned by race prejudice. They seem to suggest that they know more about the subtleties of being black and living life in this country as a black person than I do, but what they do not understand is that their assertion is deeply rooted in their belief in their own racial superiority. But I have come to forgive them, and I have come to overlook such statements because they really do not understand how such statements implicate them. How could they understand? They do not have the legacy of slavery, the memories of night riders and lynchings, the feeling of being reviled, or the constant barrage of insults that chip away at one's sense of dignity and self-esteem like water that leaves its mark to scar the earth.

I only know that when I go to a restaurant with a white person, I expect the answers to my questions to be given to my white companion. I anticipate that when our server comes to inform us of the dinner specials, the selections will be read to the white person. I expect that even if I am paying the check by credit card, my items will be returned to my white companion. I believe that most white people in this country would find it difficult to meet me, a black man, on the street in the dark, and if they encountered a group of four black men, they probably would believe the group constituted a gang. I know that when I'm in an elevator and a white woman enters, I get as far away as I can because I do not want her to think that I will pull out my ski mask, drop my pants, and rape her. When I enter my classroom as a university professor, I know that there is at least one white student who believes that he or she knows more about the subject than I and believes that I'm there only because of affirmative action. I do not assume white people will be friendly, polite, or treat me with respect and dignity. I do not presume that white people, regardless of their status, will behave as if I am a person of substance and value. I expect some whites to express that which is in their unspoken hearts: they are superior and more deserving, regardless of their status and achievements, than I am. Consequently, no matter what I accomplish and no matter what I achieve, I expect many whites to believe those achievements were either by accident or by some benevolent social handout. I know that for many whites I am inconsequential and not worthy of validation; therefore, they render me invisible. I know that the gay liberation movement addresses the oppression of gay men and women, but I wonder about the depth of their sentiments when the movement has little appreciation for the racism that is so pervasive in the gay community. So I have come to believe that the liberation of which they speak has more to do with their outrage that white gay men are reviled by other whites and that they cannot be full beneficiaries of the privileges afforded to whites in general. As I see it, the gay liberation movement has little to do with people of color. I find it difficult to understand how white gays, who should understand the effects of the yoke of oppression, can discriminate and fail to open their hearts and minds to others who are equally oppressed. I do not understand why some white people hate black people so much.

During my early years, Durham was a sleepy little southern town, but it was the fifth largest city in North Carolina. Early spring rains produced lush vegetation, but the more violent updrafts of summer produced tremendous thunderstorms. Regardless of their intensity, my sister and I were forced to ride out the thunder and lightning in a closet because our babysitter, who was a close family friend, was so terrified that we were all forced to pile into the closet and sit in absolute darkness and quiet. I do not remember exactly, but now it seems that we knew tacitly that our movements and voices would lead to our destruction. So, we sat in silence and heard the silence broken only by the sounds of thunder and the synchronized moans of terror from our frightened babysitter.

The sweltering summers were unbearable. This was a time before air conditioners were prevalent in homes. So summer also was synonymous with the ever-present electric fan or the hand-held fan that provided some relief from the humidity and unending heat. More often than not, the trees stood silent and appeared to be almost limp because no wind rustled their leaves. The air was so heavy with moisture that one thought one could merely cut out a chunk and fill a bucket. Summer was also a time for the ever-present mosquito, and the sight of large trucks lumbering down the streets spraying gullies, ditches, and any of the other places where these pests bred.

Downtown Durham had its five-and-dime, Woolworth's, and department stores that were all owned and operated by white merchants. At the height of the civil rights movement, these stores were where students from North Carolina College at Durham (now North Carolina Central University), a historical black college, picketed, stood, sat in, chanted, and prayed for the end of the segregation of public facilities and the beginning of efforts toward equal employment. But in my youth these establishments only employed white men and women. So most black people who worked for whites had the most menial, dirtiest of jobs. Once a week the garbage truck would make its way down the street where I lived. Sitting alone in the truck's cab was a white man, and hanging on to the rear of the truck were two black men. I used to think about the significance of this status difference and how hard those black men worked. Jumping from the truck, picking up one trash can after another, and yelling to the driver to drive a little farther for yet another load to lift and compress was their everyday struggle. I wonder how these men tolerated the runny, slimy ooze produced by decaying organic matter, the stench, the maggots and flies, and the blistering sun. This was the lot of black men and women of the South. One rarely saw anyone white digging a ditch, lugging a garbage can, sweating in a dry cleaner, bussing tables in a restaurant, pushing a mop or cleaning an operating room in a hospital, or sweeping the streets.

Most neighborhoods in the older part of town were filled with duplex wooden shotgun structures—the kind of house in which if you stood at the front door with a shotgun, you could shoot straight through the back door. The front was adorned with a porch swing, which became a gathering place for children. Although many of these structures were on paved streets, many of the less important side streets in the black neighborhoods were unpaved. So, when the rains came, the streets were almost impassable because of the mud. I remember many cars being bogged down and stuck in Durham's red clay. I remember the residential segregation found in the South. The only white people who entered these neighborhoods were the ones who might own shops, came to collect insurance, or deliver some other service that was not provided by black merchants. The black community was literally separated from the white community by a railroad

track, and we were literally on the other side of the tracks.

Black people had their own social institutions that employed black people. Durham always had a sizable black middle class. There was the North Carolina Mutual Insurance Company, one of the nation's older black insurance companies. There was Mutual Savings and Loan, a black bank. There were black doctors, lawyers, teachers, preachers, undertakers, and other professionals who served the black community. One of the things that I will always cherish is the fact that rich and poor lived and survived in this place together. Children from poor families went to school with children from middle-class and upper-middle-class families. However, even there, racism turned light-skinned against dark-skinned, and there was a general notion in school that if you were "high yellow," you were smarter and came from "better" stock. I remember classmates who did not have kinky hair but rather had "good" hair and who were very light receiving higher grades because their outward appearance suggested a closer link to white America. I do not have "good" hair, and I am not fair of complexion. I do have hazel-green eyes, and I was always told how pretty they were, and instead of a "nigger in the wood-pile" I saw this as a mark of a "cracker under the bed." Therefore, for some people my eyes are pretty because they are more likely to be an attribute of Europeans than an attribute of Africans.

In the midst of oppression, the church played a significant role in the life of black people of the South. When my mother died, I was reminded of my family's deep spiritual roots. At that moment, the importance of religion in my life came like a flood of memories. I can see as vividly as if it were yesterday old black women, with heads tied in handkerchiefs, standing before sinks washing dishes or clothes and humming a spiritual beseeching God's divine intervention or singing a hymn to proclaim the infinite mercy and love of God. They were faithful churchgoers and were known respectfully as "Sister This" or "Sister That" throughout the community. They sat quietly on hard wooden church pews, and the minister's mighty sermon was interrupted only by these women's sometimes collective shouts of "amen" and "hallelujah" or by their shuffling feet dancing to the beat of the holy spirit. Black churches became the inspiration for a movement, but they also became one of several social institutions that provided a moral center. I heard the speeches expressing the hopes and dreams of an oppressed race delivered by the most eloquent black men and women, and they proclaimed that the moral universe would bend toward justice. Through these institutions one derived a sense of justice, fairness, and stewardship that seemed to run counter to power and money.

During my earlier years, I struggled with being successful and the impact that success would have on my moral center. I was so insecure, and I never thought I knew enough or was capable enough. I suppose I suffered, and sometimes continue to suffer, from what one of my close academic friends at Indiana University in Bloomington refers to as the "One day they will find out that we are frauds syndrome." Certainly racism further amplifies this situation. Black men and women are new to the academy, and our role has been tenuous at best. Although many of my white counterparts may have come from blue-collar or even lower-class backgrounds, they have been able to use education as a means not only to improve their status, but also to erase any tangible signs of their origins. Moreover, whites have always been viewed as being intelligent; therefore, few individuals question whether whites belong in a university setting as thinkers or whether they are capable of determining the academic future of countless students.

But I grew up in a time when black boys and girls were not expected to achieve very much, and their family and black teachers provided the incentives to achieve, if they were lucky. Most of all, I remember a time when the only strength you had was something indefinable, something so deep inside that it was beyond expression. Yet it propelled you through life and reminded you that you had substance and value. It is perhaps from these experiences that I chart my path as a social scientist. Therefore, the roots of my work today were formed long before my life as a university professor.

When I received approximately 1 million dollars from the National Institute on Drug Abuse to investigate drugs and crime in a large urban center, my past was etched in the faces of some of the people we interviewed in the field. My field staff and I came to know many of these individuals well, and my staff also educated me about the streets. I was a novice who did not know the most basic street slang or expression. I was an "L7," or a square, but my staff and the respondents protected me. They not only educated me about the life and rhythm of the streets, they made me grow and stretch in new ways. I was the fortunate outsider who was permitted to enter the lives of poor black men and women.

One morning after going to the bank to get the money necessary to pay respondents for their interviews, I arrived at the field site to find a room full of prospective respondents. There they were, all huddled up together, waiting, as one interviewer had told them, "for her boss." I walked in with my briefcase in hand, and she replied, "There he is." I could see the surprise and amazement on their faces. He's black! Later, in an interview with one of the women who was sitting in the room that day, she remarked, "I have never been so proud as I was when I saw you walk through that door and you were in charge of this project. I thought for sure you were going to be white." The effects of racism are so profound and emerge in the most unexpected places. My field experience was a profound and spiritual journey, and it reminded me of the basic dignity that we all possess.

When I talked with my black brothers and sisters who have lived lives filled with poverty and who supported their drug habits by committing crimes, I realized again that lived experiences are complex, and move between and include times of triumph and defeat, humiliation and pride. The poor and the "other" reveal what we always knew—that life is filled with ambivalence and ambiguity. It is never neatly situated along the axes of hope or despair, pleasure or pain, dignity or defeat, good or bad. Meeting these people and thinking about my own life affirms that out of ashes many oppressed people have risen. However, many continue to experience the yoke of oppression, and the hearts of men and women must change to seek and understand the humanity of us all. We must remember that even in the darkness of racism, sexism, and homophobia, the dignity of the human spirit prevails and every road has an end.

Reflections on Black Manhood

William Oliver

"Africans," "slaves," "boys," "burr-heads," "niggers," "drug addicts," "criminals," "clowns," "gang bangers"—these are but a few of the words that have been used to define black men in the minds of the white majority. Ever since black people were brought to America in 1619 as slaves, derogatory words have been used to construct an American image of black people as being innately lazy, ignorant, crime prone, promiscuous, and irresponsible. Moreover, the linguistic stigmatization of black people and the subsequent distortion of their image as a people have been used to justify racial discrimination. For example, low expectations of black students by many white teachers, the abuse of arrest and use of force authority by police officers in incidents involving black people, and the widespread denial of credit for home mortgages to black consumers are examples of acts of racial discrimination routinely committed against black people.

One of the great tragedies associated with prejudice and racial discrimination against black people is the negative effect it has had on how black people view their worth as human beings. Through the manipulation of the educational system, religion, folklore, vaudeville shows, radio and television programs, film, and various print media, the black image in the minds of black people has been severely distorted by the construction and dissemination of untruths and stereotypes.

In a series of studies, psychologists Kenneth and Mamie Clark found that by age seven, black children internalize America's view of black people as being less intelligent, less moral, and less physically attractive than white people. One thing that cannot be refuted is that black people in America have been programmed to reject their physical characteristics and to believe that they have not made any significant contributions toward the advancement of America or the world community.

When I was a boy, I witnessed black men and women using hair relaxers to straighten their hair to mimic the hair texture and styles unique to white people. Also, from the 1940s to the mid-1960s, it was very common for some black people to use bleaches to lighten their skin color.

As the son of parents born and raised in the South, I grew up hearing many stories about how it was to live "down south." A story I will never forget is one my mother told me about an incident involving her aunt and cousin. They were walking on the side of the road when a carload of young white males drove up and stopped them. These men then raped my mother's cousin on the side of the road and, while they were doing it, told my mother's aunt that if she turned around to look, they would kill both of them.

I also recall a time when, at the age of eight, we went to Georgia to visit relatives. While there, some older cousins took me with them to the movies. After they paid the cashier for admission, I proceeded to walk through the main door of the theater. At that point, one of my cousins abruptly pulled me away from the door and said, "We have to sit in the balcony." Having been born and raised in upstate New York, I had never been denied access to any public place.

This was my first confrontation with overt racial discrimination.

Black men living in America must learn to recognize and cope with prejudice and racial discrimination. In the minds of many white people, black men are hated and feared. In the image whites have constructed, black men are perceived as ignorant and brutish. The perception that black men are prone to engage in violence plays a significant role in incidents involving white police officers and black men. White police officers have a tendency to overreact to black males who question their authority or speak to them in loud or angry tones. Some scholars of police violence suggest that the high rates of police violence against black males emerges out of racial hatred. I agree, but in addition to hatred, police violence against black males is also precipitated by white males' fear of black males. That is, white men have been socialized to believe the hype that black men are inherently violent. Thus, when white police officers encounter black men in situations in which their authority is being questioned, they overreact. In such situations, the angry or uncooperative black male is the symbolic monster that must be slain.

Not all black men are law-abiding, God-fearing, and good neighbors. Indeed, we have our share of drug addicts, criminals, and deadbeat fathers. But dysfunctional men are not limited to any particular racial or ethnic group.

What is unique about racism in America is that the heinous acts of a single black individual are often generalized to the entire black race. For example, many white people did not understand the outburst of joy when football star O. J. Simpson was found not guilty in the criminal trial in which he was charged with two counts of first-degree murder involving the deaths of two whites. The explosion of joy upon hearing the verdict emerged out of deep understanding that it wasn't just O. J. Simpson, but black people as a group who were on trial for murder. Contrast O. J. Simpson with Jeffrey Dahmer, who was convicted of killing, engaging in postmortem sex, and cannibalizing 17 minority males. In that situation, white people did not internalize or express a sense of collective guilt resulting from their racial affiliation with Dahmer, the serial killer. They simply regarded Jeffrey Dahmer as a disturbed young man whose heinous acts bespoke nothing with regard to the character and general tendencies of white people. Given the longevity and the cultural entrenchment of prejudice and racial discrimination in America, an increasing number of black people have lost faith in the belief that the white majority will ever commit themselves to the ideals of justice and equality for all. Consequently, this loss of faith has led to a resurgent emphasis on the need to implement various self-help programs to overcome social problems that adversely affect blacks.

On October 16, 1995, black men shocked America when more than one million of them convened on the nation's capital to participate in the Million Man March. Two to three weeks prior to the march, interest in the event had inspired a nationwide discussion regarding its purpose and merit. This discussion was conducted on television news programs, on television and radio talk shows, and in newspaper editorials. In addition, the march was the center of discussion at many black churches, barber shops, and other social gatherings. In these various forums a number of issues were hotly debated, for example: Why should black men travel en masse to Washington to engage in an old-fashioned civil rights demonstration? Why aren't black women being encouraged to participate in the march as equal partners? Why can't black people find a more reasonable man to listen to and follow than the racist Louis Farrakhan? What good is a march going to do to improve the lives of black people, especially poor black people? Wouldn't the time be better spent encouraging one million black men to devote a day to various community development projects rather than a march on Washington?

Like many of the old, middle-aged, and young black men who attended the Million Man March, I went to the march on faith. To be more specific, I went to the march with only a smidgen of faith that it would be a cultural and political success. The reality is that it was out of a sense of duty and obligation that I made the decision to "get on the bus."

The Million Man March was not organized to emulate the goals of the typical 1960s civil rights demonstrations, which tended to focus on demands for justice and equality from the federal government and the larger society. Rather, the march had as its primary goal to inspire black men to assume responsibility for the high rates of social problems besieging black people and to take the initiative to bring about positive change in black communities throughout America. This was a march in which black men did not impose a demand on the federal government or the white majority, but instead imposed a demand on themselves. The fact is that the Million Man March was a black cultural and political event in which black men challenged themselves to change their attitudes and behavior. Thus three basic principles were put forward for black men to adopt as guidelines to facilitate change: atonement, reconciliation, and responsibility.

Atonement refers to being humble and willing to admit mistakes and wrongs. As a cultural event, the Million Man March provided black men with an opportunity and a setting to atone for their individual and collective failings as husbands, fathers, brothers, and neighbors. Atonement also calls for a commitment to engage in some corrective action. In this sense, the Million Man March was organized to challenge black men to commit and recommit to becoming better people; to build strong, loving, and egalitarian relationships; and to struggle to make the black community a better place to live.

Reconciliation is another principle that was promoted by the Million Man March's organizers. Reconciliation means bringing oneself into harmony with others. In practice, it means that black men must actively seek to settle disputes and put aside grudges in all of our relationships. It means rejecting violence as a means of resolving disputes and committing oneself to building mutually respectful relationships.

Responsibility is the third principle of change that was promoted at the Million Man March. Responsibility means to be willing to assume obligations and duties, to be accountable and dependable.

It is too early to assess the long-term consequences of the Million Man March. However, from a short-term perspective, it was a cultural and political success. The turnout was certainly beyond my own expectations. The fact that one million black men convened in Washington has very powerful symbolic meanings regarding the image of black people, and black men specifically.

For those white people who did not invest any time to understand the purpose of the march, the event was no more than a group of black men complaining to America without just cause. It was simply the most recent attempt by black people to pressure the government and white America to do for them what they must do for themselves.

For white people who desire to see America as one nation, the Million Man

March was seen as providing an opportunity to establish self-help coalitions with progressive black community groups.

The Million Man March had a number of symbolic meanings for black people. First and most important, it represented a decision on the part of black men to stand up and be men by assuming responsibility for the survival and progress of black people. The march also symbolized the desire of black men to reconstruct their public image as men. These men wanted to send a message to black women and children proclaiming their past failures as husbands, fathers, and brothers and making a commitment to become better husbands, fathers, and brothers from this point on.

History will record that the Million Man March was a significant turning point in America. It will be regarded as a public cultural and political event that served as a catalyst for self-help; as the philosophy and cultural practice adopted and implemented by black men to bring about positive change in the lives of black people.

Discussion Questions

1. These two essays express some of the commonalities and differences in the authors' experiences as black men in our society. Discuss these similar and different experiences and perspectives.

2. What was your reaction to the Million Man March? Did the march influence how you view black men?

3. What do you regard as the major challenges confronting black people?

4. Both essays allude to the importance of religion in black communities and among the black political leadership. Why do you think religion has held such importance in black communities?

5. What are some of the ways in which racism, sexism, and homophobia intersect? ◆

Chapter 7

Stereotyping by the Media

Murderers, Rapists, and Drug Addicts

Dennis M. Rome

The crime, as the tearful young mother reported it, was demonic: a carjacking in which a thief roared off in her car with her two infants. The mother's wrenching pleas for the safe return of her sons were made to the national media, which had gathered in the small city of Union, South Carolina, to report the story's outcome in all its pathos. Much of the nation was transfixed by the pictures of the angelic infants and by Susan Smith's mask of grieving motherhood. Looming as a backdrop to these images of innocence was Smith's description of the demonic figure: an African American male in a skullcap—thus the nation's portrait of a criminal and a black devil.

But the nation soon discovered that there was no black devil. Smith, the young white mother with the tear-streaked face, possessed by demons of her own, later confessed to authorities that she had strapped her sons into her car and plunged them to their deaths in a nearby lake. But until the moment of truth, when the local police officials bluffed a confession out of her, there was that image—loose again on the surface of the national consciousness—coming out of the warped mind of ante-

bellum America, out of Thomas Dixon's 1905 novel *The Clansman* and D. W. Griffith's 1915 film *Birth of a Nation*.

The stereotype of the African American male as a criminal continues to be used to justify covert and overt racism in contemporary society. Just as Frederick Douglass' legendary argument points out how the "myth of the black rapist" was created to legitimize lynchings, the criminal image of the black male is continuously evoked today to perpetuate the dominant society's continued fear and subjugation of African Americans.

As another example, in 1989 a white Boston businessman named Charles Stuart tried to hide the fact that he had murdered his pregnant wife for her life insurance. Stuart's story that a black man killed his wife and shot him ignited a state of siege for African American men in Boston, who were harassed by police for nearly three weeks. A black man with a criminal record was eventually arrested and charged with the crime. It was not until Stuart killed himself in January 1990, as his plot unraveled, that the unjustly accused black man, as well as Boston's black community, was cleared of the crime.

Ironically, it also came to light that Jesse Anderson—the man killed with the murderous Jeffrey Dahmer in a Wisconsin prison—was serving time for the 1992 killing of his wife. Anderson, who was white, had falsely claimed that two black men had stabbed and bludgeoned his wife to death. Had Anderson's purported assailant been white, the circumstances surrounding his trial and perhaps its outcome might have been different. It is hard to imagine that Susan Smith did not know the powerful grip the image of the dangerous African American man has on the psyche of white Americans. Why else would she blame a black man? Yet, Jeffrey Dahmer, noted serial killer and cannibal, did not ignite any such fear of the white male in the minds of Americans.

The criminal depictions, often provided by the mass media and sustained by the general public's belief that most African American males are criminals, are good examples of the damaging effects of negative stereotypes. In a 1990 survey, whites were asked to evaluate, on a scale of 1 to 7, how violence-prone blacks were. Fifty-one percent chose the violent end of the spectrum (ranks 1–3). When asked the same question about whites, only 16 percent placed whites as a group in the same rank (Morris and Jeffries, 1990).

Black Stereotyping as Historical

The following historical analysis of African Americans will serve to illustrate the origin and extent to which the dominant society has used and still uses negative stereotypes to keep African Americans second-class citizens. Peter Noble, a noted film scholar, summarizes early images of African Americans in film as follows (1970, p. 143):

> The treatment of the Negro mob rivals even the treatment of the individual. American Negroes en masse are depicted with regularity as blood-thirsty, eye-rolling, demented creatures with thick blubbery lips, almost demented with hate and yelling for white blood. This distorted picture has been presented not only in such famous films as *Birth of a Nation* and *Gone with the Wind*, but also in productions such as *The Prisoner of Shark Island*. African Negroes in various Hollywood jungle films have fared no better, always being represented as hate-filled barbarians, savages, head-hunters, or cannibals, only one degree removed from the wild animals of the jungle.

When European colonialists settled in what became the United States of America, they did so in a fashion that helped chart the course of U.S. history for the next 250 to 300 years. They established a pattern of European domination of indigenous groups and transported Africans to the New World as chattel slaves, a degradation that lasted well into the twentieth century (Bell, 1992, p. 2). Chattel slaves were owned by plantation barons such as Senator Hammond, who said:

> In all social systems there must be a class to do the menial duties, to perform the drudgery of life. That is a class requiring but a low order of intellect and but little skill. Its requisites are vigor, docility, fidelity. . . . Fortunately for the South we have found a race adapted to that purpose. . . . We do not think that whites should be slaves either by law or necessity. Our slaves are black, of another, inferior race. The status in which we have placed them is an elevation. They are elevated from the condition in which God first created them by being made our slaves.

This earlier belief of African American slaves as inferior to whites is very important to understanding stereotypes because it shapes the ways in which African Americans are perceived today.

The experience of African Americans is unique in American history. No other ethnic minority group entered the country as slaves and, just as important, no other group was victimized across centuries the way African Americans were because of their original slave status. The fallout from all this is that African American/white relationships have always been characterized by intense conflicts as African Americans have tried to adjust to the dictates of living in a predominantly white society (Bennett, 1984). In fact, it has been a one-sided relationship in terms of which group has attempted to blend into the world of the other group, and which group has maintained a superior status (Davis, 1990). Kellner (1995, p. 24) reminds us:

> Radio, television, film and the other products of media culture provide materials out of which we forge our very identities, our sense of selfhood; our notion of what it means to be male or female; our sense of class, of ethnicity and race, of nationality, of sexuality, of "us" and "them." Media images help shape our view of the world and our deepest values: what we consider good or bad, positive or negative, moral or evil. Media stories provide the symbols, myths and resources through which we constitute a common culture and through the appropriation of which we insert ourselves into this culture. Media spectacles demonstrate who has power and who is powerless, who is allowed to exercise force and violence and who is not. They dramatize and legitimate the power of the forces that be and show the powerless that they must stay in their places or be destroyed.

Kellner is suggesting that African Americans are often depicted as criminals because such negative stereotypes are used as tools to imply that the subordinate group is deserving of such treatment and/or status.

Along these same lines, assimilation is difficult when white and "light" skin-based privileges exist—this preference for a lighter or fairer skin tone in our society may be traced back as far as preslavery, when an African's dark color was singled out as unusual or ugly. By 1800 blackness was seen as a critical means of sorting out people; the terms "black" and "Negro" underscored the importance of color. By the mid-1800s advocates of slavery were arguing for acceptance of the supposed apelike characteristics of the African American. In fact, in a famous article published in

the 1850s, Samuel Cartwright (1963, p. 13) wrote that Africans were a different species than Europeans "because the head and face are anatomically constructed more after the fashion of the simiadiae [apes]."

By the turn of the century, this way of insulting African Americans had taken on ludicrous forms. A low point was probably reached in 1906 when the New York Zoological Society put a small African, Ota Benga, in a cage in the monkey house of the Bronx Park Zoo as part of an exhibit. Thousands came to view the African's new home. Some African American ministers protested the degrading exhibition, but white officials as well as the white populace thought it quite entertaining (Carlson and Colburg, 1972).

African Americans were also charged with being mentally and morally inferior. Early discussions of their alleged inferiority assumed that African Americans had a small brain and a lower mental capacity than Europeans. Southern apologists for slavery embraced views of racial inferiority, views routinely legitimated by the "scientific racism" of nineteenth-century writers in Europe. Further, African American women were seen as immoral, and African American men were viewed as oversexed and potential rapists. This absurd fear of African American sexuality cannot be viewed apart from the widespread miscegenation between white men and African American women slaves. Sexual coercion was, rather, an essential dimension of the social relations between master and slave. In other words, the right claimed by slave owners and their agents over the bodies of female slaves was a direct expression of their presumed property rights over African American people as a whole. The license to rape emanated from and facilitated the ruthless economic domination that was the gruesome hallmark of slavery. Intermixing in the South had become a permanent feature of the sexual landscape, a point testified to by the lighter skin color of some African Americans (MacLeod, 1974). Angela Davis, like Frederick Douglass before her, suggests that slavery relied as much on routine sexual abuse as on the whip and the lash.

Of special interest to the present discourse is the myth of the African American rapist. This myth has a historical origin. Angela Davis (1981, p. 172) writes:

> What happens to working-class women has usually been of little concern to the courts; as a result, remarkably few white men have been prosecuted for the sexual violence they have inflicted on these women. While the rapists have seldom been brought to justice, the rape charge has been indiscriminately aimed at black men, the guilty and innocent alike. Thus, of the 455 men executed between 1930 and 1967 on the basis of rape convictions, 405 of them were black.

Susan Brownmiller (1975) claims that black men's historical oppression has placed many of the legitimate expressions of male supremacy beyond their reach. They must resort, as a result, to acts of open sexual violence. Along these same lines, MacKellar (1976) argues that 90 percent of all reported rapes in the United States are committed by black men. In as much as the FBI's corresponding figure is 47 percent, it is difficult to believe that MacKellar's statement is not an intentional provocation. She writes (1976, p. 23), "Blacks raised in the hard life of the ghetto learn that they can get what they want only by seizing it. Violence is the rule in the game for survival. Women are fair prey: to obtain a woman one subdues her. . . ."

Brownmiller and MacKellar succumb to the old racist sophistry of blaming the victim. In response, Davis (1981, p. 82) writes:

Whether innocently or consciously, their pronouncements have facilitated the resurrection of the time-worn myth of the black rapist. Their historical myopia further prevents them from comprehending that the portrayal of black men as rapists reinforces racism's open invitation to white men to avail themselves sexually of black women's bodies. The fictional image of the black man as rapist has always strengthened its inseparable companion: the image of the black woman as chronically promiscuous. For once the notion is accepted that black men harbor irresistible and animal-like sexual urges, the entire race is invested with bestiality. If black men have their eyes on white women as sexual objects, then black women must certainly welcome the sexual attentions of white men. Viewed as "loose women" and whores, black women's cries of rape would necessarily lack legitimacy.

Prior to Davis' argument, Frederick Douglass (1894) maintained that the myth of the black male rapist was a distinctly political invention. Douglass pointed out that black men were not discriminately labeled as rapists during slavery. Throughout the entire Civil War, in fact, not a single black man was publicly accused of raping a white woman. If black men possessed an animalistic urge to rape, argued Douglass, this alleged rape instinct would have certainly been activated when white women were left unprotected by their men, who were fighting in the Confederate Army.

In the immediate aftermath of the Civil War, the menacing specter of the black rapist had not yet appeared on the historical scene. But lynchings, reserved during slavery for the white abolitionists, were proving to be a valuable, politically accepted institution; however, its savagery and its horrors had to be convincingly justified. These were the circumstances that spawned the myth of the black male rapist—for the rape charge turned out to be the most powerful of several attempts to justify the lynching of black people. In this way the brutal exploitation of black labor was guaranteed, and after the betrayal of Reconstruction, the political domination of the black people as a whole was assured.

Maintaining the Stereotypes

It is important to point out that the use of the myth of the black rapist by the dominant society is not something of the past. Numerous contemporary examples abound. Two assaults worth noting illustrate how the media—newspapers in particular—not only employ the myth of the black male rapist, but also continue to bias crime reports when the offender is African American and the victim is white. Note the following description of what has come to be known as the "Central Park Case."

> The news from the hospital was encouraging. The young jogger who had been raped, beaten and left for dead in New York's Central Park emerged from her coma after two weeks. By the weekend the 28-year-old investment banker, who has suffered brain damage, was able to smile at her friends.

> As the victim's condition improved, race relations in New York took a turn for the worse. The indictment of six black and Hispanic teenagers inflamed tensions in a city that has witnessed a series of divisive cases in recent years. While many whites found their unspoken fears of minority youths vindicated, a call for the death penalty by billionaire developer Donald Trump infuriated blacks already angry at the "lynch mob" mentality of the white-controlled news media (Hatchett and McKillop, 1989, p. 40).

The rape of a New York investment banker made the front page of many daily newspapers. Ironically, at least 10 other rapes were known to have occurred in New York City on this same day. Of those 10 rapes, two ended in fatalities. Why did the rape of a white investment banker make headlines, whereas an African American woman who was raped and then pushed from a 10-story building received very little media coverage? Moreover, an Hispanic woman was also raped and killed that day, yet her case received very little media coverage. In the Central Park rape case, the offenders were either African American or Hispanic; their victim was white. Both the offenders and the victims in the two other attacks happened to have been African American or Hispanic.

Approximately six weeks after the attack in Central Park, a group of white boys raped and sodomized a mildly retarded 17-year-old female in Glen Ridge, a suburban community in New Jersey. As eight of the youths looked on, the girl was forced to perform sex acts and was raped with several objects, including a broomstick and a miniature baseball bat (Turque and Hutchinson, 1989). Not only did this assault receive less extensive coverage than the Central Park assault, in addition, newspapers appeared biased. They used very different adjectives to describe each assault, resulting in two different tones for each. For example, the African American and Hispanic youths who assaulted the white investment banker were described in one account as "vicious, sadistic terrorists," whereas the only adjectives used to describe the whites involved in the New Jersey assault were "collegiate," "former Captain of the football team," and "honor student." Note the report of the Central Park assault that appeared in the *New York Times* (Foderaro 1989, p. 2):

The teenagers began marauding. . . . A young woman, jogging on her usual nighttime path in Central Park, was raped, severely beaten and left unconscious and bloodied in an attack by as many as 12 youths, who roamed the park in a vicious spree Wednesday night, the police said.

The youths who raped and savagely beat a young investment banker as she jogged in Central Park Wednesday night were part of a loosely organized gang of 32 schoolboys whose random, motiveless assaults terrorized at least eight other people over nearly two hours, senior police investigators said yesterday.

Compare the above excerpts with those below of the Glen Ridge assault. The tone of the article, as well as the way the offenders are described, are much different from the descriptions used in the New York assault:

Of the five youths arrested, one came as a particular surprise to many in Glen Ridge. Unidentified publicly because he is 17, he is a high honors student, meaning he had at least a 3.75 grade point average. Besides playing guard and linebacker on the football team, he was a strong math student.

The real passions of the other juvenile, who has since turned 18, were football and wrestling. The son of a doctor and a nurse who live on the wealthier northern edge of town, he was described by some school staff members as sweet and obedient. He applied to fully a dozen colleges because his mother wanted him to, and was accepted by a few.

Kevin and Kyle Scherzer, twins and co-captains of the football team, were described by some classmates as the most popular students in the school. The youngest of four boys, they have lived for many years in a small, well-kept home at 34 Lor-

raine Street on the South end of town. Their father is a supervisor for the Otis Elevator Company, their mother a homemaker (Foderaro 1989, p. 2).

Whereas the youths in the Central Park assault were described as savagely beating a young investment banker as a result of a vicious spree that seemed to be normal for them, the offenders in the New Jersey assault were presented as if their behavior was surprising and unusual. Is it possible that every time a crime report "labels" African American and Hispanic offenders as "vicious," "savagely beating," or "roaming a park," the readers of daily newspapers can easily generalize these labels and come to think that African American and Hispanic offenders are acting in ways that are typical for their communities? Meg Greenfield, a national syndicated columnist, argues that such reporting is blatantly biased. She writes:

Every time we say that the vicious acts of some ghetto criminal were only to be expected and extenuate them by suggesting that they are probably the norm in that put-upon world, we are doing a disservice to the very people we should be most trying to help and whom we have the greatest reason to admire. The real stories of guts and virtue are the stories of those millions of people trapped in the poverty swamp who are resisting the temptations all around them and who are struggling mightily and honorably to do right and do well with little available to them.

I know that in saying this I enter a journalistically suspect and politically unrespectable realm. But I am not just succumbing here to the cheerful-news syndrome, the look-how-many-planes-didn't-crash-today school of reporting. I think our reflexive habit of projecting the crimes and defaults of the few onto the many, of universalizing and even, in some cases, romanticizing the worst elements of the ghetto pathology is self-indulgent, cruel, and, yes, racist. (1989, p. 86)

Another way of stereotyping African American males as criminals is by the use of "mug shots." In fact, mug shots have become commonplace in the media thanks to the programs that feature dramatizations of the crimes of *America's Most Wanted,* or those like *COPS, Super Cops, Stories from the Highway Patrol,* and *Tough Cops* that allow the public to observe actual arrests. The theme song from *COPS* poses the question: "Bad boys, bad boys, what'cha gonna do?" to a reggae beat. The "bad boys" who are shown are overwhelmingly young and black. These television programs, not unlike mug shots, depict black men as untrustworthy, dangerous, and not very intelligent.

The most famous recent mug shot is that of O. J. Simpson. Jim Gaines, senior editor of *Time* magazine, gave permission to his all-white staff to darken the mug shot of the former football star and actor. Simpson was accused of killing his former wife, Nicole Brown, and her alleged boyfriend, Ron Goldman. When Gaines was asked why he purposely darkened O. J.'s mug shot, he replied, "If I had known . . . I would have reconsidered, I think. I hope. Clearly, the effect of the cover was terrible, and it was clearly an example of racial insensitivity. . . . If there had been an African American at that place at that time, I'm sure we wouldn't have run the cover."[1]

The public relies heavily on the mass media for information about crime, law, and criminal justice (see, for example, Quinney, 1970; Graber, 1980). Crime is a prevalent topic in virtually every type of media source, including television, radio, newspapers, books, music, comics, and movies. Research indicates that public perceptions of crime are formed

on the basis of information appearing in various forms of media. For example, some researchers have found that 95 percent of those polled cited the mass media as their primary source of information about crime. The public is fascinated by crime and attends closely to what is presented (Dominick, 1978; Graber, 1980; Chaffee and Choe, 1981). Research indicates that crime is among the most frequently read newspaper categories (Swanson, 1955; Graber, 1980; Skogan and Maxfield, 1981), providing details that enable consumers to discuss the causes and solutions to the crime problem (Ryan and Owen, 1976). Criminologist Richard Quinney (1970) suggests that a conception of crime is presented in the mass media; that conception, diffused throughout the society, becomes the basis for the public's view of reality.

A contemporary example of Quinney's proposition, and yet another example of the "darkening of crime" by dominant society, is the story of Robert Sandifer, Jr. Sandifer was the 11-year-old Chicago boy whose stray gunfire killed a 14-year-old girl instead of the boy whom gang members had ordered "hit." Robert, or "Yummy" as he was called, was then allegedly murdered by his teenage compadres.

Sandifer's body was discovered by Chicago police on September 1, 1994, four days after a burst from the semi-automatic pistol he was carrying had struck and killed Shavon Dean. Reporters, columnists, and many of the sociologists, psychologists, politicians, educators, and others quoted in the media invoked the darkest "mean street of the ghetto" prose as they sifted through the details of the boy's brief, tragic life and the poor and dangerous environment in which he lived, killed, and died.

But at the same time that the larger society was bestowing so much attention on Robert Sandifer,[2] a spasm of violent acts committed by other children gushed through American society, stunning communities from coast to coast. In Wenatchee, Washington, police arrested two 12-year-old boys, Manuel Sanchez and John Duncan, for shooting to death a migrant worker. Police said the boys shot the 50-year-old man 18 times—continuing to shoot him after he was dead—apparently because the man had yelled at them for firing a gun too close to his house. On the same day that Sandifer's body was found, in High Bridge, New Jersey a 13-year-old boy shot and killed his 11-year-old friend, Jacob Tracy, because Jacob wouldn't accept an apology from a third boy. In the Bronx, New York, also on that same day, a 13-year-old boy, Moises Prado, was charged as an adult with four counts of murder in connection with the firebombing of a grocery store in which four people died. All of these incidents seemed as equally made to order for sensationalist coverage as the Robert Sandifer case. But none of them drew anything close to that attention. Why?

Because in these other cases, the young killers were not African Americans, nor were they "products" of the black ghetto, and therefore not eligible to be neatly boxed in the "mean streets" frame-up that is used to implicitly declare the problems of the ghettos a manifestation of blacks' pathological attitudes—a "black problem"—that has nothing to do with mainstream American society.

Solutions

There are at least three ways to force the dominant society to stop painting the face of crime black. The first solution is for our leaders to look racism straight in the eye and stop pretending that it no longer exists in our society.

Former President Ronald Reagan once remarked that African American leaders were using the "race card" for their own personal gain. He further argued that racism is not a problem in this country and that it is self-serving African American leaders who create racism. If racism is denied, suggesting that blacks and whites are in fact treated equally, then it follows that there is no need for programs that give preferential treatment to blacks. Recently, the University of California's Board of Regents (ironically led by an African American) took this thinking a step further and ruled that race could not be used as part of admissions criteria for the University of California branches. The states of Texas, Louisiana, and Mississippi have followed suit. The belief is that African Americans have had their chances. This move back to Jim Crow[3] also suggests that African Americans are faring well socially and economically.

Stereotyping African Americans as criminals feeds into denials of racism, with the parallel assumption that any problems faced by African Americans (or Hispanic Americans, American Indians, or Asian Americans) are their own fault. This brings us to the second solution: we must begin to change the way in which we think about crime. To use the work of criminologist Richard Quinney, for example, we must begin to question the people who are defining to the larger society what crime is. In fact, Quinney suggests that crime is created: "Crime is a definition of human conduct that is created by authorized agents in a politically organized society" (1970, p. 43).

Jerome Miller, Executive Director of the National Center for Institutions and Alternatives, maintains that crime is not only created, it is also overstated. What, then, is crime, and why is it overstated? Each semester I ask students to write down a definition of crime. Almost always, they give definitions that describe street crimes such as homicides, rapes, burglaries, and thefts. Rarely do students give definitions that describe white-collar crimes. These crimes include embezzlement, bank fraud, credit card fraud, knowingly polluting the air and water supplies, and so on. Where, then, do students and the public in general obtain these distorted conceptions? Quinney suggests that "authorized agents" are sources of this misinformation. Authorized agents include the mass media, schools, religious leaders, and, of course, government officials (especially our president).

Following Quinney, we see that most media attention focuses on street crime. Ironically, it is estimated that the total national loss for all street crimes is $11 billion a year compared to $175 to $231 billion a year for white-collar crime (Irwin and Austin, 1987, p. 16). This fact provides evidence for Quinney's first proposition:

> Crime is not inherent in behavior, but is a judgment made by some about the actions and characteristics of others. . . . Crime is seen as a result of a process which culminates in the defining of persons and behaviors as criminal. It follows, then, that the greater the number of criminal definitions formulated and applied, the greater the amount of crime. (1970, p. 16)

Quinney's first proposition can be easily extended to explain why African Americans are depicted as criminals—even though our society is affected more by white-collar offenses. The current War on Drugs campaign may be used to illustrate Quinney's point. Drug law enforcement has been disproportionately directed toward inner-city, and thereby African American and Hispanic, drug use. The National Institute of Drug Abuse has reported that African Americans make up 12 percent of people who use drugs regularly and 16 percent of regular cocaine users. Yet, more than 48 percent of those arrested for heroin or cocaine drug charges in 1988 were African Americans (Meddis, 1989). As Delaware prosecutor Charles Butler observed, "Sure, it's true we prosecute a high percentage of minorities for drugs. The simple fact is, if you have a population—minority or not—that is conducting most of their illegal business on the street, those cases are easy pickings for the police" (Berak, 1990, p. A36). With an ever-increasing amount of the federal budget allocated to the War on Drugs and President Clinton's new initiatives on crime, we can expect evergreater numbers of African Americans to be warehoused in our prisons over the coming decade and a continued darkening of the face of the street criminal (see further Chapter 9).

The third solution calls for the African American middle class, especially African American leaders, to take a more active and progressive role in the black community. Many African American leaders are falling prey to the rhetoric espoused by the Republican Party, which mainly suggests that somehow African Americans are not trying hard enough. In addition, there seems to be an increasing level of conservatism among African American leaders regarding issues of crime and poverty.

Jerome Miller suggests that there is no question about removing violent criminals from the street. Everyone wants to live in a safe environment. However, in the process of trying to remove violent criminals from the streets, Miller maintains that we are criminalizing a large proportion of nonviolent people, and, as a result, we are creating more violence (Szykowny, 1994, p. 14):

> I mean, you do not just willy-nilly arrest a father in front of a son, or break into someone's house after some kind of minor drug dealing and throw everyone onto the floor in front of screaming children and up-

set mothers, and drag people off the way we are now doing routinely in our inner cities, without having it come back at you. You create anger. It's a sad commentary, but I think eminently true, that the most honest commentators on this situation are the rap groups. What they have to say is awful to hear, but it's the clearest explication of what impact this is having. And you don't hear it from the black leadership, which is so often separated now from what's happening in the community. Here in Washington, they're mostly middle-class, they live in the northwest part of the city away from all the squalor and crime, and they're indistinguishable from the white leadership on this issue.

There are statistics that paint a bleak picture of broken families, of children born out of wedlock, of welfare dependency, of school dropouts and delinquency, and so on. But Miller's point is that the question is not whether such situations exist or whether they should be discussed, but rather how they should be interpreted: whether these observations are accepted at face value or are placed within a larger historical and social context; whether as black leaders we indulge in gratuitous moral judgments or instead explain the behavior that violates prevailing codes of morality; that is, whether we label this behavior as antisocial and treat it as self-explaining or instead establish the linkages between the behavior we can observe and the more distant and less visible social forces that are ultimately responsible for the production and reproduction of the ghetto and all its notorious ills. Paradoxically, these more remote forces are more easily discerned not at close range, but from the ivory tower at the top of the hill.

Miller's indictment of the middle-class African American community and its leaders is not unfounded. Many Afri-

can American leaders have fallen prey to the myths about African Americans and crime. Thus, policies that are the outcome of such myths are ineffective at best.

One last suggestion. Perhaps the media, and especially the news media, could survey minority media personnel. This survey would focus on attitudes, perceptions, and workplace politics. The survey would seek responses from practicing journalists, thus giving the researcher an inside perspective on the intricacies of work within the news-press industry. Minority media personnel, having life experiences that may mirror the types of issues being reported, would seem to be in a better position to report and/or address concerns of bias, especially stereotypes.

Notes

1. Jim Gaines is quoted as saying this in Atlanta at the 1994 convention of the National Association of Black Journalists.

2. For example, his picture graced a *Time* magazine cover, and *Newsweek* included an article entitled "Death of a Child Criminal: A Young Powder Keg No One Could Save."

3. The system of race relations that ultimately replaced slavery in the South was the Jim Crow system. Under this system, the minority group is physically and socially separated from the dominant group and consigned to an inferior position in virtually every area of social life. This system was once sanctioned and reinforced by the legal code; the inferior status of African Americans was actually mandated or required by state and local laws. For example, southern cities during this era had laws requiring blacks to ride at the back of the bus. If an African American refused to comply with this seating arrangement, he or she could be arrested.

References

Bell, Derrick. (1992). *Race, racism and American law.* New York: Little, Brown and Company, 2.

Bennett, Lerone. (1984). *Before the Mayflower: A history of black America.* New York: Penguin Books.

Berak, B. (1990, May 6). "Big catch: Drug war's little fish." *Los Angeles Times,* A36.

Brownmiller, Susan. (1975). *Against our will: Men, women and rape.* New York: Simon & Schuster.

Carlson, Lewis, and Colburn, George (Eds.). (1972). *In their places.* New York: John Wiley.

Cartwright, Samuel. (1963). "The prognathous species of a mankind." In Erik L. McKitrick (Ed.), *Slavery Defender.* Englewood Cliffs, NJ: Prentice-Hall.

Chaffee, S.H., and Choe, S.Y. (1981). "Newspaper reading in longitudinal perspective: Beyond structural constraints." *Journalism Quarterly,* 58 (2), 201–211.

Davis, Angela Y. (1981). *Women, race and class.* New York: Vintage Books.

Davis, James. (1990). *Minority-dominant relations: A sociological analysis.* Arlington Heights, IL: AHM Publishing Company.

Dixon, Thomas, Jr. (1905). *The clansman: An historical romance of the Ku Klux Klan.* New York: Grosset & Dunlap.

Dominick, J. (1978). "Crime and law enforcement in the mass media." In C. Winick (Ed.), *Deviance and mass media.* Thousand Oaks, CA: Sage Publications, 105–128.

Douglass, Frederick. (1894). *The lesson of the hour.* Reprinted under the title "Why Is the Negro Lynched" in Philip S. Foner, *The life and writings of Frederick Douglass* (vol. 4, 498–499). New York: International Publishers, 1950.

Foderaro, Lisa. (1989, June 12). "Glen Ridge worries it was too forgiving to athletes." *New York Times,* B1-2.

Graber, D.A. (1980a). *Coping with crime: Individual and neighborhood reactions.* Thousand Oaks, CA: Sage Publications.

———. (1980b). *Crime news and the public.* New York: Praeger Publishers.

Greenfield, Meg. (1989, May 15). "Other victims in the park." *Newsweek,* 86.

Griffith, D.W. (1915). *Birth of a nation* [Videorecording]. Chatsworth, CA: Image Entertainment.

Hatchett, George, and McKillop, Peter. (1989, May 15). "Opinions but no solutions: The Central Park rape sparks a war of words." *Newsweek,* 40.

Irwin, J., and Austin, J. (1987). *It's about time: Solving America's prison crowding crisis.* San Francisco: National Council on Crime and Delinquency.

Kellner, Douglas. (1995). "Cultural studies, multiculturalism and media culture." In Gail Dines and Jean M. Humez (Eds.), *Gender, race, and class in media: A text-reader.* Thousand Oaks, CA: Sage Publications.

MacKellar, Jean. (1976). *Rape, the bait, and the trap.* New York: Crown Publishers.

MacLeod, Duncan. (1974). *Slavery, race and the American revolution.* London: Cambridge University Press.

Meddis, S. (1989, December 20). "Whites, not blacks at core of drug problem." *USA Today,* 11A.

Morris, Richard, and Jeffries, Vincent. (1990). "The white reaction study." In Nathan Cohen (Ed.), *The Los Angeles Riots.* New York: Praeger Publishers.

Noble, Peter. (1970). *The Negro in films.* New York: Arno Press.

Quinney, Richard. (1970). *The social reality of crime.* Boston: Little, Brown and Company.

Ryan, M., and Owen, D. (1976). "A content analysis of metropolitan newspaper coverage of social issue." *Journalism Quarterly,* 53 (4), 634–641.

Skogan, Wesley, and Maxfield, G. (1981). *Coping with crime: Individual and neighborhood reactions.* Thousand Oaks, CA: Sage Publications.

Swanson, C. (1955). "What they read in daily newspaper." *Journalism Quarterly,* 53 (4), 311–421.

Szykowny, Rick. (1994). "No justice, no peace: An interview with Jerome Miller." *The Humanist,* January/February, 9–19.

Turque, Bill, and Hutchinson, Sue. (1989, June 5). "Gang rape in the suburbs." *Newsweek,* 26.

Discussion Questions

1. Beyond its guilt-evoking potential, does slavery have any value in analyzing contemporary stereotypes of African Americans? Explain.

2. What is meant by the "black male rapist?" Using newspapers, television, or films, cite present-day examples of this term.

3. In this chapter, the assault of a white female investment banker was compared to the assault of a mildly retarded 17-year-old female. The author maintained that the stories were reported differently because the race of the offenders differed. Find examples of similar crimes in your local newspaper in which the race of the offenders differed. Are there differences in the way the crimes are reported? Explain.

4. Define crime. Why does the author state that we need to look at the way in which we define crime?

5. The author suggests three solutions that will alleviate racist stereotyping. What are they, and which one(s) do you think is/are most viable? Why? ♦

Chapter 8

Stereotyping by Politicians

The Welfare Queen and Willie Horton

Donald R. Culverson

Academic and popular discourses about presidential campaigns often concentrate on candidate appeal, party ideology and strategy, fund raising, issue positions, traditional constituencies, or uncertain regional support. However, since the late 1960s, a wide range of social issues—civil rights, student activism, feminism, sexual preference, religion, and family—have infringed upon the domain of more traditional elements of political influence. For example, studies of the impact of race on campaigns have examined (1) candidates' positions on race-related policies or controversies, (2) the presence of a black or nonwhite candidate, and (3) attitudes of minority voters toward candidates. A number of the studies have demonstrated how the black vote played a key role in the Democratic victories of John F. Kennedy in 1960 and Jimmy Carter in 1976. From this perspective, African Americans exercised a "pivotal vote" in the elections (Preston, Henderson, and Puryear, 1987).

However, these approaches remain incomplete. They tend to construct race in a rather dichotomous manner—it is present or absent as a factor in the election. Scholars operating from this perspective assume that race exerts influ-

ence primarily when it serves as an indicator of the candidates' acceptance or rejection of the principle of equality. However, race may exercise a more subtle yet powerful influence in elections. It may help explain why inequalities exist, rationalize maintaining discriminatory practices, and target specific groups for punitive treatment.

This chapter examines Ronald Reagan's usage of the "welfare-queen" fable and George Bush's handling of the Willie Horton "crime-spree" story. A major contention is that these stereotypes are not just campaign strategies to demonize blacks, inmates, or poor people, but also attempt to energize more comprehensive narratives that (1) curtail public discourse on contested issues such as justice and fairness, (2) set a policy agenda for the state, as well as its allied private sector institutions, and (3) implement patterns of public investment reinforceable by economic and demographic change. These stories emerged in response to major disruptions in U.S. economic, political, and social life that were amplified by massive transfers of capital and jobs abroad. Creators of the stories drew from political ideals and cultural myths nourished by mechanisms of limited participation and representation. Understanding these stories offers insights into how coded racial messages about rights and responsibilities, taxes, and social space influence policy agendas, public discourse, and votes.

Stories as Stimulants and Depressants of Public Discourse

Social movements mobilize around an array of issues to generate resources and sustain protest drives. Although often associated with specific public policy measures, movements also contribute to the erosion of beliefs that underwrite discriminatory practices. The black freedom struggles produced the *Civil Rights Act* of 1964 and the *Voting Rights Act* of 1965, and also raised questions about the use of race as a legitimate criterion for assessing human potential. In addition to working toward ratification of the *Equal Rights Amendment,* the women's movement dislodged belief systems that confined men, as well as women, to gender-role expectations. Similarly, the antiwar movement helped end U. S. military involvement in Southeast Asia and provoked discussion about the relationship between American consumption, lifestyles, and militarization. Thus, the dialogues that accompanied popular movements became critical elements in cultivating ideas, as well as mobilizing protests.

As the claims and complaints of groups traditionally excluded from mainstream institutions gained legitimacy, they stimulated debate about who is American and what are the rights and obligations of membership in that community. These searches for new ways in which to interact with an evolving society constitute stories that furnish simple, commonsense ways to talk and think about creating meaning and order. Stories provide explanations of the origins of conflicts and their likely trajectory. They offer a cause for adherents, a sense of flow and direction for passive bystanders, and warnings to potential opponents (Michael and Anderson, 1987).

The alternative stories that emerged during the 1960s challenged the social constructions of reality that rationalized racial segregation for more than three centuries in American society. Arising from colonial notions of order, economic efficiency, racial hierarchy, obligation, and morality, traditional constructions explained a world composed of separations—causes from effects, present from future, and "us"

from "them." These stories utilized a range of vehicles—literature, religion, journalism, popular film and television, government reports, and political campaigns.

Prior to the 1954 Supreme Court decision in *Brown v. Board of Education of Topeka* that overturned the principle of separate but equal education, policymakers often endorsed broad principles of equality but maintained views about blacks that rarely diverged from myths and stereotypes circulating among the general public. The public and private comments of presidents from Harry Truman to Richard Nixon indicated that although each endorsed policy measures supportive of equal treatment of people regardless of race, stereotypes continued to influence their attitudes toward African Americans. Although Truman issued executive orders that ended segregation in the military and outlawed discrimination in federal employment, his references to blacks as "nigs" and "niggers" as late as 1946 suggest that he had not abandoned the dominant ideas about race relations acquired during his formative years in Missouri (Hunt, 1987, p. 163). Similarly, according to historian Blanche Wiesen Cook, Dwight Eisenhower sympathized with southern anxieties about the wisdom of the Court's decision in *Brown* (Cook, 1981, p. 173). Lyndon B. Johnson, who engineered much of the 1960s civil rights and Great Society legislation, did not, according to biographers, expunge the "n" word from his vocabulary even after he became president (Dallek, 1991, pp. 519–520). Yet, despite the personal experiences or beliefs of these presidents, civil rights policy developments in each of their administrations illustrated recognition of the increasing volatility of racial conflict in American society.

Popular stories of the 1960s endorsed what Thomas Byrne Edsall refers to as the "rights revolution." He defines the revolution as:

> demanding statutory and constitutional protection for, among others, criminal defendants, women, the poor, non-European ethnic minorities, students, homosexuals, prisoners, the handicapped, and the mentally ill; and second, the rights-related reform movement focusing on the right to guaranteed political representation that took root within the Democratic party. . . . (Edsall, 1991, p. 4).

Richard Nixon, however, responded to a different rights story. Nixon, who previously had a much stronger civil rights record than did John F. Kennedy, lost the 1960 presidential election in part because of his opponent's success in attracting black voter support. But after the 1962 California gubernatorial race, Nixon's political revival began through a gradual process of legitimizing the stories emanating from blocs of white voters in northern working-class and ethnic communities, as well as in the South, who felt overwhelmed by the demands that the drive for racial equality imposed on their aspirations and opportunities. To these voters, urban rebellions, student activism, the Black Panthers, and the steady increase in the number of black elected officials signaled that blacks were moving too far, too fast, at the urging of an insensitive Democratic Party concerned only about maintaining its dominance over a fragmented Republican Party.

In the 1968 presidential primaries, and later in the general election, Alabama governor and arch-segregationist George Wallace represented a conduit for white backlash stories and proved to be a valuable asset to Nixon's revival in three significant ways. First, Wallace told a forceful, emotionally laden story of whites marginalized by Democratic Party social engineering. Second, the governor spoke for the embattled South, a region where the Republican Party needed to mount a serious challenge to the Democrats. Third, Nixon could stake out a safe middle ground—conservative, yet more accommodating than that of Wallace—from which to defend the abstract principles of equality and to support the claims advanced by white constituencies that the rights revolution undermined core American values and traditions (Edsall, 1991, pp. 74–98).

Nixon's 1968 campaign strategies, which revolved around regaining the South and disgruntled white voters in northern cities, promised that law and order would be restored and the federal government's push for integration curtailed. This approach gave solace to beleaguered white voters and played a key role in Nixon's narrow victory over Hubert Humphrey. The new president attended to the concerns of an emerging conservative majority by expanding the power of law enforcement agencies against political dissent and by reducing selectively federal commitments to integration. At the same time, Nixon maintained a moderate stance on civil rights issues by appointing black officials such as Arthur Fleming and James Farmer and by supporting the notion of black capitalism. This "benign neglect" of racial problems resonated with middle and working-class whites who felt that the federal government had exhausted its obligation to assist the African Americans and that it was time for blacks to stand on their own.

Like the presidents who preceded him, Richard Nixon came from a generation that grew up in a segregated world where blacks occupied subordinate positions and where nonwhite concerns rarely altered whites' views of the community, the nation, or the world. But whereas Truman, Eisenhower, Kennedy, and Johnson adjusted to and even benefited from the entrance of blacks into the political process, Nixon moved sharply to limit their impact. In a curious way, Nixon, one of the first casualties of an energized black electorate, rebounded to exploit the symbols of black advancement, and, most of all, white fears. Nixon furnished the Republican Party with a template for responding to issues revolving around race—busing, affirmative action, racial quotas—without appearing harsh toward blacks or insensitive to the narratives expressed by an expanding white conservative bloc. Furthermore, his move to the right contributed not only to rejuvenating his faltering political career, but also to reviving a party in disarray and setting in motion a set of racial (and racist) strategies and policy agendas that framed presidential campaigns for the next 20 years.

Welfare Queens and the Violation of the Public Trust

Perhaps no president relied more heavily upon stories, and actively rejected empirical evidence, than Ronald Reagan (Green and MacColl, 1987). Reagan's career as an actor and a spokesperson for General Electric provided him with the opportunity and the audience to refine his storytelling style and to pursue a third career as an elected official. Reagan emerged as a national political figure with his 1964 endorsement of conservative Republican presidential candidate Barry Goldwater. When Lyndon Johnson defeated Goldwater in a landslide, Reagan inherited the mantle as leader of the party's conservative wing. He launched his political career in the 1966 race for governor of California, where Nixon's had nearly died four years earlier. After defeating liberal incumbent Pat Brown, Reagan made a brief but unsuccessful run for the Republican presidential nomination against Nixon in 1968. Reagan continued to learn from Nixon, not only how to revive a political career, but how to appeal to the concerns and fears of white voters without the use of overtly racist appeals.

Reagan's campaigns revolved around themes of an overzealous government trampling over the rights of the average citizen; constantly increasing taxes to pay for unnecessary, ineffective social programs; and forcing changes on states and local communities that only satisfied the needs of an expanding, predatory bureaucracy. To Reagan, welfare exemplified the abuses—both by the Great Society programs and by recipients of public assistance—that undermined the values and well-being of American families and communities. Welfare-abuse stories came to play a significant part in Reagan's message. The first one appeared in a speech he gave while campaigning for Barry Goldwater in 1964.

> Not too long ago, a judge called me from Los Angeles. He told me of a young woman who had come before him for a divorce. She had six children, was pregnant with her seventh. Under his questioning, she revealed her husband was a laborer earning $250 a month. She wanted a divorce so she could get an $80 raise. She is eligible for $330 a month in the aid to dependent children program. She got the idea from two women in her neighborhood who had already done that very thing. (Edwards, 1987, p. 565)

Twelve years later, as he challenged Gerald Ford for his party's nomination, Reagan gave a more elaborate story of welfare abuse.

> There's a woman in Chicago. She has 80 names, 30 addresses, 12 Social Security cards, is collecting veterans' benefits on 4 non-existing

deceased husbands. And she's collecting Social Security on her cards. She's got Medicaid, is getting food stamps, and she is collecting welfare under each of her names. Her tax-free income alone is over $150,000. (*New York Times*, February 15, 1976, p. 1)

This story coincided with others on welfare abuse that characterized Reagan's speeches from his years as GE spokesperson through his two terms in the White House. The speeches emphasized how "they," the abusers, enjoyed lives of leisure, whereas "we" worked harder than ever before, with little chance of ever getting ahead. The welfare-queen story played well with small-town and suburban audiences, and its reference to "a woman in Chicago" left little doubt about the implied racial identity of the abuser. The story acquired a life of its own, far more elaborate and lucrative than the actual situation of the woman charged by state prosecutors.[1] At times the "queen" had 12 names and 30 Social Security cards, and was a single mother receiving Aid to Families with Dependent Children (AFDC). Although Reagan lost his second bid for the Republican nomination, like Nixon in 1968, he discovered a formula for delivering coded messages capable of penetrating the consciousness of significant blocs of white voters across party lines.

Neither Reagan's defeat at the Republican convention nor that of the party in the general election assured retirement of the "queen" from public life. Indeed, the former governor used his popular radio commentary program and his speaking tour as a platform for accelerating his race for the White House. Over the next four years Reagan expounded the same themes of governmental intrusion, taxes, and welfare. The economic uncertainty generated by inflation and increasing rates of unemployment, especially in the steel and automobile industries, provided a receptive climate for Reagan's attacks on the Carter Administration. Reagan criticized Democratic liberals for their failure to extend and protect the basic security of American workers dislodged by foreign competition. Reagan portrayed welfare as a microcosm of the problems fostered by Great Society programs. He emphasized not just how recipients abused privileges afforded by "our" generosity, but also how intrusive federal agencies unknowingly undermined the moral commitments that sustained families experiencing material hardships.

After Reagan defeated Carter in the 1980 election, the welfare stories became the vehicle for establishing a policy agenda that penetrated the budget, the Justice Department, and the courts. Reagan was very popular during his first term, and this made it possible for him to elaborate on his philosophy of limited government. In particular, he sought to reduce social programs. Even though the 1982 recession was one of the worst since the Great Depression, Reagan succeeded in gaining congressional support for substantial program reductions. Overall spending during his first term decreased by nearly 10 percent, and AFDC and food stamp spending declined almost 15 percent (Bawden and Palmer, 1984, p. 187). The budget-cutting process introduced terms such as "the welfare mess" and "the truly needy" to policy discourse, further reinforcing the image that Reagan was committed to ending "government handouts" (Weiler, 1992, p. 229).

The argument advanced here is not that Reagan's use of welfare-queen stories singlehandedly created the momentum that led to substantial reductions in federal commitments that had originated with the New Deal. Instead, the contention is that these stories resonated with the experiences and interpretations of blocs of disenchanted white voters. The stories drew from day-to-day experiences of members of those groups—fears, isolation, alienation, hopes, and aspirations—and supplied the frame for audiences to engage in their own dialogues. The frame included three elements: (1) a diagnosis of the problem, (2) a prescription for resolving it, and (3) a rationale for action (Snow and Benford, 1988). Edsall contends that these frames imposed "racial interpretations on traditional liberal economic messages." To this group of voters, proposals for tax increases and restoration of fairness meant that government was taking money from hard-working white families and giving it to undeserving blacks (Edsall, 1991, p. 184). In their story, the welfare queen committed crimes and was unworthy of having her rights respected.

Willie Horton: Racial Fears and the Republican Selection of a Running Mate for Dukakis

Despite his long career in public service, few Americans will likely identify former Texas Senator Lloyd Bentsen as the running mate of 1988 Democratic Party presidential nominee Michael Dukakis. The name most closely associated with the Dukakis campaign is Willie Horton, a black felon featured in a series of Republican television commercials. The party's candidate, Vice-President George Bush, anticipated continuing Reagan's legacy of federal social-program reduction. Bush intensified his campaign by exploiting public fears about increased crime rates among young black males and thereby figuratively installing Horton as Dukakis' running mate. Bush's story of rampant black criminality enabled him to overcome an early 17 percent point deficit in the polls and handily defeat

Dukakis in the November election. Additionally, the Bush strategy rationalized an increasingly punitive criminal justice system and set the stage for campaign discourse on race and crime in 1992.

The ingredients in the Bush crime story began to gel during the 1988 presidential primaries. Dukakis' campaign stressed his role as a catalyst in the "Massachusetts miracle," the revival of the state's economy primarily as a result of favorable investment trends in the computer industry and other technologically intensive industries in selected regions of the Northeast. Dukakis distanced himself from other Democratic candidates with the claim that the election centered on competent administration rather than an ideological orientation toward government. But the Republicans saw another aspect of the governor's administration—the prison furlough program—and used it to nullify the importance of the Massachusetts miracle. Massachusetts, like 44 other states, authorized furloughs for selected groups of committed offenders. These programs had emerged in the 1970s as a means of enabling inmates to visit relatives, to receive medical treatment or social services unavailable in prisons, or to secure work and living arrangements for postprison life. In addition to assisting community reintegration, furloughs were viewed by prison officials and parole boards as a tool for improving prison morale and for acquiring information on which to assess an inmate's potential for return to civilian life.

The events leading to "Willie Horton" becoming a campaign moniker began in April 1987, when police in a Washington, D.C., suburb arrested William Horton, a 35-year-old black man who had escaped from a Massachusetts furlough program. Authorities charged Horton with burglary of the home of a

Maryland couple, assaults on both, rape of the woman, and theft of their automobile. A jury found Horton guilty of rape, assault, false imprisonment, and the burglary charge. The judge sentenced him to two life sentences for the rape and sentences totaling 45 years for the other counts. Horton would have to serve more than 85 years before he might be eligible for parole in Maryland.

Bush's campaign staff gravitated toward the Horton case as a result of a debate between Dukakis, Jesse Jackson, and Tennessee Senator Al Gore just before the New York Democratic Party primary. Gore, hoping to revive his faltering campaign, attacked Dukakis for allowing weekend passes for convicted felons who went on to commit additional crimes. Although Dukakis easily rebuffed Gore's charges, the exchange presented a tailor-made opportunity for the Republicans to transform George Bush, who preferred holding office much more than running for it, into an aggressive defender of the country's most cherished values. Not only had Horton escaped from Massachusetts during Dukakis' term, but earlier the governor had opposed efforts to restrict furlough programs. Additionally, the racial dimension of the Horton case enhanced its potential for capturing public attention. The perpetrator, a black male, committed a series of crimes, including rape, against randomly selected, innocent white people, whose social profile (suburban, professional, upscale, etc.) should have warranted immunity from crime. As Dukakis refused to abandon furlough programs, opponents viewed him as unwilling and incapable of protecting citizens against rampant black criminality. Although the nature of this crime spree tapped into a repository of images and stories about deviant black behavior, its electoral salience benefited from four more recent developments: (1) increased media and policymaker at-

tention to the underclass, (2) the rise of black conservatives as a constituency legitimizing social-program retrenchment, (3) the crack-cocaine industry's deeper penetration into the black community, and (4) the expansion of tele-journalism.

In the 1980s, scholarly debate on the underclass intensified. At the same time, the effects of economic restructuring continued to impose a heavy toll on the black poor and working classes (Franklin, 1991). However, early in the decade, conservative scholars accused liberals and leftists of dominating the debate and began to outline their perspectives on the causes and consequences of prolonged, concentrated poverty. Charles Murray's 1984 book *Losing Ground: American Social Policy, 1950–1980* elaborated on Ronald Reagan's claim that the Great Society programs generated higher rates of poverty. Similarly, research on the biological basis of crime by James Q. Wilson and Richard Herrnstein gave voice to ideas formerly confined to the margins of public and policymaker discourse (Wilson and Herrnstein, 1985). The underclass debate reached prime time with Bill Moyers' 1986 CBS documentary "Vanishing Black Families," which focused on young black males who fathered children with little means of supporting them.

The increased visibility of black conservatives provided a mechanism for deflecting charges that conservative proposals emanated only from whites. Economists Thomas Sowell and Walter Williams, long-time students of the Milton Friedman free-market school of economics, argued that racial discrimination played only a small, insignificant role in black economic stagnation (Williams, 1982; Sowell, 1984). Black conservatives' ideas reached wider audiences as academics, such as political economist Glen Loury and English professor Shelby Steele, took the message to opinion journals and television public-affairs programs. In contrast to Sowell and Williams, the second wave of black conservatives exemplified by Loury and Steele relied a great deal on personal experiences and observations as part of wide-ranging critiques of activist-driven redistributive measures (Roberts, 1994).

Rising public concern with crime coincided with the crack-cocaine epidemic. Crack dealing imposed its own investment, occupational, marketing, distribution, and retribution systems on inner cities. As labor-force participation rates among undereducated young black and Latino males continued to decline, the drug industry exploited this lucrative market of consumers and laborers. Lastly, the face of drug trafficking at the street level harmonized with the images of crime provided by daily doses of television news and talk shows. The proliferation of "shock" television programs, each seeking to generate higher ratings, became a forum for voyeuristic glances at the underside of economic growth and prosperity.

The domestic political climate brought a sense of optimism to Bush's campaign manager, Lee Atwater. A veteran of the post–civil rights era New South political campaigns, Atwater understood the power of using race-coded strategies to drive a wedge between the Democratic Party and its traditional white supporters. Atwater welcomed the opportunity presented by the Horton case. In June, before either party had held its convention, he reflected on its potential impact: "By the time this election is over, Willie Horton will be a household name." Furthermore, he suggested, Horton "may end up being Dukakis' running mate" (Drew, 1989, p. 332).

The Bush campaign wasted no time in linking Dukakis to Horton's crimes and accusing the Democrats of being out of touch with mainstream America. In a speech to the Illinois Republican state convention, Bush reminded his audience that Dukakis had

> let murderers out on vacation to terrorize innocent people. Democrats can't find it in their hearts to get tough on criminals. What did the Democratic governor of Massachusetts think he was doing when he let convicted first-degree murderers out on weekend passes, even after one of them criminally, brutally raped a woman and stabbed her fiancé? I think Governor Dukakis owes the American people an explanation of why he supports this outrageous program. (*Washington Post*, June 14, 1988, p. A4c)

In an address to the National Sheriffs' Association in Kentucky, Bush explained that Horton had been

> sentenced by a judge—sentenced to life in prison. Before eligibility for parole, Horton applied for a furlough. He was given the furlough. He was released. And he fled—only to terrorize a family and repeatedly rape a woman. So I'm opposed to these unsupervised weekend furloughs for first-degree murderers who are not eligible for parole. Put me down against that. When a judge says life without parole, it should mean just that. (*New York Times*, June 22, 1988, Sec. II, p. 7, 1)

Television commercials produced by the Bush campaign intensified the attack on Dukakis as being "soft" on crime. Republican commercials began to include pictures of Horton. One 30-second spot featured prisoners walking through a revolving door while a narrator described the Massachusetts furlough program.

> Governor Michael Dukakis vetoed mandatory sentences for drug dealers. He vetoed the death penalty. His revolving-door prison policy gave

weekend furloughs to first-degree murderers not eligible for parole. While out, many committed other crimes like kidnaping and rape and many are still at large. Now Michael Dukakis says that he wants to do for America what he has done for Massachusetts. America can't afford that risk. (Germond and Witcover, 1989, p. 11)

A network of "independent" groups supporting Bush aggressively linked Dukakis with Horton to portray a vote for the Democrats as a risk. Although Bush denied having influence or control over these organizations, clearly his campaign staff appreciated their zeal. Groups such as Citizens Against Unsafe Society (CAUS) and the National Security Political Action Committee (NSPAC) purchased air time in selected markets around the country to run a series of ads giving prominence to Horton. Additionally, an Illinois group distributed fliers telling voters that "All the murderers and rapists and drug pushers and child molesters in Massachusetts vote for Michael Dukakis. We in Illinois can vote against him." A Maryland Republican fund-raising letter displaying pictures of the candidate and the convict, asked: "Is this your pro-family team for 1988?" (Germond and Witcover, 1989, pp. 423–424). A Los Angeles independent group sponsored a four-state tour of Cliff and Angela Barnes, the Maryland couple that Horton was convicted of assaulting.

At the beginning of 1988, Bush faced substantial challenges in trying to succeed Reagan. He remained under Reagan's shadow, unable to claim Reagan's victories yet saddled with his scandals (e.g., Iran-Contragate). Jack Germond and Jules Witcover describe the Republican dilemma as arising from having "an uninspiring, uncharismatic political figure long on resume but short on vision, a man held in very low regard by

the voters at the outset. And yet without the benefit of a national crisis or any rallying positive issue of his own, they had turned him into a near-landslide winner" (Germond and Witcover, 1989, p. 457).

The campaign staff effectively created a crisis—the possible election of Michael Dukakis—that diverted attention from Bush's negatives and wrested control of the agenda by shifting public concern to the risks of a Democratic victory. The Willie Horton story figured prominently in constructing Dukakis as "soft" on crime, prisoners, the death penalty, and other popular measures seemingly designed to assure public safety. The racial dimension of the case enabled Bush to establish a series of associations to distinguish the Republicans from the Democrats. The use of Horton reinforced the notion of Dukakis as liberal, soft, protecting "them," and concerned with "special-interest" groups such as prisoners and blacks at the expense of average (i.e., white) Americans.[2] By contrast, Bush embraced the American flag and the Pledge of Allegiance to demonstrate his commitment to preserving public safety and preventing a return to 1960s liberalism.

Bush's inaugural speech in January 1989 reiterated his earlier commitment to developing a "kinder, gentler" nation. Yet, his administration did not retreat from the tactics and coalitions that put him in the White House. Two episodes illustrate his concern with effecting a moderate reconciliation with African Americans while continuing to allay white voters' fears. Bush vetoed the *Civil Rights Act* of 1990, claiming that although he supported civil rights, he opposed quotas. Similarly, the nomination of Clarence Thomas to succeed Supreme Court Justice Thurgood Marshall raised public doubts about the characterization of Thomas as the "most qualified candidate" (Morrison, 1992; Mayer and Abramson, 1994), and it illuminated the level to which racially coded strategies had penetrated national politics.[3]

Conclusion

This chapter has suggested that stereotypes and myths revolving around race maintain a significant, if seldom acknowledged, role in presidential campaigns. This challenges more traditional approaches that view race as having a role only when there is widespread consensus among the candidates and the electorate that such a label is appropriate. A critical turning point in the post–civil rights era has been the rise of a racially coded language that dislodged the need for overtly racist appeals. Coded messages depend on mobilizing the fears of select groups of white voters, yet thrive by detaching the problems that generate anxieties from the conditions that give rise to them.

To relegate stories to the margins of academic inquiry devalues an important method for understanding the evolving relationship between race, society, and the state. The civil rights stories, along with those of other men and women of color and white women, along with pacifists and farm workers, regardless of color and gender, offered critical tools for challenging established constructions of the nation. Inevitably, as movements spawned by those stories produced new claims, they clashed with backlash stories. Backlash stories revolve around a zero-sum, dichotomous relationship between the public and the private. They emphasize (1) the abuse of rights by previously unrepresented groups and the consequent denial of rights to whites, (2) taxes as redistributive measures that transfer resources and opportunities from whites to nonwhites, and (3) social space as indefen-

sible by state-sponsored incursions. The welfare-queen and Willie Horton stories draw not from facts or analysis, but from day-to-day experiences and interpretations, as well as the repository of collective images about race. These stories are then used creatively to diagnose selected social problems, prescriptions, and justifications for action. These stories also provide comfort to sectors of the population dislocated by structural transformation and suspicious of empirically based explanations.

Political campaigns that focus on backlash stories furnish temporary refuge from an enlarged public sphere, but they also camouflage critical issues that need sustained attention, discussion, and debate. Efforts to racialize crime ignore not only its primary victims, but also how it crosses racial lines and drains billions of dollars of resources and productive energies from society. Yet, the $25-billion-a-year prison industry depends upon a political momentum that raises few, if any, questions about the consequences of an ever-increasing, younger incarcerated population (Anderson, 1995, pp. 268–269). Each campaign presents scholars with new opportunities to decipher how candidates and the electorate respond to the salience of race. Yet, as stories have become critical media for advancing political interests—by making them seem compatible with crisis-driven, short-term needs—we must not overlook the continuing power and influence of past stories.

Notes

1. The defendant was charged with using four aliases, not 80, as Reagan claimed, and fraudulent collection of $8,000, not $150,000 (Green and MacColl, 1987, p. 85).

2. The Dukakis campaign fired Donna Brazile, a black woman, after her public accusation that the Bush staff used

"every code word and racial symbol to package their little racist campaign" (Germond and Witcover, 1989, p. 451).

3. David C. Anderson suggests that Bill Clinton's 1992 decision not to intervene in the execution of a mentally impaired black man, Rickey Ray Rector, may have been influenced by the fear of being labeled "soft" on black criminals (see Anderson, 1995, pp. 254–255).

References

Anderson, David C. (1995). *Crime and the politics of hysteria: How the Willie Horton story changed American justice.* New York: Times Books.

Bawden, D. Lee, and Palmer, John L. (1984). "Social policy: Challenging the welfare state." In John L. Palmer and Isabel V. Sawhill (Eds.), *The Reagan record.* Cambridge: Ballinger Publishing Company.

Cook, Blanche Wiesen. (1981). *The declassified Eisenhower: A divided legacy of peace and political warfare.* Middlesex, England: Penguin Books.

Dallek, Robert. (1990). *Lone star rising: Lyndon Johnson and his times, 1908–1960.* New York: Oxford University Press.

Drew, Elizabeth. (1989). *Election journal: Political events, 1987–1988.* New York: William Morrow and Company, 332.

Edsall, Thomas Byrne, with Edsall, Mary D. (1991). *Chain reaction: The impact of race, rights, and taxes on American politics.* New York: W.W. Norton and Company.

Edwards, Anne. (1987). *Early Reagan.* New York: William Morrow.

Franklin, John H., and Moss, Alfred A., Jr. (1994). *From slavery to freedom: A history of African Americans.* 7th ed. New York: Knopf.

Franklin, Raymond. (1991). *In the shadows of race and class.* Minneapolis: University of Minnesota Press.

Germond, Jack W., and Witcover, Jules. (1989). *Whose broad stripes and bright stars? The trivial pursuit of the presidency 1988.* New York: Warner Books.

Green, Mark, and MacColl, Gail. (1987). *Reagan's reign of error: The instant nostalgia edition.* New York: Pantheon Books.

Hunt, Michael N. (1987). *Ideology and U.S. foreign policy.* New Haven: Yale University Press.

Mayer, Jane, and Abramson, Jill. (1994). *Strange justice: The selling of Clarence Thomas.* Boston: Houghton Mifflin.

Michael, Donald N., and Anderson, Walter Truett. (1987). "Norms in conflict and confusion: six stories in search of an author." *Technological Forecasting and Social Change, 31,* 107–115.

Morrison, Toni (Ed.). (1992). *Race-ing justice, en-gendering power: Essays on Anita Hill, Clarence Thomas, and the construction of social reality.* New York: Pantheon Books.

Murray, Charles. (1984). *Losing ground: American social policy, 1950–1980.* New York: Basic Books.

New York Times, February 15, 1976, 1; June 22, 1988, 11, 7: 1.

Pitt, David. (1989, April 22). "Jogger's attackers terrorized at least 9 in 2 hours." *New York Times,* 1.

Preston, Michael B., Henderson, Lenneal J., Jr., and Puryear, Paul L. (Eds.). (1987). *The new black vote: The search for political power.* 2nd ed. New York: Longman.

Roberts, Ronald Suresh. (1994). *Clarence Thomas and the tough love crowd: Counterfeit heroes and unhappy truths.* New York: New York University Press.

Snow, David A., and Benford, Robert D. (1988). "Ideology, frame resonance, and participant mobilization." *International Social Movement Research, 1,* 197–217.

Sowell, Thomas. (1984). *Civil rights: Rhetoric or reality.* New York: William Morrow.

Toufexis, Anastasia. (1989, June 5). "Teenagers and sex crimes." *Time,* 60.

Washington Post. (1988, June 14). A4, c.

———. (1994, March 3). C1.

Weiler, Michael. (1992). "The Reagan attack on welfare." In Michael Weiler and W. Barnett Pearce (Eds.), *Reagan and public discourse in America.* Tuscaloosa: University of Alabama Press, 229.

Williams, Walter E. (1982). *The state against blacks.* New York: McGraw-Hill.

Wilson, James Q., and Herrnstein, Richard. (1985). *Crime and human nature: The definitive study of the causes of crime.* New York: Simon & Schuster.

Discussion Questions

1. How did the stories that inspired the rights revolution conflict with backlash stories?
2. Why do presidential campaigns present opportune moments for telling stories about crime?
3. Identify and discuss five code words most commonly used to associate race with criminality in campaign discourse (e.g., "welfare," "abuse," "special interest," "underclass").
4. Compare and contrast the way in which Reagan used the welfare-queen story as part of an ongoing political strategy with Bush's short-term exploitation of the Willie Horton story.
5. Discuss five ways in which these stories restrain public discourse about poverty, inequality, discrimination, crime, and punishment. What are the major vehicles that generate and disseminate these stories? ◆

Chapter 9

Images of Crime and Punishment

The Black Bogeyman and White Self-Righteousness

Laura T. Fishman

Introduction

During the 1950s and 1960s, the black female elder residents of Harlem's old Sugar Hill neighborhood (consisting of a variety of middle- and working-class apartment dwellings) provided me with a protective and nurturing environment. Whenever the weather permitted, my black female elders sat on park benches and conversed way into the evenings. We youngsters often hung around and listened whenever the topic interested us. We were especially interested in topics that offered us important insights into how our elders managed to survive within a segregated, white-dominated world.

With clarity, I remember how we were instructed about their notions of our vulnerability, as black females, to potentially dangerous situations that occurred in urban environments. Because these women considered the era of slavery to be just around the corner, their stories bespoke an accumulated

"wisdom" passed down from the generation of slaves to our elders' generation. Within this wisdom, however, I eventually came to learn some incorrect ideas of who we were as black females and of some of the forces that threatened us. For instance, many of their notions had their inception in slave-rooted images. These, then, became the foundation for the warnings and advice transmitted to us. I subsequently acquired from my black female elders a sense of pervasive "menace," danger, and terrifying fright.

This pervasive danger typically focused on the ability of both blacks and whites to physically harm us black females. Their stories tended to be crafted to forewarn us about how white men in general, and more specifically white police officers, believed that white male physical and sexual victimization of black women was legitimate. These women introduced us to the belief that the criminal justice system was established solely to protect the rights and property of white men, not our rights or our property.

Portions of these grim messages were extended to black men's violence, especially that of the "violent" black lower-class male. I was told that *all* black men were inherently aggressive and violent. They, like white men, could rape, plunder, assault, and murder our souls. Poor black men with Negroid features were particularly inclined to this behavior. I therefore acquired a deep-seated fear of the "savage" nature of black men who could not control their pent-up aggressiveness, hatred, and sexual urges. Believing them to be inherently criminal, my black female elders considered poor black men as the "other"—that is, not like us well-educated, hardworking, and conventionally oriented blacks who lived on Sugar Hill.

In fact, I came to believe that leaving Sugar Hill was fraught with danger. Not only was I to be vigilant about any approaching black man, I also was to be alert, although to a lesser extent, to the criminal proclivities of poor black females. I was presented with a rather narrow image of poor black women, who were portrayed as unruly women who could unpredictably turn into "masculine" monsters. They, too, were likely to prey upon a "nice" black young woman. They were likely to attack me physically, steal from me, and harass me. And when they were not preying on me, these poor black women acted as animals who could not control their sexual urges and therefore were sexually active, prostituting and/or serving as baby-making machines.

The implications of these messages were clear. We young black girls had to learn to protect ourselves against physical hurt, to figure things out in order to maximize our safety within both private and public space. To cushion ourselves against physical mistreatment meant learning to fight to defend ourselves and to win. To cushion ourselves therefore meant that we could not expect any protection from black men or, especially, from the police. I was to be on my own as a strong, independent black woman who could handle anything life threw at me.

These views, expressed by my female black elders, reflected a largely unquestioned set of societal images about blacks and their "place" in American society. My elders, as well as whites, were exposed to these images through folk tales and through what they read and viewed in the popular American media (e.g., television, movies, newspapers, and popular magazines).

This chapter examines some sets of images, common to the 1980s and 1990s, that are obsessed with black involvement in such crimes as drug abuse, drug trafficking, and violence. Attention is given to how images of black crime and criminals are often inaccurate, providing a distorted mirror of crime and an equally distorted mirror of the criminal justice system's responses to these images. Specifically, I will discuss how, spurred by the media, current members of poor black inner-city communities still give lip service to those images of black criminality presented to me by my black female elders. In turn, I will describe how these largely unquestioned sets of images and beliefs reinforce ongoing beliefs that poor blacks still present a physical danger to all "good" people.

A discussion of the societal impact of negative images begs us to unravel some reasons for the persistence of these images of inherent black criminality. This chapter discusses how these images, myths, and ideologies affect our perceptions and how they help to maintain an oppressive and racially unequal society. The flip side of this discussion focuses on the negative and positive consequences for the black community of these distorted images of black crime. Finally, I examine how these images of black crime, criminals, and criminal justice are linked to public support for punitive, crime-control–oriented policies.

Images Past and Present

There appeared to be some consensus among my black female elders, the media, and the educational system that blacks continued to follow in the footsteps of their slave ancestors. For instance, some images of black criminality were transmitted from the white planters to the slaves and became so embedded in our society that my elders and those who came after them accepted these images. In turn, they helped incorporate these images into our ways of thinking and acting. This process of defining blacks to fit white people's racist attitudes has been ongoing, working itself out according to changes in the economic and social institutions of American society.

In this section, I first highlight those crimes that the popular media recently have used to brand blacks as inherently violent, dangerous ghetto outcasts, drug zombies, and "mad" crack users. I also show how these negative images are used to scare "respectable" Americans into pressuring government agencies to employ law enforcement resources to control and contain the "menace" of drugs and violence that they believe is spilling into their suburban communities. Foremost among those crimes that have caused public hysteria are drug-related crimes and such violent crimes as rape and homicide.

The War on Drugs

The black community is suffering record rates of crime and homicide, as well as unemployment, infant mortality, AIDS infection, hunger, and homelessness. Exacerbating this deterioration, the crack-cocaine epidemic and the abuses of the drug war contribute to the ravaging of the black community. These indexes point out a more serious and deadly crisis facing the black community, namely, the poverty-driven marginalization and elimination of the black poor.

Several investigators (Inciardi, 1986; Lusane, 1991; A. W. Wilson, 1994) have argued that the media have inculcated in the public mind the frightful notion that young black men—and later in the War on Drugs, young black women as well—are the heart and core of the drug problem in America. This ongoing media scare centers on blacks using crack cocaine at alarming levels. Supposedly the use of crack cocaine contributes to the subsequent deterioration of poor black inner-city neighborhoods. Bizarre stories are presented of black "cocaine fiends" and "cocaine

sniffers" who are on the prowl for white victims. Hutchinson (1990) comments that the language used by the media to create public hysteria is considerably rougher than in previous drug scares and crime waves. The media now describe impoverished black inner-city communities as "war zones," "crack-plagued," "violence-scarred," and so forth. The warning is clear. Poor blacks, especially poor black males, continue to be a "menace" that must be contained.

The legacy of slavery persists within images of "menacing" black men. When they were first demonized, white America portrayed black men as capable of destroying genteel southern society. At the core of their destructive potential was the white belief that these "super studs" had an uncontrollable lust for the sexual pleasures of "white womanhood." These "black brutes" were animalistic, aggressive, and brutal.

The legacy of slavery also provided images of black women with some gender-specific criminal traits. They were frequently described as wanton, hot-blooded, highly sexed, and exotic, as well as very fertile. As a result, specific acts of white male sexual victimization were excused. For example, if black women were hypersexed, then why make a fuss if they were raped by white or black men (M. Wilson, 1994)? Because black women had been forced to do the same hard labor as black men, they also were perceived as possessing an excess of such masculine characteristics as toughness and aggressiveness. They were thought to be assaultive, murderous, uncompassionate, physically strong, and capable of physical abuse. This sexual objectification and defeminization of black women persists today.

Members of the black community, in contrast, are more likely to incorporate these negative images of "brutal brutes" and "black bucks" into another image, coined the "bad-ass nigger." As "baaad niggers," black men were depicted as raising havoc by stealing, maiming, and lusting for white flesh. My black female elders frequently warned me to take every precaution to minimize confrontations with these "baaad niggers." Repeatedly, I was told how both young men *and* women roamed the streets of Harlem searching for vulnerable young black women to rob and plunder, to assault and rape. Evenings on the streets of Harlem caused me severe tension. When I encountered a solitary black man, especially if he provided any signs that he was "baaad," I crossed to the other side of the street and quickened my pace. Most worrisome for me, however, were my encounters with small groups of black men, standing, drinking wine, speaking in loud tones, showing poor command of the English language, wearing stocking caps, and so forth. These cues told me that these men were primitive and brutally violent "losers." I, as well as other young black women, assumed that their values were the opposite of those held by the "decent" blacks in America. These men were our worst nightmares.

Although these images have barely changed, the media have capitalized recently on the drug plague to create some additional images of black crime that reinforce this sense of menace and danger. There appears to be agreement among social scientists (Hutchinson, 1990, 1994; Lusane, 1991; A. W. Wilson, 1994) that the media have sensationalized and propagated the erroneous and racist notion that all poor blacks, especially males, are addicted to crack cocaine, involved in drug trafficking, and/or involved in heinous drug-related crimes. These black males are also considered baaad by the white media. For instance, nightly television bombards us with scenes of young, bloodied black

men lying dead on the streets or of young black men locked up in various jails and prisons. In turn, black women are portrayed as "hos" and "bitches" who sell their bodies for drugs, neglect and severely abuse their children, and/or burden the state with the birth of crack babies usually pictured as shriveled, shaking, and trembling with unnamed pain (Leab, 1976; Collins, 1990; Morton, 1991; Parenti, 1991; M. Wilson, 1994; Burk, 1996). Interestingly, whenever black women are documented as involved in drug trafficking—still considered a male crime—their behavior is masculinized.

It must be noted that these images do not yield a sense of fear and anxiety in the black community similar to that in the white community. Many black people believe that these images are intended to deprecate us (Grier and Cobb, 1980; Stallworth, 1994; A. W. Wilson, 1994; Dyson, 1996). As suggested by Stallworth (1994) since the time of slavery, blacks have created another image based to some extent on the white notion of the "baaad" black male. This image, the "baaad nigger," has been employed more recently by "gangsta" rappers to romanticize the drug dealing in black communities. This stereotype employs the negative traits of black criminality to portray positive benefits such as that of the "baaad nigger" who "puts one over on whites" and/or "thumbs his nose at whites."

The popular media further embellish their scare campaign by announcing that the crime rate, especially the violent crime rate, is increasing. Not so. Recent data gathered by the Bureau of Justice Statistics show that there has been a steady decline in crime and in the chances of Americans becoming crime victims (see, for instance, Wozencraft, 1995).

Nevertheless, the media persist in sensationalizing who is likely to be killed. Today, to intensify public hysteria, we are told that the drug epidemic has initiated a wave of violence, and that it has led to the accidental murders of innocent people, especially children, caught in the crossfire of drug deals gone sour. Not so, says Hutchinson (1994, p. 105): "Despite the press scare stories on 'ghetto drug violence' most of the victims are not two-year-old babies, or eighty-year-old grandmothers, but the dealers and the users themselves. The murders usually stem from busted drug deals, competition for markets and disputes over turf."

What the public is barely informed about is the wave of violence and community health crisis of genocidal proportions that the current drug epidemic has unleashed (Hutchinson, 1990, 1994; Anderson, 1994; A. W. Wilson, 1994). Hutchinson elaborates (1994, p. 105):

> The growing homicide rate among young black men is higher in some cities than the casualty rate among soldiers during the war in Vietnam. One of every 1,000 young black males is murdered, and homicide is the reason for more than 40 percent of deaths for black males between the ages of fifteen and twenty-four. A young black male is six times more likely to be murdered than a young black female, nine times more than a young white male, and twenty-six times more than a young white female. Black men in Harlem have less chance of reaching the age of sixty-five than men in Bangladesh.

To conclude, some black investigators contend that the white popular media have aided and abetted these high rates of violence within the black community by perpetuating the myth that the only path to the American Dream for poor, hopeless, despairing black young men and women is through drug trafficking. Typically, these media accounts estimate that poor blacks can easily make $100 a day or more and buy some food, pay rent, and live materially better lives. Studies conducted by two black researchers (Hutchinson, 1990, 1994; Taylor, 1993) document that although racism, poverty, and greed are the combustible elements that have compelled black men and women into a cycle of violence, crime, and drugs, they are more likely to "get prison" than they are to "get rich." When it comes to profits, and occasionally the profits can be high, Hutchinson (1990, p. 54) reports that the more accurate average income from street dealing is not $700 a day but $700 a month.

Another consequence for black America is that this "monster" image created by the white popular culture has been taken over by some poor blacks. According to Stallworth (1994), young black men and women both continue to follow the patterns of slavery times. They become the monsters. Many fulfill white America's image of them legitimately by becoming successful gangsta rappers; others fulfill this image illegitimately by becoming "baaad niggers."

Rappers, therefore, reinforce the popular belief that as "baaad-ass niggers" young blacks can achieve fame, recognition, and a sense of being (somebody). If they lose, however, they face a long stay in our jails and prisons or even bodily injury and death.

Images and Reality of Popular Response

As previously noted, white America has successfully made the black man its universal bogeyman. To a lesser extent, black women have been similarly demonized. The flip side of the "bad-guy" and "bad-woman" images are the images of the "good cops" and the "just-and-fair" criminal justice system that are out there fighting to contain the "black menace." Those studying the media concur that media images convey the message that the police and other agents of the criminal justice system are doing what they are supposed to do, namely, meting out just and fair treatment.

The popular media consistently reinforce the belief that "good cops" have a difficult and dangerous job—containing and controlling the threat from brutal and menacing black criminals. No matter how many constitutional rights they might violate, they continue to be perceived as heroic and morally righteous agents of our justice system. These are the images projected in television shows such as *COPS* and *Top Cops,* in which the cops not only perform their duties with "fairness," but also share their responses to life-threatening situations. Such shows give the police more humane images and widen the gap between them and the criminals who are the threat.

White popular media also provide us with the image that these good cops have glamorous, action-filled careers and that their use of violence is legitimate (Kappeler, Blumberg, and Potter, 1996). This good-cop image complements the image of the "menacing" black criminal. The media exaggerate the black "predator" criminal and thereby bring white America's worst fears into their homes—while simultaneously assuring them that the most effective way to mitigate these fears is to have more white police out there controlling a menacing population.

Historically, the black community has never completely accepted the good-cop image as reflective of its experiences. In opposition to this image, some black filmmakers in the 1970s offered another view of the essentially good cop. Their movies focused primarily on law-and-order issues within ghet-

tos, which they depicted as war zones where corrupt kingpin-drug dealers and pushers battle for control (see, for instance, such films as *Shaft, Superfly, Coffy, Friday Foster*, and *Sweet Sweetback's Badasss Song*). In these films the white-dominated legal structure typically was portrayed as perverted and corrupt, with police who brutalized both innocent blacks and black criminals. In contrast to the white media, however, the good-guy agents of social control were primarily black males, and a few black females, acting as detectives who fought both the justice system and crime in their communities.

Several films made by black filmmakers (e.g., John Singleton's *Boyz n' the Hood* and Spike Lee's *Do the Right Thing*) that appeared in the 1990s, as well as gangsta rap music, offer another image of the police. Rather than protecting the black community, the police mission is portrayed as ensuring the continued oppression of black people through the use of force and brutality. According to Stallworth (1994), the police are seen as having a relationship to the black community similar to that of the American Army in Vietnam—that is, an occupation force that stops at nothing to control blacks.

The images portrayed in prison films and documentaries characteristically are fashioned to alleviate the public's fears and anxieties about their personal safety. These images strongly suggest that the prison system reflects the ongoing policy that incarceration and punishment remain a logical, morally just way of treating menacing criminals. As Munro-Bjorklund (1991) reports, historically there has been relatively little change in the images of convicted criminals in films.

In general, Munro-Bjorklund (1991) and Leab (1976) contend that blacks are limited to secondary roles and are not the main heroes, who test the authority of the system by organizing riots, escapes, criminal enterprises, and so forth. In contrast, black prisoners provide us with reassuring images of "Uncle Toms" who are compassionate, cooperative sidekicks to white heroes (Wiegman, 1991). They also are characterized as old, stupid, friendly, overweight, out of shape, and not too bright. In some movies, notes Leab, blacks are found only on death row, and at least one is singing spirituals. In short, black prisoners are characterized as having no minds compared to white prisoners, who tend to possess more intellect.

More recently, images of black prisoners have expanded to include those who either belong to militant political organizations and/or militant religious groups. These prisoners are portrayed as politically oriented rebels who pose some new problems for prison administrators. These films do not address the inequities of the prison system, but on the whole reinforce public anxiety about the most dangerous classes, including "baaad-ass niggers" who speak of revolution and rebellion against the system. While scaring whites, they simultaneously alleviate their fears by assuring them that the prison system is doing what it is supposed to do by containing this most violent threat to society, the revolutionary and rebellious black prisoner.

Black female prisoners fare no better than black male prisoners. According to Faith (1993), since the time of the 1950 film, *Caged*, there has been a series of women-in-prison films with fairly standard plots. A young, pretty, ultrafeminine woman (usually blond) is thrown behind prison walls with a den of raving, masculinized, lesbian, and predatory criminal maniacs. Typically, these films exploit racism by sending the message that the darker a woman is, the more dangerous she is. Black women are more likely to be depicted as having grossly Negroid and masculine characteristics. They act like men insofar as they possess deep voices and dress in a masculine fashion. These super-masculine women spend their time stalking white women, sexually molesting women, and acting assaultively and homicidally. Like black male prisoners, they are valued only when they help the white female inmates or serve as "Aunt Jemimas" who know their "place" within the prison community.

Impact of Images on the Criminal Justice System

As mentioned earlier, the media distortion of black involvement in drugs, crime, and violence has helped make the white American drug problem a "black problem" and has resulted in the War on Drugs becoming a "War on Blacks." As Tonry (1995, p. 10) argues:

> Urban black Americans have borne the brunt of the War on Drugs. They have been arrested, prosecuted, convicted, and imprisoned at increasing rates since the early 1980s, and grossly out of proportion to their numbers in the general population or among drug users. By every standard, the war has been harder on blacks than on whites; that this was predictable makes it no less regrettable.

Acting on the mandate to hold in check this dangerous population, the white police force has been allowed and even encouraged to keep "the niggers in their place"—wherever blacks reside in large enough numbers to be noticed and feared by whites (Hawkins and Thomas, 1991). To the white community, white police in black communities provide the first line of defense against the "black hordes" and assure white America that blacks and their crimes will not spill over into the white world—especially into the affluent world of white America (Hutchinson, 1990; Stallworth, 1994; A. W. Wilson, 1994; Lemelle, 1995; Wilson and Gutiérrez, 1995). Given this, there is strong evidence that the media's cultural assumptions about blacks are likely to affect the police practices directed at them.

Police Saturation of the 'Ghettos '

The current media hype about the drug epidemic in black inner-city communities has given rise to a public call for police saturation of these drug-infested black communities and for the police to target young, poor blacks as the enemy. The rationale given is that more police in these inner-city neighborhoods would dramatically reduce the violence and mayhem, lower the homicide rate, and contain, if not completely eradicate, drug-related crime. According to Hutchinson (1990) and Tonry (1995), although the same drug-related crimes that occur in inner cities are happening everywhere in America, nobody is looking at the white affluent areas. The police presence within poor black communities has reached the level of full-scale military assaults (Lusane, 1991), assuming such forms as intensified drug sweeps, raids on black apartments, ransacking homes, random vehicle checks, illegal searches and seizures, and so on. This increased police occupation force efficiently channels black males, and increasingly black females, into a crowded and violent prison system.

Who Gets Stopped, Searched, and Arrested?

A constant theme in the lives of most black men and women, regardless of class position, is their pervasive fear of the police. Some of my clearest memories consist of the numerous times I have been stopped, questioned, and even searched by the police. Each time

chilled me to the core with an icy fear. Racing through my mind were the images provided me by my female black elders: black bodies brutalized by lynchings, gun wounds delivered by the police, blood-reddened bodies shot dead on the streets by the police. I was deemed suspicious enough to be stopped simply because I was a black woman. This form of police harassment always occurred whenever I walked in white, affluent neighborhoods. Not only was I rudely questioned about my purpose for walking in these neighborhoods, frequently I was required to give proof that I was not a prostitute, heroin addict, or maniac. In one case, I was warned not to return to the neighborhood unless I was acting in a service capacity for some white household. Black women, it seemed, were not to be treated as white ladies because black women could only be cleaning ladies or ladies of the night.

These incidents are not unique. They are grounded in the history of blacks in America. A consistent finding in the literature is that blacks, and especially black males, are more likely to be stopped, questioned, searched, and arrested, both within and outside their communities. According to Berry and Looney (1996, p. 270), nearly every black male, regardless of his social class, can report a story about being stopped. An incident related by Tonry (1995, p. 51) is fairly typical:

> Harvard philosopher Cornel West writes in *Race Matters* (1993) of being stopped "on false charges of trafficking in cocaine" while driving to Williams College and of "being stopped three times in my first ten days in Princeton for driving too slowly on a residential street with a speed limit of twenty-five miles per hour."

However, others argue that police are more likely to operate with suspicion drawn from a profile of criminally suspicious black males. These correspond to such images as the black dope fiend, the black kingpin-drug dealer, the "gansta," and so forth which are current in the popular media.

Many black men have complained that regardless of their social status, they frequently are subject to police scrutiny whenever they approximate these images or simply sit in their Mercedes and are attired in gold chains. The lesson is deafening: "No matter how many achievements you have, you can't shuck the burden of being black in a white society" (Tonry, 1995, p. 51).

Not only are blacks no longer shocked about the daily harassments they and others experience from the police, unlike most whites they were not bewildered or shocked by the 1991 videotape of Rodney King, a black man, being repeatedly assaulted by 27 white police officers. The media pointed out what blacks already knew—that police use of force is a common phenomenon in the black community (Barak, 1995; Berry, 1996; Berry and Looney, 1996).

I, like so many other blacks, have witnessed the police use excessive force on many occasions. In numerous large urban environments, I observed police officers subjecting young black men and women to fairly frequent friskings on the streets. Many of these encounters left poor young blacks lying bloodied and injured on the sidewalks waiting for the ambulances to arrive or isolated in jail cells without medical attention. In my journeys down the "mean" streets of these communities, I also had the sickening opportunity to witness a police officer shoot a 14-year-old black boy dead simply because the youngster panicked when the police officer drew his gun and told him to stop.

Current research on police brutality strongly supports blacks' everyday experiences with the police. For example, recent studies on police use of deadly force consistently show that blacks are considerably more likely than whites or Latinos to be shot by the police (Reiman, 1995). Furthermore, both Hutchinson (1990) and Stallworth (1994) point out that police harassment, seizures, and shootings have caused accumulated resentment among blacks. The demonstrated hostility of the police toward blacks and the hostile response of blacks to the police can be considered a self-fulfilling prophecy. It continues to produce a deadly dynamic of mutual distrust and hostility, which in turn ignites angry confrontations, protests, and rebellions. Thus, we must conclude that the police procedures employed in black neighborhoods have not cut down on violence, and in far too many cases the police have been the *cause* of it (Hutchinson, 1990).

Stallworth (1994, p. 7) complements this observation by suggesting that perhaps gangsta rappers' lyrics are accurate in their portrayal of the police *and* the scourge of drugs that plagues inner-city black communities as being the root causes of violence in these communities. Their lyrics offer a stark portrayal of ghetto life, as experienced by its residents, as one of intense terror, brutality, repression, and oppression of black people at the hands of the police.

Finally, a major consequence of police saturation, surveillance, and harassment has skewed the arrest figures upward. There is increasing evidence that the War on Drugs has been fought in a racially discriminatory manner. As previously noted, blacks are more likely to be suspected and arrested by police who saturate black communities. Such biased police practices have become the driving force behind today's exploding prison population. Reiman (1995) elaborates upon this observation by documenting that the criminal justice system supports police racial bias by systematically failing to punish and confine *all* who are dangerous and criminal, but to disproportionately confine blacks who are dangerous and criminal.

Are We Targeting the Most Dangerous Population?

Are we really targeting the most dangerous among the black lower class? No, concludes the literature. Recent studies repeatedly provide strong and compelling evidence that most of the unprecedented numbers of people who are going to prison are guilty of petty property and drug-related crimes or violations of their conditions of probation or parole (Hutchinson, 1990; Reiman, 1995). As Irwin and Austin (1994, p. 143) put it:

> Even offenders who commit frequent felonies and who define themselves as "outlaws," "dope fiends," "crack dealers," or "gang bangers" commit mostly petty felonies. These "high-rate" offenders, as they have been labeled are, for the most part, uneducated, unskilled (at crime as well as conventional pursuits), and highly disorganized persons who have no access to any form of rewarding, meaningful conventional life. They usually turn to dangerous, mostly unrewarding, petty criminal pursuits as one of the few options they have to earn money, win some respect, and avoid monotonous lives on the streets. Frequently, they spend most of their young lives behind bars.

By arresting these petty, fairly disorganized criminals, drug abusers, and dealers, are we actually reducing the tide of drugs within lower-income communities? If so, can we then conclude that the War on Drugs is doing what it is supposed to do? No, contend Inciardi (1986), Lusane (1991), and Reinarman (1996). The War on Drugs has failed. During the 1980s, the government spent billions of our tax dollars and arrested millions of blacks and other ethnic minorities for drug possession or drug dealing. Over and over, however, the media report that yet another large-scale drug operation has been busted and kingpin-drug dealers, usually black or Latino, have been caught. These reports do not suggest the success of the war, but instead strongly indicate that drugs continue to be as accessible as they were before the new arrests. Drugs continue to flood into the poor black communities. In turn, it seems that there is an almost unlimited supply of poor black men and, increasingly, poor black women who become addicted to these hard drugs and compete—too often violently—to fill these vacant positions.

Some Benefits of Racial Images of the Black Criminal

The demonization of black men, and to a lesser extent black women, benefits white America in myriad ways. First, the ideological representations of black participation in criminal activities presented here appeal and contribute to notions of white supremacy and black inferiority (A. W. Wilson, 1994; Gray, 1995, 1996). These images of individualized black criminals reinforce the notion that blacks are still inherently different from "them," the respectable whites. Consequently, criminality generally is blamed on the individualized failure of blacks (Parenti, 1991; Gray, 1995, 1996; Surette, 1995). Given this, these images manage to convey that crime is behavior blacks freely choose, because they are not restrained in any way by normal rules and values. To be considered a failure in America, then, is to be stigmatized. To be considered simultaneously a failure, a criminal, and black is to be vulnerable to social control in the form of punishment and correction.

It seems that perceived black criminality makes whites feel good, and this need to have blacks create comfort and good feelings has its roots in slavery. Recall that the slaves' sole function within the plantation system was to provide economic and social comfort for their masters and mistresses. Today, claim Hutchinson (1990, 1994) and A. W. Wilson (1994), whites continue to criminalize blacks in order to receive a similar kind of comfort. Although images of black criminality evoke fear in America, these constructed monsters also reassure whites of their self-worth and superior moral standing. In short, argues Wilson, black criminals serve as a "negative reference group" that is vital to maintaining the white self-image of righteousness. Accordingly, the higher the arrest rates of the black population, the more self-righteous white America feels itself to be. In turn, the more self-righteous whites become, the easier it is for them to justify the domination and exploitation of blacks. In addition, by explaining black criminality as genetic in nature, whites absolve themselves of all responsibility for creating the conditions enabling crime and drugs to flourish in poor black neighborhoods.

Second, obsessing about the encroaching "menace" of black crime enables white America to deny its own criminal record, which actually poses the most severe threat to the fabric of American society (Inciardi, 1986; Parenti, 1991; A. W. Wilson, 1994; Reiman, 1995). Relatively little attention is given by the popular media to drug use and drug trafficking in the suites of corporate America, or to the role of police officers in extorting money from poor drug dealers, and certainly not to the role of government agencies in the distribution of drugs. In addition, the media hype reinforces the idea that individual exploits by relatively powerless criminals are far more serious than the institutional exploits and crimes of the powerful.

Nor is much attention given by the media to the fact that corporate criminals are seldom caught; and if caught, seldom punished; and if punished, rarely severely. Yet corporate criminals frequently resort to unfair and often illegal market practices, and they continue almost freely to violate occupational, environmental, and product safety standards, which cause more deaths and injuries and gain greater economic profits than do those engaged in street crime (Parenti, 1991; Barak, 1995; Reiman, 1995). In sum, the media's preoccupation with poor black crime effectively deflects attention from the crimes of the powerful.

The recent literature on crime and criminal justice raises an important observation. White America is the primary beneficiary of a multi-billion-dollar prison industry that processes black men and women as its basic raw material (Hutchinson, 1990, 1994; Parenti, 1991; A. W. Wilson, 1994). Prisons have become one of the largest and fastest-growing industries in the United States. The prison industry provides income for white families, vendors, construction firms, architectural firms, members of the helping professions, law and security enforcement agencies, and so forth. We cannot economically afford to eradicate black crime, contends A. W. Wilson (1994); instead, white America needs to maintain those social conditions that instigate and sustain black criminality and imprisonment.

Finally, the proliferation of hard-drug use in poor black communities provides additional benefits to white America. As Lusane (1991, p. 223) has noted: "A drugged-out community, pacified, subdued, and bent on self-destruction, is not likely to rise up against the white corporate power structure. The youth of those communities, who are most likely to rebel, are at the center of the drug epidemic and the government-sponsored drug war." The choice of incarceration as the preferred method for dealing with the drug and violence crisis also reinforces the economic marginalization of blacks and reduces the threat that they will compete with whites for scarce jobs.

It should come as no surprise that "studies have shown that blacks have a poorer chance than whites to receive probation, a suspended sentence, parole, commutation of a death sentence, or pardon" (Reiman, 1995, p. 192). What is suggested here and made more explicit in other studies is that blacks not only receive longer sentences relative to whites, but they are also more likely to spend a longer time in captivity than whites.

My research on racial minorities incarcerated in a rural, white–dominated prison system demonstrates the power of cultural images on the prison staff's treatment of prisoners of color (see also Carroll, 1974; Mann, 1993; Silberman, 1995). Pervasive and exaggerated racial stereotyping by correctional officers leads to more intense surveillance of black prisoners. This greater surveillance, in turn, increases the likelihood that black prisoners will receive frequent disciplinary reports and that, once found guilty, they will be segregated from the general population and lose some "good time," which can lead to delayed release on parole. As stated by a black prisoner (Fishman, 1994, p. 15):

> They [the white correctional staff] see black men who might be drug dealers who have nothing going for

themselves but to come up here to mess up their lives and the lives of all who have been here for years. . . . I think that they see us as the TV shows portray us. You don't get nothing good off the TV for black people. Only thing you get from black people that's good is some Bill Cosby or some Will Smith. Everything you see on the TV about black people is either they're doing drive-by shootings, selling drugs or killing somebody. What are they going to think? The first time they ever seen a black person was on TV, you know. What's he gonna come up here for and go through our neighborhood shooting up people?

Some Dysfunctions for the Black Community

To live as a black woman in the United States is synonymous with being fearful of men in general, and more specifically of black *and* white men. Nowhere in this country is a black woman as safe as a white woman or a white man. Every street in urban environments, and every forest, meadow, and swimming hole, exudes potential danger. As a black woman, I continue to deal with the legacy of slavery, namely, the existence of potential violence directed at black women. Black women were and continue to be "fair game" for both white and black male violence. Every time I walk city streets alone at night or hike in the mountains and valleys of our rural areas, I take both physical and mental precautions aimed at minimizing violence from white and black male strangers. These precautions remain far from dormant as I grow older due to the power of our cultural images. I still visualize images of the rapacious black man and the sleek, hungering white man, which I include in a series of cues to forewarn me of danger. However, I have some additional fears to add to my fear of being raped by a black man. My fears also include their potential for stealing, assaulting me, and acting like maniacs. My fears, during the years gone by, have increasingly been found to be valid. I can report many more encounters in which black men—rather than white men—have robbed me, burglarized my home, sexually threatened me, threatened me with a weapon, touched me in my private parts, and sexually harassed me.

Less talked about are the fears that black women have about each other. I remember how fearful I was of young black women walking in groups on the streets, waiting for the arrival of buses, hanging around schoolyards, and riding the subways with me. My fears were specifically directed toward those young women who "hung tough," "talked tough," "walked tough," and exuded a readiness to fight "anybody." Based on my experiences and the experiences of other females, I was well aware that these types of girls had a penchant for victimizing vulnerable, more conventionally oriented young girls and women. They were capable of jostling and shoving, tearing their victims' clothes, fighting, and robbing. I must admit, however, that neither I nor my friends have witnessed young white girls or women participating in such behavior.

I am not sure whether my female black elders based their knowledge of black men's criminal tendencies on the media or on their personal experiences. My experiences strongly suggest that the media report what white America wants to hear rather than what actually transpires. Therefore, I find it easy to agree that white America buys into the image that it is black men—not white men—who rape, torture, and kill white women. But this is not so. Blacks are more likely to victimize each other than to victimize whites.

The truth is that most thefts or robberies committed by blacks or whites occur within a few blocks of the victim's home. Most murders are committed by family members, friends or acquaintances. The same holds true for rape. A large number of the rapes stem from dates or casual relationships. Put simply: Segregation which still traps most blacks in ghettos and whites in gilded suburbs or ethnic enclaves insures that blacks target blacks, and whites target whites, they are the closest ones. (Hutchinson, 1990, p. xi)

The long history of demonization of black men and women has another negative consequence for the black community. It has built a wall of distrust, division, and disrespect among blacks. More frequently than I can count, I have heard black men and women comment upon white America's cleverness in this instance. That is, white America knows how to keep the system of racism and oppression going. They arrange matters so that we mainly fight each other; thus demonization triggers fights, robberies, rapes, and killings among blacks. It works. We are so divided and distrustful of each other that we undermine our ability to organize ourselves to redress the injustices directed at us and to fight for our liberation from oppression.

Within this context, then, the demonization of blacks also has served to give the black middle class a negative reference group. For instance, we strive not to be like poor blacks, but to be different and more acceptable to the white community. To succeed, we dissociate ourselves from the black lower class and put on a performance of respectability, conventionality, and success. Many black middle-class persons re-create themselves as "success stories." As affluent blacks, they appear to have risen from the "horror of the ghetto," thereby reconfirming the myth that "anything and everything is possible in America" (Akbar, 1984; Gray, 1995, 1996). Wilson and Gutiérrez (1995) and A. W. Wilson (1994) contend that this process encourages affluent blacks to internalize and act out the negative attitudes that white America has toward poor blacks. By projecting the image of middle-class success, blacks give lip service to the notion that the "haves," whether white or black, are better than or superior to the black "have-nots." By expressing obedience and adherence to the values and ambitions of the dominant culture, middle-class blacks demonstrate that they have overcome the deficits of being black and thus vulnerable to suspicion for every wrongdoing. Consequently, they can more effectively diminish their own unpleasant encounters with the racist criminal justice system, but they do so at the expense of their lower-class brothers and sisters.

Conclusions

We need to think seriously about the reality of life in America—a reality in which race strongly interjects itself into the images that whites and blacks hold of one another. In turn, race accentuates the sting of everyday oppression, as well as the sting of the oppression that colors the criminal justice system's differential treatment of blacks.

Of significance here is the fact that the popular American media distort the picture of crime and crime control. They not only exaggerate the incidence of black involvement in street crime and in the illicit underground-drug economy, they also project stereotypical images of blacks as criminals. This situation has worsened since the time of slavery. The mass media today have elaborated upon what Reiman (1995) terms a "carnival mirror," which continues to present a "distorted image" of the

dangers that threaten us—an image created more by the shape of the mirror than by the reality reflected.

Black America has received some potent messages about its place in American life. First of all, blacks are painfully aware of the negative impact of criminal images on their encounters with agents of the criminal justice system. A common message has evolved from this situation. Many blacks understand that they cannot depend on the white-dominated criminal justice system to protect them. They know that both the media and agents of the justice system judge them by a different standard than they do whites. It therefore behooves many blacks who compete for scarce monetary profits in the underground-drug economy to establish their own justice systems to protect themselves and their drug businesses against competitors. An unanticipated consequence of the drug war has been an intensification of black-on-black violence.

Another potent message given to the black community is the propagation of black criminal images and the actual racist practices of law enforcement. The courts and the prison system manage to make startlingly clear that black life has less value than white life. Numerous studies consistently show what blacks on the streets know. This devaluation of black life is evidenced in research showing far more serious sanctions for blacks than for whites who threaten or take white lives. Many studies have shown that when a black man kills a white, the chances are great that he will receive the death penalty (Parenti, 1991; Reiman, 1995; Tonry, 1995). Lastly, Hutchinson (1994) notes that in Dallas, Texas, a research project recently found that the rape of a white woman brings an average sentence of 10 years, whereas the sentence for raping a black woman is typically two years. This finding has been duplicated in dozens of other states. The issue is not income or gender but race.

Hawkins and Thomas (1991) report another way in which the message is conveyed that black life has little value. For decades, white officials in northern cities have allowed vice and crime to go unpoliced in black neighborhoods. This lack of protection is based on white stereotypes of blacks as having loose morals and being inclined to crime. As pointed out by A. W. Wilson (1994), police take their time answering calls in black areas and, when they finally arrive to make an arrest or to check the scene, they often treat poor blacks brutally. Many black men have died because of excessive police brutality. Seldom have police officers been punished when they kill black males without reasonable cause by beating or shooting them. According to Burk (1996), *Gannette News Service* reporter Rochelle Sharpe examined 100 lawsuits resulting from the worst brutalities. She discovered that the officers found guilty for abuse usually were not disciplined and rarely were fined. Indeed, some officers were promoted, and others were given early retirement with full disability pay after a conviction (Burk, 1996, p. 26).

Blacks' perceptions that black life is devalued have had some horrible repercussions. This message has encouraged many blacks to disrespect the law and the criminal justice system, as well as encouraged greater violence among blacks (Hutchinson, 1990; Stallworth, 1994; A. W. Wilson, 1994). It has led blacks to participate in drug distribution, drug abuse, and violence. Finally, it has invited black death rates to escalate at an alarming pace, as well as led to an escalation of pain and suffering:

> . . . African-Americans are 50 percent of emergency room admissions for heroin addiction, 55 percent for cocaine addiction, and 60 percent for PCP use.

> More than 25 percent of those treated for drugs in 1987 were blacks. Meanwhile, 25 to 30 percent of AIDS cases were black. Most of them contracted the disease through dirty needles or sexual relations with partners infected by dirty needles. In Washington, D.C. hospitals in 1988, an estimated 40 percent of the women having babies were drug addicts. (Hutchinson, 1990, p. 53)

To conclude, the images of crime and punishment propagated by the media have aided and abetted what some black investigators call "genocide" and others call "chemical warfare," with terrifying results. Whatever the terms used, there is agreement that the current drug crisis has dire consequences for the future of poor blacks. It is estimated that by the year 2000, a community-health crisis of genocidal proportions will develop in which black men will be dead or incarcerated due to their participation in the illicit-drug economy. Finally, to add to the dismal picture, Lusane (1991) points out that the AIDS virus has begun to ravage black people—especially those who are intravenous drug users and other "misfits." AIDS has overtaken homicide as the number one killer of blacks aged 25 to 44. Blacks are now surpassing the number of whites in reported new cases of AIDS (Raspberry, 1996).

As presented here, my analysis is grim and desperate. This chapter is filled with pessimistic images. I wonder how much longer poor blacks who live so close to the edge can keep themselves, much less their brothers and sisters, from going over. And I wonder whether there are enough poor blacks who can pull themselves, much less their brothers and sisters, above these cultural images of the black bogeyman and black "hos" and "bitches" that continue to assist in the racial oppression and nullification of the poor black community for the benefit of white economic gain and white self-righteousness.

References

Akbar, N. (1984). *Chains and images of psychological slavery.* Jersey City, NJ: New Mind Publications.

Anderson, E. (1994). "The code of the streets." *Atlantic Monthly,* May, 81–94.

Barak, G. (1995). "Media, society and criminology." In G. Barak (Ed.), *Media, process, and the social construction of crime: Studies in newsmaking criminology.* New York: Garland Publishing, 3–48.

Berry, V.T. (1996). "Introduction: Racialism and the media." In V.T. Berry and C.L. Manning-Miller (Eds.), *Mediated messages and African-American culture: Contemporary issues.* Thousand Oaks, CA: Sage Publications, vii–xv.

Berry, V.T., and Looney, H., Jr. (1996). "Rap music, black men and the police." In V.T. Berry and C.L. Manning-Miller (Eds.), *Mediated messages and African-American culture: Contemporary issues.* Thousand Oaks, CA: Sage Publications, 263–277.

Burk, R.E. (1996). "Intimations of invisibility: Black women and contemporary Hollywood cinema." In V.T. Berry and C.L. Manning-Miller (Eds.), *Mediated messages and African-American culture: Contemporary issues.* CA: Sage Publications, 24–39.

Carroll, L. (1974). *Hacks, blacks, and cons: Race relations in a maximum security prison.* Lexington, MA: D.C. Heath.

Collins, P.H. (1990). *Black feminist thought: Knowledge, consciousness and the politics of empowerment.* Boston: Unwin Hyman.

Dyson, M.E. (1996). *Between God and gangsta rap: Bearing witness to black culture.* New York: Oxford University Press.

Faith, K. (1993). *Unruly women: The politics of confinement and resistance.* Vancouver, BC: Press Gang Publishers.

Fishman, Laura T. (1994). *Fighting back: African-American and Latino prisoners struggling to survive HIV/AIDS infection.* Paper presented at the annual meeting of the American Society of Criminology, Miami, FL.

Gray, Herman. (1996). "Television, black Americans and the American dream." In V.T. Berry and C.L. Manning-Miller (Eds.), *Mediated messages and African-American culture: Contemporary issues.* Thousand Oaks, CA: Sage Publications, 131–145.

——. (1995). *Watching race: Television and the struggle for "blackness."* Minneapolis: University of Minnesota Press.

Grier, W.H., and Cobb, P.M. (1980). *Black rage.* New York: Basic Books.

Hawkins, H., and Thomas, R. (1991). "White policing of black populations: A history of race and social control in America." In E. Cashmore and E. McLaughlin (Eds.), *Out of order? Policing black people.* New York: Routledge, 65–86.

Hutchinson, E.O. (1994). *The assassination of the black male image.* Los Angeles, CA: Middle Passage Press.

——. (1990). *The mugging of black America.* Chicago: African American images.

Inciardi, J. (1986). *The war on drugs: Heroin, cocaine, crime and public policy.* Mountain View, CA: Mayfield Publishing Company.

Irwin, J., and Austin, J. (1994). *It's about time: America's imprisonment binge.* Belmont, CA: Wadsworth Publishing Company.

Kappeler, V.E., Blumberg, M., and Potter, G.W. (1996). *The mythology of crime and criminal justice.* Prospect Heights, IL: Waveland Press.

Leab, D.J. (1976). *From Sambo to Superspade: The black experience in motion pictures.* Boston: Houghton Mifflin Company.

Lemelle, A.J., Jr. (1995). *Black male deviance.* Westport, CT: Prager Publishers.

Lusane, C. (1991). *Pipe dream blues: Racism and the war on drugs.* Boston: South End Press.

Mann, Coramae Richey. (1993). *Unequal justice: A question of color.* Bloomington: Indiana University Press.

Morton, P. (1991). *Disfigured images: The historical assault on Afro-American women.* New York: Pantheon Books.

Munro-Bjorklund, V. (1991). "Popular cultural images of prisoners." *Social Justice, 18*, 48–70.

Parenti, M. (1991). *Make-believe media: The politics of entertainment.* New York: St. Martin's Press.

Raspberry, William. (1996, October 11). *Burlington Free Press.*

Reiman, J. (1995). *The rich get richer and the poor get prison: Ideology, class, and criminal justice.* Boston: Allyn and Bacon.

Reinarman, C. (1996). "The social construction of drug scares." In E. Goode (Ed.), *Social Deviance.* Boston: Allyn and Bacon, 224–234.

Silberman, M. (1995). *A world of violence: Corrections in America.* Belmont, CA: Wadsworth Publishing Company.

Stallworth, R. (1994). "Gangster rap: Music, culture and politics." Unpublished manuscript, revised edition, Utah Division of Investigation, Murray, UT.

Surette, R. (1995). "Predator criminals as media icons." In V.T. Berry and C.L. Manning-Miller (Eds.), *Mediated messages and African-American culture: Contemporary issues.* Thousand Oaks, CA: Sage Publications, 131–158.

Taylor, C.S. (1993). *Girls, gangs, women and drugs.* East Lansing: Michigan State University Press.

Tonry, Michael. (1995). *Malign neglect: Race, crime, and punishment in America.* New York: Oxford University Press.

West, Cornel. (1994). *Race matters.* New York: Vintage Books.

Wiegman, R. (1991). "Black bodies/American commodities: Gender, race and the bourgeois ideal in contemporary film." In L.D. Friedman (Ed.), *Unspeakable images: Ethnicity and the American cinema.* Chicago: University of Illinois Press, 308–328.

Wilson, A.W. (1994). *Black-on-black violence: The psychodynamics of black self-annihilation in service of white domination.* New York: Afrikon World Infosystems.

Wilson, M. (1994). *Crossing the boundary: Black women survive incest.* Seattle, WA: Seal Press.

Wilson, Clint C., II, and Gutiérrez, Félix. (1995). *Race, multiculturalism, and the media: From mass to class communication.* Thousand Oaks, CA: Sage Publications.

Wozencraft, K. (1995). "The cop: Waiting for good dope." In C.L. LaMay and E.E. Dennis (Eds.), *The culture of crime.* New Brunswick, NJ: Transaction Publishers, 65–74.

Discussion Questions

1. Discuss how the legacy of slavery continues to exist in present-day images of black men and women.

2. Why was the author warned to be leery of some black men and women, particularly those who were poor or considered to be bad? Compare and contrast the reasons for fearing these black men and women.

3. Identify and explain at least two police practices that are directed specifically at the black community.

4. According to the author, has the War on Drugs been a success? Why or why not? Do you agree? Why or why not?

5. Discuss at least three ways that whites benefit from the demonization of black men and women. ✦

Part III

The Color Brown

Latinos and Latinas make up the fastest-growing population segment in the United States today.[1] Although most Latinos and Latinas in the U.S. are of Mexican or Puerto Rican origin, all of the countries of South America, Central America, and the Spanish-speaking Caribbean, as well as Mexico, are represented. This very diverse population comes in all skin colors and from all walks of life.

Soon after the Spanish and Portuguese conquerors sent home word of the wealth to be found in the New World, large numbers of Spaniards and Portuguese traveled to the Americas to seek their fortune. The plantations and mines that these colonists hoped would make them rich required cheap, expendable labor. Depending upon the availability of indigenous people and on how easily they could be subjugated, either indigenous peoples or African slaves were forced to provide this labor. In some parts of Latin America, the indigenous peoples have survived with their cultures intact; in others, they were decimated by the brutal living and working conditions in mines and plantations, or they were run off cliffs into the sea.

Although some Spanish and Portuguese women made the transatlantic journey to settle in the Americas, many of the colonizers seduced or raped indigenous women or African slaves. Their children became known as "mestizos" (if Indian and white) and "mulattos" (if black and white). Of course, because historically the distribution of wealth in Latin America was tied to ancestry, direct descendants of the Spanish conquerors kept most of the wealth within a small network of families. Nevertheless, race and class relations in Latin America have always been somewhat flexible, with the result that no matter how dark or how light your skin color, if you were wealthy you were apt to be considered white, and if you were poor you were considered Indian or black (depending on which group was at the bottom of the social pile in that locale). In the United States, however, race and class are more independent of one another, such that all Latinos and Latinas, regardless of their class position, could be presumed to have certain traits in common, including laziness, a proclivity to use knives, and a preference for marijuana.

Some Latinos and Latinas migrated to the United States from other countries. Others still reside where their ancestors lived, but because of U.S. victories in its wars with Mexico and Spain, those locales are now part of the United States. Thus, many Chicanos and Chicanas living in southwestern states from California to Texas never *moved* to the United States; rather, the U.S.–Mexico border shifted dramatically, turning them suddenly into American citizens. The status of Puerto Ricans is more ambiguous, because Puerto Rico is a "commonwealth"—a legal fiction halfway between statehood and independence. As a result, Puerto Ricans are U.S. citizens, but the residents of Puerto Rico do not have the same rights of representation as do other citizens.

In addition to the Mexicans and Puerto Ricans who were part of the war booty won by the United States, huge numbers of Latin Americans have moved to the United States. Some come for short stays as temporary workers in the fields and factories; others have moved here permanently to escape poverty or war in their homelands. Mexicans, in particular, have always been our backup labor supply. When labor shortages arise, particularly in agriculture, Mexicans are encouraged to cross the border to work for wages far lower than those U.S. workers would accept but much higher than they could earn in Mexico. When the seasonal work has been completed, they are expected to leave. At times they risk staying in the United States, even though they are vulnerable to exploitation as undocumented workers. Periodically, Border Patrol sweeps attempt to force them across the border. At times, U.S. citizens and permanent residents are caught in these sweeps and deported as well. Thus, the back door swings open and shut, pulling people in and tossing them out again.

Isolated by language and racism, fearing deportation whether or not they are in the United States. legally, Latino/a communities in the United States have had to take care of themselves rather than trust the police or other governmental agencies for protection. Historically, it has been the young men of the community who have provided that protection. These age-graded groups of young men are the antecedents of today's fearful gangs.

As the authors in this part demonstrate, in many parts of the United States gangs have become synonymous with Latino youths. Yesterday's "greaser" has become today's drug-dealing "gang banger." Positive events in Latino/a communities are not often reported by the media, but every death is assumed to be gang related and makes the TV news. The involvement of young women in the gangs is even more intriguing for many. Stereotypically, Latinas are depicted as sexual objects when young and mothers (meaning cooks, laundresses, and child-care providers) once married.

The authors of these chapters explore many of the assumptions and stereotypes concerning Latinos and Latinas, and how these have been reinforced by the media and by politicians trying to show how tough they are on crime and welfare abuses—regardless of whether the data support their positions or not. They also demonstrate the effects of decades—and, in many cases, centuries—of mistrust between Latinos/as and representatives of the U.S. government, including especially Euro-American social control agents. The difficulties caused by linguistic and cultural barriers when Latinos and Latinas must interact with government authorities are also highlighted.

Note

We use the identifiers "Latino" and "Latina" rather than "Hispanic." As Suzanne

Oboler has noted, "The term Hispanic began to be disseminated as early as 1970 by government agencies . . . the term *Latino* began to emerge among grassroots sectors of the population, coined as a progressive alternative to the state-imposed bureaucratic label Hispanic. The term Latino has since been increasingly adopted, primarily in urban areas in which various Latin American national-origin groups are represented" (1995, pp. vii–viii).

References

Oboler, Suzanne. (1995). *Ethnic labels, Latino lives: Identity and the politics of (re)presentation in the United States.* Minneapolis: University of Minnesota Press. ✦

Chapter 10

Images of Latinos and Latinas

The Color of Skin Is the Color of Crime

Luis J. Rodríguez

The faces of the young men and women before me were hard and discomforting. They were brown-skinned; some had shaved heads. One of the girls, called "Baby Crazy," had tattoos on her lips and cheek, as well as harsh mascara and dark lip paint. Her arms had tattoos in old English lettering and in the barrio style, including the initials of her gang and the names of her boyfriend and two children. One of the young men had tattoos across his arms, back, and chest. On his face he had a tattooed tear below one eye and the three dots signifying "Mi Vida Loca" below the other eye; the initials of his gang were on his chin. The others were similarly marked, some with scars of bullet wounds and knifings. They wore the loose and oversized clothing known as the "Cholo" style. They had names such as Diablo, Pelon, Villain, and Whisper.

They were Latino gang members, dressed and marked in the same L.A.-gang style that has brought chills to many an outsider. Latino youths have come to represent the growing U.S. "gangsta" culture that has been portrayed in movies, the news media, and books (albeit mostly in distorted form).

As extreme as their demeanor may have been, they were also young people capable of great love, loyalty, laughter, and responsibility. Those particular young people were not on a street corner "slangin'" dope. They were, in fact, at a major conference with members of government, police, and social agencies in El Salvador, speaking out on behalf of estranged youths in their country while also lending their expertise to help obtain a measure of peace in the streets.

I was in El Salvador in late May 1996 as one of four invited international guests to present ways to work with youths, to empower them, and to utilize their vast energies for positive change. Donna DeCesere, a New York City–based photographer, and I helped bring these particular youths to the table.

For three years, Donna and I had been meeting with these young people, interviewing them and taking their photos for a collaborative book project on which we are working. It was this work, in particular Donna's slides and photos, that helped open the doors for this important dialogue.

The image and reality were definitely in conflict—yet neither could have existed without the other. (True peace can be achieved only when the so-called perpetrators of the violence are included and empowered to make peace.)

We all know that the mass media, particularly in entertainment, have a growing fascination with portraying Latino youths as cowards and vicious killers. This is far from gangsta chic. In fact, actual gangsters of European descent, such as John Dillinger and Bonnie and Clyde, and fantasy ones like those in the *Godfather* movies or Oliver Stone's *Natural Born Killers*, have most often been portrayed in a more glowing and understandable light (their motivations were made clear, despite the despicable things they may have done).

In Chicago—where the mayor and the police department have refused to sit down with African American and Latino gang youths—there is a restaurant and club called "Al Capone's" with the face of the 1920s gangster emblazoned in front. (We know that the first Richard Daley, as well as many of his cronies, had been members of a gang called the "Hamburgs" that existed primarily to keep the blacks out of the Irish community of Bridgeport.)

Image and Reality: The Color of Skin is the Color of Crime

Racist pundits such as Charles Murray and Michael Levine now use the large number of black and Latino people in prison and among crime statistics to prove the inferior and criminally inclined qualities of blacks and Latinos.

Forget the 500 years of slavery and racist oppression; forget the growing levels of poverty and deepening economic displacement; forget the social barriers that have made decent jobs and higher education virtually nonexistent for most inner-city blacks and Latinos. The color of skin is the color of crime.

Since the 1993 release of my memoir *Always Running: La Vida Loca, Gang Days in L.A.,* I have been to some of the so-called worst schools, including Roosevelt High in East Los Angeles, the most overcrowded high school in the country. I've walked the halls of schools such as Garfield and Eastside that were later depicted in the movies *Stand and Deliver* and *Lean On Me.* From Seattle to Miami, Hartford to San Diego, Chicago to Atlanta, I've been there. In "gang" schools. In schools with police officers on every floor and metal detectors at the entrances.

I've also been to various juvenile detention centers and prisons. I've met with so-called killer kids (including a sweet-faced, long-haired teenager who had been convicted of murdering her sister in Omaha). The image of crime is dark. The image of crime is poor. The image of crime is pain. Yet I also heard voices crying out for caring. Voices capable of great intelligence. Of great comprehension. Once I read poetry through a teeny slit in the door of an accused teenage murderer who closed his eyes and swayed with my words.

Don't get me wrong. I've also done workshops with upper-class white and privileged children in communities such as Bryn Mawr, Pennsylvania. All kids are great to me—regardless of their station in life. But that's the point. All kids are great. All kids are capable of great beauty. Of powerful transcendence. All are gifted and intrinsically valuable human beings.

But what soul do we murder when we declare that the color of skin is the color of crime? What stereotypes do we resurrect with every "COPS" show that depicts white, burly men of power pushing around, often degrading, impotent, mostly drugged, and beaten-down people of color? What are we saying when heroes in movies are primarily white, male, and upper-class? Yet every day we are bombarded with the same connection: the color of skin is the color of crime.

Image Versus Reality: Conflict in Truth

Those young Salvadoran gang youths were heroes to me. They had seen much tragedy, they had seen wars in their homeland and in the streets of a city to which they were forced to flee. They also saw more violence after being deported or sent back to a place where they no longer felt connected.

Were they capable of great violence? Yes, I have seen this, too. I have lived this, too. I have been both a victim and a perpetrator of such violence. But I also saw how they were willing to risk their lives (they were risking their lives every day anyway) to change the world around them. How they were tired of the killings and maimings. How they wanted to become proper fathers and mothers in a place that would accept them, hear them, and allow them room to take part.

As I have often said, when it comes to human beings, looking deeply at all the factors at play, there really is no such thing as "senseless" violence. In today's complicated, transitional, confusing, and changing times, violence makes a lot of sense. To understand the impulses, motive forces, and factors that create violence, and then to accurately, even if dramatically, portray this through art is critical for a more comprehensive sense of what we are dealing with. It is also the foundation for efforts to do something real and positive about violence. But this is far from what we see in the images on TV, in movies, or in many books.

The present-day distortion in the media of crime and color only fuels the basest emotions among us, enhancing our fears and ignorance. The results today of this disinformation are more prisons, more curtailment of our civil liberties, and more cuts in programs and educational and job opportunities (including barriers to the new technologies as the whole concept of work is being transformed before our eyes)— which, in case it isn't clear to anyone, creates the environment for more crime, more violence, and more fear.

After the Chicago Bulls won their fourth National Basketball Association championship, a number of young people, many of them in gangs, took to the streets in my Chicago neighborhood. I've known these same youths in calmer settings. But this night they were rowdy, yelling and throwing bottles. Several police officers in riot gear chased and beat down a few of them; a couple of officers were beaten in return. Again, under other circumstances, these young people would blossom; in relationship to police, to "alien" power, they were at war. I'm sure this is also true for many police officers, who include decent family men and women. But in relation to gangs, they are often violent and abusive.

We need more settings in which these young people can be expressive, creative, wise, and appreciated. They will thrive, I know.

I would rather have a tattooed and scarred hand near mine as we work to bring out the best in our people and the best of the expanding technologies than a manicured and clean hand that wants only to remove what it fears, bringing out the worst of everything in the process. You can't tell nowadays what you're dealing with just by image. You have to go deeper. You have to relate. You have to risk opening up and being next to and among those whom everyone else has abandoned. Then you will see the real place where change and peace can come from. Then you can understand why, in most cases, the image and the reality can never be reconciled.

Discussion Questions

1. Why did the images of youths attending the conference in El Salvador and the reality of what they were trying to achieve appear to be contradictory?

2. Compare and contrast the media's portrayal of youths in Latino gangs and youths in gangs of European descent, including specific examples you have encountered.

3. Explain what is meant by the statement "the color of skin is the color of crime." Do you agree with this statement? Why or why not?

4. According to the author, why does violence make sense in today's society?

5. The author claims that the present-day media portrayal of crime and color is distorted. What has been the result of this distortion? ✦

Chapter 11

Stereotyping by the Media

'Hot Blood and Easy Virtue': Mass Media and the Making of Racist Latino/a Stereotypes

Diego O. Castro

For centuries those who championed white supremacy have recorded history in their image. They have rationalized, glorified, and justified genocide and other acts of violence to excuse and explain their inhumanity to others. Nowhere has this been more visually evident than in the motion-picture industry, which has historically portrayed people of color[1] through a negative white lens. Until recently, minority actors were entirely disenfranchised by Hollywood filmmakers, and when movie roles were offered to them, people of color usually had little choice but to portray racialized and stereotyped characters.

Consequently, Latinos/as have had little success in dispelling the negative images and stereotypes projected onto them by Hollywood.[2] Filmmakers continue to flagrantly portray the Latino man as the hot-blooded, vicious killer and the Latina as the sexy and submissive woman of easy virtue. Not only do

these long-standing stereotypes remain robust, but new and more contemporary images have been constructed that portray the Latino/a in more violent and degrading ways than ever before. In an attempt to shed light on stereotypes from a media standpoint, Wilson and Gutiérrez (1995, p. 61) have stated that they are "a means of quickly bringing to the audience's collective consciousness a character's anticipated value system and/or behavior expectations" and are therefore "shortcuts to character development and a basis for mass entertainment and literary fare." However, Wilson and Gutiérrez emphasize that when stereotypes are combined with prejudices that are used to transmit good versus evil values to an audience, and the evil is always represented by a Latino or a member of another subjugated group, then this "poses a devastating obstacle to human development and understanding in a multicultural society" (1995, p. 62). In this chapter I will address Latino/a stereotypes generated and perpetuated by the media, with particular attention to the motion-picture industry, which has for the past 100 years, functioned as the primary transmitter of racist Latino/a images.

History and Development of Stereotypes

Allen L. Woll (1980, p. 3) wrote that "[t]he men of science of the Enlightenment had two-and-a-half centuries of reports from the Americas on which to base their generalizations." As an example of the images presented to Europeans in these reports, Woll quotes from the 1770 work of Abbe Raynal, who wrote that the people in the Americas were "a species of men degraded and degenerated in their natural constitution, in their stature, in their way of life, and in their understanding, which is but little advanced in all the arts of civilization" (1980, p. 3). Earlier examples of negative images and stereotypes of the people in the New World can also be found. In his diaries, Columbus invented a world that bore little resemblance to the islands or the people who inhabited them. Of the inhabitants of the Greater Antilles, which include Cuba and Puerto Rico, he wrote that they are

> a people who are regarded in all of the islands as very fierce and who eat human flesh . . . . They live together without king, without government. . . . They marry as many wives as they please; and son cohabits with mother, brother with sister . . . they have no church, no religion . . . they kill one another, and those whom they bring home captive from war they preserve not to spare their lives, but that they may be slain for food; for they eat one another. . . . (Berkhofer, 1978, pp. 6–7)

Through this type of negative imagery we can begin to envision how the seeds for the development of racialized stereotypes were planted. Because inhabitants of the Americas were depicted as savages and cannibals, people without morals, culture, or religion, stereotypes could easily be constructed and later effortlessly reconstructed to accommodate a different time period. Thus, contemporary racial stereotypes that depict Latinos as deviant, inferior, violent, lazy, and uncultured (to name but a few) had their foundation established long ago by the imagination of earlier writers who knew little or nothing of what or who they wrote about.

The indispensable collaborators throughout this conspiracy of untruths and distortion, first via the written word and more recently through cinema and television, have been the media. The media have functioned as the guardians and principal purveyors of racist images, constructing and institutionalizing stereotypes that have preserved the status quo whereby members of the dominant group stay on top while all others have been forced to linger at the bottom.

Latinos and Latinas on the Silver Screen

Since 1898, over 7,000 films have been made that have, in one form or another, negatively stereotyped Latinos and Latinas.[3] Latinos have "remained a primary ingredient for filmmakers for almost a hundred years [and] no other . . . [ethnic groups] . . . have been the subject of more Hollywood characterizations" (Richard, 1994, p. ix). The history of Latino/a stereotypes in the motion picture industry has three distinct periods. The first, which began in 1898, had by 1931 produced over 1800 films. Several key developments in the progression of Latino images are important to note from this period. It was during this period that the original negative Latino/a archetypes in the motion picture industry were created and institutionalized, initially through silent films and then in early sound films. Allen Woll, summarizing the early Latino images, stated, "[a]lthough the majority of early silent films emphasized action and violence, the Mexican bandits were clearly among the most vile. They robbed, murdered, plundered, raped, cheated, gambled, lied, and displayed virtually every vice that could be shown on the screen" (1980, p. 7).

After analyzing hundreds of films from this period, Gary Keller (1994, p. 39) found "only three distinct female roles . . . and eight male roles, and even these eleven roles were interconnected." According to Keller, "[t]he range permitted . . . female characters was very constricted because they primarily functioned in relationship to an Anglo love interest. . . . There [was] the cantina girl . . . the faithful, moral, or self-sacrificing señorita, [and] the vamp or temptress. [Moreover], given these sorts of constraints, older or nonsexual female characters rarely appear in film. . ." (1994, p. 40).

Similarly, the Latino was characterized through a limited number of roles. He was restricted to playing "bandits or otherwise badmen, good badmen, greasers, faithful Mexicans or other [Latino], Latin Lover, and two aggressively positive roles . . . the [Latino] avenger and the gay caballero. Whereas the [Latina] . . . functioned in relationship to an Anglo love interest, the [Latino] male is usually a foil to an Anglo hero. He is almost always either the physical antagonist of the Anglo or his loyal and subordinate partner" (Keller, 1994, p. 48).

As these stereotypes evolved, the images created were made even more vicious, vengeful, and sadistic. In *The Heart of a Bandit* (1915), for example, Mexicans are portrayed as outlaws and evil, cowardly half-breeds who will do anything, including kidnaping women and children, to get their way. In the end "[t]he half-breed is killed but the bandit dies honorably, sacrificing his life for the Anglo rancher's family" (Keller, 1994, p. 55).

The Latina image fares no better during this period. In *Cross the Mexican Line* (1914), the vengeful and lusting vamp "has fallen in love with a wounded Anglo whom she has nursed to health, but when events don't go her way, she arranges to have him and his Anglo love captured by Mexican bandits" (ibid.). She repents, of course, and tries to free them but fails. However, the U.S. Cavalry rides to the rescue (ibid.).

Two other important ingredients were eventually added to the Latino/a image during this period: language and skin color. Dark skin color has been used by filmmakers since the early silent-film era to depict sinister and evil characters and was "an active part of the North American national consciousness used to emphasize race or ethnicity—the darker the skin the more menacing the screen character" (Richard, 1994, p. xv). With the advent of sound came screen characters who were dark-skinned and spoke with accents or in broken English. Latino/a roles were played by white actors and actresses.

The depiction by Hollywood filmmakers of Latinos as a homogeneous group also began in the silent-film era. With the arrival of sound, this issue "created consternation . . . when to their amazement the studios discovered that Spanish was not spoken the same throughout the hemisphere and that all Latins were not alike" (Richard, 1994, p. xv). One would think that after almost 100 years some learning would have occurred; alas, the racist mind-set is as blind as it is ignorant, for both of these misconceptions continue today.

For the most part, the Latina continues to be portrayed as a promiscuous and dishonorable woman, "(a)lways easy with her favors, especially for blond hair and blue eyes. [She is] the hot blooded, fiery [Latina] whore . . ." (Richard, 1994, p. xvi). Implicit in this depiction of Latinas is the notion that they are unscrupulous, immoral, and wicked creatures who will beguile or betray just about anyone, and who want nothing more than to seduce or be seduced by any white man. Although the portrayal of the Latina has not changed substantially over time, eventually the characterization of the Latino was transformed "from his rural roots to a more urban environment bringing with him the tools of his trade, guns of course, but more essential to his screen character, the knife" (ibid.).

Whereas the first period produced over 1,800 films that depicted Latinos negatively, the second period, which characterized Latinos in a more favorable manner, ran from 1932 through 1955 and generated more than 2,100 films. During this span of 20-plus years, Hollywood added the stereotype of the happy, fun-loving musical people to portrayals of Latinos as villains and whores. The Latino-focused musicals, Keller writes, "followed the advent of the sound era. In fact, the stereotype of the Latin world as lively and musical, characterized by fiestas . . . music and dancing in cantinas carried such sway that . . . it became commonplace for music to enter Latino focused films even if they were not musicals" (1994, p. 121).

Musicals such as *Flying Down to Rio* (1932), starring Fred Astaire, Ginger Rogers, and Dolores del Rio, and *La Cucaracha* (1934), which is best known for the song "La Cucaracha," are but two of hundreds of musicals produced in the 1930s.

From 1939 to 1944 Carmen Miranda, who was Brazilian and thus of Portuguese rather than Spanish ancestry, became a huge star in the United States. She went on to

appear in eight Hollywood musicals as well as two Broadway reviews. Standard practice [in movies] was to pair her against blonds (Alice Faye, Vivian Blaine, and mostly Betty Grable), who during the war had [begun] to be perceived as incarnating Americanness. However, [Miranda] was typecast as a Latina ingenue (an artless, innocent girl), awed by North American culture. . . . In the same homogenizing spirit, . . . Miranda [was cast] in any number of Latin American nationalities. She traveled Argentine way, spent a night in Rio, a weekend in Havana, and appeared either as herself or as an equally stereotypical

Latina: Chiquita, Chita, Marina, Carmelita, and, in four films, Rosita. (Keller, 1994, pp. 124–25)

Living up to Hollywood's image of the Latina, Miranda was depicted as an "exotic, sensual, primitive, and wild" (Keller, 1994, p. 124) woman from south of the border.

This was also the era when the sexy and exciting male Latin lover stereotype grew in popularity. Movies such as *Wife, Husband and Friend* (1939), starring Loretta Young and Cesar Romero, *The Girl Who Had Everything* (1953), starring Elizabeth Taylor and Fernando Lamas, and *Latin Lovers* (1953), starring Lana Turner and Ricardo Montalban, found Latino males falling in love, lusting after, and/or cheating on white women. Of course, the male Latin lover was usually a disreputable type, a gangster or racetrack bookie, looking to cash in by marrying the rich Americana. Or he had aspirations of moving up in the world through his association with a white woman, the implication being that Latinas were less worthy, and thus confirming the stereotype that they are primitive and loathsome creatures who are not desired even by their own.

During the remainder of this period, "The number of Latin musical productions accelerated . . . , spurred on both by government encouragement and the need for escape during the war years" (Keller, 1994, p. 123). Latino imagery improved, and Latin America was "promoted in hundreds of features and short subjects as a wonderland for Anglo tourists" (Richard, 1994, p. xvi). However, it should be understood that Latinos and Latinas continued to be depicted in negative and racist ways through the use of old but reliable stereotypes developed during the early 1900s. Furthermore, Keller (1994, p. 114) notes, "[f]ilm, and subsequently television in its early period, were instruments of socialization" to facilitate "the assimilation of all racial, ethnic, and religious differences into the harmonizing credo of the Anglo-American melting pot."

Nevertheless, we need to ask, what occurred during this time span to make Hollywood filmmakers, at least for a short time, change their modus operandi? Three very significant events occurred during this period: World War II, the Korean War, and the establishment of two governing bodies, the Production Code Administration (PCA) and the Motion Picture Society for the Americas (MPSA). These organizations were developed to address two distinct but convergent interests. One was economic (exploitation) and the other was political (domination). The PCA "wanted to sell films south of the border," and the MPSA, "working closely with the CIA . . . , wanted to keep South America out of the Axis (Nazi) camp thereby making the hemisphere safe for North American democracy . . . " (Richard, 1994, p. xvi).

It doesn't take much imagination to read between the movie script lines and figure out the significance played by the two wars. It has historically been the case in the United States that Latinos and other people of color are good enough to die for the country, but not good enough for anything else. During the war years, soldiers were needed to fight on the front lines, and it just wouldn't do to have Latinos and other minority men and women depicted on the silver screen exclusively through negative stereotypes. On the home front, the scarcity of men meant that women were needed in the factories and canneries to keep the economy going and to supply the war effort. It would not do to continue to portray these women strictly as vamps, whores, and cantina girls. However, with the war's end came the end of Hollywood's love affair with the loyal and patriotic, but disposable, Latino fighting man and working woman.

The third period began in 1956 and marked the return of negative portrayals of Latinos and Latinas. Through 1993, a total of more than 3,100 films depicting Latinos in an ever more racist and mean-spirited manner were produced. The "transformation into today's vicious urban gang leader, [the] sociopath who preys on Anglo society as well as his own people, [the] vengeful street warrior at war with his black brothers for available turf" (Richard, 1994, p. xvi) began in the late 1950s with movies such as *Machete* (1958) and *The Pusher* (1959). In these two movies, Puerto Ricans and Mexicans were depicted as treacherous, knife-wielding, drug-pushing monsters responsible "for creating Anglo addicts who otherwise might have resisted narcotics" (ibid.). With the 1960s came the loosening of film production codes, making it possible for Hollywood movies to become

> much bolder in their depiction of both sex, including interracial sex, and violence. However, this was a double-edged sword for [Latinos/as] and other minorities because often they were cast in roles where their villainy was far more graphic and horrifying than the snarling but ineffective criminal or would-be rapist of blander times. In this sense, the stereotyped depictions of violence and loose morals of many [Latino/a] characters were much intensified. . . . Thus, the 1960s and 1970s were marked by far more diversity in films but also by a group of films that featured even more serious, racially damaging put-downs. (Keller, 1994, p. 150)

No longer were the bandits of old and the new urban warrior, pimp, and drug pusher just mean-spirited villains and murderers; they "were now often engaged in visually explicit and gory violence" (Keller, 1994, p. 150). No longer was the Latina just a vamp and seductress; she was now a full-fledged whore "engaged in R-rated loose sex with Anglo heroes" (ibid). Movies such as *The Alamo* (1960), *The Magnificent Seven* (1960), and *The Young Savages* (1961) are early examples of this type of film. The ever-popular musical *West Side Story* (1961), which won 10 Academy Awards and was loosely based on *Romeo and Juliet*, was nevertheless saturated with Puerto Rican stereotypes: "knives, hot blood, Spanish dancing, easy virtue, passion and vengeance were important parts of the story" (Richard, 1994, p. 66). Moreover, the Romeo and Juliet theme was used to promote the stereotype of the Latina who will do anything for her Anglo lover. In this case María, the Puerto Rican Juliet, played by Natalie Wood, goes to bed with Tony/Romeo, an Anglo, the very night he kills Bernardo, her brother, in a knife fight.

From the 1970s through the 1990s, gang films continued to proliferate, becoming more and more explicit in their depictions of Latinos as drug-dealing, gun-toting, menacing characters who daily commit unimaginable criminal acts, mostly against innocent whites.

> Latino gangs have become a widespread topic in the mainstream press, as well as a common theme of motion pictures, disseminated both in theaters and over television. . . . For example, Brian de Palma's 1983 . . . *Scarface* . . . [has] over two hours of Latino gangland killings, heroin snorting, and unrelenting sadism . . . and gave impetus to a new wave of screen Latino drug dealers, ranging from television's *Miami Vice* to such feature films as *Code of Silence* (1985), . . . *8 Million Ways to Die* (1986), *Above the Law* (1988), . . . [and] *Crocodile Dundee II* (1988). (Cortes, 1993, pp. 10–11)

For over a century, Latinas have been characterized as women who "longed for, surrendered to, and sacrificed for Anglo men" (Cortes, 1993, p. 15) and as evil and corrupt creatures, as portrayed in films like *Girl Smugglers* (1967) and *Bad Girls Dormitory* (1985). However, the depiction of the vicious, violent, brutal, and malignant Latino/a stereotypes reached their climax in the 1990s in feature films *Q & A* (1990) and *Prison Stories: Women on the Inside* (1991). The racist and disparaging representation of Latinos and Latinas by the motion picture industry in this country has come full circle. With the exception of the unimaginative but newly constructed stereotypes, Latinos are today regarded and characterized as they were 100 years ago. The question that begs to be answered is, why does a country that proclaims itself to be the most free and enlightened in the world continue to tolerate and sanction this type of injustice, these racist attitudes and behaviors?

What Does It All Mean and Where Do We Go From Here?

As thinking beings, we have a tendency to arrange and process our world in a manner that averts confusion and limits uncertainty. Stangor and Lange (1995, p. 357) have explained that one method used by people to differentiate one group from another is through "previously stored knowledge." Consequently, when we encounter certain individuals, our behavior toward them is often governed by preconceived images. If the images we carry are composites of inaccurate and/or prejudiced representations, and if our treatment of people is based on these preconceptions, an injustice will transpire.

As a society, we have entrusted the media to perform numerous functions. For example, we ask the media to inform and educate, be our watchdogs, and monitor those in power. Moreover, we expect this to be done in a fair and neutral manner. Perhaps these are unreasonable expectations. Should we believe that as agents of social control the media will perform any differently than other control agents, such as the police and court officials, who have historically demonstrated bias when dealing with people of color? Addressing this question, Bernard Cohen states that "[t]he press is significantly more than a purveyor of information and opinion. It may not be successful in telling its readers what to think, but it is stunningly successful in telling its readers what to think about" (1963, p. 13).

In a study that reviewed coverage of crime stories over a 35-year period by the newsweeklies (e.g. *Time, Newsweek,* and *U.S. News and World Report*), Robert Elias has shown that not only did these magazines regularly exhibit bias by "faithfully reproduc[ing] government definitions of crime, [but did so] despite abundant evidence that officials define crime discriminatorily" (Elias, 1994, p. 4). He adds that along with their ability to influence policy and direct public attention away from white-collar and corporate crime, newsweeklies "advocated tougher punishment for street criminals" while at the same time declaring that "for corporate criminals just getting caught was punishment enough" (ibid., p. 5). Not surprisingly, Elias (ibid.) found that over the 35-year span

> [b]lacks and other nonwhite minorities were described and pictured in the newsweeklies' crime coverage most frequently, even though these groups *do not* commit the majority of crimes. . . . In contrast, the newsweeklies described and pictured victims mostly as white people. What emerges from my study of newsweeklies is a pattern of discrimination in which criminals are conceptualized as [people of color] and crime as the violence they do to whites.

Whereas in the past distinct differences between the print media and network electronic media may have existed, today any distinction is minimal. For nearly two-thirds of the American public, television is the main source for news and information rather than newspapers or magazines (Davey, 1995, p. 90). For example, "less than one-half of the people [surveyed] say they rely on newspapers. And only 22 percent say they believe the daily papers. By contrast, 53 percent believe that television news is for the most part telling the truth" (ibid., pp. 91–92). Furthermore, "heavy television viewers were significantly more likely than others to view the world as mean, an outlook characterized by suspicion, fear, alienation, distrust, cynicism, and the belief that the world is a violent, crime-ridden, dangerous place. [The study suggests] that heavy television viewers fail to differentiate between the television world and the real world" (ibid., p. 90).

Television focuses on conflict and images, often at the expense of substance and ideas. It deals more with emotion than it does with details. It is a medium in which 30-second sound bites are used as substitutes for information. It should be understood that television news is a production in which the various networks compete for ratings, not by producing the best analysis but by having the best theme music and the spiffiest commentary, much of which is either inaccurate and/or highly opinionated.

However, newspapers and magazines are not the only sources of false and misleading information perpetuating negative minority stereotypes. Research published in books and academic journals is another source of "[r]acial stereotypes [which] are . . . *part of the suffocating web of myths* [which] ease the consciences of the thoughtful and buoy the egos of the ignorant" (Bell, 1985, p. 8). The majority of studies focusing on Latino stereotypes have involved Puerto Ricans and Chicanos/Mexican Americans. It is also the case that "many of [these] studies . . . have serious methodological flaws or have depended on nonsystematic field observations to reach their conclusions" (Marín, 1984, pp. 17–18). Moreover, it has been observed "that the data found in most studies with [Latinos] may be specific to lower-class, rural, poorly educated [Latinos] that have made up most of the samples of the majority of studies found in the literature" (Triandis, Lisansky, Setiadi, Chang, Marín, and Baetancourt, 1982, p. 423). Reliance on this limited sample means that research findings become skewed, old myths are perpetuated, and new raw material is developed for contemporary negative stereotypes, all of which add to our current cultural and societal difficulties.

Although some recent studies are methodologically sound and culturally sensitive, many continue to rely on images and terminology that have historically depicted Latinos/as in a negative manner. In addition, much of the research continues to be conducted by white academicians who practice a form of research apartheid (Rosaldo, 1989, p. xii). In a different context, Renato Rosaldo has explained that this form of exclusion occurs "[w]hen people become accustomed to privilege" and develop what "appears to be a vested right, a status that is natural and well-deserved, a part of the order of things" (ibid.). This refers to the academy's assumption that Latino researchers are incapable of studying other Latinos objectively, and therefore

that any research conducted by them is biased and without merit. In reality, this belief that whites alone are capable of conducting valid research is the response of "[p]eople who once had a monopoly on privilege and authority [and who] suddenly experience relative deprivation" (ibid.).

Specifically, studies have shown that Latinos are perceived by whites as aggressive, uneducated, lazy, and poor (Marín, 1984). Latinos have also been characterized as ignorant, cruel, and antagonistic (Fairchild and Cozens, 1981). Triandis and his colleagues (1982, p. 422) suggest that the consistent appearance of these stereotypes in research findings "may be a reflection of what is communicated by the mass media." Similarly, Marín observes that white respondents in his studies display a predisposition toward negative stereotyping even though they have had minimal contact with Latinos. And when contact has been established, the negative stereotyping of Latinos does not diminish (Marín, 1984, p. 25). He thus concurs with T. M. Martínez (1969) and Morales (1971) that this may be due to "the pervasive negative representations of Latinos in the mass media."

In a recent University of Chicago study, it was "found that three out of four white respondents believe that black and Latino people are more likely than whites to be lazy, less intelligent, less patriotic, and more prone to violence" (Carnevale and Stone, 1995, p. 276). It is well documented that the effects of "stereotyping can cause enduring psychological damage to its victims . . . , create anger . . . , stifle natural behavior . . . [and] erode energy that could otherwise be channeled into productive work" (ibid., p. 275). It is difficult, if not impossible, to communicate effectively the anguish and adversity that must be confronted each and every day by victims of racist stereotypes to those who have never experienced these feelings. How can one convey the range and magnitude of feelings accumulated over a lifetime of being the object of racist behavior? How can one explain the ceaseless pain and rage, the struggle against the constant emotional and psychological wounds inflicted on one's sense of well-being? How can one describe how it feels to have his or her humanity continuously questioned and assaulted by those who pretend they are superior?

It has been said that "[t]he true character of a nation can be judged in part by the way it treats its weakest or most vulnerable members" (Woodson, 1989, p. 1017). It has also been observed that "[h]istory has shown that racism can co-exist happily with formal commitments to objectivity, neutrality, and color blindness" (Harris, 1994, p. 741). If we were to assess the character of this country based on how it has historically treated and characterized Latino/as and other people of color, it would be difficult to argue with Elizabeth Martínez (1994), who states that "[i]n a land where the national identity is white, having the 'wrong' nationality becomes grounds for racist abuse." Latinos and Latinas are not a homogeneous group. Rather, we are rich and poor, well educated and illiterate, heterosexual and homosexual. We represent 19 separate nations that share the Western Hemisphere with the United States and Canada. Historically, however, the United States has contemptuously refused to acknowledge our existence except when it has been politically convenient, economically profitable, or strategically practical. This situation must change, and until it does, Latinos, Latinas, and all other people of color in this country will continue to be seen not as people but as images.

Notes

1. I use this term to refer to Asian Americans, American Indians, African Americans, and Latinos/as.

2. I use the term "Latino/a" and not the term "Hispanic" throughout this essay to avoid confusion and as a matter of preference. It is meant to be inclusive of all people of Spanish heritage living in the United States, as well as the 23 million plus Latinos who live in the 19 Spanish-speaking countries that are part of the Western Hemisphere (i.e., Argentina, Bolivia, Chile, Colombia, Costa Rica, Cuba, the Dominican Republic, Ecuador, El Salvador, Guatemala, Honduras, Mexico, Nicaragua, Panama, Paraguay, Peru, Puerto Rico, Uruguay, and Venezuela). The use of "o/a" signals that I am explicitly indicating men (Latinos) and women (Latinas). Both terms, "Latino/a" and "Hispanic," pose significant problems for the millions of people who are homogenized through their use. The people these terms lump together prefer to identify themselves by their country of origin. For example, when I discuss my background, I do not refer to myself as a Hispanic or a Latino; rather, I identify myself as a Puerto Rican. I believe the same holds true for others. For a detailed discussion on this subject, refer to Chapter 1 in Suzanne Oboler's 1995 book *Ethnic Labels, Latino Lives*. Also see "On Latino/ Hispanic Ethnic Identity" by Edward Murguia (1991).

3. For a complete list of the 7000 films, consult the following three volume set by Alfred Charles Richard, Jr.: *The Hispanic Image on the Silver Screen: An Interpretive Filmography from Silents into Sound, 1898–1935; Censorship and Hollywood's Hispanic Image: An Interpretive Filmography, 1936–1955;* and *Contemporary Hollywood's Negative Hispanic Image: An Interpretive Filmography, 1956–1993.*

References

Bell, Derrick. (1985). "The Supreme Court 1984 term. Foreword: The civil rights chronicles." *Harvard Law Review, 99* (4), 4–83.

Berkhofer, Robert F., Jr. (1978). *The white man's Indian: Images of the American Indian from Columbus to the present.* New York: Vintage Books.

Carnevale, Anthony Patrick, and Stone, Susan Carol. (1995). *The American mosaic: An in-depth report on the future of diversity at work.* New York: McGraw-Hill.

Cohen, Bernard. (1963). *The press and foreign policy.* Princeton, NJ: Princeton University Press.

Cortes, Carlos E. (1993). "Power, passivity, and pluralism: Mass media in the development of Latino culture and identity." *Latino Studies Journal,* January, 3–22.

Davey, Joseph Dillon. (1995). *The new social contract: America's journey from welfare state to police state.* Westport, CT: Praeger Publishers.

Elias, Robert. (1994). "Official stories: Media coverage of American crime policy." *The Humanist,* January/February, 3–9.

Fairchild, H.H., and Cozens, J.A. (1981). "Chicano, Hispanic, or Mexican American: What's in a name?" *Hispanic Journal of Behavioral Sciences,* 3, 191–198.

Harris, Angela P. (1994). "Foreword: The jurisprudence of reconstruction." *California Law Review,* 82 (4), 741–787.

Keller, Gary D. (1994). *Hispanics and United States film: An overview and handbook.* Tempe, AZ.: Bilingual Review/Press.

Marín, Gerardo. (1984). "Stereotyping Hispanics: The differential effect of research method, label, and degree of contact." *International Journal of Intercultural Relations,* 8, 17–27.

Martínez, Elizabeth. (1994). "Seeing more than black and white: Latinos, racism, and the cultural divides." *Z Magazine,* 7, 5.

Martínez, T.M. (1969). "Advertising and racism: The case of the Mexican American." *El Grito,* 2 (3), 3–13.

Morales, A. (1971). "The collective preconscious and racism." *Social Casework,* 52, 283–293.

Murguia, Edward. (1991). "On Latino/Hispanic ethnic identity." *Latino Studies Journal,* 2 (3), 8–18.

Oboler, Suzanne. (1995). *Ethnic labels, Latino lives: Identity and the politics of (re)presentation in the United States.* Minneapolis: University of Minnesota Press.

Richard, Alfred Charles, Jr. (1994). *Contemporary Hollywood's negative Hispanic image: An interpretive filmography, 1956–1993.* Westport, CT: Greenwood Press.

Rosaldo, Renato. (1989). *Culture and truth: The remaking of social analysis.* Boston: Beacon Press. Reprinted 1993.

Stangor, Charles, and Lange, James E. (1995). "Mental representations of social groups: Advances in understanding stereotypes and stereotyping." *Advances in Social Psychology,* 27, 357–416.

Triandis, Harry C., Lisansky, Judith, Setiadi, Bernadette, Chang, Bei-Hung, Marín, Gerardo, and Betancourt, Hector. (1982). "Stereotyping among Hispanics and Anglos: The uniformity, intensity, direction, and quality of auto- and heterostereotypes." *Journal of Cross Cultural Psychology,* 13 (4), 409–425.

Wilson, Clint C., II, and Gutiérrez, Félix. (1995). *Race, multiculturalism, and the media: From mass to class communication.* Thousand Oaks, CA: Sage Publications.

Woll, Allen L. (1980). *The Latin image in American film.* Rev. ed. Los Angeles: UCLA Latin American Center Publications.

Woodson, Robert L. (1989). "Race and economic opportunity." *Vanderbilt Law Review,* 42, 1017–1046.

Discussion Questions

1. What is the significance of Columbus' (and other early authors') writings in relation to contemporary images and stereotypes of Latino/as?

2. For many, use of the term "Latino" (and "Hispanic") eradicates history and creates the illusion of a homogeneous group that does not exist. What social issues are germane to this problem? What public policy recommendations would you make to correct this situation?

3. What movies have you recently seen in which Latino/a stereotypes discussed in the chapter were depicted? Describe them. Were any of

the images different, and if so, in what way? What inferences can you make if they have not changed?

4. It has been suggested in this chapter that television, newspapers, and weekly news magazines in this country are agents of social control, reporting news in a manner that intentionally perpetuates racist Latino stereotypes. Define the term "agents of social control." Discuss at least one example of a racist stereotype from each of these three sources.

5. Often we are given different and/or conflicting versions of the same story by the media. For example, one reporter covering an alleged gang shooting in a Latino neighborhood will focus on guns and drugs, whereas another will highlight poverty and education. What do you think accounts for these discrepancies? Should restrictions be placed on how certain stories are reported? By whom? Would this interfere with First Amendment rights? In what ways? ◆

Chapter 12

Stereotyping by Politicians

Immigrant Bashing and Nativist Political Movements

Alberto G. Mata Jr.

This chapter examines stereotyping of Latinos and Latinas by politicians as the latest example of race-card politics. The use of stereotypes to scapegoat Latinos and curry favor with the white American electorate is clearest when one examines local, state, and regional political contests and referendums in areas with large concentrations of Latinos and Latinas.

Playing the race card appeals to those troubled by the growing numbers and visibility of Latinas and Latinos (Boyarsky, 1993). Many Americans continue to view Latinas and Latinos as foreigners—the latest wave of immigrants (Gallegley, 1993a, b). Some consider Latinos to be harmful to their interests, a drain on their communities, and a threat to a way of life many believe to be under siege. It is not clear whether the use of racialized fears reflects politicians' true feelings and beliefs, is a campaign tactic designed to challenge the opposition and solidify support, or reflects a convenient opportunity to make a once narrowly appealing political agenda more palatable to the unsettled, disaffected, and undecided. In any case,

politicians' uses of the race card and scapegoating of Latinos—knowingly or unwittingly—play into efforts that go beyond the contest of the day (Simon, 1993). These invectives serve to heighten interethnic suspicions, tensions, and conflicts and to call into question social and political reforms that have helped improve the lives of men and women of color, as well as white women.

Elected officials, political candidates, and political organizations cater to racial fears and use them to polarize voters (Bustamante, 1993). In so doing, they assume that their actions carry few risks to their campaigns or deleterious societal consequences. For some political activists, the play on racial fears, concerns, or issues is less an appeal to base instincts than a return to what they see as having made this country great. It is, in other words, a form of nostalgia. For others, taken by Pat Buchanan's frankness, the concern is to draw attention to the threat that undesirable elements pose and to their prescription for measures to stem the tide, recapture control, and return the inheritance to its "rightful" owners—whites. But what makes such previously questionable claims and agendas now palatable? How are the strident, narrow interests of fringe elements made acceptable to segments of the larger society? What may make these claims appealing to individuals whose personal lives may be subject to unsettling changes beyond their control or influence? In some instances, the answer may lie in the economic restructuring of the past two decades, resulting in changes in their quality of life and standard of living, or in the viability of their social networks and mediating institutions (e.g., schools, churches, synagogues, and mosques).

It is also unclear whether the use of racial fears as a tactic to gain advantage over the opposition and enhance one's own candidacy is portable across groups and regions. Clearly, embracing strident messages linked to narrow political agendas in order to present oneself as a champion of the unsettled and disaffected voters remains key to certain campaign strategists and managers. Grass-roots backlash groups are not timid about courting those uncomfortable with the growing number of racial/ethnic minorities in this country. They are not reserved in their criticisms of efforts to improve conditions for minorities and white women when they perceive that those avenues are not available to them or when opportunities for others appear to come at their cost. Regardless of motive, they play into the hands of smaller nativist groups of hatemongers who see the need to reverse the gains of people of color just because they look, sound, or act "different."

The Latino population in the United States is large, young, and growing. Their overall educational and economic statuses are lower than those of their Anglo counterparts, and odds are that they will not attain the "American dream" that many white youths expect. Yet this very diverse population reflects a variety of political perspectives; lifestyles, tastes, buying power; and views about the appropriate roles for men and women. Some Latino families have lived here for centuries, when those parts of the United States where they live once belonged to Mexico. They never immigrated here but just stayed where they were and became U.S. citizens when the border changed. For others, specifically Puerto Ricans, their territories were ceded to the United States. Still others migrated here from Mexico, the Caribbean, and Central and South America in search of better jobs or to escape political repression in their homelands.

Nevertheless, those employing race politics ignore history. They tend to pro-

mote homogeneous images of Latinos as drug lords aiming to destroy America's youths through drugs, as dangerous gang bangers who shoot anyone unfortunate enough to stumble through their neighborhoods, or as poor peasants sneaking across the border to have babies in U.S. hospitals so that their children will become American citizens and thus inappropriately be eligible for a broad range of entitlements. These suspect images of Latinos/as as criminal, vicious, and sneaky 0are very powerful and mute calmer voices claiming otherwise.

Latinos/as trying to promote, enhance, and assure the progress and well-being of their communities are mindful of the need for vision, voice, and action in local and national political forums. As the numbers, visibility, and claims of Latinos/as for a better life grow, the more culturally conservative and xenophobic Americans have come to see these claims and efforts as *prima facie* evidence of further threats and encroachment (Tanton and Lutton, 1992; Reese, 1995). The Latino community's growth and visibility also seem to draw out this element's baser instincts, rancors, resentments, and crusading predilections. When Latinos/as counter and rebuff racist and nativist claims and actions, the nativists stiffen their resolve. The result is increased polarization between groups, and an expanded base for and manifestation of 1990s-style race politics into the next century.

The new race politics involves a range of American conservative groups including far right, nativist, and hate groups (Auster, 1990; Brimelow, 1992; Evans, 1994; Plafox, 1996). Nativism is an ideology that asserts the primacy of the native born as a country's "true" sons and daughters over naturalized citizens and legal immigrants. Originally, nativists in the United States were aligned with the Know-Nothing Party.

Most were suspicious of Catholics and new immigrants generally. Later, beginning in the 1880s, nativists turned on eastern and southern European immigrants and adopted anti-Semitic tendencies. Whenever Asian and Mexican laborers threatened to encroach on jobs desired by white workers, they became targets for nativist backlashes. Fear and hatred of foreigners and racial minorities, and unbridled nationalism, seemed to coincide with periods of marked social or economic change (Lipset, 1993; Calavita, 1996).

When we speak about the new race politics, we are not just referring to state-of-the-art negative campaign themes involving racially coded messages, but rather to a range of actions from fervent social crusades to more organized networking efforts. These efforts reflect a sense of threat, resentment, and opposition to past ideologies ranging from Franklin Roosevelt's New Deal politics to the liberal social agenda of the 1960s. Race politics target and scapegoat Latinos as part of the larger campaign to mobilize moderate and undecided angry citizens. By aligning aspects of their agenda with the larger society's concerns, fears, resentments, and rancors, they hope to expand their base and reduce the risk and impact of changes that they perceive to be threatening.

In some instances, political campaigns seek to enhance their candidates' fortunes while simultaneously silencing American racial/ethnic minorities' cultural, political, and social claims to meaningful involvement in national decision making (Chavez, 1991; Skerry, 1993; Schuck, 1995). The remainder of this essay focuses on two key examples of the new race politics—the English Only movement and the SOS movement rallying around Proposition 187. These case studies illustrate the nature, size, and consequences of such anti-immigrant, and specifically anti-Latino, political movements.

The U.S. English Only Movement

The specter of America harboring more than 40 million non-English-speaking residents frightens some Americans (Buchanan, 1991; Huddle, 1993; Hawkins, 1995). Prior to the 1970s, undocumented immigrants labored in agricultural sectors and on the fringes of urban metropolitan areas. By the mid-1970s, a major shift to urban occupations increased the visibility of these workers and their families (Muller and Espenshade, 1985; Acuña, 1988). The swelling of the native Latino/a population, combined with the large numbers of immigrants, refugees, and undocumented workers coming from Mexico and Central and South America, fed Anglo-American fears of being overwhelmed (Butler, 1985).

The English Only movement seeks to mandate English as the only language to be used in official U.S. business, including government offices and voting ballots. The movement reflects the fear that foreign languages might become more widespread than English (Brimelow, 1995), even though only 10 percent of the population speaks a language other than English. Of this group, over 13.5 million are Spanish speakers, and only 12.5 million speak the entire range of other foreign languages (Hernández-Chavez, 1978; Piatt, 1990). Thus, the primary target of state and national English Only campaigns is the nation's ever-growing Spanish-speaking population, especially in the southwestern U.S. and Florida (Chavez, 1991). Ultimately, English Only proponents fear any efforts to promote a more multilingual and multicultural society, believing that this would diminish western European (i.e., English-speaking) traditions and institutions in favor of others that they perceive as inferior.

English Only's proponents added it to their legislative agendas in over 27 states, although its consequences were greatest in the Sunbelt. In the 1996 presidential campaign, Bob Dole, Pete Wilson, Pat Buchanan, and Ross Perot added it to their campaign agendas. Only Wilson and Buchanan, however, unabashedly championed English Only without concern for its implications for Latino voters' support. In Pat Buchanan's words (1994, http//www.buchanan/timeout/):

> If America is to survive as one nation one people we need to call time out on immigration, to assimilate the tens of millions who have arrived. We need to get to know one another, to live together, to learn together America's language, history, culture and traditions for tolerance, to become a national family, before we add a hundred million more. And we need to soon bring down the curtain on the idea of hyphenated-Americanism.

Since the 1960s, three major policy issues have shaped national and state debates on these matters. The designation of English as the official language at national, state, and local levels is seen as no less important than the questions of whether or not we should have bilingual education or language rights in the electoral process. In more mundane terms, foreign languages in the workplace are seen as obstructing common business and governmental operations.

The growth and increasing visibility of Latinos and Latinas throughout southern California and in most major metropolitan areas has added to feelings of being overwhelmed, of losing control of borders and communities, and of the need for defensive action. A popular image is one of hordes of illegal aliens seeking to gain what they do not deserve at the expense of U.S. (read, white) taxpayers (Tanton and Lutton, 1992). Many critics argue that both legal and illegal immigrants come primarily to derive such benefits as public education and health care at the expense of taxpayers whose quality of life is threatened or declining. In a 1996 speech, presidential candidate Bob Dole indicated support for Representative Elton Gallegly's (R.-California) bill to cut funding for the education of children of illegal aliens. He cast the issue in this manner: "We shouldn't stick the states with billions and billions of dollars of extra expenses, particularly . . . California. . . . It's not that we don't care, it's not that we're not compassionate. . . . [But] where do you draw the line?" (cited in Seelye, *New York Times,* June 20, 1996, p. A:16).

Other images depict illegal aliens as drug traffickers, gang members, and terrorists. As former Central Intelligence Agency (CIA) Director William Colby once said, "The most obvious threat for the U.S. is the fact that . . . there are going to be 120 million Mexicans by the end of the century. . . . [The Border Patrol] will not have enough bullets to stop them" (cited in Acuña, 1996, p. 115).

In addition to the fringe right's diatribes, English Only's reports in the electronic and print media largely repeated their unchecked claims, adding their sensationalized flair to bulletins about the "Latino invasion" (Butler, 1985; Auster, 1990; Brimelow, 1995). The immediate effect of the media's sensationalism was to further strain white–Latino/a relations and heighten suspicion (Acuña, 1996). Many large urban centers throughout the United States faced fiscal crises. Their public schools, public health centers, and other social services overflowed with more clients than they could serve. Soon local neoconservatives' attacks on bilingual education and transitional services began to argue that these efforts were unwarranted and needless expenditures. Programs like these, critics argued, were draining otherwise limited resources and exacerbating local and state fiscal crises (Chavez, 1991; Acuña, 1996).

Neoconservatives' calls for action encouraged legislators and policymakers to retreat from earlier commitments to and support for bilingual education, limited English proficiency programs, and even English as a second language (ESL) programs (Chavez, 1991). In California, especially in the Los Angeles Unified School System's understaffed and underfunded bilingual programs. This led to the adoption of structural immersion programs, such as teaching English to limited-English speakers by immersing them directly in classes with native English-speaking students (Cooper, 1994). Bilingual education programs and multicultural and diversity programs were seen as too expensive. Thus, establishing the primacy of English in the conduct of official government business and publicly funded programs was portrayed as simply being fiscally responsible (Stefancic and Delgado, 1996).

But more fundamentally, the underlying issue for this movement concerns the implications of perpetuating "our common English culture" (Chavez, 1991). For the more fervent proponents, like Terry Robbin, the former head of English Only in Florida, the movement is not just needed for language preservation: "It's precisely because of the large number of Latinas and Latinos who have come here, that we ought to remind them, and better educate them to the fact that the United States is not a mongrel nation. We have a common language, it's English and we are damn proud of it" (Stefancic and Delgaldo, 1996, p. 9).

In a similar vein, ex-CIA Director William Colby held that Mexican immigration was a greater threat to the United States than was the Soviet Union (Acuña, 1996, p. 115). Fueling the debates on the need for an English Language Amendment, a 1986 special report by the Council for Inter-American Security claimed that "Hispanics in America today represent a very dangerous, subversive force that is bent on taking over our nation's political institutions for the purpose of imposing Spanish as the official language of the United States" (cited in Stefancic and Delgado, 1996, p. 17).

Concerned about charges that they were anti-immigrant, xenophobic, and nativist, if not outright racist, the leadership of English Only quickly asserted, in their personal statements and in their literature, that they are the only true champions of ethnic and linguistic non-discrimination. They proudly pointed to the fact that their membership included minority-group members—a few of whom were in leadership positions, although most were rank-and-file members.

Nevertheless, claims that English Only proponents were nativist and racist could not long be denied. In 1986, English Only co-founder John Tanton wrote his assessment of the consequences of immigration to California for a study group known as Witan:

> "To govern is to populate." Will the present majority peaceably hand over its political power to a group that is simply more fertile? As Whites see their power and control over their lives declining, will they simply go quietly into the night? Or will there be an explosion? Can "home contraceptives" compete with "home *progenitiva*" if borders aren't controlled? Or is advice to limit one's family simply advice to move over and let someone else with

greater reproductive powers occupy the space? Perhaps this is the first instance in which those with their pants up are going to get caught by those with their pants down. Since the majority of the retirees will be non-Hispanic Whites, but the workers will be minorities, will the latter be willing to pay for the care of the former? They will also have to provide the direct care: How will they get along, especially through a language barrier? (Cited in Stefancic and Delgado, 1996, p. 119)

In 1988, Tanton's study paper was discovered and disclosed during Arizona's English Only campaign. For many, Tanton's essays demonstrated underlying assumptions and premises that were truly nativist and racist at their core. For Linda Chavez and Walter Cronkite, Tanton's Witan paper was troubling and disquieting, leading both to resign from the organization. After Tanton's resignation, two years of struggle followed for English Only's membership. The close scrutiny and criticism of the press did not, however, dissuade English Only's proponents or lead to the group's dissolution. In fact, the English Only campaign regrouped and regained its loyal following shortly thereafter. In 1991, they convened a national kickoff rally to create momentum for their next campaign: Campaign for Our Common Language. The underlying goal is to return us to traditional Western European-American core values to help us weather and withstand the coming invasion and subsequent imposition of "lesser" cultures (Schlesinger, 1992; Cheney, 1995).

It is not clear how most Americans view the origins and dynamics of such groups as English Only, U.S. English, and English First or their collusion with and support of attacks on bilingual education, multicultural education, and affirmative action. Clearly, most of those who challenge English Only, U.S. Eng-

lish, and English First actions do not see these efforts as the passing acts of a few crackpots, the dispossessed fringe, or disaffected members of the middle and working classes. Unlike other neoconservative organizations, English Only derives most of its operating funds from membership dues and direct-mail campaigns. Its fund-raising letters and pamphlets capitalize on American fears of a "linguistic Babylon," the Balkanization of the United States, and the squandering of limited educational and social service dollars (Stefancic and Delgado, 1996, p. 30). Although many English Only adherents are xenophobic and socially conservative, most probably do not see themselves as nativists, racists, or white supremacists. They do not see their animosities, antipathies, and dislikes as exaggerated or unwarranted. Of course, some recognize that their actions lend support to supremacists and hate groups' causes, but they see this as the price of getting things back to "normal."

Proposition 187: Fiscal Crisis, Illegal Aliens, and Public Services

In the fall of 1993, Ron Prince convened a small group of southern California grass-roots activists to discuss illegal immigration, its consequences, and alternatives to unrelenting invasions of American society by illegal aliens (Stefancic and Delgaldo, 1996). By the end of the day, these 10 individuals, many previously unknown to each other, had decided to launch a statewide referendum, Proposition 187. This measure would prohibit undocumented immigrants from receiving publicly funded medical care, education, or social services. Proposition 187 would also require schools, health centers, and social service agencies to report suspected illegal immigrants and their children to state and federal authorities (Acuña, 1996; Calavita, 1996). Aligning currents of unrest with race politics is not new. Yet, unlike the repatriations of unwanted Mexican workers (*braceros*) in the 1930s and 1950s (Acuña, 1988), this measure seems to be linked to the growing populations of Latinos and their expectations of a meaningful partnership with, and inclusion in, the body politic.[1]

In May 1994, an initiative to stem "the alien invasion and their unlawful use of educational, social, and medical services" was filed by a coalition of anti-immigrant groups (Bunting, 1993). The coalition became known as the California Coalition for Immigration Reform (CCIR), and their theme was *"Save Our State (SOS)."* It was put to the voters as a referendum in November 1994, passing by a 59–41 percent margin.

The campaign was tuned to a range of Anglo anxieties and fears: a declining standard of living and quality of life; a faltering and changing economy; a sense of being overwhelmed by a range of cultures and peoples of color; and concern for dilution of American values, institutions, and ways of life (Simon, 1993; Quiroga, 1995). In due course, it would come to be championed by a converging range of interests: the Republican Party, United We Stand, Buchanan for President, and even some "new" Democrats. Governor Pete Wilson's faltering presidential campaign soon wrapped his candidacy in the SOS message of the "invasion's" imminent dangers: the government's inability to protect our borders; the economic crisis brought about by this last wave of immigrants; and the growing influence and size of the Latino population in the United States, especially in combination with other Third World immigrants.

The message was an appeal to the California electorate to support and elect an uncompromised, conservative state political leadership willing to get tough to check the unrelenting tide of immigration and force the federal government to change its ways—whether or not such changes would ultimately be found constitutional. Calavita (1996) argues that this symbolic aspect was crucial to the success of Proposition 187 and to Wilson's improved ratings. California voters were angry about the economic changes that had hit the working poor and middle classes, making them vulnerable to layoffs arising from downsizing, mergers, and movements of factories overseas. It was easy to lay the blame for the current fiscal crisis on immigrants and to assume—regardless of whether the assumption was based in fact—that immigrants really were obtaining more from the state or federal government than they paid into it.

By early 1994, Governor Wilson's ratings had plummeted. But soon after he endorsed Proposition 187, his ratings increased. The improved ratings can be attributed to the remolding of his image as a moderate—one willing to get tough and champion immigration reform as no other potential national party standard bearer had been willing to do. His immigrant-bashing theme clearly distinguished him from the other candidates and served as a spearhead theme in his next two campaigns. Yet according to Acuña (1996), several of Wilson's critics found him more than willing to ignore or distort data and findings about the costs of services used by immigrants and the tax dollars immigrants bring into the state. For example, Wilson "alleged that the County had spent $946 million dollars in 1991–92 on services to recent immigrants, adding that the county had only collected $139 of the $4.3 billion dollars a year in federal, state and local taxes paid by immigrants" (J. Flanigan, *L.A. Times*, July 11, 1993, p. D1).

The challenge to SOS's claims came from journalists, state government watch groups, the Urban Institute, and even RAND, which is generally considered a conservative research institute. These journalists and researchers questioned the basic assumption that immigrants took more from federal, state, and local services than they put in, suggesting that contradictory findings are due to very different assumptions about the number of undocumented workers in the U.S., their use of social services, and their contributions to Social Security (see further Calavita, 1996). For instance, an Urban Institute report demonstrated that over 50 percent of welfare benefits go to U.S. residents who are 65 years of age or older (Fix and Passel, 1994). Moreover, local, state, and federal taxes paid by immigrants more than offset the costs of services immigrants receive, with a net annual surplus of at least $25 billion, although variation exists from city to city (Fix and Passel, 1994; see also Lee, 1993; Fix and Zimmerman, 1995). Other critics, including a 1993 California Senate report, argued that too many politicians were using immigrants as scapegoats for problems with the state's economy. They further chided these politicians, and SOS leaders, for their failure to heed admonitions that scapegoating immigrants won't begin to solve the state's economic woes.

The immigrant-bashing theme was fueled in part by a decade of marked demographic change in many southern California communities (Cornelius, 1993; Acuña, 1996). These communities displayed wide differences not only in household income, but also in family size, median age, education, and, of course, ethnicity. These changes must also be linked to a major plunge in southern California real-estate prices, a downturn in the economy, and plant closings in what was once termed the "miracle economy."

By 1994, the prior decade's immigrant bashing had reached unexpectedly high levels of anti-immigrant and minority hysteria. Both Republican and Democratic candidates distorted this issue and embraced this concern as their own. The levels of acrimony soon reached such heights that few dared to challenge the backlash against immigrants as divisive, hysterical, a dangerous resurgence of nativism, and quite possibly legalized racism (Acuña, 1996; Stefancic and Delgado, 1996).

In the end, Democratic and Republican politicians joined in the fray, adding their spin on how to close the borders, thus stemming the tide of illegal immigration. Most, however, were not as vicious as Proposition 187's supporters, perhaps because they recognized that the Supreme Court had decided in 1982, in *Plyer v. Doe*, that the Texas policy of allowing public schools to bar undocumented children was unconstitutional, violating the equal protection clause of the Fourteenth Amendment. Or perhaps they realized that excluding undocumented pregnant women from prenatal care, and their children from receiving inoculations, posed serious and costly public health risks. Ultimately, Proposition 187 divided key Republican leaders into two camps, with William Bennett, Jack Kemp, William Kristol, and Steve Utz choosing to oppose the referendum while Pete Wilson and Pat Buchanan sought to expand Proposition 187 to other states and the federal government (Brimelow, 1995; Chavez, 1991; Acuña, 1996). Access to public education, health care, and other social services for immigrants—whether legal or undocumented—continued to be a major theme in the 1996 elections and in pending congressional legislation in 1997.

Closing Observations

Latinos who promote and work to assure the Latino/a community's progress and well-being understand the need for meaningful involvement in local and national political forums. As our numbers, visibility, and claims to "a better life" grow, some whites experience unsettling anxieties and increasing frustrations about racial/ethnic minorities. Politicians and grassroots campaigns exploit both old and new stereotypes about Latinos and Latinas to give themselves decisive advantages in campaigns. In periods of insecurity, stereotypes may be linked to other fears. Thus, Latinos/as are scapegoated as the cause of fiscal crises in California and elsewhere. Challenges to such scapegoating by Latinos, demonstrating, for example, that whites are the primary users of public assistance, seem only to encourage further hyperbole, spin, and counter claims. The heat of political campaigns and elections increases polarization. Sometimes, this polarization passes and is not of lasting consequence—at least for the major political parties and the majority of the electorate. For those touched by these scapegoating efforts, however, the pain and scars remain long after the specific political campaign is over. Occasionally, the scapegoating escalates to proportions well beyond the bounds that most Americans are willing to accept.

Numerous internal tensions, differences, and conflicts are found between moderate and far-right fringe conservatives, and between leaders and advocates and their grassroots. But, there is little doubt about their need to reach and enlist the angry, disaffected, and imposed-upon. Race politics, then, can be seen as an effort to pursue and mobilize moderate and undecided voters' anger, frustrations, and fears. In this contest, Latinos and Latinas continue to be convenient scapegoats for politicians and political groups seeking electorate support.

Yet of all the groups allied with SOS, those who pose the greatest concern today are the ones who fervently oppose the political and social claims of Latinos (and other people of color). This is a political coalition that seeks to lessen minority cultural, political, and social claims for a say in political decisions. It seeks to recapture and redirect government at all levels away from progressive and liberal directions towards a more conservative orientation and tone. These politicians and right-wing movement activists seek to lessen government's scope, and to undo liberal and progressive agendas dating back to FDR. They call for a return to the politics of the past, before the rise to prominence of liberal and progressive interests and groups, thereby deflecting, diluting, and disregarding the gains of all women, and of African American, Latino/a, Asian American, and American Indian men.

While many conservative social reformers and crusaders share similar worldviews, values, and behaviors, they differ in particular emphases, priorities, and targets. However, their agendas' focal concerns are generally linked and buttressed by other conservative groups' precepts. Many times, another group's causes and concerns serve as background. For example, English Only and Proposition 187 proponents were able to further their own interests by working cooperatively. To supporters, Latinos/as, like all people of color, remain racially and ethnically suspect. The increasing numbers, visibility, and claims of Latinos/as to "a better life" serve as clear evidence of their threat and encroachment.

It is not hard to fathom why many Americans' disbelief, distaste, and disgust continue to grow with each new political campaign, and why they are troubled by the current state of race politics. With each new election, the campaign seems to grow and reach new levels of acrimony and negative campaigning. Stereotyped Latino/a, African American, and women's rights groups are targets for these campaigns. Thus it is important to make sure that moderating influences remain, are visible, are voiced, and are active.

Note

1. During the period 1942 through 1964, the U.S. entered into a series of agreements with the Mexican government to create and maintain a foreign-contract labor system known as the "Bracero Program." This program provided agribusiness with a seemingly endless supply of cheap labor. Throughout this period, undocumented immigrants continued to cross the border in search of jobs. Employees who objected to exploitive and often dangerous work conditions found themselves without contracts and thus deportable, generally without being paid for the work they had done. For these and other reasons, agreements between the U.S. government, agribusiness, other business sectors in the United States, and the Mexican governments occasionally broke down. The best known of those occasions was in 1954, when Operation Wetback was launched. Having decided in 1953 that there were too many undocumented workers, known as "wetbacks," the Immigration and Naturalization Service deported tens of thousands of persons—including many U.S. citizens of Mexican descent—replacing them with Mexican workers imported to the United States under contract (for a full analysis of the Bracero Program see Calavita, 1992).

References

Acuña, Rudolfo F. (1996). *Anything but Mexican: Chicanos in contemporary Los Angeles.* New York: Verso.

———. (1988). *Occupied America: A history of Chicanos.* 3rd ed. New York: Harper & Row.

Auster, Lawrence. (1990). *The path to national suicide: An essay on immigration and multiculturalism.* Monterey, VA: American Immigration Control Foundation.

Boyarsky, Bill. (1993, August 18). "A thin border between security and prejudice." *Los Angeles Times,* B1, B2.

Brimelow, Peter. (1995). *Alien nation: Common sense about America's immigration disaster.* New York: Random House.

———. (1992, June 22). "Time to rethink immigration." *National Review.*

Buchanan, Pat. (1994). *Immigration timeout.* Available: www.buchanan.org/timeout.html.

———. (1991, August 28). "America has a right to preserve identity." *Conservative Chronicle.*

Bunting, Glenn. (1993, February 8). "Wilson's huge bill to U.S. uses sleight of hand." *Los Angeles Times,* A3.

Bustamante, Jorge. (1993, August 13). "Mexico bashing: A case where words can hurt." *Los Angeles Times,* B7.

Butler, R.E. (1985). *On creating a Hispanic America: A nation within a nation.* Washington, DC: Council for Inter-American Security.

Calavita, Kitty. (1996). "The new politics of immigration: 'Balanced-budget conservatism' and the symbolism of Proposition 187." *Social Problems, 43* (3), 285–305.

———. (1992). *Inside the state: The Bracero Program, immigration, and the I.N.S.* New York: Routledge.

Chavez, Linda. (1991). *Out of the barrio: Towards a new politics of Hispanic assimilation.* New York: Basic Books.

Cheney, Lynne. (1995). *Telling the truth: Why our culture and country have stopped making sense.* New York: Simon & Schuster.

Cooper, Marc. (1994, October 4). "The war against illegal immigrants heats up." *Village Voice.*

Cornelius, Wayne. (1993, July 12). "Neo-nativists feed on myopic fears." *Los Angeles Times,* B7.

Evans, G. Russell. (1994). "The crisis of illegal immigration." *Conservative Review*, March/April.

Fix, Michael, and Passell, Jeffrey S. (1994). *Immigration and immigrants: Setting the record straight*. Washington, DC: Urban Institute Press.

Fix, Michael, and Zimmerman, Wendy. (1995). *Immigrant families and public policy: A deepening divide*. Washington, DC: Urban Institute Press.

Flanigan, James. (1993, August 15). "Blaming immigrants won't solve economic woes." *Los Angeles Times*, D1.

Gallegley, Eltan. (1993a, August 17). "Why not restrict citizenship?" *Los Angeles Times*, B7.

———. (1993b, April 6). "Illegal immigration to the U.S.: A crisis that must be handled."

Hawkins, William R. (1995). *Importing revolution: Open borders and the radical agenda*. Monterey, VA: American Immigration Control Foundation.

Hernández-Chavez, Eduardo. (1978). *Language maintenance, bilingual education and bilingualism*. Washington, DC: Georgetown University Press.

Huddle, Donald L. (1993). *The net national costs of immigration*. Washington, DC: Carrying Capacity Network, July 20.

Lee, Patrick. (1993, August 13). "Studies challenge view that immigrants harm economy." *Los Angeles Times*, A1.

Lipset, Seymour. (1993). *The encyclopedia of democracy*. Washington, DC: Congressional Quarterly Press.

Muller, Thomas, and Espenshade, Thomas J. (1985). *The fourth wave. California's newest immigrants*. Washington, DC: The Urban Institute.

Piatt, Bill. (1990). *¿Only English?: Law and language policy in the United States*. Albuquerque: University of New Mexico.

Plafox, José. (1996). "Militarizing the border." *Covert Action Quarterly*, Spring.

Quiroga, Angélica. (1995, April). "Copycat fever: California's Proposition 187 epidemic spreads to other states." *Hispanic Magazine*, 18–24.

Reese, Charley. (1995, April 12). "Preserve America or lose it." *Conservative Chronicle*.

Schlesinger, Arthur. (1992). *The disuniting of America: Reflections on a multicultural society*. New York: W.W. Norton and Company.

Schuck, Peter H. (1995). "The message of 187." *American Prospect* (Spring).

Seelye, Katharine Q. (1996, June 20). "Dole opposes public education for illegal aliens." *New York Times*, A16.

Simon, Julian. (1993, August 4). "The nativists are wrong." *Wall Street Journal*, A8.

Simon, Richard. (1993, November 24). "The activists for immigrant rights battle erosion of public support." *Virginia Times*, A24.

Skerry, Peter. (1993). *Mexican Americans: The ambivalent minority*. New York: Free Press.

Stefancic, Jean, and Delgado, Richard. (1996). *No mercy: How conservative think tanks and foundations changed America's social agenda*. Philadelphia: Temple University Press.

Tanton, John, and Luttan, Wayne. (1992). "Welfare cost for immigrants." *The Social Contract*, Fall.

Discussion Questions

1. To what sectors of the voting public were Proposition 187 and the English Only referendums designed to appeal? What was their appeal?

2. Explain the term "race politics."

3. Do you think the Proposition 187 and English Only referendums are examples of immigrant bashing? Why or why not?

4. What factors do you think need to be considered when assessing whether immigrants take more from the U.S. economy than they contribute or contribute more than they take from it?

5. Do you think English should be the official language of the United States? Why or why not? ✦

Chapter 13

Images of Crime and Punishment

Latinos, Gangs, and Drugs

Edwardo L. Portillos

"If it walks like a duck and talks like a duck, it must be a duck." This idiom is frequently cited by police officers when asked how they determine that a given youth is a gang member. Certainly the walk, dress, speech, and mannerisms of some barrio youths indicate involvement or association with gangs. Similarly, gang tattoos signify current or prior gang membership. Nevertheless, this image quickly becomes the unofficial profile for identifying gang members, even though it fits nongang as well as gang youths. As a result, many young Latinos who are not involved in gangs are also harassed and degraded by law enforcement officers (Mirandé, 1987).

The image of the gang member also carries other baggage, such as that of a violent criminal who uses drugs. Consciously or unconsciously, many people make these connections, and these images become a primary means of defining Latinos, especially in suspicious or questionable circumstances. That is, the assumption is frequently made that if you are a young Latino, and especially a Latino male, you are a gun-wielding,

drug-selling gang banger unless proven otherwise.

On a warm summer night in Phoenix, Arizona, in 1996, a crowd gathered around a man lying spread-eagled off the roadway. Near him, hanging off the curb, was a mountain bike. The crowd began to speculate about what had happened. One man believed someone had run him off the road. A woman commented, "Maybe someone tried to rob him and knocked him unconscious," since his watch was hanging loosely around his wrist. Another person replied, "Maybe he's a drunk, a thief, or a drug user who stole the bike." Soon the group was joined by another man who informed them that he had called for an ambulance.[1]

That night there was only one Chicano at the scene, except for the Latino man on the ground, who might also have been Chicano.[2] Some of these conjectures bothered the Chicano because they were associated with criminal images. Also, no one bothered to check to see if the unconscious man was breathing. So the Chicano checked for a pulse to see if he was okay. While he tried to determine if the bike rider was alive, another bystander asked if he knew the man on the ground. The Chicano was stunned by the question but politely responded, "No."

He then began to tap the unconscious man on his back and ask if he was all right. There was no response, so he tapped again. One young woman warned, "I wouldn't do that. If he awakes, he might get violent." The Chicano began to think, sure, it was late at night, and maybe she was saying this out of sincere concern for his safety. But could there be more to this, as the man laying before him was noticeably brown?

A few minutes later help arrived, but an ambulance wasn't dispatched; rather, a police officer was sent to the scene. Was this man hurt or a criminal on the streets? The presence of the police, without an ambulance, suggested that we already had our answer. I was the Chicano in this story, and my reaction to the situation was complete disbelief. The crowd assumed that because we were both brown, that we knew one another. They associated an unconscious Latino man with criminal activity while knowing nothing but his ethnicity. Moreover, they held the predisposition that the Latino man would act violently when he awoke, when they should have been concerned for his welfare.

This story illustrates some of the overt and covert images of Latinos in our society. The dominant image is of a dark brown young man involved in gangs and selling drugs. This image becomes even more menacing when the young person dresses in baggy pants, white T-shirt, and a baseball cap. Young Latinos who dress as gang members are viewed as violent individuals who prey on unsuspecting citizens, and their alleged drug use and drug selling contribute to this violence. This image of Latinos also applies to undocumented immigrants, who are thought to bring drugs in from Mexico and South America.

In this chapter, we will look at some of the images that demoralize and degrade Latinos and Latinas all across this country while simultaneously ignoring the vast differences among them. Latinos and Latinas face problems with a criminal justice system that does not allow for their heterogeneity of cultures, with intense police monitoring and informal police profiles that target people with dark skin, and with a lack of sufficient court interpreters. Throughout, images of Latinas are analyzed in terms of distinct gender differences in arrest and incarceration. It is important, therefore, to begin with an understanding of the origins of these images.

Where Do These Images Come From?

Mexicanos settled what is now called the Southwest well before this region was of interest to whites from the East Coast. During the 1800s, the United States viewed these lands, which were held by Mexico, as essential to achieving manifest destiny. To create a country that extended from coast to coast, whites began to move into the Southwest (Montejano, 1987). The American Indians and Mexicanos/as who occupied these lands came to be seen as impeding manifest destiny for whites. It would not be long before there was a war with Mexico, known as the "Mexican-American War," to acquire land.

The war ended with the Treaty of Guadalupe Hildalgo. In the treaty, the United States acquired what today is called California, New Mexico, Nevada, and parts of Colorado, Arizona, and Utah. One provision of the treaty allowed Mexicans to remain in the United States as citizens and affirmed that the United States would recognize the land grants given to Mexicans by Mexico. Needless to say, many land grants were not acknowledged. Language problems and a legal system that favored whites helped whites to steal these lands from Mexicans.

The atrocities during the war and the stealing of Mexico's land were legitimized by creating an image of the Mexican as inhuman and were displayed in anti-Mexican attitudes (Mirandé, 1987). Common images of Latinos, at least in the Southwest, are rooted in their historic treatment and in their assumed difference from whites their "otherness." As was also the case with American Indians and African Americans, this led to many racial epithets and stereotypes (Mirandé, 1987). Mexicanos were viewed as primitive, inferior, backward, alcoholic, and dirty (Mirandé, 1987). The men were also assumed to be horse stealers, born criminals, and wife beaters. The women were accused of inducing white men's desire for them and therefore of being promiscuous (Montejano, 1987).

These images were carried into the twentieth century, but they took a new form. One common stereotype of the 1920s associated marijuana use with the Mexican community (Regoli and Hewitt, 1991; Mann, 1993). Many people at this time believed that using marijuana made Mexicans even more backward. A common belief was that Mexicans and Chicanos who used marijuana were involved in homicide and other violent crimes (Mann, 1993). When bands of youths gathered, people often assumed that these cliques were delinquent. Certainly, some of them engaged in delinquent acts, but not all of them did so. Nor did youths who engaged in delinquent acts do so all of the time (Moore, 1991).

In the 1930s and 1940s, the image of a young Chicano or Mexican male was the pachuco in a zoot suit. Young Chicanos wore zoot suits as a means of conforming to American styles, but they did so in a way that created their own dress, thus setting them apart (Mirandé, 1987). Their unique styles of dress and dancing and their use of a street language known as calo (Chicano slang that uses both Spanish and English), combined with their ethnicity, created a group of young people who were viewed as different. Mirandé (1987) argues that the pachucos' unique dress became a 'badge of crime.' The perception of them as dangerous criminals made close monitoring by the police appear normal and appropriate. These notions developed from racist attitudes and fear of the "other," especially during periods of high immigration and economic hardship in the United States.

The media reinforced these negative perceptions of Mexicans (Mirandé, 1987; Mann, 1993), which were then generalized to all Latinos in the United States. Today's media continue to depict young Latinos as violent gang members or drug users. Every day, the news shows Latinos in crime stories involving gangs and drugs. Rarely are positive aspects of the Latino community addressed by the news media. These images are also bolstered by television shows and movies, where Latinos come to represent gang members or drug users. Latinas also face the same negative stereotypes and characterizations, as well as the image of the young mother who conceives children to draw a larger welfare check.

The Images and the Police

For many young Latinos growing up in the barrio, these stereotypes seem to lump all youths in their community into one group: the gang member. Involvement with a gang is seen as synonymous with drug use and abuse, selling drugs as an organized business enterprise (Padilla, 1992), and being involved in criminal activity to support drug addiction. Studies do find that there is drug abuse in the barrio, and in many places drugs are a business enterprise (Moore, 1978; Fagan, 1989; Padilla, 1992; Bourgois, 1995). Nevertheless, drug use and sales are not necessarily related to gangs. In fact, some gangs look down on drug abuse, seeing it as a liability for the gang. A gang member addicted to drugs can't be trusted to think of the group's needs before his or her own need to get high (Curry and Spergel, 1992).

However, police officers who patrol the barrio are more often white and have internalized these images of young Latinos. The gangster dress, which can include baggy work pants called "Dickies" and nicely pressed, oversized shirts, often becomes an indicator of gang involvement. Police have tremendous discretion in choosing whom to pull over and whether to issue a warning or arrest the person. Police often work with official profiles of criminals, which are believed to aid police work (Zatz, 1987). Unfortunately, police also use unofficial profiles of criminals that are related to the images we have discussed.

To many Chicanos in the barrio, police operate on the basis of these stereotypes and are prejudiced against them because of the color of their skin. In these communities the police are not trusted. Young men and women think the police see them as enemies. They have had their civil liberties violated through police beatings and racist overtures meant to degrade young Latinos (U.S. Commission on Civil Rights, 1970; Mirandé, 1987; Rodríguez, 1993; Padilla, 1992; Portillos and Zatz, 1995). There are many examples of cases in which excessive use of force resulted in the death of young Latinos and became the overarching perception of what the police can and might do.

Miguel offers an example of a youth growing up in the barrio. Many people in Miguel's barrio and in surrounding communities believe that their neighborhoods have been overrun by gangs. In fact, Miguel's older brother has been involved with a gang since he was 11 years old. Growing up in his barrio, Miguel has seen friends, some of whom were involved in gangs and others who were not, die because of gang violence. He has also seen others die at the hands of police.

For the most part, Miguel considers himself a regular kid. He has never sold drugs or robbed anyone. He willingly admits his drug use, which he considers purely recreational. He excels in school and is involved in extracurricular activi-

ties. Miguel's friends are no different from the kids in Boy Scout troops on the other side of town. Miguel often hangs around with gang members because some are his cousins and others have been his lifelong friends who drifted into gang membership while he shunned it. He knows all of them want to grow up to have a family, a good job, a pleasant house in short, the American dream. He also knows that many of his friends will not realize this vision. Often these aspirations are cut short by death or entanglement with the criminal justice system.

One night Miguel and his cousin stopped at a convenience store while their friends waited in the car. A police officer stood outside the store. As they walked past the officer, they were met with a suspicious glare. While Miguel walked through the store looking for chips and a soda pop, he was closely monitored by the officer. For Miguel this was a part of life. He always felt that he was being watched, and that most people are waiting and looking for the slightest sign of his evil criminal core. What occurred when he left the store was also a regular part of growing up. As they walked out, the officer called to him, "Hold on, buddy, where do you think you guys are going?" He then asked for their identification, as well as that of their friends in the car. He began to search them, and Miguel asked, "Why do you need to search us? We didn't do anything." The officer replied, "For my safety." Quickly two other cars swarmed to the scene. Since his cousin was a known gang member, the others also were considered to be gang associates. For nothing more than being brown, wearing a certain style of dress, and his relationship with his cousin, Miguel's name was added to the gang list. Because of a criminal image associated with people who looked like Miguel and his friends, he had to endure the humiliation of a search and the stares as people drove past.

Miguel, like so many other young Latinos, learned at a young age that the police are more likely to monitor them than to provide help. Police are quick to point out that those who criticize their work are the first to call them when they need assistance. It is true that when confronted with a violent or dangerous situation, most people will call the police. Those growing up in Latino communities perceive, however, that the response time for the police is longer in their communities than in the suburbs (Portillos and Zatz, 1995).

Problems also arise when white officers who patrol Latino/a communities do not have adequate Spanish language skills to communicate effectively with the citizenry and to provide assistance. Often, younger children must translate for their parents and the police officers. While this provides information for the police, is it reliable, especially in traumatic situations?

Latinos/as and the Courts

One problem associated with intense police monitoring of Latino and Latina urban poor is their overrepresentation at multiple stages of the juvenile criminal justice systems. Many of these arrests are related to moral panics concerning gangs (Zatz, 1987) and their perceived relationship to drugs. Chicano youths involved in gangs are also more likely to be prosecuted than youths not involved in gangs (Zatz, 1985). A study in Maricopa County, Arizona found that Latino/a youths make up 24 percent of the population, yet they comprise 30 percent of all referrals to juvenile court, 37 percent of all detainees, and 44 percent of youths committed to secure juvenile institutions (Bortner, Burgess, Schneider, and Hall, 1993, p. 34). Overall, minority youths

have a higher chance of being arrested than whites. The study found that 70.8 percent of African American youths and 42.9 percent of Latino youths are likely to be referred to juvenile court by age 17 compared to 38.9 percent of white youths (Bortner et al., 1993, p. 34). Similar patterns of overrepresentation are found throughout the country and within the adult justice system (Donziger, 1996; Miller, 1996; Walker, Spohn, and DeLone, 1996).

In the following story, Luis and his mother, María, exemplify another problem often encountered with the juvenile justice system: a language barrier. Luis' gang involvement started at age 13. Prior to this time he had been a model son. He played in youth basketball leagues. He was an above-average student, and the teachers regarded him as a future leader of his community. María and her husband both worked very hard to provide more than the basic necessities of life for their children.

Little Luis was not considered at high risk for gang involvement because he had a stable family environment and a strong support network at school. Suddenly, things changed. María learned from the school and police officials that her son was robbing houses and using marijuana. Nothing is sadder than the tears of a mother who cries for her children as she sees them throw their lives away. Many nights she sobbed herself to sleep, and she dreaded the night she might receive a phone call or a knock on the door telling her that her son was dead. Her fear was real, as there were many nights when he came home beaten after a fight with rival gangs.

María also cried every time she went to court. She felt so alone in the world and embarrassed by her son's involvement in delinquent activities. She wanted her husband to help, and he didn't. He simply said, 'Calm down, vieja, he'll soon grow out of it.' She wanted the judge to help, and he yelled at her. She wanted the probation officer to help but she couldn't understand his orders. María was not stupid; she was monolingual. Although she knew some English, it wasn't enough to allow her to understand the courtroom proceedings. Nor did it allow her to understand the stipulations of Luis' probation.

María had never been in a courtroom before and did not know how formal the proceedings would be, including the appropriate dress for her son. She was criticized by the judge for allowing Luis to dress like a gang member. Both María and Luis were forced to leave the courtroom until he was properly dressed. Going to court was humiliating for María, who had worked so hard to be a good mother. Once the judge asked her a question, and she responded in broken English that she did not understand. The judge then asked, 'How long have you been in this country? 'Fifteen years,' she replied. 'You should be ashamed of yourself, living in this country for fifteen years and not knowing English,' he chided. A translator was not provided for her, so she had to rely on the information that her son gave her about his probation rules. Sure, she had received paperwork from the probation department, but the papers were all in English. And although the probation officer knew some Spanish, he wasn't fluent enough to clarify the probation stipulations. If only she knew that her son was to be home at a certain time, she would have made sure that he was!

María's experiences with the juvenile justice system are similar to the experiences of other Latinos and Latinas. The overrepresentation discussed earlier is the result of a cluster of factors. One factor is the common shortage of translators, which results in Latinos/as often not understanding the court proceedings. Also, they are intimated by such a formal white system. Government business in Mexico and other Latin American countries is conducted much more informally. Economics is also a factor. In some cases, Latinos are assigned lawyers because they do not have the money to provide their own. These lawyers may not speak Spanish, and because they may have many other cases, they may not take the time to get to know the family, expecting instead to be trusted immediately with what the family views as its shame.

Also, parents who are poor cannot provide alternatives to incarceration such as private psychological counseling, or drug or alcohol treatment. These actions are looked upon favorably by the juvenile justice system and show that the parents are involved in their children's lives. Courts also look at the family history. Youths from single-parent families are more likely to be incarcerated than those from two-parent families because of concerns about how closely they can be supervised. Many urban poor Latino/a youths live in single-parent families. Finally, their own and their families' involvement in gangs will determine how they are processed through the system. Youths involved in gangs are more likely to be detained and later committed to secure facilities than are youths who are not involved in gangs (Zatz, 1985). The perception of gang youths is that they are more violent and more apt to be involved in criminal activity than youths who are not in gangs. Juvenile court officials also look down on families whose brothers, fathers, uncles, and other relatives are current or past gang members. They perceive that multigenerational-gang families set youths up for failure, and that they are better off in an environment where they are not influenced by the gang.

Latinas and the Criminal Justice System

Young Latinas face many of the same problems as their brothers and also fit the tough gang profile. In addition, they are assumed to be welfare queens and irresponsible mothers who raise young gang members. Outside the realm of motherhood, contemporary images of Latinas emphasize their sexuality and drug use. For young women of color, and in this case Latinas, juvenile justice officials see themselves as the ultimate saviors. The perception held by some juvenile officials and police is that if these young women are left alone on the street, they soon may become pregnant. So the juvenile justice system acts as a paternal father to protect these young women. The question, of course, is: does the system really protect them? Young women of color are often stopped, arrested, and processed through the juvenile justice system to keep them away from male gang influence, including crime and drugs.

Similar to males, Latinas are overrepresented in both federal and state prisons. Research suggests that the overrepresentation of Latinos/as in federal prisons is correlated with the War on Drugs (Walker et al., 1996). According to the National Criminal Justice Commission, only a small percentage of all people are arrested for violent and dangerous crimes; most are drug-related offenses (Donziger, 1996). The following young woman's story epitomizes what can happen to women as they move through the criminal justice system.

Lupe is now 25 years old and is serving a 10-year sentence for marijuana possession with the intent to sell. Her involvement with drugs began in eighth grade, when two of her friends convinced her to share a joint in the bathroom. At first Lupe wasn't interested in the drug, but she knew many other kids who had already tried it. Soon marijuana became her drug of choice, and in fact she liked it better than alcohol. She believed that marijuana was no different from beer, so she continued to use it, mostly when she was with her friends.

The first time she was arrested for possession was when she was hanging out with some friends from the barrio. She was 15 at the time, and they were on their way to a party. Flaco asked Lupe if she was ready to get 'budded up' (high) when they arrived at the party. Lupe liked Flaco and she sweetly replied, 'You know I'm down.' En route to the party, the driver noticed a police car following them in his rear-view mirror. Flaco asked Lupe to hold the joints for him because he was on probation, and if caught with them, he would be sent back to a juvenile facility. She agreed and was subsequently arrested for her first marijuana possession. She spent that weekend in a detention center scared out of her mind, but this didn't deter her.

In time she experimented with harder drugs such as crack, speed, and methamphetamines, but still she preferred marijuana. She accumulated other arrests, but they were related to purely recreational use. At 23, she was living with a boyfriend, and together they had a child whom Lupe loved with all her heart. She also adored her boyfriend, who occasionally sold drugs for extra income to pay for diapers and baby formula. Lupe didn't like the fact that he sold drugs, but she also knew how hard it was for him to get a job in the barrio, where jobs were limited.

One day a narcotics officer served a warrant and found drugs in her apartment. Now that the government had declared a renewed War on Drugs, her previous adult drug record resulted in Lupe's receiving a long prison sentence (Tonry, 1995; Díaz-Cotto, 1996). Lupe felt she didn't belong in prison; those drugs weren't even hers. She was a recreational user who was trying to raise her child in a very difficult marginal environment in the barrio. Now her child must stay in a foster home until she is released in the year 2000. It breaks her heart that she can't see her child every day, and she is saddened to think about the impact this will have on him.

Some Responses

One response to the image of a young Latino as involved in either gangs or drug use is to understand that Latinos are no more violent or dangerous than any other group of people. Similarly, if Latinos are involved in crime, it is not necessarily because of gangs and drugs. Yes, many young Latinos and Latinas are involved in gangs and drugs, but many others are not.

The Latino population is very diverse. It consists of people from many different countries and regions: Mexico, Central America, South America, Puerto Rico, and other Caribbean nations. Each region and country has a distinct culture, which may be very dissimilar to the culture of those countries that surround it. Although Latinos share a common language, there are distinct differences in dialect, the use of particular words, and the speed with which the language is spoken.

Workers within the criminal and juvenile justice systems must remember this diversity. More Spanish-speaking officers are needed in the field to understand and relate to the Latino community. Preferably, these should be officers who grew up in those neighborhoods and have some understanding of the difficulties of growing up in the barrio. Additionally, to give Latinos/as some hope of equality before the law, more interpreters are needed. The juvenile justice system must remember that it is not only youths who need interpreters but also their parents. Only then can the parents play a vital role in deterring their children from crime. Lawyers are also needed who desire to serve Latinos/as, including helping them to understand their legal rights. Again, in-

terpreters or, even better, bilingual attorneys are needed so that Latinos and Latinas can understand the proceedings and voice dissatisfaction if their rights are impeded just as any other citizen can do.

Finally, and perhaps central to truly implementing any of the above recommendations, is the need for a change in the 'get tough on crime' attitude. The War on Drugs and "get tough on crime" initiatives such as 'three strikes' will result in an even larger overrepresentation of blacks and Latinos in the justice system (Tonry, 1995; Miller, 1996). A new approach is needed to replace the largely ineffective initiatives that have led many states to set aside more money for building prisons than for educating children. We should reconsider locking up small-time drug users and instead provide drug rehabilitation that is sensitive to cultural differences. Prison is still needed for the rapists and murderers in our society, but not for many of the poor people of color who are incarcerated for drug-related offenses. These policies have led to a sorrowful life for many Latinos/as and their families.

Conclusion

This chapter has attempted to depict commonly associated images of crime and punishment as they relate to Latinos. The images of crime are of young Latino males who are involved in gangs and drug use. These images also impact young Latinas, who must further contend with stereotypes associated with their gender and ethnicity.

From the perspective of Latinos/as, these stereotypes create unfair punishment at every level within the juvenile criminal justice system. The images allow police to equate Latinos with certain crimes and to target youths who may not be involved in gangs, are former gang members, or are current gang members. Young Latinos assume the police are their enemies, and that all police are prejudiced and discriminate against them because of their ethnicity. Moreover, there are language barriers at all levels within the system. The assumption is that everyone should know English to some degree, especially if they have lived in this country for a number of years. To alleviate these problems, Spanish-speaking officials are needed.

There are also cultural barriers, particularly with the formality of the proceeding and the correct protocol in courtroom proceedings. The experiences with the criminal justice system, particularly with the police, lead some Latinos to believe that the criminal justice system in its present form is unfair. Moreover, some Latinos feel that they have been targeted by current crime policies that have led to their overrepresentation in juvenile facilities and in state and federal prisons.

Notes

1. The phone call for help had identified the man on the ground as Latino.
2. The term "Latino/a" reflects the diversity of this population, which includes people from Mexico, Puerto Rico, Central America, and other Caribbean islands. I use 'Mexicanos' and 'Mexicans' interchangeably to refer to people from Mexico. I refer to 'Chicanos/as' as U.S. citizens of Mexican descent. When I follow the Spanish spelling, I use the nomenclature 'Mexicano' (and 'Latino' and 'Chicano') to refer to men and 'Mexicana' (and 'Latina' and 'Chicana') to refer to women.

References

Bortner, M.A., Burgess, Carol A., Schneider, Anne L., and Hall, Andy. (1993). *Equitable treatment of minority youth: A report on the over representation of minority youth in Arizona's juvenile justice system.* Phoenix, AZ: Governor's Office for Children, Equitable Treatment of Minority Youth Project.

Bourgois, Philippe. (1995). *In search of respect: Selling crack in El Barrio.* New York: Cambridge University Press.

Curry, G. David, and Spergel, Irving A. (1992). "Gang involvement and delinquency among Hispanic and African-American adolescent males." *Journal of Research in Crime and Delinquency, 29,* 273–291.

Díaz-Cotto, Juanita. (1996). *Gender, ethnicity, and the state: Latina and Latino prison politics.* Albany: State University of New York Press.

Donziger, Steven A. (Ed.). (1996). *The real war on crime: The report of the National Criminal Justice Commission.* New York: Harper Perennial.

Fagan, Jeffery. (1989). "The social organization of drug use and drug dealing among urban gangs." *Criminology, 27,* 633–700.

Mann, Coramae Richey. (1993). *Unequal justice: A question of color.* Bloomington: Indiana University Press.

Miller, Jerome G. (1996). *Search and destroy: African-American males in the criminal justice system.* Cambridge: Cambridge University Press.

Mirandé, Alfredo. (1987). *Gringo justice.* Notre Dame, IN: University of Notre Dame Press.

Montejano, David. (1987). *Anglos and Mexicans in the making of Texas, 1836–1986.* Austin: University of Texas Press.

Moore, Joan W. (1991). *Going down to the barrio: Homeboys and homegirls in change.* Philadelphia: Temple University Press.

———. (1978). *Homeboys: Gangs, drugs, and prison in the barrios of Los Angeles.* Philadelphia: Temple University Press.

Padilla, Felix. (1992). *The gang as an American enterprise.* New Jersey: Rutgers University Press.

Portillos, Edwardo L., and Zatz, Marjorie S. (1995). *Not to die for: Positive and negative aspects of Chicano youth gangs.* Paper presented at the annual meeting of the American Society of Criminology, Boston.

Regoli, Robert M., and Hewitt, John D. (1991). *Delinquency in society; A child-centered approach.* New York: McGraw Hill.

Rodríguez, Luis J. (1993). *Always running, La vida loca: Gang days in L.A.* New York: Touchstone.

Tonry, Michael. (1995). *Malign neglect: Race, crime, and punishment in America.* New York: Oxford University Press.

U.S. Commission on Civil Rights. (1970). *Mexican Americans and the administration of justice in the Southwest.* Washington, DC: U.S. Government Printing Office.

Walker, Samuel, Spohn, Cassia, and De-Lone, Miriam. (1996). *The color of justice: Race, ethnicity, and crime in America.* Belmont, CA: Wadsworth Publishing Company.

Zatz, Marjorie S. (1987). "Chicano youth gangs and crime: The creation of a moral panic." *Contemporary Crisis, 11,* 129–158.

———. (1985). "Los Cholos: Legal processing of Chicano gang members." *Social Problems, 33* (1).

Discussion Questions

1. The problem of overrepresentation of minority youths is attributed in part to intense police monitoring and to a judicial system laced with Anglo values that ignore the experiences and culture of other racial groups. What are other possible causes of this overrepresentation of minorities (e.g., racial tension, economics, family values)?

2. Based on the images discussed in this chapter, can Latinos and other ethnic minorities ever receive equal justice? Also, how can you, as a possible future employee within the criminal justice system, help deal with these images?

3. Because only a small percentage of people in jail are violent criminal offenders, what other policies would be useful for dealing with crime other than "getting tough?"

4. What impact do you think a new policy aimed at reducing the number of drug offenders in our jails would have? Would the overrepresentation of minorities change? Would there be more crime?

5. Imagine that you are driving down the street and the police pull you over because you look like a suspected felon. You are asked to exit the car with your hands on top of your head. With weapons drawn, you are then searched for weapons. A background check is run to validate the information on your identity that you have provided the police. During the entire process the police are condescending, assuming that you are lying. How would you respond to such an incident, which seems to violate your dignity? Would your response be different from that of a young Latino male who experiences such stops regularly because of his ethnicity? ✦

Part IV

The Color Yellow

Coming to the U.S. from what is literally the other side of the world, Asians are thought of as exotic, inscrutable, and different (Takaki, 1979, 1993). Asian women are seen as sexy; Asian men as evil, the "yellow peril." Most American men know of Asia and Asians only through their wartime experiences fighting the Japanese—for the World War II generation—or the Koreans or Vietnamese—for the Korean War and Vietnam War generations. Most American women know even less about Asia and Asians.

Yet large numbers of Asians have immigrated to the United States since the mid-1800s, beginning with the Chinese laborers recruited to build the Central Pacific Railroad. Desired by business owners in cities all over the U.S. because they performed the hardest, dirtiest, and most menial jobs at far lower pay than Euro-Americans demanded, and hated by whites who saw them only as competition, these early Chinese immigrants were victims of exclusionary policies that prohibited them from becoming U.S. citizens. To coerce these men to return home, the number of Chinese women who could enter the U.S. was severely limited. The *Chinese Exclusion Act*, passed in 1882, was not rescinded until 1943, when the Chinese were our allies in World War II. The Chinese were also the victims of other discriminatory laws aimed solely at them, such as the *San Francisco Opium Ordinance*, which only prohibited the *smoking* of opium, as was the Chinese custom, rather than all use of opium, which would have affected Euro-Americans as well. This is but one example of how drug laws have historically been aimed at a particular racial/ethnic group.

Drugs, prostitution, and gambling are the types of crime most closely associated with Asians and Asian Americans. Yet in many cases, the persons seeking the drugs, prostitutes, and gambling opportunities are Euro American. The allure of Asian and Asian American women for Euro-American men is also discussed by several of the authors in this section. Prostitution is a viable occupation only if you have sufficient customers, and the stereotype of Asian women as exotic and submissive played a large part in determining that Thailand and the Philippines became major rest-and-recreation sites for men in the U.S. military.

The Germans and the Japanese were our primary enemies in World War II. Why, the authors in this section ask, were Japanese Americans imprisoned in internment camps while German Americans were not? The answer seems to be that we—as a society—trusted German Americans to be Americans first and of German ancestry second, but we were unwilling to make the same assumption about Japanese Americans. We must ask ourselves why. Similarly, when faced with a scandal surrounding campaign contributions from countries in *Asia* in the spring of 1997, the Democratic National Committee telephoned *Asian American* supporters to ask whether they were citizens. As Nash and Wu (1997, p. 15) suggest, "the questions aimed at Asian Americans reflect the same stereotyping that has portrayed all Asian derived people as foreigners, even if they are fifth-generation Californians."

Today, Asian Americans are our "model minority." Hardworking, studious, excelling in math and business, they are assumed to be perfect—the model for other people of color. This appears on the surface to be a very positive stereotype. However, it has several serious consequences. First, the image of the model minority hides the very real diversity across and within different Asian American groups (e.g., Vietnamese, Cambodian, Chinese, Japanese, Korean, Thai). Second, if all Asian Americans are presumed to have "made it" in the U.S., then it follows that there is no need for social services for those who are struggling economically. Similarly, if all Asian Americans are models, then there is no need to develop culturally appropriate resources, such as drug and alcohol treatment centers, for the Asian American communities. Finally, the stereotype of the model minority pits Asian Americans against other minorities, as well as against Euro-Americans. In recent years, these conflicts have flared into violent confrontations between Korean Americans and African Americans in major cities on both coasts. The anti-immigrant and anti-affirmative-action climate in the United States today has also contributed to increased numbers of hate crimes against Asian Americans who are seen as encroaching on what was previously an area of Euro-American privilege. The implications of this stereotypic image of Asian Americans as the model for other minorities are so important that each of the authors in this section addresses them, though they approach the issues in slightly different ways.

References

Nash, Phil Tajitsu, and Wu, Frank. (1997). "Asian Americans under glass." *The Nation, 264*, (12), 15–16.

Takaki, Ronald T. (1993). *A different mirror: A history of multicultural America.* Boston: Little, Brown and Company.

——. (1979). *Iron cages: Race and culture in nineteenth-century America.* New York: Alfred A. Knopf. ◆

Chapter 14

Images of Asian Americans

'Senator Sir, Meet Susie Wong and the Inscrutable Fu Manchu'

Karen Joe Laidler

I remember when the movie *The World of Susie Wong* first came out in the 1960s. I was just a small girl filled with excitement as everyone in my apartment building gathered around my auntie's black-and-white television set to watch the premiere. It was a big deal on my block in Chinatown, partly because it was one of the few movies about a Chinese woman but also because my auntie was in the movie as an extra in one of the crowd scenes. I was fixated on the screen as I watched Susie Wong. She was unlike any Chinese woman I had ever seen or met. She was a real "sex kitten," dressed up in a very tight form-fitting Chinese dress (*chong-sam*), with flawless makeup and hair. She had this erotic yet submissive allure about her. She seemed to have some special seductive hold on the white guy in the movie. She was my first introduction to the "oriental beauty."

This popular image of Asians was only one of many from the movies I used to watch as a child. On Sundays, while my father was at work and my mother was doing the laundry, I got to watch the afternoon movies. I couldn't relate to Shirley Temple; she was much too innocent and cutesy for me. I was most fascinated with the *Inscrutable Fu Manchu* series. Fu Manchu was this scary, mysterious foreign devil who was always causing evil and mayhem. He had slanty eyes and bushy eyebrows like master sleuth Charlie Chan's in his movie series. I found Charlie Chan a curious character, too, because he also seemed to lurk in the shadows of "evil-dom" and had an exaggerated look of "Chineseyness." I suppose the real mystery for me was that, despite being Chinese and living in Chinatown, I didn't know anyone who looked or acted like those guys. I was still too young to realize that Fu Manchu and Charlie Chan weren't even played by Chinese actors.

Some people would argue that times have changed. Asian American actors and actresses are now appearing on television and in major films. Blockbuster Hollywood movies like *The Joy Luck Club* are meant to sensitize and enlighten the Western community to the distinctive culture and heritage of Chinese women. But the "yellow-peril" images created through characters like the inscrutable Fu Manchu and Charlie Chan have not dissipated and, instead, have continued to thrive in contemporary films like *Year of the Dragon*. This movie contains all the images from the past packed into a two-hour gangster-police drama and set in the congested streets of New York's Chinatown. The hero, a good ol' Irish cop (played by Mickey Rourke), sets out to destroy the organized crime efforts of the Chinese Mafia and, in the process, hopes to bring down their young, fearless, and violent recruits. The real target for justice is the suave and ruthless gang leader who aspires to control all of Chinatown's illicit operations—gambling, prostitution, and extortion. While the Irish cop is tracking down leads, he meets and becomes enraptured by a seductive oriental beauty.

Ironically these characterizations of Asian men and women as devious and mysterious stand in distinct contrast to the other popular stereotype of them, namely, that of the "model minority." The media, in all its various forms (television, newspapers, magazines, movies, documentaries, etc.), also cast the Asian as the well-assimilated immigrant, who through diligence, hard work, and obedience is working toward the American dream. This characterization assumes that there are no differences in the histories, immigration experiences, and cultural traditions of the more than 34 different ethnic groups that are lumped into the category "Asian." This model minority stereotype also assumes that all Asians abide by the cultural values of self-discipline, perseverance, and a strong sense of family. Moreover, these values, combined with their desire to become "American," mean that *their* community does not experience social problems like domestic violence, substance abuse, delinquency, poverty, and mental illness.

At first, these images and stereotypes might seem harmless and sometimes entertaining. But stereotypes need to be challenged because they take on a life of their own, becoming real, especially for people who have had little or no interaction with those who are being typed. Social typing often is used as a substitute for really knowing the individual or situation. And as W. I. Thomas said, "If men define situations as real, they are real in their consequences" (1928, p. 572). In other words, if we believe that these characterizations are real (even though they aren't), then we will inappropriately base our actions on them (rather than on what is actually real).

What does this mean? People in positions of power and authority will be making decisions about social policy and community programs based not on the real situation, but rather on what is projected as being real (that is, the stereotypes). Let me give you just two examples.

Over the last decade, public concern has been captivated by youth gangs and their association with drugs and violence. The media, the police, and several members of Congress have identified Chinese gangs as being especially problematic. They are more dangerous and violent than other minority-youth gangs because of their alleged links to the Chinese Mafia and organized crime (including international heroin trafficking). Senator Sam Nunn had this to say: "Chinese organized crime . . . is in many ways as mysterious, if not more so than its portrayal in movies such as *Year of the Dragon*. For example, this criminal subculture is rooted in distinct groups—triads, tongs and gangs—that are completely unfamiliar to most Americans" (U.S. Senate, 1991, p. 2).

Senator Nunn appears to link the real Chinese gang scene with that portrayed in *Year of the Dragon*. Such views gain even more credence in the media:

> Today, Chinese gangs are not just bands of teenagers that once prowled Chinatown exclusively, extorting protection money from shop owners and occasionally mugging tourists. They have evolved into sophisticated groups that deal in narcotics and operate money laundering rackets using legitimate business fronts as covers. They have forged new links with Hong Kong and Taiwan syndicates, which have traditionally dominated the supply of heroin smuggled into the United States (Leung, 1987, p. A8).

These characterizations of Chinese gangsters—slick, violent, fearless, sophisticated—have taken on a life of their own and, consequently, have led to the development of several aggressive law enforcement suppression policies that specifically targeted Asian gangs (Joe, 1994). This first example demonstrates the unfortunate consequences of negative stereotypes of Asians as the mysterious foreign devil.

The second example is based on the contrasting assumption that Asian Americans are the model minority. One of the many negative consequences of this stereotype is that Asians are assumed to have few personal, familial, or social problems. The Asian immigrant is assumed to go through a period of "adjustment" in which he or she must learn the ways of "becoming American." This is typically perceived as a temporary period until the newcomer assimilates. Accordingly, successive generations are absorbed into the mainstream of American culture, and when problems arise, they are attributed to cultural and generational gaps. Moreover, it is assumed that any social problems will be handled internally by the individual or within the tight-knit family or community.

As a result, policymakers have little knowledge about the realities and problems of Asian Americans and, in turn, are more likely to divert monies for prevention, intervention, and educational programs to other communities. Many Asian ethnic community organizations—Filipino, Japanese, Korean, Chinese, Vietnamese—have joined forces to educate policymakers and to lobby for and develop culturally appropriate programs, including drug treatment programs, in various parts of the U.S. They are constantly struggling to survive in a period of government cutbacks. With existing resources, services can be extended only so far to a population that includes culturally diverse groups.

It is critical, then, to move beyond these stereotypes and look at the realities of Asian Americans. Among the Asian Americans I know, no one fits the popular characterizations—not that of the model minority without any social problems or that of the slick, violent gangster or that of the erotic, submissive woman. In fact, many of the Asian Americans whom I have encountered—both in my social or professional experience—face problems similar to those of other Americans. The reasons for and ways of coping with these problems, however, are shaped by different cultural and social factors.

Johnny's Story

I've known Johnny since childhood. We grew up together in San Francisco's Chinatown. It was a very cool place to grow up because the neighborhood was only a few square blocks, with markets and businesses, surrounded by apartment buildings and a big housing project. Many people lived in this small area, and everyone knew one another (and their business).

The housing project where Johnny lived was especially crowded because several generations often resided under the same roof. Johnny's place was a one-bedroom apartment and had a mix of people living there: his grandparents, his mother, his two brothers, his sister and her husband and baby. He never said where his father was. It was so noisy and packed in this tiny place that Johnny constantly sought peace and quiet on the street. This is when he started getting into trouble:

> I left home at an early age and went to live with my cousin. I was 11, my cousin was 10. Then my cousin and I started staying at a friend's house. At first when I left home it was fun, and we stayed out until we got tired from playing. Instead of going to my

cousin's house, we just started sleeping on roof tops or at the laundry room at the housing project. We never went outside of Chinatown, stuck mostly around the projects and the markets.

We started hanging around gangs; they were our role model. They gave you a feeling of power and security because when you are on the street, you know that by hanging around the gang that it sort of makes you feel safe. I would never admit that I was scared. It is more like you want to believe that you are really bad and that you fit in. So we got involved in the gang. I was hanging around the Rainmakers. Most of them were ABCs [i.e., American-born Chinese]. We was just into a lot of mischief stuff, nothing major.

I switched over to the Disciples because I was more on the streets. We started getting into a lot of fights, especially with the ABCs. The B.D.s were immigrants, born in China or Hong Kong. They were called FOBs [i.e., fresh off the boat]. I didn't really fit into either group, I guess, because even though I was born in China, I came here when I was a baby. So really I am both, I guess. I was caught in the middle because I used to hang around ABCs and FOBs. I tried to stay out of those fights because I knew both sides. I mostly got into the racial fights with white guys. First we were just jumping [i.e., beat up] them; then later we started taking their money. What was really amazing, though, is when the ABCs and FOBs joined together to fight the black guys at school. Even though the ABCs and FOBs hated each other, they had that common enemy. They said, "We will fight against each other tomorrow, but today we are our own kind." That came first.

I felt more natural with the Disciples because we all had heart. The Rainmakers were afraid because they were taught that if you do this

you go to jail. But the Disciples weren't so scared. They would stick up for you; you'd know they'd be right there for you. I think a lot of guys that belonged to the Disciples joined the gang because there weren't any jobs, and they had nothing else to do but hang out in the street. The Disciples were FOBs, and they felt that Chinese that lived here didn't like them, that they were too Chinesey. The Disciples felt like outcasts, and so that's why they used to stick together.

Social workers used to come down to Chinatown; they kept telling us that they were trying to get money for us so we could have jobs. Give us something to do. But Chinese don't have problems. They had no trouble. It was that stereotype, you know. It's the same with drugs; they say that Chinese don't use.

My only income was ripping off: stealing, robbing, strong-arm robbing. Anywhere I could get money. We were into extorting businesses as well, the restaurants and stores. The merchants were expected to "show respect" by paying us protection monies, and they usually paid because they were scared. The Chinese don't get into trouble because they never hear about it, Chinese people don't usually like to go to the police. I guess that they don't trust them. That's another reason why those stereotypes live on.

The other things we used to do was cruise, look for girls, and crash parties. When we went to dances, we would push our weight around and most of those dances turned into fights. For me, I enjoyed the fighting. You know, growing up Chinese, you aren't supposed to show that you are hurting, especially if you're hanging out on the street. It is considered weak. It was one way for me to get out my frustration.

I also got a sense of pride and power out of it all and a sense of belonging. It is like you don't know any other way. I grew up thinking that to be a man you got to go out there on your own.

By the time I hit my fifteenth birthday, I got sent to Log Cabin [secure juvenile detention]. Later I went to California Youth Authority three times. My cousin and I were always getting arrested. The counselors would look at us with surprise and say, "What are you doing here? You're Chinese." As much as I hate the stereotype, we tried to use it to our advantage, being all humble and stuff, and sometimes they would let us go. But usually I would be out a month, two months, then I was back in. In and out.

I was really scared, though, when I got sent off. The big tough guys always trying to get the advantage. You're in there, scared as hell, and swearing that you ain't gonna do it again. Then you get out and be with your friends and act like it was nothing. You got to keep up that "I'm bad" image. Reputation is everything. To get a reputation, you gotta establish that you are crazy and will do anything. The more crazy you are, the less people will mess with you. Weird thing is that you start believing that you are really that person. You really start to believe the lie.

Every time I got out, though, being on parole, the police would come by and hassle me. They didn't need a warrant because I was still part of the system. Every time someone got killed, the police knew how to track you down, thinking you were involved. The fighting in Chinatown got worse, and then three bodies turned up dead underneath the bridge. That's when my cousin and I decided we were just going to stay out of it. We went back to school for a while. My cousin was working down in Chinatown, and he got into a hassle with some guys down there. They jumped him and cut his throat and arm. So he started

recruiting for his group. I was married by then and had a daughter. He didn't want me to get involved. But we always watched each other's back. He said, "If you went out there and got killed, I couldn't face my niece." He wouldn't even hear of me taking care of things from the outside. My cousin really got into it, and finally he got sent away for murder.

I started in the drug scene when I left home, so I was pretty young. The Disciples weren't into drugs, but the Rainmakers were into smoking weed. I started out sniffing glue. That was the thing. I later got into weed, then downers, sleeping pills, reds, yellows, and later, acid. The gangs weren't into using drugs. Neither of the gangs were into it at all. And the Disciples eventually said that no one was allowed to hang out when they were fucked up because business came first.

I saw myself moving into heavier stuff; I wanted to try everything. I just did it because I liked it. I just kept using like sleeping pills, then acid and mescaline, and THC. In my own eyes, it was okay because the doctors prescribed these. It wasn't shooting heroin. Heroin was a drug. I kept telling myself, I ain't no dope fiend or junkie. But eventually I did get into that.

My wife and I split up, and then I got really heavy into the heroin. In Chinatown, even though you don't hear a lot about druggies, most of them break away from everyone they know, so you don't see it. And if you don't see it, it ain't a problem, eh? I think they retreat somewhere else in the city because they don't want anyone to know. It's an embarrassment for them and for their families. You know, everyone seems to know everyone. So it's easier to disappear and no one sees anything.

I been in the drug thing for nearly twenty years, using and dealing, but never with the gang. I broke away and started hanging out in another district of town. Eventually it all came down on me, and I got shot four times because of a bad drug deal. That's when I hit rock bottom.

Johnny tried at several points during the 20 years of his use to get help with his drug problem. He found the first three attempts at treatment unsuccessful, due partly to what he perceived as a lack of appropriateness of the mainstream counseling and intervention strategies. In returning to his old neighborhood, he met an outreach worker and, after waiting several months, was able to get into a treatment program designed specifically to address the cultural issues and problems facing Asian Americans using illicit drugs.

Linda's Story

Linda's experience with drugs was quite different from Johnny's. I met her many years ago when I went to live in Hawaii for a summer. She was going through a difficult time then, trying to stay off the dope (on her own), recuperating from breast cancer surgery, and coping with her husband's death. She seemed to be constantly maneuvering through an endless number of life's roadblocks. Dope seemed to have a medicinal effect, helping her to cope with all of these obstacles.

She was born in Hong Kong and moved to Hawaii with her mother and stepfather when she was three-years-old. Her mother was from a wealthy merchant family in Peking. When the Communists took over, her family fled to Hong Kong through an underground network and lived in poverty with a distant cousin. Her mother was 16 and unmarried when she gave birth to Linda. Linda's natural father and his family decided that, given the mother's undesirability, marriage was out of the question. Linda's mother then met and mar-

ried an American, moved to Hawaii, and had another daughter and a son. They were on welfare for several years until the two younger children were old enough for school. Linda believes that her troubles began when her parents took on extra work to keep afloat on the margins of the working class:

Things started to change. I started to hang around the corner market where all the drug dealers were. I think it was because my parents started being home a lot less. Mom was working all the time. Dad was working two jobs, and I think he had somebody on the side as well. It was pretty much just me, alone, with my little sister and brother. We started hanging out, got to know the guys down there. It was better than staying home and watching TV. I was around 12. One of the first things those guys taught me was how to have an attitude. So, of course, I got into my first fight shortly thereafter.

It was with this blonde girl that was after my boyfriend. A little bimbo! I didn't want to fight, but everybody kept on telling me that I had to do it. So I did it, and I just totally beat the shit out of her. It was horrible. She ran off, and I remember her running down the street with only her panties on. Somehow I had taken off all her clothes, shoes, and everything. The cops came with her parents. Nothing happened, though, and the guys all were so proud of me. I felt shitty afterwards, and I went over to her house to apologize. We were friends two days later.

The guys were mostly selling weed and acid. No coke, though. They would grow it and then bring it on down to sell. They'd mostly sell joints and small bags to people passing by. A lot of them were cousins, all distantly related. My first joint was with my dad. Back then they used to have those little rolling machines, and my dad would have ounces of weed in his freezer. So we'd sit there eating ice cream and rolling joints and making bags.

My mom used to smoke dope. I remember watching her smoke dope and doing coke. She denies that she ever did coke. I remember watching her do a couple of lines. I didn't get on with my mom too well. She used to beat the shit out of me, bloody me up, bruise me, hack me with hangers and high heels. She used to drag me out by my hair and throw me down the stairs and shit. It was wild. When I was 13, we moved to the East Side, and that's when she started using chairs and lamps and sticks to beat me. She never hit my sister or brother. I think I probably ruined her life. She used to tell me that. She used to say, "Fuck, I hate you!" She hated me, I think, because I pretty much cramped her style. She was so young when she had me. Totally huge responsibility. She was like a party animal, and then I just cut the whole scene for her.

I remember the last time she beat me. I couldn't walk. She broke some stick on my back, and I was laid out for four or five days in bed. That was when my stepfather started sexually abusing me, for two years, on and off. He used to protect me from her as much as he could, but he was never at home. She never knew about the abuse.

I left home when I was 14. At first, I ran to my girlfriend's house for a couple of days. Then her parents took me home. The second time, I lived down in the central area for about six months. I had to get out of there. The abuse was physical, sexual, emotional. I knew I would be better off by myself. I used to live on the beach, met some guys down there and sold bogus weed. We'd do deals in hotels and rip people off. You know, I'd set people up, and we'd take the money and eat. We

just moved from one place to another.

Then one day we were at the pool hall and I met this guy. We stayed together for four and a half years. He was five years older than me. That's when I started doing heavy drugs. At first, I took acid. It was so smooth and so good. We used to sell it for our friend. Me and my boyfriend would take acid and stay up for days. When I met him, he was on methadone. We used to live at the pool hall. He made a lot of money, all illegal. Whatever money I made dealing drugs supplemented our income. We made a couple of thousand dollars a month in cash.

He turned me on to quaaludes, different kinds, Lemons and Rorers. We used to buy them in little Life Saver packet rolls with ten to a roll. I was doing this for months. Every day I'd take two or three in the morning, and when I started coming down, I'd pop a couple more. I really liked downs. I started doing reds, Darvons, and Percodans; whatever we could get, we'd do.

Occasionally I'd be picked up by the police for being a runaway. I'd go to the detention home, and from there I'd get farmed out to social agencies and placements. I'd go to the placement and then I'd stay there for a little while, then I'd run away. I'd always end up back at the pool hall. Sometimes I'd go back home when there was no other placement or the social worker said, "Well, you should try it." And I'd try it. This went on from 14 till I was 17. I'd always leave my mom, though. I always had a boyfriend to run to. When I started college, I went home periodically.

When I was around 16, my first boyfriend and I started doing coke. He taught me how to cook coke, smoke it. Later we were banging it. I shot cocaine for about eight months. I liked it. I entered a surfing contest and I kept on going to the bathroom to shoot up, and it's a good thing he was there. He dragged me out of the bathroom and beat the shit out of me right there in front of all my friends. That's when I quit. Because I knew I was totally fucking out of control.

I stopped smoking dope, too. I felt stupid when I smoked. I just was kind of unsociable, withdrawn. I couldn't think clearly. I wanted to eat, watch TV, and vegetate. I don't like just sitting still and not doing anything. If I'm gonna sit someplace, I'd like to be amping so I can think. Dope was boring.

Acid made me laugh. Acid was good. I was dealing that but stopped when I was 18. I was doing a lot of it and hanging out at the beach. One day, I was in the water. I was real high and punched somebody out in the water. Some guy dropped in on me [i.e., encroached on her space in the water], and I went over there and beat the shit out of him. Later on, the next day, I thought, "That's not really funny, that wasn't really too cool." I think that had a lot to do with me quitting acid. I just had sheets and sheets of the shit.

It got to the point back then that I wasn't making any money. You start off making money. Then you start doing it. Then you start turning people on, and you start doing more. Pretty soon, you're selling just to do it. Next thing, you wake up, and somebody's knocking at your door. They say, "Hey, you were suppose to give me so much money ten days ago. Where's the money? You have no money, you have no drugs."

I eventually dumped that boyfriend. I met somebody else. This other person was a real person. I was with him for two years. He smoked a lot of dope. I still don't smoke dope. We did a lot of coke. We lived together. He was probably the only person that was really supportive of my school. He was totally smart and would work with me.

Then we'd go out and party till the sun came up.

After I left him, I partied more and more. I got back into coke. I started working in a nightclub, and people would give me coke. I worked days, nights, and on call, so I was up a lot. When I wasn't working, I liked to dance. I had a lot of money and I had a lot of drugs.

After I quit working there, I continued using it, and then one night, I went to a dealer's house to pick up some coke. That's when I saw ICE. He said, "You guys want to try this?" We started feeling kinda crispy. It was good. There was no rush like coke; it just kept you up there for a long time. My friends and I went back and got some more of that. Then I started smoking it some, but mostly I stuck with coke. I liked the taste of it. I liked the rush. I liked the numbing effect. My gums and stuff. It would drip down the back of your throat.

I finally quit coke when I got pregnant; that was about three years ago. I quit too because I spent $15,000 on coke in one month. I married the guy; it was my mother's idea. I should have told her to marry him!

Linda and I became quite close that summer. When the fall came, however, she dropped out of sight. She'd call me about once a month to keep in touch. The calls and letters became less frequent. I hope she didn't start using again.

Discussion

We must ask ourselves now whether the stereotypes of Asian Americans bear any resemblance to the life experiences of Linda and Johnny. Neither of them fits the image of the model minority or the deviant stereotypes of mysterious foreign devils. Johnny did not fit the image of the slick, sophisticated immigrant gangster, but rather that of the young marginal male who is frustrated with a dense living environment and limited employment opportunities. This situation, combined with intense male peer pressure, was the setting in which Johnny grew up and tried to develop a sense of manhood. Linda also did not fit the stereotype of the submissive, weak, and alluring sex kitten. In fact, she showed an extremely strong and independent character in her attempts to leave a chaotic family situation where her mother abused her physically and emotionally and her stepfather sexually molested her. It was her stepfather who also first introduced her to dope. Her experiences clearly dispel the simplistic characterizations of the obedient and complacent Asian family, and instead illustrate the constraints and problems facing some families more generally.

Equally important, popular characterizations of Asian Americans do not go unrecognized, nor are they passively accepted. Johnny was not blind to the stereotypes of Asians as obedient, passive, and without social problems. He resisted these images and instead ironically used them to his advantage when dealing with the police and detention counselors. Linda was also aware of the problems with gender typing in her encounters with authorities when she ran away from home. The authorities—social workers, police, counselors—wanted her to end her "rebelliousness" and return home to her mother. Assumptions about her "character" and "femininity" rather than her family situation (i.e., physical and sexual abuse) became the basis for juvenile and family court decisions.

One final point merits our discussion. Johnny was also well aware of the implications of the Asian American stereotypes. As he rightly points out, when Asian Americans are portrayed and viewed by outsiders as having no social problems like unemployment, illicit drug use, crowded housing, and crime and delinquency, few efforts will be made to address the realities within their community. Moreover, as his experience illustrates, the Asian family and community can't solve the problems internally. The social workers with whom he interacted were unable to obtain external resources to develop any employment opportunities or programs.

We must question the complex ways in which stereotypes gain a reality inconsistent with the life experiences of people like Linda and Johnny. If we hide behind these stereotypes and do not address the real issues, then we are setting Linda and Johnny up for failure. Johnny was not able to stop using drugs until his fourth attempt. Perhaps he was finally ready to quit or perhaps getting into a treatment program designed specifically for Asian American drug users was the key to his success. We don't know. Linda's strong character may account for her quitting on her own, although it is unclear what she is doing now. Once we have set people like them up for failure, it is all too easy to dismiss them as evil.

References

Joe, Karen. (1994). "Myths and realities of Asian gangs on the West Coast." *Humanity and Society, 18,* 3–18.

Leung, J. (1987, November 3). "Chinese gangs' widening role in U.S. crime." *San Francisco Chronicle,* A8.

Thomas, W.I. (1928). *The child in America.* New York: Knopf.

U.S. Senate. (1991). *Hearing on Asian organized crime.* Hearing before the Permanent Subcommittee on Investigations of the Committee on Governmental Affairs, U.S. Senate, 102nd Congress, First Session, October 3, November 5–6. Washington, DC: U.S. Government Printing Office.

Discussion Questions

1. Discuss the significance of the title "Senator Sir, Meet Susie Wong and the Inscrutable Fu Manchu."

2. Compare and contrast the stereotypes of Asian American men and women.

3. Discuss W. I. Thomas' notion that "if men define their situations as real, then they are real in their consequences." Then examine the implications of this notion for public policy using a contemporary example.

4. Explain how Johnny's and Linda's experiences dispel current stereotypes of Asian Americans and how their experiences can specifically inform public policy.

5. If you were asked to design drug treatment programs appropriate for Johnny and Linda, what social and cultural factors would you need to consider? ◆

Chapter 15

Stereotyping by the Media

Framing Asian Americans

Thomas K. Nakayama

Asian Americans have long been concerned about the representations of Asians and Asian Americans in the media—an issue often overlooked by many non-Asian Americans. This concern stems largely from the apparent difficulty in distinguishing between Asians and Asian Americans. This confusion does not seem to arise in the case of Africans and African Americans or Europeans and European Americans. Yet, as the U.S. Civil Rights Commission observes: "The distinctions between citizens of Asian nations and citizens or intending citizens of the United States who happen to be of Asian ancestry have remained largely unarticulated by the media" (1992, p. 181). The conflation of Asians and Asian Americans raises particularly important concerns because of the historical patterns of discrimination that resulted from those misunderstandings.

One of the historical foundations for this concern emerges from the experience of Japanese Americans, who, during World War II, were seen as Japanese, not Japanese Americans. This confusion led to their internment in concentration camps. They were not charged with any crimes, nor were their rights of due process recognized. My own parents and grandparents were neither charged with any crimes nor given a trial to determine any wrongdoing. Yet, they lost considerable property, as well as civil rights guaranteed by the U.S. Constitution. This experience marked my parents in significant ways and perhaps fuels other Asian American concerns with media representations of Asians and Asian Americans. After all, my parents would tell me, it is *not* the U.S. Constitution that guarantees rights to U.S. citizens; it is the perceptions and beliefs of the American people. Having U.S. citizenship did not guarantee their rights or their property. These are things that can always be taken away, despite constitutional guarantees. The powerful media stories of that period played into and often reinforced anti-Japanese fears, particularly in California.

But this historical memory is not the only reason for continuing concern about media images of Asians and Asian Americans. We live in a society in which hate crimes against Asian Americans and Asians are increasing. This violent context forms an important backdrop against which we must read these media images. We do not live in a society that is race blind. Hate-based violence against Asians and Asian Americans is based largely on appearance. For example, the suspected murder of Thien Minh Ly, a Vietnamese American, appears to be racially motivated: "The words, 'Oh I killed a Jap . . .' were found in a letter penned by Lindberg [the alleged murderer] to a friend, along with a gory blow-by-blow account of the murder" (Hasegawa, 1996, p. 3). Distinctions between various Asian and Asian American groups is largely irrelevant, as is nationality (citizens or not), in these racially motivated crimes.

It is this fear of what other people might do that motivates much of the concern about negative media images of

Asians and Asian Americans. *Year of the Dragon* and *Rising Sun* are just two of several recent movies that have led to protests because they reinforce stereotypes of Asians while insidiously redefining other groups of Americans as *not* Asian Americans. Both of these movies, along with the Broadway musical *Miss Saigon*, have demonstrated the continuing need for careful scrutiny of how Asians and Asian Americans are portrayed by the media. We cannot view and understand media images outside of the social contexts in which they function; that is, media images are given their power and meaning in relationship to everything else that occurs in a given society.

In this chapter, I will introduce two stereotypes about Asian Americans in the media, particularly as they relate to issues of crime. It is only by knowing the social context in which these stereotypes function that we can begin to understand the concerns and debates over media images.

Asian Images

It is difficult to understand the media images of Asian Americans without being attentive to the historical construction of Asian images. Europeans have long discussed, thought about, and constructed stereotypic images of "Orientals" and "Asiatics." In part, these images were based upon the information available at the time and upon the projection of European cultural anxieties onto these "others." For example, stories about "deviant" sexual activities, particularly homosexuality, are projected onto these others as a way of deflecting deep European cultural anxieties.

The development of this entire system of thinking about "Orientals" led to an ideological system known as "Orientalism." Orientalism, as discussed by Edward Said (1978), took a different direction in Europe than in the United States. In Europe, he notes, one is more likely to think of the Near East or Middle East, whereas in the United States, one is more likely to think of the Far East in reference to the Orient. Of course, "Near," "Middle," and "Far" East arc near, middle, and far from a European-centered way of thinking about the world.

In the United States, these cultural differences were not simply interesting, but rather threatening and problematic for the dominant Anglo Americans. Dennis Ogawa notes that "Anglo-Americans have been notorious for their illtreatment of non-Anglos. The American Indian, the Catholic, the Irish, the Negro, the Mexican, the Spanish, the East European have all felt the heavy hand of Anglo discrimination and stereotyping" (1971, p. 8). He continues by noting that Japanese have not been exempt from this process. Difference, then, has tended to be considered threatening and negative. The use of these stereotypes has instilled a particular way of viewing the world and dealing with racial and ethnic differences.

The ways that difference is deployed in media representations largely depends upon the meaning it conveys (Neale, 1979). Storytelling and narration are predicated upon the notion of "difference." It is vital to narration that difference exists, as difference is a driving force for narration. In the case of many narratives, the difference can be gender, in which the male and female characters see things differently and act accordingly. For example, in the film *The Bridges of Madison County*, the gender difference drives the narrative. We understand the love story because we understand the heterosexual gender relations at work.

In narratives involving race, difference must be constructed in such a way that it appears substantial and concrete. If everyone were "just people," it would be difficult—if not impossible—to have movement in the narrative. Often differences among characters help us to understand the driving force in the narrative; for example, someone is the "good guy" or the hero and someone else is the "bad guy" or the villain. Narrative demands difference, and it is this that makes nervous those who are constructed as different. The other, that group that is constructed as different, is an ideological construction (O'Barr, 1994). Not only do these differences then communicate particular meanings, but they also help us make sense, common sense, out of the ways we are asked to view the world and others.

Within the context of media images, the representations of Asians far overwhelm the images of Asian Americans. Rarely do we see media images of Asian Americans. Exceptions such as *All-American Girl*, starring Margaret Cho, have not long survived on the screen. Within the U.S., the notion that "they all look alike" has led to the creation of an Asian "other" or orientalism, as discussed previously.

Orientalism in the United States led to strict laws and debates governing the lives of Asians and Asian Americans. In the nineteenth century, tremendous concern over immigration issues and settlement patterns led to the passage of exclusionary laws in many places. Chinese, for example, were restricted to living in a particular part of San Francisco that came to be known as Chinatown. Other cities and towns in the United States did not allow Chinese to live within the city limits at all. In the twentieth century, the spread of "yellow peril" propaganda created enormous anti-Asian sentiment that led to numerous legal and social restrictions. The media were major players in this propaganda effort.

These images of Asians were sometimes specific to particular subgroups; at other times, they were generalized. Fears about the impossibility of Asians integrating into U.S. society formed much of the rhetorical discourse leading to severe restrictions on immigration, land ownership, naturalization, and interracial marriage. Today these discourses have changed, although some of the older forms of orientalism remain and others lie dormant, with the potential to return. Next, I highlight two of the dominant themes of contemporary orientalism—the construction of differing sexualities and the rise of the model minority.

Sexual Stereotypes

Asian sexuality has a long history of deforming constructions in the media and in U.S. society at large. In the context of tremendous fears of Asian immigration, Asian domination, and Asian intermarriage with Euro-Americans, a number of states and the U.S. government passed laws restricting immigration from Asian nations and land ownership by Asians, as well as miscegenation laws (laws restricting interracial marriage). Through the Hays Code, Hollywood, too, forbade images of interracial sexual relations or romance. Filmmakers were able to sidestep some of these regulations by casting white actors in "yellowface." Earlier fears of Asians as sexual demons have given way to more "domesticated" images of Asians as either asexual eunuchs or sexually available for white pleasure.

In D. W. Griffith's 1919 movie *Broken Blossoms*, an asexual Chinese male tries (unsuccessfully) to save and protect a brutalized white female. Julia Lesage speculates: "Perhaps reacting against the charges of racism which *Birth of a Nation* had provoked, Griffith clearly wanted *Broken Blossoms* to be considered anti-racist" (1981, p. 54). In the context of intense anti-Asian attitudes in the United States at that time, with its attendant fears of a yellow peril and miscegenation, Griffith's film may indeed be seen to challenge racist attitudes. Yet, as Lesage notes, we see "the Chinese man as being in many ways not fully a man, but as woman-like" (1981, p. 52). "[T]he Chinese man seems to elicit from the audience a common social accusation: that of effeminacy. [That] is, time and time again, the viewer seems led to conclude, 'That's an effeminate man—or effeminate gesture, or article of clothing, etc.' The young Asian man's robe is excessively ornate; in the exterior shots, its shirts conspicuously blow in the wind. It is shapeless, making the shape beneath it androgynous in form" (Lesage, 1981, p. 52). Through their many cinematic conventions, the media inadvertently remind us that images are simultaneously racialized and gendered. Here antiracism apparently requires a masculine white male and an effeminate Asian male. Whatever Griffith's intentions, the development of distorting sexual stereotypes of Asians and Asian Americans has continued unabated despite a shifting social context.

By now, the asexual Asian male has become a staple of media stereotyping. The continual effeminate construction of Asian masculinity is reflected in films such as *Sixteen Candles,* in which there is nothing sexually attractive about Long Duck Dong. He simply plays the Asian fool. The romantic, desired male is, of course, white. In other films and in television shows as well, Asian masculinity is devalued and generally effeminate or asexual.

For example, *Showdown in Little Tokyo* is a Hollywood movie that typifies the martial arts genre in many ways. This story concerns two Los Angeles Police Department officers who rid the Lit-

tle Tokyo district of Los Angeles of Japanese criminals. The white male hero, Detective Kenner, played by Dolph Lundgren, is portrayed as far more masculine, serious, stern, and in charge than his comedic sidekick, a biracial Asian American, played by Brandon Lee. The narrative begins with Kenner, and it is through him that "the narrative unfolds. Central to the functioning of racial and sexual difference, then, is Kenner's focal position" (Nakayama, 1994, p. 167). It is Kenner, the white male hero, who eventually gets the girl and kills the evil Asian nemesis, Yoshida.

Conversely, the overly sexual Asian female is stereotyped in stark contrast. Driven by differing historical forces, such as the deployment of U.S. military men to Asia during various wars and police actions, the Asian woman is stereotyped as erotic and exotic, submissive, and a good wife. These well-known stereotypes have led to "the Caucasian male's irrefutable preference for Asian women" (Chan, 1990, p. 1). The development of an elaborate mail-order business that helps white men meet Asian women points to the prominent place this cultural image holds in the United States (Halualani, 1995). The sexuality of Asian women is clearly marked as different from that of white U.S. women. As Peter Feng (1996, p. 27) observes: "In the American popular imagination, Asian women are depicted as ultrafeminine sexual objects for white men, and that sexual formula leaves Asian men literally out of the picture."

Asians and Asian Americans, like whites and humans in general, exhibit sexual characteristics that span the diversity of sexualities. From heterosexual to gay or lesbian, from single to married/partnered, Asians and Asian Americans are not reducible to any one sexual category. The questions we must ask, however, are: What would drive the media construction of such odd stereotypes? Whose interests are served by these deformed media images? Who benefits from thinking about Asians and Asian Americans in these ways? The ideological constructions surrounding Asian male and female sexuality appear to serve the needs of white heterosexual masculinity quite easily by decreasing masculine competition and threats from Asian males while making Asian females desirable.

More recently, we have seen the return of the earlier image of the sexually perverse Asian. *Rising Sun* constructs an overly sexualized Japanese masculinity. These images are not new but were utilized 100 years ago to justify differing social and legal needs. Within *Rising Sun*, Nguyen notes: "They [the Japanese characters] are sexist, treating their white women like chattels, objects of such exotic practices as sex by asphyxiation and sushi on a naked body. (They even have a boudoir behind the sliding door of the huge conference room and a private bordello full of Anglo-Saxon looking women). Sex maniacs, all of them, is what one is inclined to think" (1993, p. 3).

The return to these stereotypical images from the late nineteenth and early twentieth centuries calls for an examination of the similarities between the contemporary period and the racial politics of 100 years ago. Fears about Japanese—and Asian more generally—masculine sexuality were drawn on to justify fears of rape and interracial marriage.

The Model Minority

A more recent media stereotype has emerged that constructs Asian Americans as a "model minority." The emergence in the 1960s of Asian Americans as an idealized minority group departs significantly from earlier, fiercely nega-tive stereotypes of Asian Americans. One of the major media moguls of the era, William Randolph Hearst, utilized the media to spread racist imagery: "Motion pictures, as well as the printed word, were used by Hearst to preach the yellow peril gospel" (Daniels, 1962, p. 76; see also Miller, 1969; Ogawa, 1971; Takaki, 1985).

In an earlier study (Nakayama, 1988) that I conducted on the model minority discourses in the media, I was struck by the sudden emergence of this seemingly new stereotype. Given the persistence of earlier stereotypes, I wondered what might be driving this new image. The answer, I concluded, lay less in the situation of Asian Americans and more in the context of increasing critiques of the status quo in light of the U.S. civil rights movement. What I found most unsettling was the use of Asian Americans to defend the "unbiased" character of U.S. social institutions such as the educational system.

The rise of the model minority stereotype, in which Asian Americans are viewed as harder-working and smarter than other minorities, coincides neatly with fears and concerns raised by the civil rights movement. This movement challenged many of the deeply held ideological assumptions about U.S. society, including notions of freedom and equality. The construction of the model minority was not promulgated or constructed by or for Asian Americans. It is a media image that offers a comforting vision of the United States as a country in which anyone who is willing to work hard can succeed. For example, in the midst of the civil rights movement, *U.S. News and World Report* wrote that "At a time when it is being proposed that hundreds of billions be spent to uplift Negroes and other minorities, the nation's 300,000 Chinese-Americans are moving ahead on their own—with no help from any-one else" (1966, p. 73).

The construction of this media stereotype, which often focuses on the Confucian ethic, strong Asian families, and hard work, tends to deflect attention away from the social and structural constraints that lead to inequality in the United States. Focusing on the characteristics of Asian Americans allowed the media to ignore the multiple and complex ways in which U.S. society was segregated, by law and by custom, during this period. During the 1960s, for example, Asian Americans in California did not face quite the same barriers as African Americans in the South. Although an in-depth analysis of these differing experiences would be helpful in understanding the civil rights movement, as well as provide deeper insight into the ways that these experiences have stratified racial and ethnic groups in U.S. society, that discussion has been deferred in favor of invoking an idealized stereotype of Asian Americans.

We should also note that these practices tend to create and reinforce the notion that the contemporary system is based upon merit. That is, it is a meritocracy in which those who are more meritorious (more intelligent, harder-working, more athletic, etc.) are rewarded. From this perspective, people earn (or don't earn) what they deserve. As one response to the U.S. civil rights movement, invoking Asian American experiences seems convenient indeed, particularly as they are now represented as an integral part of U.S. society.

As we have seen from our analysis of the sexual stereotypes of Asians and Asian Americans, these media representations are not innocent. We must again ask: Whose interests are served by these images? In what ways do they continue to reinforce the status quo? How might dominant groups benefit from this deflection of attention away from

the existent social structure? At this point, I again speculate that the powerful ideologies behind these images continue to serve the interests of white Americans whose families, work ethic, and cultural beliefs do not come under media scrutiny in these discussions. They remain the hidden beneficiaries of these comparisons of African American and Latina/o experiences against Asian American experiences.

Alternatives

Resistance to distorting and negative images led to the creation of the watchdog organization Media Action Network for Asian Americans (MANAA) in 1992. MANAA is charged with monitoring and changing media representations of Asians and Asian Americans, protesting mainstream media images, and developing alternative, independent media productions. Richard Fung notes:

> Given the historical misrepresentations of mainstream media, I am not surprised that most independent films and videotapes produced by North American men and women of Asian descent seek redress from white supremacy. They perform the important tasks of correcting histories, voicing common but seldom represented experiences, engaging audiences used to being spoken about but never addressed, and actively constructing a politics of resistance to racism. (Fung, 1994, p. 165)

Similarly, Queer New Wave Asian American filmmaker Gregg Araki argues: "There is a genuine need for the under- and misrepresented to identify themselves via the cinema machine. The world really doesn't need any more wannabe hack Hollywood directors" (1991, p. 69).

For example, Asian American director Steven Okazaki uses film to counter some of the powerful ideologies perpetuated by the mainstream media. In his recent film *American Sons,* he utilizes a documentary format to portray four Asian American men who resist and speak out against the exhausted stereotypes of Asian masculinity. Peter Feng notes: "Ironically, *American Sons* may have done too good a job of redefining Asian American masculinity. Many fans of popular Asian American media may not recognize these men!" (1996, p. 29). By ending with real-life stories of anti-Asian hate crimes, Okazaki draws a clear connection between these distorting media images and the everyday realities of life in the United States.

Richard Fung raises serious questions about the possibility of an alternative system, yet makes a passionate call for one:

I do not think that it is possible to create innocent images of Asians either; to ignore the overbearing history of Hollywood and of television, we must somehow learn to place ourselves at the centre of our own cultural practice, and not at the margins. (Re)creating ourselves in our own terms requires constant re-evaluation of the master narratives that have bracketed our lives. For this we need to understand the history and language of images, we must grasp this language and make it our own. (Fung, 1991, p. 67)

The tremendous weight of these media representations makes resistance to them a difficult task. There is never an easy escape from history.

Outlook

As I noted at the outset of this essay, the primary crime issue facing Asian Americans that is tied to the media is hate crimes. Hate crimes and other types of discrimination reflect the deep racial problems facing this country. Hamamoto (1994) reminds us:

Hate crimes are usually explained away by government officials as acts committed by misguided individuals rather than as being symptomatic of deep racial divisions that have been exacerbated over the phony battle against black and Hispanic "drug lords," Japan bashing by certain politicians and high-profile corporate executives such as Chrysler CEO Lino "Lee" Iacocca, and the manifest anti-Arab racism of the Persian Gulf War. These are all signals to a dispossessed, alienated white working class and a large segment of the financially faltering middle class that it is open season on people of color. (Hamamoto, p. 167)

The recent controversy over the images perpetrated by the Broadway musical *Miss Saigon* exemplifies how these sexual and racial politics set the stage for increasing hate crimes. Asian American activist Yoko Yoshikawa notes:

"Miss Saigon" is yet another name to add to the roster of pop culture stereotypes: Suzy Wong, Charlie Chan, Fu Manchu, "Chink," and "Gook." *Miss Saigon* contributes to an entrenched system of racist and sexist images that straitjackets relationships between Asians and Westerners. This system is backdrop to increasing incidents of violence against Asians and Asian Americans across the United States, and paves the way for exploitation in massage parlors, mail-order bride business, and Asia-based tourist industries where women, children, and sometimes men are sold as commodities. (1994, p. 280)

Narrow, limiting stereotypes do not offer us much room to maneuver our interpretations of media images of Asians or Asian Americans. These images only have meaning against the backdrop of history. While the alternative film and video producers are challenging these stereotypes and ways of "reading" images of Asians and Asian Americans, other challenges are also being mounted. As I have noted, activist groups have taken on the mainstream media and protested against the continued use of stereotypical images. Taken together, these two approaches offer some new ways of thinking about racialized media stereotypes.

Set within the context of a shifting global economy, the changes in media images of Asians and, increasingly, Asian Americans will be encouraged by increasing markets in Asia and international trade. As O'Barr speculates:

> Perhaps one of the consequences of the globalization of markets, the increase in the availability of the same goods and services around the world, and the emergence of generic consumers who are portrayed as sharing common desires will be a decrease in the otherness of foreigners. A Japanese girl drinking a Coke has a lot in common with a French or Brazilian girl drinking a Coke. . . . But in speculating about what more advertisements of this sort might mean, we should not assume too quickly that otherness will disappear. (1994, p. 200)

Given these economic pressures and incentives, the configurations or stereotypes of others will have to shift rather than disappear. In order to facilitate international marketing, the older, more traditional stereotypes of Asians must be eliminated to help market goods to Asians. And as a fast-growing group, the Asian American population is going to demand new images to sell products.

Yet it would be a mistake to use such a narrow lens in looking to the future. Increasing trade tensions with Japan, debates over most favored nation status with China, and other U.S.-Asian tensions only exacerbate the stereotypical views perpetrated by the media to "help" us understand Asia. Within these international conflicts, Asian Americans have historically been victimized, and it is this concern that drives the activism and anger directed against the stereotypes of Asians. When they serve particular ideological interests, Asian Americans are easily represented as Asians; at other times, with other ideological agendas, they are just as easily configured as model Americans. Without seeing any end in sight to the U.S.–Asia international tensions—tensions that are not often played out against Britain, France, and other Western European nations—it is difficult to envision an end to the persistent use of these stereotypes in the U.S. media.

References

Araki, Gregg. (1991). "The (sorry) state of (independent) things." In Russell Leong (Ed.), *Moving the image: Independent Asian Pacific media arts.* Los Angeles: UCLA Asian American Studies Center and Visual Communications, Southern California Asian American Studies Central, Inc., 68–70.

Chan, Melissa. (1990, December 19). "Gentlemen prefer Asians: Why some Anglos are only attracted to Asian women." *The Rafu Shimpo (1)*, 3.

Daniels, Roger.(1962). *The politics of prejudice.* Berkeley: University of California Press.

Feng, Peter. (1996). "Redefining Asian American masculinity: Steven Okazaki's 'American sons.'" *Cineaste*, 22 (3), 27–29.

Fung, Richard. (1996). "Looking for my penis: The eroticized Asian in gay video porn." In Russell Leong (Ed.), *Asian American sexualities: Dimensions of the gay and lesbian experience.* New York: Routledge, 181–198.

———. (1994). "Seeing yellow: Asian identities in film and video." In Karin Aguilar-San Juan (Ed), *The state of Asian America: Activism and resistance in the*

1990s. Boston: South End Press, 161–171.

Hamamoto, Darrell Y. (1994). *Monitored peril: Asian Americans and the politics of TV representation*. Minneapolis: University of Minnesota Press.

Halualani, Rona. (1995). "The intersecting hegemonic discourses of an Asian mail-order bride catalog: Pilipina 'oriental butterfly dolls' for sale." *Women's Studies in Communication, 18* (1), 45–64.

Hasegawa, Lisa. (1996, April 23). "The murder of Thien Minh Ly." *The Rafu Shimpo*, 3.

Lesage, Julia. (1981). "Broken blossoms: Artful racism, artful rape." *Jump Cut, 26*, 51–55.

Miller, Stuart Creighton. (1969). *The unwelcome immigrant*. Berkeley: University of California Press.

Nakayama, Thomas K. (1994). "Show/down time: 'Race,' gender, sexuality in U.S. popular culture." *Critical Studies in Mass Communication, 11* (3), 162–179.

——. (1988). "'Model minority' and the media: Discourse on Asian America." *Journal of Communication Inquiry, 12* (1), 65–73.

Neale, Steve. (1979). "The same old story: Stereotypes and difference." *Screen Education, 32* (33), 33–37.

Nguyen, Lan. (1993, July 1). "'Rising Sun' presents damaging portrayal of Japanese, Asians." *The Rafu Shimpo*, 3.

O'Barr, William M. (1994). *Culture and the ad: Exploring otherness in the world of advertising*. Boulder, CO: Westview Press.

Ogawa, Dennis M. (1971). *From Japs to Japanese: The evolution of Japanese-American stereotypes*. Berkeley, CA: McCutchan.

Payne, Robert M. (1996). "Total eclipse of the SUN." *Jump Cut, 40*, 29–37.

Said, Edward W. (1978). *Orientalism*. New York: Random House.

Takaki, Ronald T. (1985). *Iron cages*. Seattle: University of Washington Press.

U.S. Civil Rights Commission. (1992). *Civil rights issues facing Asian Americans in the 1990s*. Washington, DC: United States Government Printing Office.

U.S. News & World Report. (1966, December 26). "Success story of one minority group in U.S." 73–76.

Yoshikawa, Yoko. (1994). "The heat is on Miss Saigon coalition: Organizing across race and sexuality." In Karin Aguilar-San Juan (Ed.), *The state of Asian America: Activism and resistance in the 1990s*. Boston: South End Press, 275–294.

Discussion Questions

1. What are some of the contemporary social forces that influence the media stereotyping of Asians and Asian Americans?

2. What images come to mind when you think about Asian sexuality?

3. What movies or television shows can you think of that portray Asians in nonstereotypical ways?

4. What other stereotypes of Asians and Asian Americans are you familiar with?

5. Do you think that stereotypes of Asians and Asian Americans will change in the next 50 years? In what ways? Why or why not? ✦

Chapter 16

Stereotyping by Politicians

Asian Americans and the Black-White Paradigms

Bong Hwan Kim

Conservatives like to use their stereotypic views of Asian Americans as hardworking people who don't complain about what's due them but put their noses to the grindstone and earn their share of the American dream. A leading Republican state assemblyman in California once told me that he was so proud of the way Koreans have pulled themselves up by their bootstraps, sending their children to college, and starting businesses. I couldn't help but read between the lines of his statement—Korean Americans don't need any assistance from the government. But another message is also implicit—that if only more blacks and Latinos could learn from the "model minority," they would be much better off. This extremely paternalistic attitude toward Asian Americans is based more on "their" worldview or political/policy-making agenda than on any real concern for the welfare of our community or awareness of the real challenges we have faced and the successes we have achieved—as we perceive them. Asian Americans have become a useful tool

for the rhetoric of the right, asserting that America is about rewarding individual hard work, strong "family values," and God-fearing Christians as the foundation upon which this nation was built and to which we must return.

Asian Americans as a Wedge Between Whites and People of Color

This stereotypical view of Asian Americans, combined with their relatively weak political clout, makes it easy to use them as examples of minorities who achieved the American dream without any handouts and to justify cutting more government assistance to blacks and Latinos. That Asian Americans have succeeded in education and business is true, but it is also true that they made inroads despite the many institutionalized social, economic, and political barriers erected in this country against people of color. Moreover, Asian Americans from middle-class professional backgrounds in their native countries are the ones achieving academically. Completely invisible to the mainstream are the high rates of poverty among many Asian immigrants and refugees dependent on the federal welfare support system. For example, 40 percent of Vietnamese and Cambodian families are welfare-dependent and have large numbers of youth gangs that the Los Angeles Police Department considers to be among the most violent in the city. Sixty percent of the Mien community, a nonliterate nomadic mountain tribe from Vietnam who were recruited to assist the Central Intelligence Agency during the Vietnam War, are welfare-dependent.

Conservatives view American history in ways that justify their public policy approaches to solving today's most visible social problems such as crime, poverty, and unemployment. The majority of Asian Americans today are foreign-born, having immigrated after the passage of the 1965 *Immigration Act.* Most are unaware of the history of the civil rights movement and the long history of struggle of people of color fighting for their rightful place as equal Americans in this country. Most entered the United States after the civil rights movement and thus have little to no understanding of the tremendous impact that era had in shaping the policies, laws, and institutions that are in place today. Most also come from relatively homogeneous societies, so they are unaware of the powerful social dynamics among majority whites and minorities. Moreover, many don't view themselves as Asian Americans but rather as Vietnamese, Cambodian, Korean, and so forth, which presents unique challenges to organizing political leverage. Aside from the more established Asian American communities (Chinese/Japanese American), most recent immigrants remain isolated in their own ethnic-specific enclaves.

Asian-Pacific communities in large urban cities are geographically dispersed, fragmented islands. Limited in their ability to engage in mainstream civic life by language and cultural barriers, many turn their attention inward and seek to isolate themselves within their own enclaves. These communities easily fall prey to aggressive and exploitive fund-raising strategies of politicians. As one colleague noted, Asian Americans are viewed by many politicians as ATM machines. City councilmen, state senators, and other politicians think they can just flash their business cards and the money will follow, with no more effort than it takes to put their bank cards in an automatic teller machine.

In my own experience, Koreatown becomes a parade for politicians from all levels of government in election years. Most are never heard from again. The city councilman for Koreatown in Los Angeles, an African American, has become very proficient in tapping Korean American dollars. This practice is also widely known and apparently condoned in the African American community (which comprises the majority of this district) because he's managed to hold office for three successive terms. In private discussions about the need for more effective representation of Korean American concerns at City Hall, he would reply that I need not worry because he would take care of our "people." And furthermore, he felt Korean Americans were not appreciative enough of all that he had done for them. This paternalistic attitude is very similar to the attitudes of white Republican conservative politicians described previously. It is estimated that Korean Americans have donated over half of his campaign war chest. Many take it for granted that politicians know what they are doing and that they wouldn't have been elected had they not been responsible people. A naive attitude, maybe, but one must also keep in mind that Asian Americans have the highest percentage of self-employment among all ethnic groups—mostly in small mom-and-pop-type family-run businesses. They are very preoccupied with daily economic survival issues, compounded by language and cultural barriers, which keep them from participating more fully in the civic and political life of this country.

Tapping Asian Americans for their money has brought our communities to the attention of the mass media and government reformers. John Huang was a highly placed player in the Democratic National Committee (DNC) charged with raising money in the Asian American communities.[1] He was involved in the most sensational controversy of the

1996 presidential election when the media seized upon the fact that large donations had come from a foreign-owned Indonesian conglomerate (his former employer before joining the DNC). The partisan political brouhaha and media frenzy triggered by this controversy again lumped Asians and Asian Americans in the same pot, painting us as the stereotypical yellow horde of evil foreigners scheming to gain favors with President Clinton. *Newsweek*'s cover of John Riady, CEO of Lippo Bank, where John Huang worked before taking a position with the Clinton Administration, evokes strong stereotyped images of Asians as evil, unscrupulous agents poised to corrupt alleged Western integrity.

The stereotypic Asian face evokes powerful images in the collective memory of America—Pearl Harbor, lynchings of Chinese railroad workers, Japan bashing, and the South Korean rice scandals, to name just a few. Such focused, sensationalized coverage using powerful racist images grabs the attention of readers, further reinforcing the secret fears of many white Americans that Asians are evil geniuses scheming to overtake them. While racist images are being reinforced, attention is being diverted from the ultrarich multinational companies that have much greater influence over elected officials and public policies. The total amount of money raised by John Huang is a drop in the bucket compared to the feeding troughs of both Democratic and Republican politicians. These have been fed for years by powerful multinational corporations as well as other foreign governments. What the media have seized upon, as they always have done, is a means of capturing the interest of their readers through the lens of race. This adds a different flavor to the humdrum problem of campaign-finance reform. Campaign financing improprieties and violations must be pursued, but singling out Asian Americans and lumping them with overseas Asians is typical of the racist treatment Asian Americans have had to endure for centuries in this country.

Black-Korean Relations

My closest interactions with the African American political and community leadership occurred in the aftermath of the death of Latasha Harlins—a 16-year-old African American girl shot and killed by a Korean American merchant, Ms. Soon Ja Du. The modern version of the recurring racist stereotype of the yellow peril has become one of greedy, gun-toting merchants preying on poor, vulnerable African Americans. During the height of black-Korean tensions in Los Angeles, many Chinese and Japanese American colleagues from other cities told me that they were now being mistaken for Korean. The ramification is that many Asian Americans are seen in this image as rude store owners who can't get along with black folk.

The tragedy of a young girl's death was effectively exploited by some opportunistic African American politicians in their reelection campaigns. They saw this as a way of gaining more visibility for themselves among black voters. One slogan appearing on campaign literature in a county supervisor race—"our community will not be sold out for a $1.79 bottle of orange juice"— referred to the *Los Angeles Times'* description of the incident.

The controversy significantly heightened resentment and hostility against Korean American merchants, ultimately involving the entire community. The overwhelming sense was that Korean American communities were being unfairly scapegoated for the unfortunate act of one individual. But it was clear from the tone, rhetoric, and message of some of the most vocal and divisive black community leaders that

Korean Americans were depriving African Americans of economic opportunities by operating stores in their neighborhoods without hiring local residents or contributing their profits to their customers. This made little sense to a largely immigrant community who understood that America was the land of opportunity and that business was about meeting a demand for goods and services—all you had to do was go for it. In other words, immigrant communities had no understanding of why so many African Americans felt as strongly as they did about perceptions of mistreatment and prejudice. In turn, many African Americans viewed Korean Americans as foreigners sent here in cahoots with the American and South Korean governments to keep the African American community from making economic gains.

Then-Mayor Tom Bradley, the first African American mayor of a major urban city, showed some concern for the issues being raised by Korean American leaders. However, he failed to engage the African American leadership in developing constructive approaches to resolve the controversy. In the end, and throughout the series of controversies, the conflict was not about race or ethnicity. The real source of conflict was political power and access to determine which issues were to be dealt with and how and which concerns were to be ignored. If the store owner had been Latino or Jewish, the political dynamics in the aftermath would have been handled in a much more balanced and accountable manner because both Jews and Latinos had political clout which assured that their concerns were weighed in along with the concerns of African Americans. The political impotence of Korean Americans left them completely vulnerable to the political whim of those who had access. Bradley was very cognizant of the criticism that he had spent much of his political capital developing a downtown skyline at the expense of the poorest, most disenfranchised areas of South Los Angeles—an area that is largely Latino but regarded as the political turf of African Americans.

Another case involved the shooting death of an African American customer attempting to rob a store owned by a Korean American. The Los Angeles Police Department's (LAPD's) investigation determined that this was a justified homicide. This incident, however, occurred a few months after the first airing of the Rodney King beating, which had dropped the credibility of the LAPD (particularly in much of the African American community) to an all-time low. A high-profile boycott of Korean American small businesses resulted. A deal was cut whereby African Americans received concessions in exchange for calling off the boycott.[2] This deal was cut over the objections and behind the backs of those of us involved in the negotiations to that point because we viewed it as a form of extortion to pay off the boycotters (in exchange for ending the boycott) when the merchant was attempting to defend himself from being robbed. The deal left Korean Americans with nothing, as it failed to recognize the right of store owners to conduct business in safety wherever they chose. Merchants' rights were being swept away under the tidal wave of widespread resentment against Korean American store owners. This fueled the frustrations of many Korean Americans, who pointed to the dozens of merchants shot and/or killed in their stores since the early 1980s.[3]

These events preceded the Los Angeles civil unrest by two years. The tragic timing of the Latasha Harlins incident, followed by the Rodney King videotaped beating approximately one year later, would frame an image of rude Korean American store owners along with abusive police officers and the institutionalized racism of the criminal justice system in the minds of many African Americans. Extreme resentment and overt hostility arose; many blacks felt that, in addition to the risk of being assaulted by the police, they were being treated badly at their corner grocery store.

The controversy surrounding rebuilding of liquor stores burned down during the 1992 civil unrest provided yet another opportunity to lay the blame for excessive crime, joblessness, and drug/alcohol addiction on Korean American merchants. The civil unrest, which resulted in 54 deaths and over $1 billion in economic damage, was unleashed when the four white police officers involved in the brutal beating of Rodney King were acquitted of all charges. Korean American stores were heavily targeted, sustaining over 40 percent of the total damage, even though Korean Americans made up less than 1 percent of the city of Los Angeles.

Frustration because the rights of Korean American merchants were being ignored for political expediency was widespread. I was criticized for leading a compromise effort. The criticism was that I gave the African American political leadership an easy out—not having to offer assistance to riot victims—by forging a compromise that supported local zoning controls but also calling for assistance to merchants who, through no fault of their own, lost their sole source of livelihood. Looking back, I feel it was the right tack to take. The Korean American leadership was extremely divided and disorganized but, most important, it lacked political clout. There was nothing to lose by attempting to work out a consensus position that, it was hoped, would create some room for politicians and government agency staff—many of whom were sympathetic to the plight of small-business victims—to begin developing some concrete forms of assistance.

The scapegoating of Korean American store owners (and, by extension, the Korean American community) was so strong that African American leaders had little choice but to voice these frustrations to the larger public, using the occasion as an opportunity to bring attention to the ongoing neglect of the poor and disenfranchised. Progressive leaders of established African American civil rights organizations confided to those of us seeking constructive alternatives that the black-Korean conflict was not high on their prioritization of issues. Viewed strategically, there was little political capital to be gained from engaging in such an emotionally charged and "media-cized" debate. Having no political clout, Korean Americans had nothing to "put on the table." The best that progressive leaders could do was to be silent on the issue lest they be branded as sellouts. More political capital could be gained through conflict because, unlike mediation and reconciliation efforts, it *never* failed to receive widespread media coverage. For better or worse, conflict kept the issue of poor, disenfranchised African Americans in the public consciousness. Unfortunately, it was at the expense of Korean Americans and, by extension, Asian Americans. Recognizing the potential for political gains, opportunists actively engaged in and supported organized efforts lending visibility to these issues. Korean Americans became the new villains who had to be purged from their community if black economic development was to be realized. African American politicians at all levels of government made little, if any, effort to reach out to community leaders to communicate mutual concerns or to attempt any constructive solutions. A well-known African American congresswoman representing South Los Angeles, appearing before a community rally organizing support for the recall of Judge Karlins (who sentenced Ms. Du to 500 hours of community service in lieu of jail time), insinuated that it was just to take the lives of Korean Americans because they were killing African American children.

Interethnic tensions are just another extension of the legacy of racism and skin-color preference that established its roots in Native American genocide and in bringing over slaves from Africa. Many people of color have to fight with each other for political space on the margins of mainstream America. Political and economic influence has shifted significantly to the majority white suburbs, leaving the remaining residents and immigrants to cut a deck with fewer and fewer cards left in it. African Americans are feeling threatened and alienated as the struggle for political representation, gained at the expense of many lives, is being cut back by the declining urban economy and immigrants eager to get a share of the shrinking pie.

In California, where many residents are people of color, political power mongers are devising divide-and-conquer strategies such as Proposition 189—anti-immigration legislation directed largely at Latinos and Asians—and Proposition 201—anti-affirmative action legislation directed largely at African Americans and other people of color. These political strategies are deepening the racial divide in America—whites from people of color, people of color from each other, men from women, and so on. It is a very effective political strategy to appeal to people's fears rather than provide constructive solutions based on a forward-looking agenda.

In closing, the predominance of racism in America affects everything in society. It exists like an invisible cloud of ether affecting the behavior of individuals, communities, and institutions. Asian Americans have been effectively used to put down African Americans, Latinos, and others who "don't measure up" to our standards. This allows society's power holders to continue to tend to their self-serving agendas. The challenge for Asian Americans is to see through the thinly disguised yet powerful veil of racism, to reject the notion that skin color and the quality of a person's character and intelligence are linked, and to keep our eyes on the prize of that elusive but powerful vision called America.

Notes

1. John Huang was a fund-raiser for the Democratic National Committee in Clinton's reelection campaign. Controversy erupted when it was learned that millions of dollars came from noncitizens and foreign companies allegedly seeking special favors from the President. Major policy reforms are underway to strictly limit foreign interests in political fund-raising.

2. Leaders of the Korean American Grocers' Association (KAGRO) agreed to provide a certain number of jobs to African American residents. Danny Bakewell, the store owner, president of the Brotherhood Crusade and leader of the boycott against Tae Sam Park, received $250,000 from City Hall to begin a small business development program.

3. The Los Angeles County Human Relations Office established the Black-Korean Alliance in 1983 in response to a rash of shootings of Korean American merchants in South Los Angeles.

Discussion Questions

1. Why are most Asian Americans unaware of the history of the civil rights movement, as well as the struggles of other people of color in the U.S.?

2. Discuss the reasons for the lack of participation in civic and political life by many Asian Americans.

3. Why did Korean Americans become the villains of the black community?

4. Elaborate on at least two divide-and-conquer strategies. Why were these strategies implemented? What has been the result?

5. What are the ramifications for Asian Americans of the confusion in distinguishing between Asians and Asian Americans? Between different Asian ethnic groups (e.g., Korean versus Chinese, Vietnamese versus Japanese)? ◆

Chapter 17

Images of Crime and Punishment

Vice Crimes and Asian Americans

Taiping Ho

According to the 1990 census, Asian Americans constitute approximately 3 percent of the total U.S. population. However, although they are presently a relatively small part of the population, their numbers are growing rapidly. They are characterized by an extensive diversity of original nationalities. To the extent that the different Asian American groups have had common experiences, these would include cultural conflicts, political alienation, economic depression, and social injustice. Nevertheless, as noted in previous chapters, Asian Americans are sometimes referred to as a "model minority" (Nakanishi, 1988). This designation primarily emphasizes Asian Americans' educational achievements rather than their political and/or social attainment in American society. Most unfortunately, as Walsh (1993) indicates, the image of Asians as immigrant role models has disguised the enduring poverty of some, as well as the political feebleness of this group as a whole.

Stereotypes of Asian Americans can be discovered in many areas of American society, ranging from talk shows to films saturated with degrading contents about Asian Americans (see further Chapters 14 and 15). Kim (1986) indicates that there are two types of Asian stereotypes in American popular culture: the "bad" Asians, depicted as sneaky or greedy or as sinister villains and brute hordes bent on sheer destructiveness, and the "good" Asians, who pose no threat and are portrayed as helpless heathens, loyal sidekicks, docile servants, or seductive females. Both the bad and the good Asian stereotypes serve to reinforce the moral and physical superiority of Anglos vis-à-vis Asians.

Since the U.S.-supported South Vietnamese government collapsed in 1975, a massive number of Southeast Asian refugees entered the United States. The vast majority of Indochinese refugees were uneducated and lacked English proficiency; in turn, they relied heavily upon the American welfare system (Bach, 1979; Montero, 1979; Stein, 1979; Nguyen and Henkin, 1982). A few of the refugees continued their traditional occupations of farming or fishing, but in some places conflicts with American fishermen have escalated. Local fishermen in Galveston Bay, Texas, for example, were outraged about Vietnamese refugees operating shrimp boats. Three of the refugees' boats caught fire after they received threats from the Ku Klux Klan. Arson was suspected, but no further investigation has confirmed it (Kelly, 1981). Such a racially motivated crime against Vietnamese fishermen reflects an anti-immigrant backlash that is escalating across the country, apparently because large numbers of poor immigrants—whether they enter the United States legally or illegally—are competing with persons born in the U.S. for jobs, social welfare, and other resources (Church, 1993; Gray, 1993; Mutt, 1994).

The American criminal justice system usually deals with crimes against Asian Americans inappropriately. In

1982, for example, a young Chinese American, Vincent Chin, who was misidentified as a Japanese was brutally beaten and killed by two unemployed auto workers in Detroit who blamed the Japanese for having taken their jobs away. Initially, the offenders were sentenced to three years of probation and fined $3,780. However under tremendous pressure from the Asian communities and other organizations, the court changed its sentence to 25 years in prison. The defendants' attorneys appealed the conviction and claimed that the prosecutor misled witnesses' testimony. A retrial ordered by the U.S. Justice Department took place in Cincinnati, an industrial city like Detroit. Not surprisingly, the defendants were acquitted. Such unjustifiable "justice" has raised a reasonable doubt concerning whether all persons, regardless of ethnicity, are treated equally under the laws of American society. This incident has also raised the question of whether prevailing stereotypes of minority members, Asian Americans in particular, contribute to discriminatory treatment in American institutions, including the criminal justice system.

Images of Asian Crimes

In the 1992 U.S. Senate hearings about Asian organized crime, Senator Roth (U.S. Senate Hearing, 1992, p. 4) stated:

> While we recognized that the vast majority of Asian Americans are law-abiding, hard-working and extremely productive members of society, we also heard disturbing evidence that Asian organized crime groups . . . were engaged in a wide variety of criminal activities, including drug trafficking, alien smuggling, money laundering, loan sharking, extortion, illegal gambling, prostitution, home invasion, and other crimes.

Researchers have rarely examined crime patterns among Asian Americans and their associated causes. Crime statistics (see U.S. Department of Justice, *Sourcebook of Criminal Justice Statistics*, 1994) show that among a total of 11,741,751 people arrested and charged with a variety of crimes in 1993, 66.8 percent were whites, 31.1 percent were blacks, 1.1 percent were American Indians or Alaskan Natives, and 1.0 percent were Asians or Pacific Islanders. Asian Americans are also underrepresented in both federal and state prisons. Charges against Asian Americans were primarily for nonviolent offenses such as gambling, prostitution, or commercialized vice. The image of "sinister" Asian Americans, brilliant but arrogant and cruel, which is frequently portrayed in films and literature (Kim, 1986), does not fit the crime statistics.

Racially laden labels of criminality have been shown to contribute to systematic patterns of discrimination against African Americans in the criminal justice system (see, for example, Peterson and Hagan, 1984; Spohn and Cederblom, 1991). However, researchers have rarely examined the effects of racially based images of Asian American criminality. This chapter helps to fill that gap by showing how popular images of criminality among Asian Americans, such as alien smuggling, prostitution, and gambling, are historically derived from laws and practices that discriminated against Asian Americans. It also clarifies the ways in which racial stereotypes contribute to racialized images of crime.

Alien Smuggling: Issues of Immigration

In 1993, six people died off New York City's Long Island from a tramp freighter smuggling Chinese illegal immigrants into the United States. More than 285 people were detained by the Immigration and Naturalization Services (INS), with many jumping into chilly waters in an attempt to escape. The most shocking news was that such massive alien smuggling was operated by Chinese organized crime groups. Recent Chinese immigrants, the vast majority of whom are uneducated laborers, are easily hoaxed by an old Chinese saying that "the streets are paved with gold in the United States." At the same time, legal channels for poor Chinese seeking to immigrate are virtually blocked. Consequently, smuggling illegal immigrants into the United States has become a lucrative business for Chinese organized crime groups in recent years. Each illegal immigrant pays between $35,000 and $50,000 to Chinese smugglers; however, most of them sign a "contract" to pay the fee after arriving in the United States. In order to exchange freedom and smuggling fees, Chinese illegal immigrants become "contracted slaves," working in sweatshops in the garment district, restaurants, laundries, or other labor-oriented industries. These indentured servants must work for at least three years, 12 hours a day, seven days a week, for subminimum wages to pay the smuggling fees. They are likely to live in filthy apartments with numerous other illegal immigrants. Some are lured into making even quicker money to pay back the smuggling fees, "voluntarily" engaging in prostitution, drug smuggling, or other criminal activities for Chinese organized crime groups (U.S. Senate Hearing, 1992).

Nearly 300 Chinese immigrants who attempted to enter the United States illegally in 1993 are still detained in state penitentiaries, with their cases for political asylum pending. The suspected Asian organized crime members who operated the alien smuggling rings are still at large. Historically, Asian Americans have been discriminated against by U.S. immigration and naturalization laws (Chiu, 1986). Due to the need for cheap labor in farming, mining, and railroad construction, the first wave of Asian immigrants arrived in the United States during the 1850s. During periods of economic depression, American workers sensed job competition with Asian immigrants. The Chinese, in particular, were scapegoated in labor disputes. Poor Chinese workers were accused of taking jobs away from white men because they were willing to work for less pay. In 1879, as Ching (1976, p. 193) described, *Harper's Illustrated Weekly* printed a picture of an African American and a Chinese with the words "The Nigger Must Go" and "The Chinese Must Go" on the front page. The author also portrayed the Chinese and the African American as "barbarians" who could not be civilized within American society. Increasingly, the Chinese were victimized by individual and collective racially motivated violence, but they had no legal right to accuse white men (Tracy, 1980; Sowell, 1981; Chan, 1991). Mann (1993) noted that the legal system became a weapon against the same population that once was welcomed as a source of labor for jobs shunned by Euro-Americans.

In 1882, the U.S. Congress passed the *Chinese Exclusion Act* designed to prohibit Chinese immigration to the United States. This law was revoked in 1943, mainly because the United States was allied with the Chinese Nationalist government during World War II. The U.S. immigration laws adopted the national origins principle in 1924 to allocate "quotas," a system that has continued to be unfavorable to Asian immigrants (Chiu, 1986; Knoll, 1986). The Asian population did not increase until 1965, when the immigration laws were revised in favor of highly educated professionals. Unfortunately, a massive number of Asian immigrants, most of whom are unskilled and uneducated, are also attempting to enter the United States illegally. Moreover, immigrants from countries whose governments generally have good relations with the United States typically do not receive political asylum, and this includes most Asian immigrants.

Other sets of laws also illustrate hostility and discrimination against Asian immigrants in the past. For example, the State of California passed the *Alien Land Act* in 1913, which prohibited land ownership by immigrants, the Japanese in particular. The anti-Japanese sentiment among Americans escalated during World War II when Japan bombed Pearl Harbor on December 7, 1941. President Roosevelt signed an executive order mandating that military commanders evacuate persons of Japanese ancestry to "relocation centers" in isolated semidesert areas. Thus 8,000 to 20,000 residents were restricted to army barracks similar to penitentiaries surrounded by barbed-wire fences and guard towers (Miyamoto, 1986). The U.S. Supreme Court concluded in 1943 that such an evacuation measure was not discriminatory against Japanese Americans. In the case of *Hirabayashi v. United States*, the Court stated that "in time of war, residents having ethnic affiliations with an invading enemy may be a greater source of danger than those of a different ancestry." Such discriminatory action exclusively against Japanese Americans must be seen as racially motivated, because no Americans of German ancestry were restricted or relocated during the World War II period (Chiu, 1986). Indeed, according to Ching, the Assistant Chief (whose name was not mentioned) of the Army's Western Defense Command's Civil Affairs Division justified the evacuation of Japanese Americans to detention camps during World War II, saying, "In the case of the Japanese, their Oriental habits of life, their and our inability to assimilate biologically . . . made necessary their class evacuation on a horizontal basis. In the case of the Germans and the Italians, such mass evacuation is neither necessary nor desirable" (Ching, 1976, p. 200).

It is clear that Asian Americans were historically perceived as racially undesirable and culturally unassimilable into the mainstream of American society. Such images may account for the recent anti-immigration backlash against the massive number of Asian immigrants attempting to enter the United States illegally. On the other hand, racially laden standards of "desirable" Americans not only undermine the images of Asian Americans who have successfully assimilated into the American mainstream but also stereotype those potentially desirable Asian immigrants who will be valuable to the American society.

Prostitution and Gambling: A Historical Linkage

Since the mid-nineteenth century, Asian immigrants, particularly from China and Japan, have emigrated to the United States as sources of cheap labor for railroad construction, gold mines, the lumber industry, or farms. The early Asian immigrants, predominantly young males who left their wives behind, wished to put in several years of hard labor and then return to their home countries wealthy. These immigrants lived in communities consisting almost solely of Asian males. The family, which traditionally and culturally has been valued by Asian Americans, was almost nonexistent. The previously mentioned *Chinese Exclusion Act* of 1882 prohibited U.S. entry to Chinese workers' wives until Congress revoked the law in 1943. Antimiscegenation laws were also enforced to prohibit interracial marriage. The discriminatory nature of such laws becomes evident when one considers the massive numbers of European immigrants and their families who were allowed to emigrate to the United States during that time.

Discriminatory laws also affected Japanese immigrants from 1905 to World War II. For example, the San Francisco Board of Education ordered all Japanese school children segregated into "Oriental" schools. White hostility and hatred of Asian Americans in the past contributes significantly to the tendency of Asian Americans to remain socially segregated from the mainstream of American society today (Miyamoto, 1986).

The early Japanese immigrants were able to establish families through the "picture bride system" (Ching, 1976; Knoll, 1982), whereby Japanese females were allowed to immigrate to the United States even though they had not previously met their husbands. Sexual imbalance, however, was still significant. Many Japanese women were lured to the United States and forced into prostitution (Okihiro, 1994). In contrast, Chinese immigrants were not granted the privilege of seeking female mates from their home countries but instead lived in male-dominated quarters (i.e., Chinatowns).

Gradually, the Chinese established clan associations or secret societies (e.g., tongs) in their communities. Tongs originally served economic and social functions for the first- generation Chinese immigrants who worked in gold mines or on railroads. However, a few tongs that were closely associated with triads (Chinese organized crime groups) were heavily involved in a variety of illegal businesses in Chinatowns, such as gambling, prostitution (smuggling in Chinese females as prostitutes), and opium dens (U.S. Department of Justice, 1988; Toy, 1992). Accordingly, Chinese immigrants lived in bachelor communities, where their recreation was primarily limited to gambling and prostitution; some were also heavily involved in drugs (i.e., opium). In 1900, for example, the sex ratio was 36:1 within Chinese communities (Daniels, 1988). This vicious lifestyle persisted for many decades, until the immigration laws favored family reunification in the mid-1960s.

In more recent congressional hearings (U.S. Department of Justice, 1988; U.S. Senate Hearing, 1992), law enforcement agencies indicated that prostitution and gambling have become major sources of revenue for Asian organized crime groups in the United States. Both crimes are also associated with other illegal activities such as alien smuggling, conspiracy (fraudulent documents), money laundering, and extortion. For example, the vast majority of Asian women who illegally enter the United States and work as prostitutes are likely indentured to Asian organized crime groups. Some Asian women enter the United States with fraudulent marriage documents. Asian organized crime members have paid some U.S. military serviceman up to $10,000 to "marry" Asian women in order to allow them to enter the United States legally. Then, after they arrive in the United States, they separate from their "husbands" and work in brothels.

As was discussed in Chapters 14 and 15, stereotypes of Asian Americans are often tied to sexuality. Kim (1984, 1986) further suggests that images of Asian women as sexual and sensual have created a demand for pornographic films featuring Asian women and prostitution-related businesses (e.g., bath houses). Such images of Asian women as seductive sex servants may directly contribute to the booming sex trade within Asian communities and the business of mail-order brides from Asian countries.

The blending of cultural conflicts with racial stereotypes about Asian Americans has contributed to the involvement of increasing numbers of Asian Americans in the criminal justice system. Using prostitution as an example, the stereotype of the sexual servility of Asian women may significantly promote prostitution and increase the likelihood of being caught by the police. Most Asian prostitutes who are assisted by Asian organized crime groups are smuggled in from Korea, Taiwan, China, or Hong Kong. They are told that prostitution is legal in the United States and, owing to their limited education and cultural ignorance, they believe these tales (U.S. Department of Justice, 1988). They do not have the social skills, linguistic proficiency, or legal immigration status to seek better jobs, so they eventually become indentured prostitutes. Not surprisingly, racial stereotypes are always overgeneralized. Images of Asian prostitutes are likely to be portrayed inaccurately by the media, intentionally or unintentionally, as characterizing all Asian women. This is fallacious and misleading. Kim (1986, p. 108) indicates that "the popular image of Asian women as obedient, eager to please, and simple to satisfy makes it all the more difficult for them to overcome race and sex discrimination."

Discriminatory policies against Asian Americans in the past may contribute significantly to the issues of gambling and prostitution in Asian communities. Prostitution and gambling, which as I have shown were derived from discriminatory immigration policies, gradually became an accepted part of life within Asian communities, particularly for the first-generation Asian immigrants. Due to lucrative profits, Asian organized crime groups are actively involved in gambling and prostitution. Consequently, prostitution and gambling still prevail in Asian communities and become major crime problems among Asian Americans (U.S. Department of Justice, 1988; U.S. Senate Hearing, 1992).

Theoretical Implications of Stereotypes and Criminality Among Asian Americans

Biases or prejudices frequently present themselves in stereotypic processes toward a particular ethnic group if that group is involved in controversial social issues and is regarded as undesirable (Jussim, Mannis, Nelson, and Soffin, 1995). Such prejudices still prevail in American society. For example, Chinatowns are not only regarded as exotic locations for tourists but also are perceived historically by the general public as peculiar communities filled with dens of opium, gambling, smuggled-in sex slaves (prostitutes), and gang-related violence. Racially laden stereotypes have a tendency to exaggerate social reality (Judd and Park, 1993). Accordingly, the criminality or deviance of minority groups, as influenced by the media, is quite often affiliated with stereotypic labels to portray the group members as a whole as "prototypical criminals" or "undesirable residents."

Similar to the experiences of the first generation of Chinese Americans, the recent issue concerning illegal Chinese immigrants has magnified the perception that all Asian immigrants are poor, uneducated, and unassimilable. Asian immigrants and Asian Americans have also become the scapegoats during economic recessions, accused of taking away "American" jobs and lowering the "American" standard of living. On the other hand, Japan has recently gained economic supremacy in many industrial areas, such as the automobile industry, intensifying malice toward Japanese Americans. Furthermore, some

Japanese businessmen have purchased land in America and invested in resort hotels and golf courses, which, similar to their images during World War II, has strengthened the stereotype of the Japanese as an invading enemy.

One criminological theory that may be valuable in explaining the criminality of Asian Americans is cultural conflict (Sellin, 1938). This theory implies that crimes likely evolve from conflicts of values or norms between different ethnic groups in a heterogeneous society. In American society, Euro-American values and conduct norms are enacted into the criminal laws that dominate the definitions of crimes. Therefore, the criminal justice system becomes a powerful tool for controlling the minority groups and "reflects the unequal distribution of power in society" (Walker, Spohn, and DeLone, 1996, p. 76; also see Turk, 1969; Quinney, 1970). Accordingly, a particular behavior could be considered appropriate within a particular minority-ethnic group but unlawful in the majority-ethnic group because of conflicts over social norms or values. Cultural conflicts may also, directly or indirectly, impact on political equality, economic status, and social justice in American society.

Each Asian ethnic group has its own distinctive history, culture, and heritage. Unfortunately, Asian Americans as a whole are generally perceived as unassimilable into the mainstream of American society. Ironically, the image of Asian Americans as a model minority, derived primarily from their work ethic and other purportedly unique aspects of their cultures, is also seen as the main source of their unassimilability. Because the earlier Asian immigrants came to the United States as cheap laborers, Asian Americans were perceived as intellectually inferior and thus unassimilable into American society (Kim, 1986). Similar to African Americans, Asian children were segregated from white children and sent to different schools. Once the desegregation policies were enforced, the educational achievements of Asian Americans began to attract a great deal of attention from the general public. However, the majority of Asian Americans are still clustered into labor-intensive occupations and ethnically segregated communities.

After the immigration laws were revised in the mid-1960s, the influx of Asian immigrants intensified racial confrontations with whites, as well as involvement with the criminal justice system. Owing to linguistic and cultural barriers, newly arrived Chinese youths, for example, who experienced adjustment problems (e.g., alienation or educational failure) and cultural conflict in the United States were actively recruited by the tongs (secret societies, some of which had close associations with Chinese organized crime groups) to be warriors or enforcers and to engage in a variety of criminal activities in Chinese communities (Joe and Robinson, 1980).

Lack of cultural awareness also accounts for racial stereotypes of Asian American women. Constrained by culture, education, and socioeconomic status, Asian American women are often clustered into sweatshops and other low-prestige and labor-intensive jobs. Additionally, compared with other ethnic minorities, Asian American women are less likely to be integrated into the mainstream of American culture because of linguistic barriers and traditional gender-role socialization (Loo and Ong, 1987). Asian American women are coping with two coexisting cultures: American culture accentuates women's liberation, whereas Asian culture values traditional gender roles in the patriarchal family structure. Undoubtedly, Asian women endure substantial hardships, struggling with un-justifiable stereotypes while trying to assimilate into the mainstream of American society.

Conclusion

The civil rights movement during the 1960s, led by Dr. Martin Luther King, Jr., enhanced the quality of life and equality of opportunity for minority groups. This movement has significantly benefited Asian Americans, who shared a history of racial oppression with African Americans. In particular, Asian Americans have benefited in the areas of education and immigration, with a small proportion of Asian Americans using educational advantages to raise their socioeconomic status. Asian Americans as a whole, however, are still segregated from the mainstream of American society socially, economically, politically, and racially.

Immigration became one of the major issues in the 1996 presidential campaign (see Chapter 12). The current immigration laws are under revision in the U.S. Senate, and much more restrictive immigration policies are anticipated. "Seeking a better life in America" has been associated with different ethnic groups for many generations. For ethnic minority groups such as Asian Americans, however, the assimilation process has been plagued with racial prejudice, political disenfranchisement, physical violence, and social injustice.

A series of special television news broadcasts and congressional hearings has raised public concerns about "Asian" criminal activities such as alien smuggling, prostitution, money laundering, and drug smuggling in the United States. However, investigations of Asian organized crime groups and their associated criminal activities are difficult because law enforcement agencies have insufficient knowledge about Asian organized crimes and lack international law enforcement cooperation (U.S. Senate Hearing, 1992). Asian organized crime members with abundant illegal profits may easily avoid legal sanctions for alien smuggling, whereas poor and illegal immigrants may become the scapegoats for punishment.

Owing to cultural ignorance and language barriers, many Asian Americans distrust the criminal justice system. They tend to resolve their problems, including victimization, privately and rarely seek assistance from law enforcement (Vigil and Yun, 1990; Chin, Fagan, and Kelly, 1992). Victims are so intimidated or fearful of retribution that they are unwilling to cooperate with the police. Accordingly, crimes against Asian Americans are tremendously underreported to the police and the "Asian" criminals are seldom punished. Unfortunately, crime and punishment among Asian Americans remain underresearched in criminology.

This chapter has illustrated the historical linkage between racial stereotypes and criminal activities such as prostitution, but further research is needed to determine whether and how images of Asian Americans result in racial disparities in criminal justice processing, sentencing, and treatment. Especially important, future research must address ways in which our thinking about crime and punishment may be biased by a historical pattern of systematically excluding the various Asian American populations from our theorizing.

References

Bach, Robert L. (1979). "Employment characteristics of Indochinese refugees." *Migration Today*, 8 (3), 10–14.

Chan, Sucheng. (1991). *Asian Americans: An interpretive history*. Boston: Twayne Publishers.

Chin, Ko-lin, Fagan, Jeffery, and Kelly, Robert J. (1992). "Patterns of Chinese gang extortion." *Justice Quarterly, 9,* 625–646.

Ching, Frank. (1976). "The Asian experience in the United States." In Frank J. Coppa and Thomas J. Curran (Eds.), *The immigrant experience in America.* Boston: Twayne Publishers, 192–214.

Chiu, Hungdah. (1986). "Asian Americans and American justice." In Hyung-chan Kim (Ed.), *Dictionary of Asian American history.* Westport, CT: Greenwood Press, 55–59.

Church, George J. (1993). "Send back your tired, your poor." *Time, 141* (25), 26–27.

Daniels, Roger. (1988). *Asian American: Chinese and Japanese in the United States since 1850.* Seattle: University of Washington Press.

Gray, Paul. (1993). "Teach your children well." *Time, 142* (21), 69–71.

Joe, Delbert, and Robinson, Norman. (1980). "Chinatown's immigrant gangs: The New York warrior class." *Criminology, 18,* 337–345.

Judd, Charles M., and Park, Bernadette. (1993). "Definition and assessment of accuracy in social stereotypes." *Psychological Review, 100* (1), 109–128.

Jussim, Lee, Manis, Melvin, Nelson, Thomas, and Soffin, Sonia. (1995). "Prejudice, stereotypes, and labeling effects: Sources of bias in person perception." *Journal of Personality and Social Psychology, 68* (2), 228–246.

Kelly, James. (1981). "Closing the golden door." *Time, 117,* 24–27.

Kim, Elaine. (1986). "Asian Americans and American popular culture." In Hyung-chan Kim (Ed.), *Dictionary of Asian American history.* Westport, CT: Greenwood Press, 99–114.

———. (1984). "Sex tourism in Asia: A reflection of political and economic inequality." *Critical Perspectives, 2* (1), 225–229.

Knoll, Tricia. (1986). "Asian Americans and American immigration law." In Hyung-chan Kim (Ed.), *Dictionary of Asian American history.* Westport, CT: Greenwood Press, 51–54.

———. (1982). *Becoming Americans: Asian sojourners, immigrants, and refugees in the western United States.* Portland, OR: Coast to Coast Books.

Loo, Chalsa, and Ong, Paul. (1987). "Slaying demons with a sewing needle: Feminist issues for Chinatown's women." In Ronald Takaki (Ed.), *From different shores: Perspectives on race and ethnicity in America.* New York: Oxford University Press, 186–191.

Mann, Coramae Richey. (1993). *Unequal justice: A question of color.* Bloomington: Indiana University Press.

Miyamoto, S. Frank. (1986). "Japanese in the United States." In Hyung-chan Kim (Ed.), *Dictionary of Asian American history.* Westport, CT: Greenwood Press, 7–12.

Montero, Darrel. (1979). *Vietnamese Americans: Patterns of resettlement and socioeconomic adaption in the United States.* Boulder, CO: Westview Press.

Mutt, Andrew. (1994). "Immigrants in the valley." *Newsweek, 124* (26), 115–116.

Nakanishi, Don T. (1988). "Seeking convergence in race relations research: Japanese-Americans and the resurrection of the internment." In Phyllis A. Katz and Dalmas A. Taylor (Eds.), *Eliminating Racism.* New York: Plenum Press, 159–180.

Nguyen, Liem, and Henkin, Alan B. (1982). "Vietnamese refugees in the United States: Adaption and transitional status." *Journal of Ethnic Studies, 9* (4), 101–116.

Okihiro, Gary Y. (1994). *Margins and mainstreams: Asians in American history and culture.* Seattle: University of Washington Press.

Peterson, Ruth D., and Hagan, John. (1984). "Changing conceptions of race: Towards an account of anomalous findings of sentencing research." *American Sociological Review, 49,* 56–70.

Sellin, Thorsten. (1938). *Culture conflict and crime.* New York: Social Sciences Research Council.

Sowell, Thomas. (1981). *Ethnic America: A history.* New York: Basic Books.

Spohn, Cassia, and Cederblom, Jerry. (1991). "Race and disparities in sentencing: A test of the liberation hypothesis." *Justice Quarterly, 8,* 305–327.

Stein, Barry N. (1979). "Occupational adjustment of refugees: The Vietnamese in the United States." *International Migration Review, 13* (1), 25–45.

Toy, Calvin. (1992). "A short history of Asian gangs in San Francisco." *Justice Quarterly, 9,* 647–665.

Tracy, Charles A. (1980). "Race, crime and social policy: The Chinese in Oregon, 1871–1885." *Crime and Social Justice,* Winter, 11–25.

U.S. Department of Justice. (1994). *Sourcebook of criminal justice statistics.* Washington, DC: U.S. Government Printing Office.

———. (1988). *Report on Asian organized crime.* Washington, DC: U.S. Government Printing Office.

U.S. Senate Hearing. (1992). *Asian organized crime: The new international criminal.* Washington, DC: U.S. Government Printing Office.

Vigil, James D., and Yun, Steve C. (1990). "Vietnamese youth gangs in Southern California." In C. Ronald Huff (Ed), *Gangs in America.* Thousand Oaks, CA: Sage Publications, 146–162.

Walsh, James. (1993). "The perils of success: Asians have become exemplary immigrants but at a price." *Time, 142* (21), 55–56.

Discussion Questions

1. A typical "bad" stereotype in American culture refers to Asians as sinister villains and brute hordes bent on sheer destructiveness. Why do crime statistics (e.g., *Sourcebook of Criminal Justice Statistics*) not reflect those images? What are the contributing factors in stereotyping Asians in American society?

2. Taking immigration as an example, why were Asian Americans historically perceived as racially undesirable and culturally unassimilable into the mainstream of American society?

3. According to crime statistics such as *Uniform Crime Reports*, Asian Americans are underrepresented in the criminal justice system, and criminal charges against Asian Americans are primarily for nonviolent offenses such as gambling or prostitution. Why have Asian Americans been involved in gambling and prostitution since the mid-nineteenth century?

4. Use the cultural-conflict theory (Sellin, 1938) and prostitution as examples to discuss why this theory can explain stereotypes and criminality among Asian Americans.

5. Why has the criminal justice system responded so poorly to crimes against Asian Americans? ◆

Part V

The Invisible Color White

For Euro-America, being white is the norm. When Euro-American men and women walk into an office, classroom, or store, there are usually a lot of other Euro-American people in the setting and the newcomer is unlikely to be stared at because he or she doesn't seem to belong. And yet, although Euro-Americans may distinguish among themselves as Irish or Norwegian or French, these are in-group comparisons that do not lead them to say of other whites, "they all look the same to me." Ironically, then, Euro-Americans can both blend into a crowd comfortably and be distinguished from one another.

White represents power, purity, virginity, cleanliness, and goodness. The White House is the seat of power and privilege. Effective detergents make your wash "snowy white," "white lies" aren't all that serious and are told for good reasons, white is the color worn by virgin brides, and "white magic" is good.

Most analyses of race and crime ignore Euro-Americans. They focus on criminal acts committed by African Americans, sometimes by Latinos/as, and rarely by anyone else. With very few exceptions, when researchers *do* specify Euro-Americans as the offenders, they do so only as the standard against which to judge others. When crimes in which Euro-Americans are the typical offenders are discussed (e.g., white-collar crimes, serial murders), *race* isn't mentioned as a factor. It is almost as though the offender's whiteness was invisible. White-collar crimes, in which wealthy Euro-American men are the typical offenders, are not even recognized by the *Uniform Crime Reports.* Thus the *crimes*, as well as the offenders, become invisible. Why is it so easy to ignore Euro-Americans?

The authors in this section problematize whiteness. They speak explicitly about the unearned privilege that whiteness provides. When Susan Smith, a Euro-American woman, pushed her car containing her children into a lake and drowned them, and when Charles Stuart killed his pregnant wife, both blamed African American men. And both were believed, at least initially. When it becomes overwhelmingly apparent that Euro-Americans commit these and other heinous crimes, the media play up the angle that some personal tragedy or trauma befell them, perhaps in early childhood, and can explain this abnormality. Euro-Americans typically appear only as the victims of crimes—or rather, as the victims who matter. The overwhelming pattern in our country is for the death penalty to be requested by prosecutors, and handed down by judges and juries, when an African American man kills a Euro-American man or woman, far less so when the victim is African American, and almost never when a white person kills a black person.

Hate crimes, which are almost invariably committed by Euro-Americans, have only recently been taken seriously by police officers, prosecutors, and the general public. Yet hate crimes have a long and sordid history in the United States, beginning with the genocide practiced by Euro-American settlers against American Indians who were in the path of their westward expansion, continuing through the lynchings of African American men accused of crimes against Euro-Americans (including charges of simply looking at white women), to today's church burnings and the beatings, rapes, and murders of people of color. Why, the authors in this section ask, are Euro-American offenders and typically "white" crimes so invisible? ✦

Chapter 18

Images of Euro-Americans

White Privilege, Color, and Crime: A Personal Account

Peggy McIntosh

In 1988, I published an autobiographical account of my experience of having white-skin privilege by contrast with African American female colleagues who work in the same time, place, building, or line of work, doing research on and programs about women (McIntosh, 1988). I listed 46 ways in which I experienced daily conditions of unearned overadvantage by contrast with these colleagues. I listed conditions that seemed to me a little more connected with race than with class, region, religion, ethnicity, or sexual orientation, though I wrote that I saw all of these factors as intricately intertwined privileging systems that bear on any one person's experience.

I explained that I did not ask for the unearned advantages that I put on my list. They came to me because of my placement within systems of privilege and disadvantage that do not have to do with merit. I had come to see white privilege as an invisible package of un-

earned assets that I could count on cashing in each day but about which I was meant to remain oblivious. White privilege is like an invisible, weightless knapsack of special provisions, maps, passports, codebooks, visas, clothes, tools, and blank checks. Seeing this, which I was taught not to see, made me revise my view of myself, and also of the United States' claim to be a democracy in which merit is rewarded and life outcomes are directly related to deservedness.

Among the 46 conditions of white privilege I listed in the 1988 paper were a few that pertain specifically to my relation to the law, to crime, and to the courts. At the invitation of the editors of this volume, I am giving examples from the original list, and I have expanded it in order to illuminate my experience of having white skin privilege with regard to crime and the courts in particular.

My method remains autobiographical. In the 1988 paper, I compared myself only to African American female colleagues with whom I came into daily or fairly frequent contact. For this analysis, I have broadened the sample to include friends and colleagues in other racial/ethnic groups who are engaged in a variety of occupations outside of this building and line of work. Once again, I know something about their experiences and have heard some of their stories. It is by contrast with these that I tell of my own experience, and of the racial overadvantage that makes my life markedly different from theirs in most circumstances, including many involving law, crime, and the courts.

Before turning to this list, I want to make clear again the focus of my original analysis. The point of my work is not to make me or other Caucasian people feel blamed or guilty for benefiting from inherited systems of systemic overadvantage. We did not invent them, and in my analysis, we were taught not to see them. I observe that the people who benefit most (in the short run) from privilege systems in the United States are kept most blinded to the existence of privilege systems, to preserve the myths of moral and managerial meritocracy and the belief that democracy is working as it should.

Rather than creating a sense of guilt or blame, the point of my work is to help those with the most power to recognize that privileging systems exist and that the existence of unearned disadvantage usually involves a corresponding existence of overadvantage. Without this understanding, it is impossible, in my view, to either make sense of or to do effective work to improve race relations and most other power relations that exist in U.S. society. In this chapter I raise again my question of 1988: Having seen unearned power or permission to dominate, how can I use my unearned power to distribute power more fairly and to weaken systems of unearned privilege?

I will start with some general points from my earlier list, then repeat those that related most specifically to crime, the courts, and the law, and then add further points about white privilege, crime, law, and the courts, in my experience.

In 1988, I wrote that the African American women in the same building and line of work whose stories and lives I knew something about could not, as far as I could see, count on most of the 46 conditions I listed. Readers are reminded that my list was and is context-specific and autobiographical; it is about what I knew and does not claim to be about the privileges of all white people everywhere relative to all people of color. Some readers may wish to make their own autobiographical lists grounded in their own daily circumstances and perceptions.

1. I can, if I wish, arrange to be in the company of people of my race most of the time.

2. The day I move into new housing that I have chosen, I can be pretty sure that my new neighbors will be neutral or pleasant to me.

3. When I am told about our national heritage or about "civilization," I am shown that people of my color made it what it is.

4. I can be sure that my children will be given curricular materials that testify to the existence of their race in all classes, in all subjects, at all grade levels.

5. If I want to, I can be pretty sure of finding a publisher for this work on white privilege.

6. I can go into a supermarket and find the staple foods that fit with my cultural traditions, or into a hairdresser's shop and find someone who can cut my hair.

7. I can swear, or dress in second-hand clothes, or not answer letters without having people attribute these choices to the bad morals, the poverty, or the illiteracy of my race.

8. I can do well in a challenging situation without being called a credit to my race.

9. I am never asked to speak for all the people of my racial group.

10. I can remain oblivious of the language and customs of persons of color who constitute the world's majority without feeling in my culture any penalty for such oblivion.

11. I can criticize our government and talk about how much I fear its policies and behavior without being seen as a cultural outsider.

12. I can easily buy posters, postcards, picture books, greeting cards, dolls,

toys, and children's magazines featuring people of my race.

13. I can go home from most meetings of organizations to which I belong feeling somewhat tied in, rather than isolated, out of place, outnumbered, unheard, held at a distance, or feared.

14. I can choose blemish cover or bandages in "flesh" color and have them more or less match my skin.

At this point, I turn to conditions on my 1988 list that relate most closely to color and crime.

15. I can turn on the television or open to the front page of the newspaper and see people of my race widely and positively represented.

16. Whether I use checks, credit cards, or cash, I can count on my skin color not to work against the appearance of financial reliability

17. I can arrange to protect my children most of the time from people who might not like them.

18. I can take a job with an affirmative action employer without having co-workers on the job suspect that I got it because of race.

19. I can choose public accommodation without fearing that people of my race cannot get in or will be mistreated in the places I have chosen.

20. I can be sure that if I need legal or medical help, my race will not work against me.

21. If my day, week, or year is going badly, I need not ask of each negative episode or situation whether it has racial overtones.

22. If a cop pulls me over, or if the IRS audits our tax return, I can be sure it is not because of my race.

23. If I get angry and ask to s "person in charge," I ca sure I will be talking to a my race.

24. I did not need to teach our children about systemic racism for their own daily physical protection.

25. I can go shopping alone in department stores near my house without being followed or harassed by store detectives on the grounds that I may be shoplifting or soliciting.

26. We were able to teach our children that the police were their allies, and that they should dial 911 if they had an emergency.

What follows here are further points explicitly related to color and crime.

27. In my neighborhood, I can be sure that the police will not harass me because of the color of my skin.

28. In my neighborhood, any police officer who might need to arrest people in my family is likely to be a person of my race.

29. Criminality is not imputed to me as a genetic component of racial character; I am not assumed to belong to a group of people predisposed to crime.

30. The word "criminal" in the dominant culture does not conjure up the faces of people whose skin color is like that of my father, mother, brother, sister, husband, nieces, or nephews.

31. I have never heard or read the suggestion that all the people of my color ought to be locked up or killed. Even Islamic fundamentalists do not call for the killing of all people of my color, only certain "morally corrupt" ones.

32. In World War II my grandparents, despite having German ancestors

two generations ago, were not locked up by the U.S. government in internment camps on the suspicion or pretext that they might be traitors.

33. Nearly all of the lawyers and judges who study, write about, argue, debate, and practice law in the U.S. are people of my race.

34. Lawbreaking by the U.S. government with regard to treaties with Indian people was not taught to me as a criminal aspect of my racial heritage.

35. Deceiving Indians is not described as a genetic or inherited trait of Caucasians.

36. Refusing to honor Indian treaties today is not shown to me as lawbreaking by white people.

37. The U.S. government has never made it a crime for me to speak my native language or observe the religious ceremonies of my parents and grandparents.

38. The prison system is thoroughly controlled by people of my race.

39. The Constitution I am subject to was created by people of my ethnic heritage to apply to some people of my ethnic heritage and to not apply to people of other races.

40. I am assumed to be entitled to whatever legal defense I can afford, even if it allows me to be acquitted of a crime I have committed.

41. If I am suspected of being guilty but am acquitted, I will be seen as someone who got through the cracks rather than as a person who especially deserved not to get through the cracks.

42. Those who have been able to afford the high costs of legal training have

been, for the most part, people of my race.

43. Lawyers featured as experts by the media are overwhelmingly people of my race.

44. Those who have been able to pay lawyers' fees and legal costs have for the most part been people of my race.

45. A successful tax evader in my ethnic group is usually portrayed as a cheater or even a victor, but not as an innate criminal or a representative of a whole race of people who drain society.

46. A deadbeat dad in my ethnic group is portrayed in the media as financially but not sexually irresponsible.

47. When I walk into the courthouses of my country, I can expect respectful treatment from the receptionists.

48. As a child, I heard jokes and sound tracks that cast people of other races as habitually dumb and coarse, or else sneaky, shifty, sly, malicious, or underhanded, and left people of my race protected from such typecasting.

49. The voiceovers of criminals, shifty individuals, and villains in Disney films and in ads rarely sound like people of my racial/ethnic group.

50. If I stand in line at a bank teller's window, no one looks strangely at me, as though they have a problem with my being there.

51. If I suffer damages and decide to take a case to court, the people I see in the legal system will probably be people who were trained to trust my kind and me.

52. I can stand behind another person at an ATM machine without being feared as a potential mugger.

53. If I am laughing with friends on a street at night, it is not assumed that we are in a gang.

54. A realtor has never discriminated against me to "protect property values."

55. No one has ever suggested that I might have dealt drugs in order to afford a certain car or house.

56. The men of my race who took 400 billion dollars in the 1994 U.S. S & L (savings and loan) scandal are not branded as criminals or seen as enemies of the U.S. people, even though the money has never been returned.

57. When I think of prisons, I do not have to think of people of my race as disproportionately serving time in them, having longer than average sentences, and being executed in greater numbers.

58. I am allowed to believe, and encouraged to believe, that people of my race are in general law-abiding rather than law-breaking.

59. TV shows and films show people of my color as the main defenders of law and order, cleverest detectives, best lawyers and judges, and wiliest outlaws.

60. Portrayals of white males on TV as criminals and violent individuals do not incriminate me as a Caucasian; these males, even the outlaws, are usually presented as strong men of a quintessentially American type.

61. Illegal acts by the U.S. government, in the present and in the past, around the world, are not attrib-

uted by whites to Caucasian immorality and illegality.

62. Bad race relations in the United States are not attributed by whites to criminal behavior, despite a history of race-related breaking of laws by whites over the entire span of Anglo-European life on this continent.

The list could expand much further. The examples are hard to allow into my awareness, however, because these truths are so unpleasant to face and so disruptive of my acculturated sense of myself in moral and political worlds.

My conscious mind was schooled to believe that to some extent justice will be done through the legal system of the United States; it balks at the realization that continual unnamed injustices result from the projection onto my race of being on the side of law or being an admirable, individualistic challenger to the law, while people of color are subtly portrayed as beyond the ethics and rules of law and order, whether by being shiftless, exploitive, unreliable, violent, or criminal.

The bad behavior of a person of color, when it occurs or is thought to occur, is unfairly projected onto his or her entire group, whether it is the stereotype of inscrutable shiftiness attributed to Asian Americans, the gangsterism attributed to Latino men, or another of the myriad common projections and stereotypes. Meanwhile, people of my Anglo-European ethnicity escape mass negative projections by the media and by other white citizens. Projections onto Italians that they are connected to the Mafia, onto Jews that their main value is making money, or onto the Irish as drunken drivers do occur, but they do not so clearly incriminate them without trial. And the Anglo-European character perpetually bobs up, like a Weeble doll, as the norm of uprightness that

negative attributions cannot desta-
bilize, except for very short periods, in
particular instances of crimes that are
seen as committed by individuals.

I am struck by the magnitude of the
effects of unincriminated "whiteness."
As a case in point, white-collar crime is
considered to be unlike other crimes.
There is a lack of public acknowledgment in the media of the damage it
does to the society. Men like Michael
Milken and Donald Trump and even the
S & L scandal perpetrators continue to
be lionized for their ruthlessness in
breaking laws. The $400 billion "lost" in
the S & L scandal has never been traced,
but the white men who are sitting on the
money are not known as white crooks if
they are thought of as crooks at all.
Imagine what would have happened in
the United States if black or Chicano
men had made so much investors'
money disappear.

The reason I see a need to *do the
arithmetic of unearned overadvantage as
a function of unearned disadvantage* is
that without it I am allowed to consider
myself as a person neutrally placed in
relation to these matters of law. Then I
do not need to bother myself about "the
forces for law and order" as long as I
behave myself and do not run too many
red lights. But in fact, the forces for law
and order, because they do not deal
evenly with us, are a threat both to me
and to my colleagues of color, bringing
them an absence of legal protection and
security and bringing trepidation, anxiety, and anger, if not outright harassment and persecution. If I am let off
what they endure, then I have an unearned advantage in the form of freedom from danger, fear, and anger, and I
become a target for their legitimate anger. I do not think it is good to be made
a target of others' legitimate anger.

Several years ago, the teenage friend
of a black colleague of mine was
stopped by the police as he drove to his
family's suburban home one night. The
police made him wake up both of his
parents in the middle of the night to
prove that he belonged in the mostly
white neighborhood, that is, that his
credentials were not forged. The memory of the police hostility and the humiliation will never disappear from that
family and their community; for this
family, I think the town's police can
never be seen as allies. But can I see
them as my allies? How are they my allies if they humiliate and try to intimi-
date my neighbors?

The police claim they do such things
in order to protect "our" neighborhood.
But it is a protection racket. They are
creating a problem of bad race relations
that they then claim to protect the
neighbors against. Meanwhile, white
privilege might be seen to insulate my
family against such treatment and the
knowledge of such treatment. We do get
unearned freedom from fear, anger, and
preoccupation with the question of
what the police may do to us. But the
bad race relations are not a favor to
whites. They surface in the schools and
in the streets, and they lower the quality
of life for everyone, including whites,
who become targets for anger they do
not understand and are kept from
understanding by the silence surrounding privilege.

I fear the police sirens when I am
pulled over for speeding, but even then
I can observe the processes by which police officers decide to let me off with just
a warning. I am a late middle-aged
white woman with her hair in a bun
who speaks with a soft voice and lives
on a well-known street in a mostly white
town. I can see the officers' inclination
as they talk to me and look at my license,
to feel that I am not as much of a danger
on the road as, say, a young black man
would be. Yet I think I am every bit as
dangerous on the road as the next
speeder.

While writing this chapter, I had a vivid experience of how white privilege works in my favor in my place of work. Campus police found computer equipment on the porch of the building at 11:00 p.m, saw computer equipment in the back seat of my nearby car, and after searching the grounds came into the building. They thought they had interrupted a robbery. I could tell by their faces, though, that they believed me when I said that I was just working late, and that earlier that day some new computer equipment was installed, and we were told we could take away old equipment if we would pay for the repairs. I think that an African American colleague found in this apparently incriminating situation would not have been so easily believed, and would have had much more reason to be scared in the situation, if she had dared to work in this building so late at all.

In the nine years since I published the original white privilege paper, I have done more than 90 co-presentations with persons of color on the subject of privilege systems. Many co-presenters have said that within the last few days preceding our co-presentation, their financial credentials had been doubted or in stores they had been asked for more kinds of personal identification than had others. It does not matter whether they are full professors or owners of their own businesses; they get incriminated through whites' racial and ethnic projections onto them of financial unreliability and habitual dishonesty. I escape these projections. I can thus live naively, out of touch with what life in the United States is, out of touch with the society we actually have, and unthinking on the question of how I reside in that society and it resides in me.

I was in Sweden when the O. J. Simpson criminal trial verdict was announced. My Swedish colleagues had trouble believing the rejoicing and relief at his acquittal among many people of color. They knew U.S. race relations involved discrimination, which they could understand, but not white privilege, which they had never conceived. Skillful lawyers with good legal resources and winning arguments have often allowed white murder suspects to go free. Many African Americans, in addition to feeling that the racism of the Los Angeles Police Department cast doubt on the whole way they got evidence on Simpson, observed that finally a black man had been defended by a highly competent, confident, and large legal team that won the case.

I think that the anger of many white people in the United States that Simpson got off in the criminal trial reveals more than their feeling that he was guilty, which I share. I think it also reveals an assumption of white privilege: whites' belief that they deserve whatever legal power they can muster, whereas people of color are immoral if they can afford and obtain lawyers to make a successful defense in the face of evidence of guilt. The second, civil case deepened the bitterness of many people of color, who felt that whites had gone to special lengths to see "justice" done in the case of this black celebrity.

There have been two main misreadings of my analysis of white privilege. Some well-meaning white readers have felt that they will now just divest themselves of unearned advantage. It is not that simple. Doors will continue to open for us whether or not we want this to happen. I have, however, identified at least 10 ways in which I can, in my own circumstances, use power to share power and use unearned privilege to weaken systems of unearned privilege. There are ways to collaborate, work as allies, and create change within institutions, policies, and individuals.

My own forms of activism have especially involved choosing to work with women and men of color and trying to diversify all-white groups if I work with them (this is related to point one on my list); organizing for integration of my neighborhood (point two); challenging and changing curricula, scholarship, and teaching methods to create more critical and more inclusive knowledge and education (related to points three and four); co-presenting on white-skin privilege with persons of color to share podium time and honoraria (point five); asking the local supermarket buyers why they will stock specialty Chinese but not specialty African American foods (point six); writing to Hallmark and Crayola's executives about both racism and sexism in their product lines (point 12); trying to listen and then respond as an ally to participants of color in mostly white organizations (point 13); doing homework on, taking seriously, and disseminating words and works by those who do not have white privilege (points 1–62); getting and using money to spread understanding of privilege systems (and denial of them) through school-based faculty development seminars, consultancies, talks, articles, letters, and conversation, including family conversation (points 1–62); understanding how much I have to learn from people I was taught to overlook, fear, or avoid; learning some of what they have to teach and being awed and grateful for that; and putting my life on a more inclusive and generous base, aware that white privilege both helps and hinders this effort.

There are also people of color who misread the original paper in a way that deepens the conspiracy theory, that is, that white people know all about our racial status and behavior as whites. These readers think that I was saying things that all white people know. On the contrary, I was carefully taught in hundreds of ways not to know, not to see, what I wrote in that paper. I was

taught that I didn't have a race. The word "race" referred to other people. I was just "normal." And I was taught to see racism only in individual acts of meanness, not in invisible systems conferring dominance on my group. People who benefit most, in the short term, from privilege systems are kept most blinded to them for they interfere, as I have said, with the ideology that democracy has been achieved and is working well.

I can understand that some people of color find that everything I have written confirms their experience and observations: it is obvious to them. This is what makes some readers conclude that we whites must all know of our unearned privilege and that I just blew the cover of my race. But white people are socialized, conditioned, and educated to not know about white-skin privilege, even more thoroughly, I think, than males are raised to be oblivious to male privilege. To use a parallel and telling example with fewer political and social ramifications: most right-handed people cannot tell you about right-handed privilege. They were not taught to be aware of it. Left-handed people have a lot to say on the subject of being left-handed, which comes as a surprise to the dominant group.

The white readers who have found the analysis most unsurprising are in general those who, through interracial relationships, cross-cultural adoptions, and other "border crossings" are positioned so as to have double or triple perspectives, seeing on both sides of lines of privilege. White women who become keenly aware of male privilege may also get, as I did, to the insights on race privilege if they are able to decenter themselves, as we have asked men to do. But in doing so, we forego the moral high ground that many of us found so empowering in being the people with justice on our side. It can feel sickening to be decentered when you have felt centered for the first time ever.

I originally found that going into this subject deeply shook up my sense of being a moral and a nice person. It complicates the whole matter of moral worth. But it has nothing to do with niceness. It has to do with being oppressive through privilege and oblivious to one's oppressiveness, again through privilege. One white privilege is not to know about white privilege. This has nothing to do with whether one is nice. It is about the sense of entitlement with which people of my color took permission, or what we read as permission, from God, or nature, to fill the turf, the time, the payrolls, the centers of recognized authority, including the courts of law. And then not to know that this is our racial history.

I believe that when this happens, the centers of recognized authority within the psyche also take on a cast of white dominance, and replicate the larger society in the inner self. And then the forces of law and order, or of brave domination, in the psyche can feel they are holding at bay the forces of lawlessness and all the projections that they have acquired. To me, it feels as if forces in my personality that are privileged in the wider society for whites become forces in a multiple, interior self that have license to govern, imprison, or ride roughshod over the rest of my personality and perceptions. Then what I call interior colonization occurs (McIntosh, 1990). The self gets taken over by just a segment of itself, and the rest gets identified with the Other, imprisoned, or silenced, while the authorities can deny that any repression is occurring.

Through my work on these problems, I have found it is hard to keep alert to myself as white. It requires diligent reflection on the relation between what I send out to the world in my projections and what I receive. I find that the an-

cient Greek idea of seeing as a two-part process is useful, though we learned about it in school in order to learn that it was inaccurate. Yes, I do seem to send out "eyebeams" that pick up some things and not others, so that what I send out bears on what I get back. One's racial and other social understandings go forth and pick up what they have the capacity to see. Keeping alert to the racial origins of my eyebeams is appropriate but taxing. I was not taught to see myself as white, let alone to see my seeing as influenced by whiteness. And I was taught to see myself as on the side of the law and of fairness. It seems now that my Anglo-European eyebeams saw lawfulness where people of my color were in control and the scene was quiet.

This work on seeing privilege is epistemologically dizzying as well as emotionally hard. It is hard to learn you are being decentered when you were not aware of being central to begin with. I think that for heterosexual white males it has been especially hard, like a one-two-three punch, first having "maleness" problematized and then "whiteness" and then "straightness." I think that many people who are trying to be reflective are feeling a kind of epistemological nausea from being whirled around so suddenly, as it seems to them. And I myself find that a retreat from the subject of being consciously white is tempting. I see it as curling up and falling asleep, and sleep has its place. But nightmares will come. And I would rather be awake, and not a sleepwalker. I now feel that being a white sleepwalker through the world of white control perpetuates a zombielike incapacitation of the heart and mind.

It is only a hypothesis, but I would guess that white oblivion about, and inculturated denial of, privilege acts as a psychological prison system that costs white people heavily in terms of preventing human development. Walking obliviously through our own racial experience may perpetuate the imprisonment of the heart and intelligence in a false law-and-order of tyrannizing denial about who, what, and where we are. So the societal systems of color and crime may reside also in the psyches of white people, where an equivalent of bad race relations or white supremacy damages the civic health and balance of the soul.

References

McIntosh, Peggy. (1990). *Interactive phases of curricular and personal re-vision with regard to race*. Working paper #219. Wellesley, MA: Wellesley College Center for Research on Women.

——. (1988). *White privilege and male privilege: A personal account of coming to see correspondence through work in women's studies*. Working paper #189. Wellesley, MA: Wellesley College Center for Research on Women.

Discussion Questions

1. Talking in a group of four or five others in your class, name and describe some effects of one unearned *disadvantage* you have had in life. Plan for equal time for each speaker, and time the speakers. Anyone who takes more time than is allotted may be privileging himself or herself.

2. Next, talking in a group of four or five others in your class, name an unearned circumstance of *advantage* you have had in your life that has not been mentioned. Again, plan for an allotment of equal time for each speaker, and keep track of the time. To repeat: Anyone who takes more time may be privileging himself or herself through dominance in the taking of "air time."

3. In a group of four or five (still using equal time), discuss a way in which you have seen white privilege at work in the context of law school, justice studies, or the courts. (This discussion will require more time altogether.)

4. Name one way in which you can use your power to share power in your context or use privilege to weaken systems of unearned privilege. (Take equal time, and keep track.)

5. In the small group, have each person discuss some frustrations, difficulties, and/or payoffs in structuring the uses of time in this way during the discussion of privilege, color, and crime. I am hoping that time-use habits will be seen as one more aspect of privilege, and that being democratic can also entail stringent controls, at times, on the sharing of power. (Take equal time.) ◆

Chapter 19

Stereotyping by the Media

The Caucasian Evasion: Victims, Exceptions, and Defenders of the Faith

Jody Miller and Peter Levin

Introduction

We recently came across a political cartoon drawn by Tim Jackson that illustrates concisely much of what is notable in the media treatment of race and crime. In the first frame is a middle-aged white male newscaster reading the "Los Angeles Headline News" with an expression of boredom on his face: "A child is gunned down in yet another random act of violence in the mean streets—yadda, yadda, yadda. . . . WAIT! This says the victim was White this time?!?" In the second frame, with a look of rage, fists clenched, the newscaster leans toward the camera and says, "Why you sick filthy street thugs! We're sick of these senseless acts of violence! This behavior simply will not be tolerated! We mean business!!!" The meanings behind this cartoon are layered: "street thugs" are people of color, their victims are usually also people of

color (and implicated as potential thugs themselves), and the only "true" victims of crime are innocent whites caught in the crossfire or preyed upon by these dangerous others.[1]

This imagery also implies that whites who do commit violent crimes are somehow unique—they don't reflect white culture and society more generally. When the media focus on street crime, they typically do not pay attention to the routine participation of whites in these activities, although the majority of individuals engaged in street crime are actually white. The invisible white street thug is, thus, an important stereotype. It is often hard to recognize, however, because it is the white thug's very invisibility, his absence in media accounts, that makes him so stereotypic. One way to focus in on this ephemeral stereotype is to examine what images of whites and crime the media *do* pay attention to. For this chapter, we decided to examine media stereotyping of whites and crime by looking at a number of recent prominent criminal cases in the media that involved whites. In doing so, we uncovered three important themes.

The first theme is an emphasis on whites as crime victims. This imagery is specifically class-based (with a focus on the victimization of middle-class whites) and is often gender-based as well (with a focus on white women as victims, often of sex crimes). What is compelling about these media stories is not just that whites are crime victims, but that they are the innocent targets of crimes by "street criminals," who most often (in the stories that make the news) are men of color. These images create a contrast between those crime victims who are most "innocent" and thus "deserving" of public sympathy and a continuum of less innocent and less deserving victims.

The second and third themes we discuss both focus on white criminals, but in ways that differ from media depictions of criminals who are not white. Scholars who study the impact of race on the educational system have noted a contrast between a "discourse of potential" and a "discourse of deficit," as applied to white students versus students of color (Powell, 1997). The discourse of potential, typically applied to white students, presumes that these students bring with them ability and talent. This belief in their potential follows them unless they prove otherwise via poor school performance. In contrast, the discourse of deficit, typically applied to students of color, takes as its premise that these students have deficiencies that will require special assistance in order to be overcome.

Although this discussion of education may seem far removed from our focus on crime, we suggest that a similar pattern can be seen in the popular media's treatment of race and crime. Whites are presumed to be noncriminal by nature; thus their crimes are in need of special explanation. As a result, in many celebrated cases in which the criminal is white, a great deal of time and space are dedicated to exploring those life factors that may have contributed to the creation of someone capable of committing the given crime. These include early childhood traumas, abuse, depression, mental illness, and so on—psychological and psychiatric causes of the crime. In contrast, when people of color commit crime, there is little attempt to explore the question of "why?" Because the question is not asked, the answer is implicit: it is in their nature.

Finally, there are romanticized media images of the white criminal. Here, the individual white criminal is particularly intelligent and/or heroic, and the crimes reflect these valued traits. These images are specifically masculine and middle-class. Because they mirror dominant values in our society, the crimes are met with understanding and the criminals with sympathy or admiration. As a result, the overall notion of white potential and goodness remains unchallenged. In the sections that follow, we will explore each of these themes in greater detail, discussing prominent examples to illustrate our points. Although we primarily examine nationally celebrated cases, we believe the handling of these cases by the media represents more common patterns. Occasionally we will provide examples that are not national to illustrate how these images operate in local news media as well.

Whites as Crime Victims

Perhaps the most consistent historical theme within the media regarding the relationship of whites to crime is the image of the white crime victim, assaulted by a man of color, typically an African American. Often the representation is that of a white woman whose victimization is explicitly sexual. As Chapter 7 highlights, the media have long been fascinated with portraying African Americans as violent and, in particular, with the image of the black rapist (see also A. Y. Davis, 1981). The flip side of this image is that of the victim, who is frequently depicted as white. *Birth of a Nation*, one of the earliest feature-length films ever made, included a storyline about a young, innocent, blonde white woman chased off a cliff by a black man intent on ravaging her. This theme has carried through to the contemporary era. Specifically today, when a case arises that fits this stereotype (a black stranger assaulting a white woman), it is the case most likely to get media attention and to be treated most harshly by the criminal justice system (Estrich, 1987; Walsh, 1987).

The image of the young, attractive, middle-class, white (often blonde) female rape victim is the epitome of our society's construction of the innocent victim of street crime. Perhaps the most telling contemporary case along these lines was the 1989 attack on the woman known as the "Central Park jogger" (see also Chapter 7). A 28-year-old investment banker on Wall Street, the woman was jogging through Central Park one spring evening when she was attacked by a group of African American and Latino youths, who bound and gagged her, beat her with fists, stones, and a metal pipe, gang-raped her, and then left her for dead (Kunen, 1989, p. 106). The woman had lost two-thirds of her blood by the time she was found, and she remained in a coma for 13 days suffering a skull fracture and injuries to her brain. She survived the attack, and the young men involved were found guilty of rape (though they were acquitted of attempted murder) (Podolsky, Balfour, Eftimiades, and McFarland, 1990).

This attack fit the prototypical media stereotype of the crime victim: she was young, attractive, financially successful, and the innocent victim of a random attack by strangers. The strangers who attacked her were a group of young men of color on the streets looking for trouble. The story was a media sensation, with multiple articles in national news outlets detailing the assault and following both her recovery and the ensuing trials. The media stories surrounding the attack had two themes: portraying the young men who committed the crimes as savage, animalistic, and unremorseful and portraying the victim as innocent, good, and a fragile but brave survivor. A columnist for the *San Jose Mercury News* captured these themes succinctly when she wrote, "They were predators. She was Bambi" (in Hackett and McKillop, 1989, p. 40).

The jogger typified all that makes a crime victim innocent in the media. She was described as young, well educated, ambitious, hard-working, and attractive, but also generous and appreciative of her privileges. A woman who had "lived her life with singular grace and compassion," she was a "spirited and spiritual girl" who volunteered to help those less fortunate than herself, and who jogged at night because "she had too much faith in humanity" (Kunen, 1989, p. 106). Her physical appearance was important as well. For example, it was noted that she had "blond hair, large eyes, and [an] elfin figure" (Kunen, 1989, p. 106), and her height and weight were mentioned in multiple stories about the attack (see, for example, Kunen, 1989, 1990; Trippett, 1990). One story even described her "manicured hand(s)" (Kunen, 1990), a symbol of the jogger's middle-class status. The media's focus on the jogger as a fragile, brave survivor is perhaps best captured in the following description of her testimony during the trial:

Now the door swung open, and a young woman hobbled up the steps to the witness chair. Carrying only 90 lbs on her 5 ft. 5 in. frame, with her blond hair cut in a pixieish wedge, she bore a resemblance to actress Sandy Duncan. After being sworn in, her hand trembling on the Bible, she was asked to state her name. She gave it in a strong, clear voice, and in that instant reclaimed herself from the headlines. She was no longer a symbol, but a woman— somebody's sister, somebody's daughter, a human being who looks in the mirror each morning and sees a scarred face looking back. (ibid., p. 32)

The youths involved in the attack were depicted as animals. In an article tellingly entitled "Wilding in the Night," a *Time* magazine writer described a "band" of teenagers who "roamed" Central Park, until "one pack" came upon the jogger attacked in the case (Gibbs, 1989, p. 20). New York Mayor Ed Koch described the youths as "engage[d] in a wolf-pack operation" (in Gibbs, 1989, p. 20). They were described by police and quoted in the media as being "smug and remorseless" (Gibbs, 1989, p. 20). Billionaire developer Donald Trump took out full-page ads in four newspapers calling for the death penalty. Interviewed for *Newsweek,* he said, "I'm sick and tired of watching this kind of thing being perpetrated on an innocent public" (in Hackett and McKillop, 1989, p. 40). As one author critical of the media's handling of the case noted, the Central Park rape fit well with the "white love affair with the notion of the inevitability of black antisocial behavior" (Greenfield, 1989, p. 86). Another noted that "many whites found their unspoken fears of minority youths vindicated" (Hackett and McKillop, 1989, p. 40).

The point of our discussion is *not* to suggest that this attack was not incredibly brutal, that the victim was not worthy of tremendous sympathy, that she was not a brave survivor, or that the perpetrators did not deserve to be prosecuted to the full extent of the law. Instead it is to question what makes one victim more deserving than another. The prosecutor in the case, Elizabeth Lederer, called the Central Park attack "one of the most vicious and brutal crimes in the history of New York" (in Kunen, 1989, p. 106; Trippett, 1990, p. 40). But in 1989 alone, there were 3,254 forcible rapes reported to the police in New York City (Podolsky et al., 1990). There were hundreds of homicides. What made this assault so special that it was not just vicious and brutal, not just one of the most vicious and brutal assaults in 1989, but one of the most vicious and brutal assaults *in the history of New York?*

One of the most significant problems with media stereotypes of this sort is that they create a hierarchy of deserving and less deserving victims. What about those crime victims who are not young, attractive, blond, financially successful, and so on? What about those crime victims who are not white? The media present a particular image as representative of the quintessential innocent crime victim. Consequently, all other crime victims are compared to this ideal, and many can't measure up. They are deemed less worthy of sympathy and their lives of less value. This may seem like a strong statement to make, but the evidence is quite compelling. It is not just the media that judge cases along these lines, but police agencies and the justice system and much of the public as well.

A local case is illustrative. In Kankakee, Illinois, in 1995, two youths ended up as murder victims, but the media, the public, and the police responded to them in very different ways. A 10-year-old white boy disappeared from a riverbank and a 13-year-old African American girl disappeared but was suspected of running away. The boy's case "riveted the region for two weeks, prompting an extensive search and relentless media coverage" (White, 1995). Television news crews from Chicago traveled 70 miles to Kankakee and covered the story around the clock, and the case (unlike the girl's) was covered by the Associated Press. After the boy's body was found, "a throng of media chronicled [his] burial" (ibid.). In contrast, the girl's saga didn't make any TV newscast. In fact, Kankakee's newspaper, the *Daily Journal,* wrote only three brief stories about her death. On the day the body's identity was reported, the demise of 'Whitey,' a blind horse, got more ink" (White, 1995). This story is but one example of a consistent pattern within the media of perpetuating a hierarchy of more and less deserving victims, according to factors such as race and social class. This particular comparison only made the news because the Kankakee police chief was struck and disturbed by the contrast and spoke out.

There are numerous examples of this phenomenon. In Los Angeles, gang violence became a serious focus in the media when violence left the "ghetto" and moved into the predominantly white neighborhood of Westwood Village, near UCLA. When a young woman was accidentally killed there by a gang member in 1987, press coverage shifted dramatically from its prior coverage in South Central and East Los Angeles (M. Davis, 1992, pp. 270–271). Gang violence had suddenly posed a threat to the "innocent." Likewise, police and media in Columbus, Ohio, recognized the existence of gangs in that city only after two incidents in which the mayor's son and the governor's daughter were each assaulted by gang members (Huff, 1990). These examples hearken back to the cartoon described at the opening of this chapter.

There are other consequences of these stereotypes as well. Given the strength of media images of African American criminals victimizing innocent whites, it is not surprising that white criminals have attempted to escape responsibility for their crimes by calling upon these popular stereotypes. Perhaps the two most noted recent cases are those of Susan Smith and Charles Stuart. In 1994, Smith drowned her two young children and told authorities they had been kidnapped when she was carjacked by an African American man in a knit cap. In 1989, Stuart drove to the outskirts of a predominantly African American neighborhood in Boston, shot and killed his pregnant wife, shot and injured himself, and then claimed they had been the robbery victims of an African American man in a jogging suit. Each evoked racial symbols of white fear to shift attention away from themselves.

Both Smith and Stuart were eventually found out, but not before each spent time as sympathetic media figures. Smith stood before television crews while a nationwide hunt ensued, pleading for the return of her children: "they are missed and loved more than any children in this world" (Dougherty and Sider, 1994, p. 50). Stuart, even more so, was cast as a devoted, heroic husband and father-to-be who, even after the horrible attack, still tried to save his family. In an interview for a story that ran in *People* magazine, the 911 operator who took his call described Stuart as "incredible. . . . Here's this poor man, shot, his wife beside him, and he had the ability, the guts and gristle to get help to his family. If there's a hero in all of this, it's him" (Brower, Mathison, and Brown, 1989, p. 52). Likewise, a director for the show *Rescue 911*, which aired a segment on the "attack," described arriving on the scene to find Charles Stuart's arm around his dying wife, noting, "it was as if even at that moment he was still trying to protect her" (ibid.).

Early on, the media and police treated the Stuart case as "*the* symbol of senseless urban violence" (Stanko, 1990, p. 1). The neighborhood in which they were "attacked"—near the hospital where they had attended Lamaze class—was described in *People* magazine as "menacing" and "crime-plagued." The magazine described "the sentiment that . . . echo[ed] throughout Boston's middle-class neighborhoods: 'This doesn't happen to us. Not to us'" (Brower et al., 1989, p. 52). Within hours, police swept into the community where the shooting took place, stopping and frisking hundreds of young African American men, and the mayor "ordered all available detectives to work on the case" (Carlson, 1990, p. 10). Even Governor Michael Dukakis attended Carol Stuart's funeral. In a later article in *People* magazine, as the media examined their own participation in Stuart's hoax, the authors surmised, "to the press, police and much of the public, Charles had become both hero and victim, and his tragedy a paradigm of society's battle between decency and decline" (Hewitt, Mathison, Brown, Verner, Sawicki, and Carswell, 1990, p. 66). The deep public outrage and sympathy that the case triggered was a direct result of the belief, fostered by media coverage, that a menacing black criminal had destroyed the lives of a decent, loving, white, middle-class family.

The Psychology of White Criminals

Whereas the African American perpetrators in many celebrated cases with white victims are described as animalistic and savage, many white criminals are viewed as tragic anomalies. Particularly when the criminals are middle class, a great deal of energy is spent trying to figure out why they have gone astray—why their enormous potential has been lost. This has certainly been the case with Susan Smith. Charles Stuart committed suicide when it became apparent that his version of the attack on his wife was unraveling. Because his demise ended the case abruptly, opportunities for the press to examine his psychological state and attempt to "understand" him were foreshortened. It is impossible to say with certainty whether these psychological analyses would have occurred had he lived to face prosecution. If other famous cases involving gruesome and heinous homicides by whites are any indication, however, the likelihood would have been quite high.

As we noted in the introduction, given a presumption in the media that whites are not violent or criminally inclined by nature, individual whites who deviate from this image need to be explained. The search for understanding may reflect, more than anything, the need to distinguish these individuals from whites as a whole in order for the presumed purity of the category to remain intact. Thus ensues a struggle, played out in the media, to figure out what makes these individuals so different from "the rest of us." Although it may not be the primary drive behind the psychological analysis of offenders, an additional result is the humanization of these individuals. This includes both recognition of the ways in which they have been shaped by their life histories and opportunity for redemption. Nowhere is this search for understanding and its consequences more clear than in the case of Jeffrey Dahmer.

Dahmer's crimes are without question some of the most gruesome in recent history. A serial killer who confessed in 1991 to murdering 17 people, he sodomized, mutilated, dismembered, and cannibalized the bodies, storing body parts throughout his apartment. However, even while early media depictions of Dahmer used language such as "evil," "chamber of horrors," and "monster" in reference to him and the case (Chin, 1991; Chua-Eoan, 1991), from the start the focus was on examining the traumas of Dahmer's childhood in search of an explanation for his behavior.

For example, a story in *People* magazine noted that Dahmer was "raised in [a] well-to-do community" (Chin, 1991, p. 33) and that his "ordinary, even banal background at first seemed to mock efforts to fathom what lay behind such evil" (ibid.). However, the article quickly focused on his early childhood. Chin noted that "Dahmer was traumatized at an early age. At eight, he was sexually abused by a male in the neighborhood" (ibid.; see also Prud'Homme, 1991). His homicidal behavior was also linked to his parents' "bitter divorce" when Dahmer was a senior in high school. In the article Dahmer's stepmother explained, "'Jeffrey was left all alone in the house with no money, no food and a broken refrigerator. . . . The desertion [by his mother] really affected him'" (ibid., p. 34). As if to offer proof of his stepmother's analysis, this statement was immediately followed in the *People* article with Dahmer's acknowledgment that "he committed his first murder that June" (ibid.). Dahmer was described as a "quiet loner" whose "inner disturbances continued to erupt to the surface" (ibid.). His stepmother also speculated in the *People* article that during a short stay in prison for child molestation a year earlier, "something happened to him that he would never talk about. . . . Everyone knows what happens to a child molester in prison. I don't know if that's what happened, but when he came out he was hardened, and he hated black people [his primary homicide victims]" (Chin, 1991, p. 34). In a companion story in the same issue of *People*, a psychologist who studies serial killers explained that " 'all have been abused, emotionally, physically and quite often sexually' " (Norris in Tayman, 1991, p. 36).

Numerous follow-up articles about Dahmer appeared in the media—when he stood trial, was convicted and sentenced; when books about him and the case came out (including his father's); and finally when he was himself murdered in prison. Dahmer's media story was ultimately one of redemption. This was accomplished in three ways. First, as previously noted, was the attempt to understand how traumatic life experiences had contributed to the creation of a man whose "inner furies" (Chin, 1994,

p. 38) drove him to commit his crimes. Dahmer's father published a memoir on the topic, and Dahmer himself was interviewed on *Dateline NBC* in the quest to understand what went wrong.

Second, from the time of Dahmer's arrest on, media stories highlighted his progressive religious conversion. After his arrest, it was noted that he "spen[t] his days reading the Bible" (Treen and Tamarkin, 1992, p. 75). After his attempt to plead insanity failed, Dahmer was quoted as explaining, "I knew I was sick or evil or both. Now I believe I was sick. I know that I will have to turn to God to help me get through each day. I should have stayed with God. I tried and failed and created a holocaust" (in Schneider, 1992, p. 38).

In the *People* magazine story on Dahmer's death (tellingly entitled "The Final Victim" after he was murdered in prison), much of the story was devoted to describing "Dahmer's budding religious beliefs" (Gleick, 1994, p. 126). According to the article, Dahmer was baptized in the Church of Christ. His minister, Roy Ratcliff, "submerged Dahmer in the prison whirlpool, saying, 'Welcome to the family of God.' Dahmer, dripping but smiling, sputtered his thanks" (ibid.).

This and other articles focused on his newly contemplative Christian lifestyle: "Dahmer kept to himself in Cell 648, smoking cigarettes, voraciously reading religious materials and listening to tapes of classical music, Gregorian chants and humpback whales" (Gleick, 1994, p. 126; see also Chin, 1994). He was even described as unwilling to press charges after an inmate in prison tried to slit his throat (Gleick, 1994). Of Dahmer's murder, his minister is quoted as saying that Dahmer was "a very nice, decent guy. . . . He was ready to meet his maker. I believe he is in the hands of God."

The focus on Dahmer having "found God" was tied explicitly to the third and most significant way in which Dahmer was able to find redemption and forgiveness through the media's construction of him. This was the focus on Dahmer's deep remorse and his stated desire to die in order to provide justice for the families of his victims and atone for his sins. At the trial, he was described as "quietly apologetic," with "his head bowed in seeming humility" (Schneider, 1992, p. 38). This particular article ended with a statement made at the trial by Dahmer: "I have seen [the victim's families'] tears, and if I could give up my life right now to bring their loved ones back, I would do it. I am so very sorry" (ibid.). Dahmer's desire to die was perhaps key to his redemption, as it was described as his means of atoning for his sins. After he was killed, it was noted that "Dahmer, like the families of many of his victims, felt he deserved to die" and "yearn[ed] to be removed from this earth" (Gleick, 1994, p. 126). The religious significance of these statements was confirmed by his minister, whom the article quoted as noting that "Dahmer often contemplated 'the question of death,' asking Ratcliff if he was 'sinning against God by continuing to live'" (ibid.).

Although Dahmer's case represents an extreme—given the gruesome nature of his crimes and the number of victims—the same themes are nonetheless present when we examine other celebrated cases with white defendants. The focus is on the psychological state of mind of the individual(s) in question and the life experiences that may have pushed them to commit their crimes. This is particularly the case with white female criminals, who have presumably gone against their nature both as whites and as women. The goals, again, are to understand what caused these individuals to behave against their nature, as

well as to create distance between them and the category/ies to which they belong (e.g., white women). The implication is that without some traumatic causal mechanism (childhood abuse, psychological problems, etc.), the crimes would not have taken place. This does not imply that media discussions absolve white offenders of responsibility for their crimes, but rather that they are much more likely to examine the question of "why?" when the offender is white.

To further explore this theme, and to contrast it with the treatment of people of color, we will return to the case of Susan Smith, as well as the cases of two other women implicated in the homicides of their children: Hedda Nussbaum and Awilda López. As noted above, Smith's attempt to blame the disappearance of her two young sons on a black carjacker was short-lived. As her story fell apart, she eventually confessed to drowning the boys and told authorities where they could find the bodies. Hedda Nussbaum and her common-law husband, Joel Steinberg, were arrested in 1987 after the beating death of their six-year-old daughter, Lisa. Both were white and upper middle class. Steinberg was a lawyer, and Nussbaum had been a children's book editor. Charges against Nussbaum were eventually dropped when evidence suggested that Steinberg had repeatedly abused and tortured both Nussbaum and their daughter. The case brought national attention to the issue of family violence. Awilda López, who is a Latina, was arrested in 1995. She also was charged with the beating death of her six-year-old daughter, Elisa, after several years of suspected abuse. The case made the national media specifically as an indictment of the child-welfare system, which had failed to remove the child from her mother's home despite repeated reports of abuse.

When Smith's crimes came to light, the press immediately began the search for an explanation. In addition to focusing on childhood traumas, the stresses of an unfaithful husband, a failed marriage, and subsequent single parenthood were themes (Gibbs, 1994; Levitt, 1994). An article in *Time* magazine even detailed her financial troubles: "She took home $1,096 a month, but her $344 mortgage, $300 in daycare—plus car payments, utilities and other costs—added up to $1,284" (Gibbs, 1994, p. 42). Describing the proceedings at Smith's trial, a *Time* magazine article noted that Smith's ex-husband—father of the murdered boys—broke down on the stand. The article went on:

> But the jurors could also grieve for Susan Smith. The defense argued that she snapped after a long history of depression, suicide attempts, abuse and abandonment. Her brother Scotty Vaughan cried as he described how their father had shot himself when Susan was just six. "The Susan I know wouldn't have made a decision to harm Michael and Alex," he said. "The Susan I know was never at the lake that night." And there was also testimony on Smith's behalf from her stepfather Beverly Russell, a formerly upstanding citizen of Union who has admitted to molesting her as a teenager and continuing sexual relations until just months before the murders. Reading a letter he sent to her on Father's Day, he said, "I must tell you how sorry I am for letting you down as a father. . . . All you needed from me was the right kind of love. You don't have all the guilt in this tragedy." (Gleick, 1995, p. 31)

As in the case of Dahmer, stories about Smith following her incarceration focused on her tremendous remorse but, even more so, on the intense pain she suffers from having to live with the knowledge that she murdered her children. She was described as "spen[ding] much of her time in jail weeping and talking to photos of her sons" (Hewitt, Wescott, and Sider, 1995, p. 76), as "weep[ing] every day for . . . the children she drowned," and as " 'confused' and 'seriously depressed and suicidal' " (Cerio and Sider, 1995, p. 69). Her lawyer explained: " 'She is suffering torments that are so beyond anything the legal system could ever inflict' " (ibid.). Consequently, articles written at the conclusion of the Smith case (when she was sentenced to life in prison) focused on the themes of understanding and forgiveness. People from her hometown were quoted as saying, "let's pray for her," and individuals close to the case were described as feeling "compassion" for Smith (Hewitt et al., 1995, p. 76). An article in *Time* magazine concluded by noting, "the process of forgiveness may have already begun" (Gleick, 1995, p. 31).

In the López case, there was little attempt in the popular media to try to understand the causes of the mother's actions. To state that she was a "crack addict" who became pregnant with Elisa while staying in a homeless shelter seemed answer enough (Peyser with Power, 1995; Van Biema, 1995). Article after article, detailing and psychoanalyzing every incident of abuse and every trauma that may have triggered her treatment of her daughter, did not occur. Instead, López was described by Peyser and Power (1995, p. 42) in *Newsweek* as "ranting, wild-haired," and screaming when she was arrested, and police said she had "shown little emotion" since her arrest. Under the headline, Peyser and Power's story began: "How a mother—now charged with murder—got away with years of grisly abuse" (ibid.). It was mentioned only in passing that López was the repeated victim of serious spouse abuse, including an incident in which her husband stabbed her 17 times, leaving her hospitalized.

In contrast, *Time* ran a story about the Steinberg/Nussbaum case entitled "Hedda's Hellish Tale," which began as follows:

> She still limps. Despite plastic surgery, her nose is crushed and her upper lip is permanently split. But when she testified last week in a Manhattan courtroom against her former live-in lover, who is accused of beating to death their illegally adopted six-year-old daughter, Hedda Nussbaum spoke in a firm, clear voice. What emerged was a bizarre tale of violence, drug abuse, isolation and mind control inflicted by disbarred lawyer Joel Steinberg. Asked why she never escaped from Steinberg's thrall, Nussbaum had a simple reply: "I worshipped him." (Ellis, 1988, p. 32)

Nussbaum, like López, was reported to be addicted to cocaine; however, whereas López was poor and Latina, Nussbaum was upper middle class and white. She and Steinberg reportedly freebased cocaine together after their daughter was beaten unconscious prior to calling for help (Ellis, 1988; Hackett with McKillop and Wang, 1988). Nussbaum's victimization at the hands of her abusive partner resulted in the charges against her eventually being dropped after prosecutors became "convinced she had been so battered psychologically and physically that she could not have participated in beating Lisa" (Ellis, 1988, p. 32). Instead, Nussbaum testified against Steinberg in the death of their daughter.

The flip side of the López case is that, perhaps because the victim was also Latina, the case itself did not receive repeated popular media coverage. Elisa's brown skin meant that she didn't make as gripping a victim as Susan Smith's white sons, Nussbaum and Steinberg's white daughter, or even Nussbaum herself. Whereas the popular press followed these cases from start to finish, including multiple articles in *Newsweek*, *Time*, and *People* magazines, only *Time* and *Newsweek* ran stories about Elisa's death and only in one issue (Peyser with Power, 1995; Van Biema, 1995). The focus of these stories was the failure of the child-welfare system to intervene and remove Elisa from her mother's home—not to understand or examine what social factors and life traumas created a mother capable of killing her own child. When López was convicted of her daughter's murder (and sentenced to 15 years to life), it was noted in two sentences in *Time*'s "Milestones" section.

Smith's and Nussbaum's cases were followed by lengthy media stories such as *Newsweek*'s "Why Parents Kill" (McCormick with Miller and Woodruff, 1994) and "Prisoners of Pain" (Gelman with Elam, 1988) and *Time*'s "Parents Who Kill" (Van Biema, 1994). These stories sought to explore the social and psychological dynamics of the crimes to help explain and understand these and other individuals' involvement. The articles offered answers to such questions as "Why didn't she leave?" and "Why didn't she protect her child?" in the case of Nussbaum and other battered women. Mothers kill their children, it was surmised, only as a result of poverty, child and spousal abuse, or mental instability (Van Biema, 1994).

We are not implying that individuals such as Jeffrey Dahmer, Susan Smith, and Hedda Nussbaum do not deserve the attempts to understand their actions, or even to offer them redemption or forgiveness. Instead, we highlight the fact that this process tends to be reserved exclusively for whites. Cases such as Dahmer's and Smith's come to resolution by emphasizing the individual's remorse, sorrow, and suffering they experience as a result of their crimes—not suffering meted out through criminal justice punishment but internal suffering caused by the deep guilt they live with for their crimes. This emphasis on remorse, contrition, and ultimate forgiveness is in direct contrast with media constructions of many individuals of color who have committed violent crimes. The contrast between Smith and López is exemplary, as are the descriptions, noted above, of the Central Park rapists as smug, remorseless predators. Psychologists' attempts to explain these young men's actions were rejected by media commentators. One noted:

> The boys have not yet been taught to say they did it because of rage, pain and despair, because of the sins whites have visited upon them and their ancestors. But they will be taught. By trial time, they will be well versed in the language of liberal guilt and exoneration. . . . What distinguishes these boys is not their anger—Who is without it?—but their lack of any moral faculty. (Krauthammer, 1989, p. 104)

The media's consistent attempts to answer the question of why a particular white criminal has committed his or her crimes illustrates the extent to which whites as a category are not perceived as capable of crime by nature (see similarly Chapter 18). In contrast, the question "why" is not the focus when the defendant is a person of color. This lack of attention presumes that the answer is obvious, and thus not in need of asking. The implication is that somehow it is in his or her nature, to be expected, or at least not surprising.[2] For whites, the question is of critical importance—how could someone whom we know to be good by nature turn to behavior that is bad? The result of the media's intense pop psychology is that white criminals

are seen in human terms. They are granted a degree of sympathy and understanding, and ultimately can achieve forgiveness and redemption, no matter how heinous their crimes. This type of humanization typically does not occur when the criminal is a person of color.

The Romanticized White Criminal

The images of white criminals in many cases serves to reinforce the dominant values of our society. In contrast to their depictions of people of color, the media sometimes choose to romanticize white criminals. These images of white criminals pick out dominant and valued themes in American society and portray the perpetrators as "criminals, but . . ." where "but" could take the form of crime as resistance to the failures of the social system, crime as a means of achieving economic gain, or crime as the display of intelligence and intellectual savvy. By examining two case studies, we can better understand why some criminals are portrayed differently than others.

The portrayal of white criminals as fighting against a failed social system elicits sympathy for criminal behavior on the grounds that the crimes are protecting a larger social order. On December 22, 1985, Bernhard Hugo Goetz was accosted on a New York City subway by four black teenagers. After he was asked for the time, then for a match, and then for $5, Goetz pulled out a handgun and shot and wounded all four youths. For his crime, Goetz was charged with attempted murder, assault, reckless endangerment, and illegal possession of a firearm.

The Goetz case was striking in the way his vigilantism was framed as illegal yet heroic. Immediately after the incident, Goetz began to receive supportive phone calls from many sympathetic New York residents. Rather than being seen as a dangerous criminal, Goetz represented the failure of public safety. As one editorial put it, telling people that vigilantism is wrong makes sense only if police can provide security to the public. Otherwise, "the vigilante is elevated to the status of hero" (Raspberry, 1985, p. 5A). For another observer, who more pointedly supported the crime, Goetz spoke "for all of us weary of being terrified on the streets, and of the sentimental view of youthful crime that seems to license it" (Yoder, 1985, p. 5A). Apparently, the jury felt the same way. Goetz was acquitted on the 12 counts stemming from the attempted murder, assault, and reckless endangerment charges and was only convicted of illegal possession of a firearm.

This image of an otherwise good white man taking the law into his own hands in the face of a system that has broken down was the subject of the fictionalized film *Falling Down*. Michael Douglas played the lead role of a man who "snapped" in the face of a series of events that conspired against him. Nameless throughout three-quarters of the film, Douglas is laid off from his job as a defense engineer. After snapping in his car on an overcrowded freeway in Los Angeles, Douglas moves across Los Angeles with escalating violence as he attempts to see his ex-wife and daughter. He notes the deterioration of "American" values as he travels across the city. Becoming better and better armed as the film progresses, he finds himself "standing up" for an America he sees as no longer existing.

In the face of this breakdown, Douglas retaliates. He smashes up a Korean grocer's store after screaming at the owner about his lack of English skills; encounters gang members who won't let him be; shoots up a fast-food restaurant that represents all that is wrong with American business; kills a neo-Nazi who believes his vigilantism was influenced by white supremacist ideals; and accosts a rich old man on an exclusive golf course. Douglas epitomizes the "angry white man" who simply went too far.

Both the real-life Goetz incident and the fictional *Falling Down* illustrate a common portrayal of white criminals. Although both Goetz and Douglas are eventually brought to justice, both also elicit sympathetic responses to their railing against the system. It is the romanticization of vigilantism, and the protection of American values at any cost, that are highlighted in these two cases. As one of Goetz's neighbors put it, Goetz was a "very quiet and a very smart guy. He's not the violent type . . . but he's also not the type to let people abuse him" (Daley, 1985, p. 3B). And in the final scene of *Falling Down*, Douglas asks rhetorically "I'm the bad guy? How'd that happen? I did everything they told me to."

The second way that white criminality is romanticized is through white-collar crime. This type of criminalization is often overlooked in the popular imagination about crime, yet it has a far greater economic cost than most violent crimes. But it is not only the nonviolent nature of crimes like fraud, embezzlement, and securities infractions that set them apart from more violent crimes. The conformity of white-collar crime to dominant American values, combined with the mostly white, professional stature of the criminals, make these criminals worthy of our collective admiration.

Michael Milken is such a criminal. In 1990, Milken pled guilty to six felony counts of fraud and agreed to pay $600 million in penalties for violating the laws of the Securities and Exchange Commission in connection with junk bonds. These high-risk instruments were used to finance companies during the mid-1980s. Their often risky nature, combined with Milken's expertise in convincing investors to use them, resulted in a highly lucrative income for Milken. However, Securities and Exchange Commission officials accused Milken of working these bonds by misleading investors, manipulating markets, and often bribing other stockbrokers to go along with his schemes. When Milken pled guilty to the six counts in 1990, it was part of a plea-bargain agreement. Though he was ordered to pay $600 million in penalties, estimates of his income suggest that between 1983 and 1987 Milken earned over $1 billion, with one year's salary during that time topping out at $550 million. In fact, Milken's lawyer at the time worried that if the case went to trial, Milken's wealth would prejudice jurors against him (Paltrow, 1990).

Milken's character was romanticized in the film *Wall Street* (with Michael Douglas once again playing the lead role), but it is not necessary to look even as far as Hollywood to show how Milken was glorified. For instance, after the conviction, the *Los Angeles Times* attempted to rank Milken among the great financial "rogues" of history. It noted that only time will tell if Milken will be derided (as one official pointed out) as "among the worst violators of securities laws in U.S. history" or as a man "who breathed life into corporate have-nots with a new means of financing and who fell because he crossed the line in an age when many on Wall Street seemed to have done the same" (Richter, 1990, p. 1D).

In fact, it is Milken's financial knowledge and his accumulation of wealth that placed him on a par with America's captains of industry rather than with America's most wanted. In 1993, Milken was invited to co-teach a series of lectures at UCLA's graduate school of management. In justifying paying a known felon to teach graduate students in business, Bradford Cornell, who co-taught the course with Milken, argued that "this is not a class on ethics. UCLA is not saying that Milken is a role model . . . but his practical experience and knowledge about the workings of American capital markets are unparalleled" (Cornell, 1993, p. M5). Cornell made an interesting analogy: if you teach a class on heart surgery, you want the best surgeon to speak to the class; if you teach a class on mass media, you want Ted Turner [owner of Turner Broadcasting], "and if you are teaching my class, you want Milken" (ibid.).

The question that needs to be addressed is, why are these criminals romanticized? Part of the answer is the fact that they are white and male. Patricia Williams argues that it is impossible to even imagine a scenario in which a lone black man firing on a group of white youths under the same circumstances as Bernhard Goetz would receive support from the New York community. She goes on to argue that although sympathetic responses might vary, the consensus would probably be to imprison or institutionalize the black man (Williams, 1991, pp. 76–77). Goetz's whiteness allowed him to become a "defender" of dominant social values in a way that is virtually impossible for women or nonwhites. The interesting aspect of *Falling Down* is that Michael Douglas was a good man in a bad world. His criminality was rooted in the fact that, rather than deviating from the dominant values of society, he simply went too far in trying to conform to them. In the case of Michael Milken, we can see that it is not just race and gender but also class that distinguishes the degree of criminality we assign to deviant behavior. Because of his business smarts (in addition to the large sums of money he has given to universities and to private medical research foundations), Milken is seen as a brilliant investor who, again, just went too far.

Thus, how the media choose to portray criminals depends in part on their race, gender, and social class and in part on how closely these criminals conform to the dominant values of American society. Hollywood correctly picks up on the fact that some criminals are perceived as less criminal than others. As one commentator put it in the Goetz case, "although my mind tells me that Goetz was wrong, my gut aches with understanding for him" (Kilpatrick, 1985, p. 5A). Likewise, Milken was a financial guru who was caught crossing the line. However, his expertise warranted a lucrative teaching position at UCLA to teach the "practical" workings of capital markets. In both cases, we can see that the images of criminality depend heavily on the race and gender of the criminal, as well as on the degree of conformity between the crimes they commit and the dominant values of American society.

Conclusions

There are a number of significant consequences of the imagery of whites and crime in the media, all of which function to perpetuate racial inequality and the oppression of people of color in America. The media continue to present an image of criminal victimization that fails to capture the realities of crime in America. As one social commentator notes, "random violence against the white middle class [does] not constitute the bulk of crimes, or even a very large minority of them. Why give them so much more than their share of attention?" (Anderson, 1995, p. 9).

One result of this attention is that these images play into the public's fear of crime. White women, in particular, report higher levels of fear of crime than other groups, even though their likelihood of victimization is lower than that of most groups (Ortega and Myles, 1987). In addition, this fear of victimization focuses on public crimes—crimes by street criminals and strangers. As such, it diverts attention away from many forms of private violence. Though women report heightened levels of fear of crime by strangers, women's experience with violence is mostly private—date and acquaintance rape, domestic violence, and so on (Stanko, 1990). Media attention to stereotypical crimes diverts the focus away from these important issues.

In addition, these media images project a hierarchy of victims in which some victims are seen as more deserving of public attention, outrage, and sympathy than others. When people of color are victims of crime, their cases are deemed less newsworthy by the media, ultimately sending the message that their lives are of lesser value. Evidence suggests that these beliefs are carried through into the criminal justice system as well. For example, researchers have found that the harshest sentences in rape cases are meted out to African American men who rape white women, whereas the least severe sentences are given to men who rape African American women, whose victimization is taken less seriously, regardless of the race of the perpetrator (Walsh, 1987).

The media also differ in their treatment of white offenders compared to offenders of color. First, because crime is not seen in media stereotypes as a white phenomenon, white participation in ordinary street crime typically does not make the news the way it does when an African American or another person of color is involved. The category "white" is not associated with crime in the media in the same ways that the categories "black" or "Hispanic" are. White criminals who make the news are discussed and understood in ways that don't challenge the fundamental assumption that whites as a whole are noncriminal. This is in contrast with media portrayals that insinuate that people of color are criminal by nature.

We have described two categories of white offenders that appear in the media: the psychologically troubled criminal and the romanticized criminal. The most significant aspect of the media's focus on the social and psychological causes of white offenders' crimes is that these criminals are presented in human terms and, as such, are offered understanding and even forgiveness for their crimes. White criminals who are presented in romanticized ways are those whose crimes in some way mirror dominant values in our society. Their crimes, as well, elicit understanding and sometimes even admiration. Troubled or romanticized, the result is the same: the notion of white potential—that whites are noncriminal by nature—remains unchallenged.

Notes

1. In this chapter we make a broad distinction between whites and people of color. This does not suggest that the treatment of people of color should be perceived as unified (or the treatment of whites, for that matter). Rather, we make the distinction in order to contrast the treatment of the dominant racial category in the U.S. (whites) with that of various other racial-ethnic groups, all of whom experience racial oppression in our society.

2. A local case is illustrative. In East St. Louis, a young African American man accused of throwing rocks onto the freeway during rush hour was undergoing psychiatric evaluation to determine if he could stand trial. In the local paper, a man whose car had been struck in the incident was quoted as being angry that the young man's mental health was at issue: "He didn't look disturbed. He just looked like your typical hoodlum kid" (Matthews, 1995, p. B3).

References

Anderson, David C. (1995). *Crime and the politics of hysteria: How the Willie Horton story changed American justice.* New York: Times Books.

Brower, Montgomery, Mathison, Dirk, and Brown, S. Avery. (1989, November 13). "A dark night of the soul in Boston." *People*, 52.

Carlson, Margaret. (1990, January 22). "Presumed innocent." *Time*, 10.

Cerio, Gregory, and Sider, Don. (1995, July 10). "Death on trial." *People*.

Chin, Paula. (1994, March 28). "Sins of the son." *People*, 38.

——. (1991, August 12). "The door of evil." *People*, 32–35.

Chua-Eoan, Howard G. (1991, August 12). "The uses of monsters." *Time*, 43.

Cornell, Bradford. (1993, November 28). "Milken expertise bridges a gap." *Los Angeles Times*, M5.

Daley, Suzanne. (1985, January 2). "IRT suspect is charged as fugitive." *New York Times*, 3B.

Davis, Angela Y. (1981). *Women, race and class.* New York: Vintage Books.

Davis, Mike. (1992). *City of quartz: Excavating the future in Los Angeles.* New York: Vintage Books.

Dougherty, Steve, and Sider, Don. (1994, November 14). "The lost boys." *People*, 50.

Ellis, David. (1988, December 12). "Hedda's hellish tale." *Time*, 32.

Estrich, Susan. (1987). *Real rape: How the legal system victimizes women who say no.* Cambridge, MA: Harvard University Press.

Gelman, David, with Elam, Regina. (1988, December 12). "Prisoners of pain." *Newsweek*, 65.

Gibbs, Nancy. (1994, November 14). "Death and deceit." *Time*, 42.

——. (1989, May 8). "Wilding in the night." *Time*, 20.

Gleick, Elizabeth. (1995, August 7). "No casting of stones." *Time*, 31.

——. (1994, December 12). "The final victim." *People*, 126.

Greenfield, Meg. (1989, May 15). "Other victims in the park." *Newsweek*, 86.

Hackett, George, and McKillop, Peter. (1989, May 15). "Opinions, but no solutions." *Newsweek*, 40.

Hackett, George, with McKillop, Peter, and Wang, Dorothy. (1988, December 12). "A tale of abuse." *Newsweek*, 56.

Hewitt, Bill, Mathison, Dirk, Brown, S. Avery, Verner, Gayle, Sawicki, Stephen, and Carswell, Sue. (1990, January 22). "A cold killer's chilling charade." *People*, 66.

Hewitt, Bill, Wescott, Gail Cameron, and Sider, Don. (1995, March 13). "Tears of hate, tears of pity." *People*, 76.

Huff, C. Ronald. (1990). "Denial, overreaction, and misidentification: A postscript on public policy." In C. Ronald Huff (Ed.), *Gangs in America*. Thousand Oaks, CA: Sage Publications, 310–317.

Kilpatrick, James J. (1985, January 11). "Subway shooting: Life in the jungle." *Los Angeles Times*, 5A.

Krauthammer, Charles. (1989, May 8). "Crime and responsibility." *Newsweek*, 104.

Kunen, James S. (1990, July 30). "Risen from near death, the Central Park jogger makes her day in court one to remember." *People*, 32.

——. (1989, May 22). "Madness in the heart of the city." *People*, 106.

Levitt, Shelley. (1994, November 21). "Portrait of a killer." *People*, 54.

McCormick, John, with Miller, Susan, and Woodruff, Debra. (1994, November 14). "Why parents kill." *Newsweek*, 31.

Ortega, Suzanne T., and Myles, Jessie L. (1987). "Race and gender effects on fear of crime: An interactive model with age." *Criminology*, 25 (1), 133–152.

Paltrow, Scot. (1990, April 21). "Milken to plead guilty to fraud." *Los Angeles Times*, 1A.

Peyser, Marc, with Power, Carla. (1995, December 11). "The death of little Elisa." *Newsweek*, 42.

Podolsky, J.D., Balfour, Victoria, Eftimiades, Maria, and McFarland, Sabrina. (1990, September 3). "As the Central Park jogger struggles to heal, three attackers hear the bell toll for them." *People*, 47.

Prud'Homme, Alex. (1991, August 12). "Milwaukee murders: Did they all have to die?" *Time*, 28.

Raspberry, William. (1985, January 11). "Subway shooting: Life in the jungle." *Los Angeles Times*, 5A.

Richter, Paul. (1990, April 29). "Ranking Milken among the rogues." *Los Angeles Times*, 1D.

Schneider, Karen S. (1992, March 2). "Day of reckoning." *People*, 38.

Stanko, Elizabeth. (1990). *Everyday violence: How women and men experience sexual and physical danger*. London: Pandora.

Tayman, John. (1991, August 12). "The lambs connection: Fiction pales. *People*, 36.

Treen, Joe, and Tamarkin, Civia. (1992, February 3). "Probing the mind of a killer." *People*, 75.

Trippett, Frank. (1990, August 27). "Guilty, guilty, guilty." *Time*, 40.

Van Biema, David. (1995, December 11). "Abandoned to her fate." *Time*, 32.

—— (1994, November 14). "Parents who kill." *Time*, 50.

Walsh, Anthony. (1987). "The sexual stratification hypothesis and sexual assault in light of the changing conceptions of race." *Criminology*, 25 (1), 153–174.

White, Ed. (1995). "Chief: Race played a role in reaction to murders." *Belleville* (Illinois) *News-Democrat*.

Williams, Patricia. (1991). *The alchemy of race and rights*. Cambridge: Harvard University Press.

Yoder, Edwin M., Jr. (1985, January 11). "Subway shooting: Life in the jungle." *Los Angeles Times*, 5A.

Discussion Questions

1. In what ways do the authors suggest that media handling of race and crime creates a hierarchy of victims, who are seen as more or less deserving of public sympathy?

2. How did media stereotypes play into the cases of Charles Stuart and Susan Smith?

3. Compare the media's attempts to explain Jeffrey Dahmer's crimes with

their explanations of the crimes of the young men who raped the Central Park jogger. What are the consequences of these differences?

4. How does the image of Michael Milkin compare with the image of a "typical" street criminal?

5. What are some of the consequences of the media's treatment of whiteness and crime? How do the media contribute to the perpetuation of racial inequality in the United States? ✦

Chapter 20

Stereotyping by Politicians

The Politics of Race and Crime

Jerome Miller

It is no accident that the great analysis of American democracy by Alexis DeToqueville began as a commentary on American penal practice. Similarly, Charles Dickens in his "Travels in America" spent an inordinate amount of time describing the youth and adult institutions for offenders in Massachusetts, New York, and Philadelphia. Why this interest?

It was because these elements in a society are, in effect, relatively good barometers of what a society is about and where it is headed. The canard that one can judge the degree of civilization in a society by entering its prisons was the same bellwether that led DeToqueville to comment on America and to point out its political contradictions—among them the abiding issue of race and slavery. Two hundred years later, Gunnar Myrdahl (1962) would call it the great "American Dilemma"—hinting (as did DeToqueville) that it contained the seeds for the undoing of the American democratic experiment.

The reasons for the current flight from decency in our treatment of young offenders are contained in the statistics regarding who they are likely to be. Over the last two decades, an ominous pattern has emerged that will probably alter American society in the most fundamental ways.

On an average day in many American cities, one-half or more of the young black male residents (ages 18–35) are under the onus of the criminal justice system—in prison or jail, on probation or parole, out on bond, or being sought on arrest warrants (National Center on Institutions and Alternatives, 1992a, 1992b, 1997). At least 75 percent of African American males can now anticipate being arrested before their 35th year—thereby acquiring a formal criminal record. More than half of the men who enter the nation's state and federal prisons are black. This stands in sharp contrast to the place of black men earlier in the century, when their representation in the general population was approximately what it is now. For example, in 1926, approximately 21 percent of new admissions to state and federal prisons were black men. By 1995, spurred on in particular by the War on Drugs, at least 56 percent of prison admissions nationally were black men (Miller, 1996, p. 55). Another 20 percent were Latino/Hispanic.

Of 1,000 arrestees charged with misdemeanors (most having to do with curfew violations) during the Los Angeles riots following the Rodney King police beating verdict, more than 600 had "criminal" records and nearly a third were on probation or parole. An earlier 1991 study revealed that nearly one-third of all the young black men aged 20–29 living in Los Angeles County had been jailed at least once that same year (Austin and Irie, 1992). A similar study of the Cook County Jail in Chicago showed that 29 percent of all the young black men aged 20–29 living in Chicago were jailed in 1990 for an average of 32 days (Austin, 1990). This pattern was unknown even in the heyday of segregation.

All of this means that we have reached a point where Caucasian males now make up less than 25 percent of all new admissions to state and federal prisons nationally. This new reality has redefined the political debate and changed the rules of the game in a profound way. It has drained the system of any impulse on the part of the general populace to be humane or rational in the treatment of offenders. It has fed a culture of punishment and retribution. Replete with images of dark-skinned predators, crime has been forged into a metaphor for race—hammered home nightly on TV news and "reality-based" crime shows. The racial composition of the "stuff," so to speak, of the criminal justice system is now clearly made up of young black and Latino men.

The Rhetorical Wink

These portents have been effectively ignored or forgotten. Contemporary politicians of both major parties vie with one another in the delivering of pain to those who are perceived as real or even potential lawbreakers. Crime has seldom been more effectively exploited by politicians than in recent years. At times, one wishes for ready access to the delicious words used by Victorians in describing certain types of contemporary politicos—"tufthunters," "lickspittles," or "cringing parasites and toadies."

This fact has led white politicians—liberal and conservative alike—into the era of the "rhetorical wink" whereby code phrases communicate a well-understood but implicit meaning while allowing the speaker to deny any such meaning (Guinier, 1993, p. A29). The wink has become all but blinding when the discussion turns to matters of crime and punishment. Politicians can now shout "crime" and, with a wink, ensure that their audiences will hear "race."

When we talk about "criminals," most now see a black or brown face. The word "black" or "Latino" need never be uttered. In fact, racial references are assiduously avoided. They are simply understood. This, more than anything, has conditioned the punitive approaches of the past decade. Moreover, it has placed the nation in a posture of mimicking the "line in the sand" criminal justice model in dealing with a host of other problems—welfare, immigration, family disputes, children's services, drug treatment, and school administration, to name a few.

Were our political leaders to think for a moment that 75 percent of the nation's young white males were being arrested (mostly for minor charges) and saddled with a criminal record, we would be in the throes of a national emergency. Were they to discover that half of the young white male population is under criminal justice supervision, we would witness a quick retreat from the vicious shibboleths that now masquerade as public policy.

Broken Windows

Though the problem has grown exponentially in recent years, the relationship of the criminal justice system to African American males has historically been fraught with problems for our democracy. Equating convict labor with slavery was a central theme following Reconstruction and well into the twentieth century. "After the [Civil] War," wrote one observer, "the crime problem in the South became equated with the 'Negro Problem' as Black prisoners began to outnumber White prisoners in all Southern prisons . . . the terms 'slave,' 'Negro,' and 'convict' were interchangeable" (Vining-Brown, 1975, pp. 18–19).

Likewise, the now common practice of arresting massive numbers of minorities on petty public-order charges (referred to alternately as "zero tolerance" or, in another context, as "broken window theory") has a long tradition. Citing the studies of H. Donaldson on the Negro migration of 1916–1918, University of Michigan sociologist Shirley Vining-Brown (1975) noted that many blacks migrated to the North in the late 1800s and early 1900s to escape these arrest tactics of southern law authorities.

Sheriffs (the most political of politicians in the South) were paid by the head for every man arrested. Large numbers of black men found themselves with what amounted to a bounty on their heads. They were picked up for petty infractions like littering and disorderly conduct. Fines were set at such high levels that those who had been arrested could not afford them, thereby having to stay in jail or prison. Mark Carlton (1971) found that black men tended to be picked up when the labor market was in short supply or workers were needed for county road work and other local duties.

These practices followed black men to the North in the twentieth century. In Pittsburgh, arrests of blacks for petty offenses, including the crime of "suspicion," nearly doubled. A Department of Labor study conducted at that time in Cleveland revealed that in 1916–1917 extraordinarily large numbers of black men were being sent to prison for this "crime," accounting for much of the "Negro Crime" in the United States reported during this period.

As Vining-Brown put it, "In the South, both the facilities and the philosophy of prison were tailor-made for Black convicts in the post-Civil War period. . . . [T]he crime problem in the South became equated with the 'Negro Problem' as Black prisoners began to outnumber White prisoners in all Southern prisons. . . . The sudden change in the racial composition of Southern prisons produced changes in various penal practices." These involved a kind of "privatization" of the prisons in the "prisoner lease system," whereby inmates were leased to local farmers and plantation owners as a way of making a profit for the penal system and avoiding some of the costs of maintenance for the inmates. As one southern sheriff put it, "Before the war we owned the Negroes. . . . But these convicts we don't own em. One dies, get another." Vining-Brown (1975, pp. 18–19) concludes that "once a Black man was convicted in the South, he was viewed as incorrigible and any attempt to rehabilitate him was considered wasted money."

Providing the Rationale

In tandem with this political mood, the major academic/policy advisors of the right (e.g., James Q. Wilson, John DiIulio, and Charles Murray) have eagerly provided a "scientific" rationale for a culture of punishment, retribution, and exile. Terms like "super-predators" and "moral misfits" are manufactured on cue. The message is to ignore root causes in pursuit of immediate control. The political model is that of the meritocracy. British criminologist Jock Young characterized Wilson's approach, for example, as evolving "a series of measures which would step beyond the bounds of justice in order to defend the existing order. . . . If one does not wish fundamentally to restrict the economic and judicial system," he adds, "then coercion and discipline are the only alternatives to maintain order" (Young, 1994, p. 118).

Wilson routinely assumes the garb of the righteous protector of society. In the tradition of other moralists (Savanorola and Cotton Mather come easily to mind), he has charged that the justice system had "trifled with the wicked" and "encouraged the calculators." In pursuit of his agenda for harsher punishment, he has characteristically had little time for so-called root causes.

> "[When I hear the phrase] 'Crime and drug addiction can only be dealt with by attacking their root causes'," he wrote, "I am sometimes inclined, when in a testy mood, to rejoin, 'Stupidity can only be dealt with by attacking its root causes.' I have yet to see a 'root cause' or to encounter a government program that has successfully attacked it, at least with respect to those social problems that arise out of human volition rather than technological malfunction." (Wilson, 1975, pp. xiv–xv)

In a later treatise, *Crime and Human Nature*, written jointly with the late Harvard educational psychologist Richard Herrnstein, Wilson gave a strong hint as to where his views led, at least when it comes to offenders (Wilson and Herrnstein, 1985)—that is, to the vaunted genetic predispositions among certain racial groups, blacks in particular. *Crime and Human Nature* anticipated by a decade Charles Murray's collaboration with Herrnstein on *The Bell Curve* (Herrnstein and Murray, 1994)—a book of little scientific merit, but of relatively great political import—touting putative genetic deficiencies among blacks as limiting their possibilities in contemporary societies.

In the wake of Wilson's, Murray's, and Herrnstein's relative successes, other criminologists and behavioral scientists came out of the closet, given leave, so to speak, to utter what heretofore had been frowned upon—at least since the discoveries following the occupation of Germany. We were treated to a view of how all this might play out on the contemporary American scene as we confronted domestic crime. Among others, there were calls for sterilization, experimentation on inmates, and making the prison experience as torturous

as possible.[1] While granting that prisoners probably couldn't "be subjected to the same terrible tortures in prison as Dante dreamed up for Hell of Purgatory," Graeme Newman, then associate dean of the criminal justice department at the State University of New York at Albany, recommended that as an alternative they be used for "risky medical research" (1979, p. 69).

The 'Supermax' as Metaphor

The new "supermax" prisons probably provide the best metaphor for the country's moral bankruptcy when it comes to crime and corrections. By 1997, one had a sense of how far down the punitive road we had ventured. In August, *USA Today*, the TV-generation national newspaper, featured a relatively positive front page "cover story" on the new generation of maximum security prisons that were springing up throughout the country—the "supermax" facilities. As I read the article, I was struck by the ease with which the material was handled. There was no evidence of embarrassment or an attempt to hide the obscene treatment. It were as though one were reading a "Style" section "Tour of Buchenwald." "Serving superhard time: New prisons isolate worst inmates" screamed the headline (*USA Today*, August 4, 1997, pg. 1A). Spilling over to fill most of the second page, the story continued—topped in boldface with a quote from the recently appointed director of Texas' newest supermax to be occupied that week. "Some people," he opined, "deserve to be treated like animals." Significantly, race was not mentioned.

USA Today described the regimen of the new Texas facility—built at a cost of $170,000 per cell:

> Looming behind two rows of razor wire is a low-slung menacing place

designed to cage—not house—the worst of Texas' expanding inmate population. . . . Inside, most of the 660 prisoners who begin moving in today will spend 23 of every 24-hour day locked in un-airconditioned concrete stalls. There will be no televisions, no newspapers, no books. Human interaction, even between inmate and guard, will be strictly limited. Food will be shoved through a crack in the door. The most unruly prisoners will be served an unappetizing concoction of deboned meat, vegetables and gelatin desserts churned into a lumpy puree, then baked into bricks called "food loafs.". . . If there is an amenity here, it is the single hour that inmates are first stripped naked . . . then led in handcuffs wearing only their underwear to another cage. There for 60 minutes, they can pace an 18-by-20 foot concrete floor.

No mention was made of the fact that the racial disparities in the supermax facilities are even more extreme than the already gross differences in ordinary prisons and jails. In fact, the supermax facilities are mostly reserved for "obstreperous" black and brown men. William Chambliss' 1994 survey of the Maryland supermax prison in Baltimore revealed that 283 of its 288 inmates were African American (Chambliss, 1995, p. 254).

Moreover, though these facilities are touted as handling the "most dangerous" inmates in prison, they contain mostly those who have become management problems in the general prison population—unrelated to whatever crime they might have committed on the street. They are, in fact, designed primarily to manage emotionally disturbed and psychotic inmates in a system that has given up on providing adequate services to "criminals." The supermax suggests that if the system is not working , it must be due to poor management. It represents a manager's approach to what Christie refers to as the efficient management of pain. In this sense, it comes with a long history.

Continuing a Tradition

The American historian Richard Maxwell Brown has noted that the 3,224 recorded lynchings that occurred between 1889 and 1918 targeted almost exclusively young black males. The macabre ritual was less likely to be hanging than one in which "the doomed victim was burned at the stake—a process that was prolonged for several hours, often as the black male was subjected to the excruciating pain of torture and mutilation . . . climaxed, ordinarily, by the hideous act euphemistically described as 'surgery below the belt.' " "Souvenirs" taken from the mutilated body were then passed out (Brown, 1993, p. 217).

Our current approach to crime and corrections in general, and the emergence of the supermax in particular, should be viewed within a context of how elements in the white majority have traditionally feared the black male. In 1906, for example, southern newspapers waged a campaign calling for the castration of all black men who had been involved in incidents with white women. Indeed, some newspapers proposed that, as a preventive measure, all black women be "unsexed" early in life to forestall the rise of another generation of rapists (ibid., p. 336).

The supermax facilities are, in a broad sense, a reiteration of this tradition. They are designed to break the recalcitrant and to display the results of this handiwork publicly for all to see. For many in the white majority, it provides a psychological substitute for the reassurance that lynching once gave them.

The supermax stands as mute testimony to the fact that we can no longer recognize, much less acknowledge, that nexus where the criminal impulse merges with the dark predilections of the dispensers of pain. I trust that my friends in the sociological academic community will forgive me for this brief indulgence in resorting to my own clinical experience, but the question must be posed—Where did all this come from? Surely not from any credible scientific research on human behavior. It might be well to place it in a historical and social-psychological context.

The procedures that characterize the day-to-day routines in supermax facilities cannot be understood by looking in a criminology text or scanning a prison management manual. Instead, they should be more properly relegated to a psychoanalyst's casebook, better deciphered by perusing the *Naked Lunch* fantasies of a William Burroughs. Surely, properly filmed and produced, the regimens of the average supermax could be well positioned to attract the S&M segment of the pornography market.

Drinking Gin From a Bottle

Providing a constant drumbeat for the culture of retribution are a news media drowning in kitsch and talk show ethics. Garrison Keillor put it more bluntly. "Every murder turns into 50 episodes. It's as bloody as Shakespeare but without the intelligence and the poetry. If you watch television news you know less about the world than if you drank gin out of a bottle."[2]

In August 1997, the Center for Media and Public Affairs (CMPA) published a study of the media and crime, noting that from 1993 to 1997 overall crime news tripled; and the coverage of murders increased by 721 percent during a time when real-world homicide rates were dropping dramatically. The coverage had all the elements of creating what the sociologists refer to as a "moral panic"—a situation in which the realities of a particular social phenomenon do not warrant the attention given them in the public concern and in the media (Media Monitor, 1977).

Under the heading "If It Bleeds It Leads," the Center noted:

No trend in news coverage has been more striking over the past seven years than the soaring number of stories about crime. Since 1990 one out of every ten stories on the network evening news has dealt with this topic. Crime was a significant part of the new agenda even during the early 1990s. But crime news took on a life of its own in 1993, as the coverage doubled in a single year from 830 to 1,698 stories. That made crime the leading TV news topic for the first time since CMPA began tracking the news agenda in 1987. But the coverage continued to grow, reaching 1,949 stories during 1994 and 2,574 during 1995, more than triple the total recorded only three years earlier. (ibid.)

The Center went on to note that while news coverage of crime increased by 240 percent, violent crimes in the real world were dropping significantly.

These findings confirmed a trend pointed out three years earlier. Then, as now, while both government crime reports and victimization surveys showed that the overall national crime rate was stable or declining in 1993, the three major TV network evening newscasts had more than doubled their coverage of crime. Moreover, they developed crime-oriented features like NBC's "Society under Siege," which focused on urban violence and street crime. The director of the study, Robert Lichter, commented at the time, "I'm not arguing there is no crime problem, but when the media make more of it than they have, the media coverage can really ratchet up public concern. . . . People's fear of crime doesn't come from looking over their shoulders. It comes from looking at their television screens" (Edwards, 1994, p. C1).

Again, race was not mentioned in any of these studies. Had it been, it likely would have confirmed the impressions of *The New York Times'* television critic Walter Goodman that "[t]he suspects seen on television being arrested in muggings and shootings are almost always black men in their teens and 20s, and they figure hugely in the prevailing anxiety, among blacks as well as whites over personal safety. . . . No positive stories can compete with the recurrent images of shackled black youths" (Goodman, 1993, p. 14).

Pandemic Viciousness

To look upon the politics of contemporary American criminal justice is to see stereotyping and viciousness in every arena. Offenders are now routinely "objectified" to ensure their place as a breed apart. As this has taken place, the criminal justice system—described by George Herbert Mead (1917) as the "hostile procedure of law"—has come to define a wide array of social, family, personal, and economic problems.

In the wake of the changing color of its clientele, probation has likewise been so distorted and removed from its original roots that it is barely distinguishable from police roles. Probation officers sit with the prosecution at sentencing. The new "attack" probation officers resemble SWAT teams—in some cases even resorting to the black uniforms and employing the armamentaria more suited to an antiterrorist strike force than a "helper" (as was John Augustus, its inventor and founder). Social workers, school counselors, teachers, "child protective" workers, and therapists have all found a new author-

ity and identity with a law enforcement approach to solving social problems.

Some European scholars have begun to note that the current political mood in the United States regarding crime and punishment is uncomfortably reminiscent of that observed by the Danish sociologist Svend Ranulf when he looked across the border into the Germany of the early 1930s (a time not unacquainted with racial and ethnic hysteria).[3] Ranulf was primarily concerned with the anticrime policies of National Socialism. Again, the criminal justice procedures betrayed the direction of the larger society. Everywhere Ranulf saw "a disinterested disposition to punish." He called it "disinterested" because "no direct personal advantage seemed to be achieved by calling for the harsh punishment of another person who had injured a third party" (Ranulf, 1964, pp. 1–2). Noting that this punitive inclination was not equally strong in all human societies, and was entirely lacking in some, Ranulf concluded that it didn't arise out of concern for deterrence. Rather, he saw it as a kind of "disguised envy"—less a response to crime rates than tied to the economic insecurities of the middle class.

The politicians of that time assessed the atmosphere, bolstered the stereotypes, and fed the public's worst impulses. The anticrime program proffered by the Prussian Minister of Justice in 1933 called for aggravated penalties for criminal acts already subject to punishment; mitigation would be allowed only in the most rare and exceptional cases; attempts would be dealt with as severely as accomplished crimes; drunkenness would be an aggravating rather than an extenuating circumstance; and prisons would be made harsher, with "dark cells and hard couches." Disciplinary measures would be applied at the discretion of prison wardens without the intrusion of outside monitors, and there would be more liberal recourse to capital punishment. Criticizing the alleged permissiveness of the previous Weimar Republic, the Minister ended this crime policy statement with a familiar slogan. "It seemed," he wrote,"that the welfare of the criminal, and not the welfare of the people, was the main purpose of the law."

The essential elements of this "crime control" program could have been promulgated last week in Washington or seriously proposed in the legislative chambers of most states. Indeed, these proposals are relatively mild when placed alongside those of many contemporary American politicians and criminologists.

The Swing of the Pendulum

One wonders not *when* but *whether* the pendulum will swing back again to a more humane and rational approach to crime as a social problem. I tend to think not. In the current state of American criminal justice, though, *race* has become the definer and separator; it need never be mentioned. The paradigm provides a refuge for all from accusations of racism—most significantly, for traditional liberals. Politicians in search of votes no longer look to an era of mandated segregation or blatant discrimination. The criminal justice system has raised the race game to new levels of sophistication. Why "race-bait" when one can "crime-bait" with impunity?

The urge is to ask how we reached this point. The answer is contained in the framing of the question. We didn't come to this as a detour in the nation's journey. We've never solved the dilemma—preferring to toy with it from the beginning. Rather, the question is: what has happened to make brutally manifest what has lain latent for so long?

We are only now beginning to confront the implications of this new state of affairs. If prison populations continue to grow at their present rate—and if the racial patterns are sustained—we will shortly see an absolute majority of the nation's black men in prisons and camps. The tenor of current political leadership can only accelerate the process.

We have created our own fictitious entities and are busily going about the task—to paraphrase Graham Greene (1991)—of contriving to educate our citizens to suppress any lingering sense of guilt or indecision of mind that might remain. Unfortunately, our political leaders are going about the same dirty business with a vengeance.

Notes

1. Newman (1979) had put forth the thesis that "some people may be born with a physiology that is likely to predispose them (or in some rare cases determine them) to become killers." Similarly, as president of the American Society of Criminologists, C. Ray Jeffrey had posited a connection between criminal behavior and genetically determined low I. Q. Curiously, he rejected the idea that genes had any relevance whatsoever to white-collar crimes, saying that they "should be regarded not as a problem in criminology but as a problem of politics and economics" (Platt and Takagi, 1979, p. 8). Taking a somewhat different tack, behavioral geneticist David Rowe introduced his own Darwinian "evolved genetic theory" of delinquency, basing it on the "mating strategies" of baboons, monkeys, and cuckoos. Applying this theoretical model to inner-city crime and welfare, Rowe proposed that we concentrate on identifying (presumably through a statistical correlational process) those as yet unspecified genes that maximize "mating" and minimize "parenting" among "certain groups and individuals." In assessing the public-policy options necessary to remedy these deficits, Rowe—chary of "interventions aimed at

altering family conditions"—suggested that "a biologically based trait . . . raises the possibility of using biological as opposed to social interventions" (Rowe, 1996). Race was not mentioned.

2. Garrison Keillor, "News from Lake Wobegon," on National Public Radio's *Prairie Home Companion*, December 1993.

3. Among them the eminent Norwegian criminologist Nils Christie, a student of the Nazi death camps and Eastern European gulags, in remarks made at the International Conference on Imprisonment, Academy of Science, Oslo, Norway, April 28, 1992.

References

Austin, James. (1990). *1990–2000 briefing report, Cook County Department of Corrections*. National Council on Crime and Delinquency. San Francisco: National Council on Crime and Delinquency.

Austin, James, and Irie, Donald. (1992, August 21). *Los Angeles County Sheriff's Department jail population analysis and policy simulations: Briefing report.* San Francisco: National Council on Crime and Delinquency.

Brown, Richard Maxwell. (1993). *Strain of violence: Historical studies of American violence and vigilantism.* New York: Basic Books.

Carlton, Mark T. (1971). *Politics and punishment.* Baton Rouge: Louisiana State University Press.

Chambliss, William J. (1995). "Crime control and ethnic minorities: Legitimizing racial oppression by creating moral panics." In Darnell Hawkins (Ed.), *Ethnicity, race, and crime: Perspectives across time and place.* Albany: State University of New York Press.

Edwards, Ellen. (1994, March 3). "Networks make crime top story: Survey says coverage fanned public's fear." *Washington Post,* C1, C8.

Goodman, Walter. (1993, December 23). "Critic's notebook: 'Crime and black images in tv news.'" *The New York Times,* 14.

Greene, Graham. (1991). *Reflections.* London: Reinhardt Books.

Guinier, Lani. (1993, October 19). "Clinton spoke the truth on race." *The New York Times,* Op-Ed., A29.

Herrnstein, Richard, and Murray, Charles. (1994). *The bell curve: Intelligence and class structure in American life.* New York: Free Press.

Matthews, Jayne. (1995, August 30). "Suspect's status angers victims." *The Belleville* (Illinois) *News-Democrat,* 3B.

Mead, George H. (1917). "The psychology of punitive justice." *American Journal of Sociology,* 23, 577–602.

Media Monitor. (1997, July/August). *Network news in the nineties,* 11 (3).

Miller, Jerome G. (1996). *Search and destroy: African-American males in the criminal justice system.* Cambridge: Cambridge University Press.

Myrdahl, Gunnar. (1962). *An American dilemma.* 2nd ed. New York: Harper and Row.

National Center on Institutions and Alternatives. (1997, August). *Hobbling a generation revisited: African Americans in D.C.'s criminal justice system.* Alexandria, VA: National Center on Institutions and Alternatives.

———. (1992a, March). *Hobbling a generation: African American males in the District of Columbia's criminal justice system.* Alexandria, VA: National Center on Institutions and Alternatives.

———. (1992b, September). *Hobbling a generation II: African American males in Baltimore, Maryland's criminal justice system.* Alexandria, VA: National Center on Institutions and Alternatives.

Newman, Graeme. (1979). *Understanding violence.* New York: J.B. Lippincott.

Ranulf, Svend. (1964). *Moral indignation and middle class psychology: A sociological study.* New York: Schocken Books. (First published by Levin & Munksgaard, Ijnar Munksgaard, Copenhagen, 1938.)

Rowe, David C. (1996). "An adaptive strategy theory of crime and delinquency." In J. David Hawkins (Ed.), *Delinquency and crime: Current theories.* New York: Cambridge University Press.

USA Today. (1997, August 4). "Serving superhard time: New prisons isolate worst inmates." 1A

Vining-Brown, Shirley Ann. (1975). *Race as a factor in the intra-prison outcomes of youthful first offenders.* Ph.D. thesis, University of Michigan.

Wilson, James Q. (1975). *Thinking about crime.* New York: Basic Books.

Wilson, James Q., and Herrnstein, Richard. (1985). *Crime and human nature: The definitive study of the causes of crime.* New York: Simon & Schuster.

Young, Jock. (1994). "Recent paradigms in criminology." In M. Maguire, R. Morgan, and R. Reiner (Eds.), *Oxford handbook of criminology.* Oxford: Clarendon Press.

Discussion Questions

1. What is the "rhetorical wink?" How does the author use this figure of speech?

2. How are demographic and economic changes related to changes in penal practices in the South?

3. According to the author, why does the Supermax prison provide the best metaphor for moral bankruptcy about crime and corrections? Who is the typical inmate in Supermax prisons?

4. According to the author, how are the Supermax prisons comparable to lynchings?

5. What is a moral panic and why is this a useful term for explaining recent crime policies? Give two examples of moral panics you have seen developed in the media. ◆

Chapter 21

Images of Crime and Punishment

The Laundering of White Crime

Mark S. Hamm

In the year 1006 A.D., Leif Eriksson's brother, Thorwald, came ashore somewhere along the northeastern coast of North America. According to Viking legend, Eriksson and his men discovered a village of natives—whom they called Skrellings—and seized the place with violence, killing eight Indians in the process (Josephy, 1968).

This is the oldest known account of contact between peoples of the Old World and the New; and given the immediate resort to bloodshed, it was a strange encounter to be sure. Nevertheless, 10 centuries later, United States President George Bush stood on the site of Eriksson's launching in Norway, and proclaimed that he was one of the "great heroes" of world history (Hamm, 1993).

In one way or another, this institutionalized racism—or, more precisely, *institutionalized white supremacism*—has been the wellspring of Western violence throughout the second millennium. It brought about the genocide of some three million Native Americans during the nineteenth century. It gave rise to American slavery, and then to the Ku Klux Klan and a reign of terror against an untold number of blacks fol-

lowing the Civil War. In recent years, it has led to rampant violence across the United States, to a spectacular increase in hate crimes, and to the Oklahoma City bombing—the greatest act of domestic terrorism in American history (Hamm, 1994, 1996, 1997).

It should come as no surprise to the student of American criminology, then, to learn that the majority of violent crimes are committed by young white males. Nationwide, whites account for 54 percent of the yearly arrests for murder, rape, robbery, and aggravated assault (Donziger, 1996; Miller, 1996). Most of the other violent crimes are committed by young black males from urban areas. And much of *that* violence is connected to the trade in crack cocaine and heroin (Fagan, 1992; Boyum and Kleiman, 1995). By and large, this illicit drug market is supported by middle-class white males. They are the largest category of users, the ones who sustain the drug trade economically (Chambliss, 1994).

Yet strangely enough, criminologists and the general public seldom focus on the race of these criminals. Consider the reporting of crimes by your local evening television news program. If the perpetrators of a violent crime are young African American men, reporters typically refer to them as "black males." Yet the distinction "white males" is almost never used in the same context.

But what about the criminal image of whites, the group actually responsible for most of the violence in America today? For them, color is transparent; it takes on meaning only when compared to the color black. The transparency of white criminality is linked not only to the legacy of institutionalized white supremacism but also to the dominant language of the society. In defining the word "white," *The American Heritage Dictionary* uses such terms as "unsullied and pure," "bloodless" and "devoid of hue." It also says that white is the "antagonist of black." History shows that this antagonism applies to crime as well.

How did all of this come about? In the following pages, I shall attempt to answer that question by referring to several key waves of American history. As we shall see, these historical waves served to diminish—to make transparent—the "whiteness" of white violence. Not only that, but in the tradition of the Viking Thorwald Eriksson, they also transformed the most violent white men of American history into folk heroes.

The First Wave: The White–Indian Conflict

The longest and deadliest conflict in American history was unquestionably the one between whites and Indians that began in Virginia in 1607 and continued, with intermittent truces, for nearly 300 years, ending in the massacre of the Sioux by United States troops at Wounded Knee, South Dakota, in 1890 (Brown, 1989). It is likely that no other factor has had a more brutalizing influence on the character of white America than the Indian Wars. Three centuries of broken treaties, along with rape, pillage, plunder, and the slaughter of thousands of defenseless women and children, would become, in the words of President John F. Kennedy, "a national disgrace" (1961, p. 8).

History teaches that three important developments set the stage for the mass killing of American Indians. First, from the early seventeenth century to the middle of the eighteenth century, a secure European foothold was established in what would later become the northeastern region of the United States. This period also marked the development of several strong alliances between the Europeans and various Indian tribes throughout the region. Foremost among these was the alliance between British traders and the Iroquois. They had a common interest: to protect themselves against the French—a formidable enemy.

The second development was related to population growth in the new colonies of the Northeast. A rising birth rate during the early 1700s created among the colonialists a moral fervor that, in turn, led to increased white economic expansion in the region. This moral determination led to the widespread belief that the extermination of local "savages" was necessary (Guillemin, 1989).

At first, however, the white–Indian conflict was limited to minor local skirmishes and brief retaliations. This changed with the coming of the American Revolution, the third deciding factor of the genocide. For with the Revolution came the military intervention of the state. This not only brought organization to the conflict but would eventually increase dramatically the scale of retribution against the Indians.

By the 1770s, most of the Six Nations of the Iroquois were under the leadership of a brilliant Mohawk chief, Thayendanegea, known also as Joseph Brant. When the Revolutionary War broke out, an Englishman known to history as Sir William Johnson made his home with the Six Nations and strongly encouraged Brant to side with Britain (Wissler, 1966). This he did, and the British employed their Iroquois allies in raids on the Pennsylvania–New York border, threatening to cut the colonies in two along the Hudson River.

In the summer of 1779, Commander-in-Chief George Washington responded by dispatching 4,000 militia men under General John Sullivan. They burned villages, chopped down orchards, and trampled cornfields to lay waste to the Iroquois homeland. Then Sullivan's troops withdrew, leaving the

Iroquois to face the winter without food and shelter. Broken in power and spirit, they migrated to Canada or turned to liquor (Wissler, 1966; Josephy, 1968).

Before Sullivan's raid, white–Indian violence was sporadic and nonsystematic. With Sullivan's raid, a new epoch in white violence began.

The Second Wave: The Indian Wars

After the Revolutionary War, the United States government signed a number of treaties with the Indian tribes. As was discussed in Chapters two and three, most of these treaties have been broken. Military might was used repeatedly to force Indian nations to bend to white desires for land (Josephy, 1961). My purpose in discussing the Indian Wars here is to clarify how the actions of white settlers, soldiers, and politicians constituted some of the earliest instances of white supremacist crimes in what is now the United States.

The Indian Wars were based on one thing: the need of white Americans to acquire more land. This land had been home to various Indian tribes for generations of history, and their people had developed a deep spiritual connection to it. Time after time, treaties were broken and revised in favor of mining, railroad, and land speculation interests. Each of these occasions broke a solemn promise of the United States and led to a thorough Indian distrust and hatred of anything American. General George Crook, perhaps the most effective peacemaker of the Indian Wars, summed up this process: "Greed and avarice on the part of whites—in other words, the almighty dollar is at the bottom of nine-tenths of all our Indian troubles" (Josephy, 1961, p. 342).

Along with the wars came increased lawlessness on the part of opportunistic white men drawn to the West in search of fortunes in cattle, railroads, and gold. These men deliberately created their own wars with the tribes due to a sincere belief that the Indians should be wholly exterminated. "Let our motto be extermination, and death to all opposers," said a California newspaper in 1854 (Josephy, 1961, p. 311). To encourage Indian submission in the Great Plains region, the military encouraged roving bands of white men to slaughter the big buffalo herds, the Indians' principal source of food (Josephy, 1968).

These conditions gave rise to the bounty hunters, who marked an important chapter in the history of white American violence. Driven by the powerful profit motive and often fueled by whiskey, they engaged in unspeakable atrocities against the Western Indians, atrocities that not only went unpunished by frontier law but were actually sanctioned by the federal government. This was especially so under the administration of President Ulysses S. Grant (1869–1877) and his commander of the army, General William Tecumseh Sherman, who once called for the "utter extermination" of all Indians (Josephy, 1961, p. 313).

Examples of such vigilante killing abound in history. For instance, one historian writes of "three unauthorized squads in one sector of Oregon [that] killed between 12 and 18 savages per squad in less than a week in 1853, in each case by inducing the savages to lay down their arms under pledges of peace and then shooting them" (Josephy, 1961, p. 312). The policy of vigilante killing was so well applied during the California gold rush that California's Indian population was reduced by some 50,000 between 1849 and 1852 (ibid.).

The Indian Wars also produced legendary American heroes, such as the frontiersman Kit Carson. In June 1863, Carson and some 700 militia men invaded the vast homeland of the Navajo in northern New Mexico. They applied what can best be described as a scorched earth policy. By the following April, Carson's troops had destroyed the Navajo's cornfields and slaughtered their herds of sheep, thereby reducing some 10,000 Indians to starvation and death (Josephy, 1961; Carter, 1968).

These years also saw a disastrous new round of military provocations. As Riding In and Harjo discussed in Chapters two and three, the massacres at Sand Creek and Wounded Knee are especially noteworthy for their brutality and the numbers killed. These assaults sent the tribes of the Central Plains into united warfare.

The beginning of the end of the Indian Wars occurred in July 1876 with the defeat of Lieutenant Colonel George Armstrong Custer's Seventh Cavalry at the battle of the Little Big Horn in Montana. This battle, which killed Custer and some 250 of his men, was the moment of reckoning for President Grant and the white political establishment. Such a humiliating defeat simply could not be tolerated in a modern nation now approaching 40 million people, especially in light of the fact that the nation had just celebrated its 100th anniversary. And so, the United States Army doubled its efforts against the protagonists of the Little Big Horn battle—the Sioux and Cheyenne leaders Crazy Horse, Sitting Bull, and Gall (Josephy, 1968). But they proved elusive, and the ending went on for years.

By the late 1880s, extermination, starvation, disease, and harsh prison conditions had reduced the Western Indian population to less than 300,000 from the estimated pre-War figure of nearly three million. That was when the messiahs appeared. One was a Nevada Paiute named Wovoka. He began what has been called the Ghost Dance because it foretold the disappearance of white men and the return of the buffalo and dead Indians who would help living Indians in their final hour of extremity. A great revival spread among the embattled Indians of the Plains, and the authorities feared the excitement might lead to a new round of hostilities. At this point, Sitting Bull, the great apostle of the Ghost Dance, was captured and murdered.

Then, three days before Christmas in 1890, a 500-man unit of the Seventh Cavalry massacred a band of some 400 Sioux, two-thirds of whom were women and children, on suspicion of hiding Crazy Horse. How it started is unclear, but the troops suddenly opened fire at point-blank range into the Sioux camp. The shooting went on as long as any one—man, woman, or child—remained to be shot at. In the center of the camp, a group of young girls knelt in the snow and covered their faces with their shawls so that they would not see the troopers come up to shoot them (Josephy, 1961). It was the greatest military victory of the Indian Wars. It took place on ground immortalized in the last line of a poem by Stephen Vincent Bénet:

> I shall not rest quiet in Montparnasse . . .
> I shall not be there, I shall rise and pass.
> Bury my heart in Wounded Knee.

The Third Wave: Slavery

Abraham Lincoln described slavery as America's original sin. Historians often date the beginning of this sin to the year 1670, when the first Africans arrived in what is now the state of South Carolina (Wood, 1974; Joyner, 1984). By law, these people were deemed "chattels . . . in the hands of their owners. They are, generally speaking, not considered as persons but as things" (Butterfield, 1995, p. 6). Instead of simply considering them different by virtue of their skin color, then, the law viewed blacks as innately inferior to whites.

Over the next two centuries, some 700,000 Africans were forcibly transported across the Atlantic to the United States, where they were enslaved on plantations producing sugar, tobacco, coffee, rum, and cotton. The United States eventually became the world's leading user of slave labor, not because it participated heavily in the slave trade (Brazil led the world in that category) but because of natural increase. That is, an unusually high number of African Americans were born into slavery. By 1825 there were about two million slaves in the southern United States (Fogel, 1989). By the time Jefferson Davis was elected President of the Confederacy in 1860, the number had risen to some four million (Davis, 1982).

Slavery, the "peculiar institution," as southerners called it, was the ultimate American experience with white supremacy. At base, slavery permitted one group of people (whites) to exercise tight, legal, and wholly unrestrained personal domination over another group of people (blacks). The extreme degree of social domination required by this system provided the essential conditions for crime. Physical cruelty became necessary on the part of whites so that they could sustain domination over blacks. The vast forces needed to run a society based on domination and cruelty had a brutalizing effect on both the black slaves and their white masters. In time, it would lead to a tradition of violence among descendants of both groups (Butterfield, 1995).

Two features of slavery, then, would add to the character of white American violence. First, the goal of slavery was historically unprecedented. In the case of the Indian Wars, the goal was the utter extermination of the tribes. But in the case of slavery, it was to control the slaves in the pursuit of economic profit. And second, as a result, slavery was a more deliberate, systematic, and well-executed crime against humanity. Slavery therefore not only created a cultural tradition of violence among whites but also led to a penchant for white political extremism.

According to criminological theory, two essential elements are necessary to accomplish a successful crime: ideology and skill (Sutherland and Cressey, 1978). Extreme white supremacy supplied the ideological justification for slavery. The skills were more complex. They demanded that slave owners inflict cruelty on slaves but, at the same time, keep them alive so that they could work the plantations, thereby fulfilling their economic function. This led, first and foremost, to the practice of lynching.

Lynching originated in the South Carolina back country in the 1760s. But it wasn't until the days of the American Revolution (around 1776) that it became encapsulated into law. It was then that a Virginia colonel of Scottish-Irish descent, named Charles Lynch, passed into Virginia law a means to punish British loyalists. Lynch's law became so popular that a city was named after him—Lynchburg, Virginia.

After the Revolutionary War, Lynch and his supporters extended the law to cover all "lawless men." In legal terms, lynching was "the practice or custom by which persons are punished for real or alleged crimes without due process" (Brown, 1989, p. 36). For the next 100 years, various versions of the "lynch law" provided southern states with legal permission to inflict all manner of physical cruelty on the slaves. As a result, vigilante violence became an official instrument of southern justice.

This required that white plantation owners learn numerous skills in corporal punishment. Whipping came first, primarily because it was the only form of corporal punishment mentioned in the Bible. The Old Testament stipulated that a miscreant be struck a total of 39 times, "well laid on with hickory withes, whips, or any readily available instrument," as the South Carolina law stipulated (Brown, 1989, p. 36). Whipping even began to acquire an ideological dimension of its own. "Spare the rod and you spoil your Negroes" read a banner headline in a South Carolina newspaper in 1858 (Butterfield, 1995, p. 29).

Slaves could be whipped for anything, and they were—by the thousands (Fogel, 1989; Litwack, 1996). The case of a slave named Randal is typical. On the afternoon of May 8, 1844, Randal was riding a mule through a freshly plowed field on a plantation near Edgefield, South Carolina. His overseer, Seabourn Randolph, began chasing him on horseback. Randolph caught the slave, knocked him to the ground, hit him in the face, and then tied him up. Upon returning to plantation headquarters, Randal was stripped to the waist and given 500 lashes with a cowskin whip. After inflicting the blows, Randolph and another overseer washed Randal with salt and water to make the wounds sting more. Then Randal drank some water, vomited, and died (Butterfield, 1995).

This case clearly illuminates the image of white American violence brought about by slavery. Under the law, Randal's murder was justifiable. The white men who did the killing were not criminals. Instead, by the cruel inversions of southern justice, Randal was the criminal. Hence, the "whiteness" of white violence was made transparent by the permissions afforded in law. Without permission, violence is aberrant and forbidden. But with permission, it is laudable, patriotic, and professionalized. By the late 1860s, this tradition was so deeply entrenched in southern culture

that a new social movement arose in actual costumes of white transparency.

The Fourth Wave: The Ku Klux Klan and the Lynch Mobs

In Beaufort, South Carolina, near the edge of town, there is a giant old tree known as Emancipation Oak. It was here that a tax collector named Brisbane first read Abraham Lincoln's Emancipation Proclamation to the Negroes of South Carolina. Thereafter, it became a sacred place (Davis, 1982). But the road to freedom was a long and bloody one. By the time Robert E. Lee surrendered to Ulysses Grant at Appomattox on April 9, 1865, the Civil War had claimed the lives of 600,000 men. Mathematically, one soldier had died for every six slaves who were freed (Potter, 1976). Less than a week after Lee's surrender, on April 14, President Lincoln was assassinated by a Confederate sympathizer named John Wilkes Booth. That proved to be a harbinger of the extraordinary violence and extremism that would grip the South during the post–Civil War era.

Three days after the federal elections of 1868, a mob of men dressed to resemble ghosts—in white gowns, with white masks over their faces and white covers over their horses—attacked the home of a black farmer named Pickens Stewart near Mount Willing, South Carolina. They had come to punish Stewart for being "too smart, running to town too often to speeches," and trying to vote (Butterfield, 1995, p. 39). The mob seized Stewart at gunpoint, blindfolded him with a towel, tied him to a tree stump, and beat him until he was senseless.

So began the history of the Ku Klux Klan. Over the next several years, the sight of hooded Klansmen, burning crosses, night riders, and lynching would terrorize blacks throughout the rural South. The original Klan probably was the greatest perpetrator of vigilante violence in American history, rivaled only by the bounty hunters of the Indian Wars. How many black southerners were lynched, beaten, whipped, mutilated, or quietly murdered in order to enforce deference to white supremacy will never be known. As one historian has correctly noted, there will never be a full accounting of "the severed ears and entrails, the mutilated sex organs, the burnings at the stake, the public display of skulls and severed limbs as trophies" (Litwack, 1996, p. 121).

Not all the killings, assaults, and mutilations of the Reconstruction period can be attributed to the Klansmen, however. They simply were the most visible participants in southern opposition to the northern military, to the "carpetbaggers," and to the emerging participation of blacks in the affairs of government. Two features of Klan violence, though, would leave an indelible mark on the character of white American violence.

First, similar to the exhibitionism displayed by United States troops after the Sand Creek massacre, the Klan brought a carnival-like atmosphere to the character of white violence. In other words, the Klan's random and excessive brutality, combined with its bizarre costumes and rituals, had the effect of suspending reality—of being both out of place and out of consciousness. In time, this carnival of violence would develop other grotesque features, thereby attracting all sorts of white men from the lunatic fringes of American society (Hamm, 1993; Ezekiel, 1995; Presdee and Carver, 1996). Second, because the Klan had the sympathy of most white southerners, its campaign of terror was ultimately successful: By the mid-1870s, former slave owners had resumed control of state governments throughout the South and blacks, though still legally free, were effectively resubjugated (Gurr, 1989). Once again, blacks had been "put in their place"—a place of economic dependence, political impotence, and social and cultural subservience (O'Brien, 1989).

Although the original Ku Klux Klan formally disbanded in 1872, its political function was continued through the segregationist policies of state and local governments; its carnival of violence was continued through lynch mobs. Between 1882 and 1903, at least 1,985 southern Negroes were killed by these mobs. Supposedly the lynch-mob hanging (or, too often, a ghastly burning alive) was reserved for black rapists—"black beasts" who preyed upon "fragile" white women—or murderers, but statistics show that blacks were frequently lynched for lesser crimes or in cases where there was only the mere suspicion of one (Brown, 1989; O'Brien, 1989).

The carnival of violence reached full flower in 1894, when a total of 134 southern blacks were lynched by white mobs. Unlike the Klan atrocities—which were usually conducted quickly, in the dead of night, in secluded rural areas by costumed men hiding their faces—the lynchings became public spectacles. Carried out by large mobs of white men who seldom concealed their identities, observed by hundreds and sometimes thousands of spectators, including women and children, they received wide coverage in the press. The more heinous the alleged crime, the more sadistic the punishment. Alleged rapists would often have their genitals burned off with acid or branding irons. Body parts—fingers, toes, ears, teeth, and bones—became souvenirs. The mutilated bodies, sometimes burned beyond recognition, were photographed, often with one or more of the lynchers standing by.

In 1906, 43 years after Lincoln signed the Emancipation Proclamation, white mobs in Atlanta lynched, murdered, and assaulted scores of blacks and plundered their homes and stores. Much of the violence fell on the most industrious, respectful, law-abiding, and best-educated blacks, many of whom owned property. These victims were teachers, physicians, lawyers, clergymen, and merchants. In the words of one rioter, the action was taken to teach "uppity, smart-ass niggers" lessons they would never forget. Among those driven from their homes was Dr. W. F. Penn, a prominent black physician, a graduate of Yale University, and a community leader. "What shall we do?" he asked a gathering of Atlanta whites after the riot. "If living a sober, industrious, upright life . . . is not the standard by which a colored man can live and be protected in the South, what is to become of him?" (Litwack, 1996, p. 121).

The answer came: in one more round of cruelty. The black man would now become an entertainer in a pornography of racism. He would be caricaturized as lazy, shiftless, immoral, and occasionally dangerous in the white-dominated southern newspapers. He would be given these roles in minstrel shows, in vaudeville acts, and then in cinema.

Hollywood released its first motion picture in 1915. It was D. W. Griffith's epic movie *The Birth of a Nation*—a viciously racist portrayal of the original Ku Klux Klan as the protector of white womanhood and southern rights against rapacious blacks, greedy carpetbaggers, and vengeful, Lincolnesque Republicans (Toy, 1989). Within a matter of months, a new Klan was born. A national movement that would eventually enroll more than two million people, this Klan was not only anti-black, it was also anti-Semitic, anti-Catholic, and against anyone else Klan members regarded as "immoral."

Meanwhile, the lynchings continued unabated. Between 1915 and 1920, a total of 328 blacks fell victim to the hangman's noose. And despite the observance of lynchings by numerous spectators and the constant press coverage surrounding them, lynchers were rarely arrested, seldom indicted, and virtually never convicted (O'Brien, 1989). After a particularly brutal lynching in Little Rock, Arkansas, for example, the local newspaper wrote: "This may be 'Southern brutality' as far as the Boston Negro can see, but in polite circles, we call it southern chivalry, a southern virtue that will never die" (Litwack, 1996, p. 121).

This, then, was the image of white American violence near the turn of the century. The vicissitudes of institutionalized white supremacy had unleashed a blond beast. The ordinary modes of white violence—hidden from public view by the remoteness of the Indian Territory and the peculiar mechanism of slavery—no longer satisfied the emotional needs of the body politic. Grown men now hoisted their children on their shoulders to get a better view of the spectacle—of criminals who went about their deadly business in the confident manner of cultural heroes.

The Fifth Wave: The Social Bandits

When 15-year-old Henry Antrim rode out of Silver City, New Mexico, in 1875, he was a skinny, buck-toothed, girlish-looking boy with few prospects.[1] His mother had recently died of tuberculosis, he had dropped out of school and had begun stealing, and he was being pursued by the local sheriff after escaping from jail. Little did anyone know—they couldn't—that within a few short years this boy, nicknamed "Kid" because he was known to associate with men, would become a giant of American folklore. More than that, he would set in motion a series of events that would ultimately redefine the image of white American violence.

Young Henry arrived at the Hooker Ranch near Fort Grant, Arizona, sometime in mid-1876, where he briefly worked as a cow puncher. But that didn't last long, and he soon began running with a gang of cattle rustlers and horse thieves. After stealing one horse too many, Henry attracted the attention of the Gila County sheriff and was subsequently locked up in the Globe City jail. That also failed to hold him, and Henry escaped. He was rearrested twice more by the constable, and twice more he slipped away from custody.

By midsummer 1877, he was back in the Fort Grant area, where he quickly ran into trouble. On the night of August 17, Henry got into a fist fight with a man named Francis "Windy" Cahill in a saloon. Henry finished the fight by drawing his pistol and shooting Cahill in the stomach, killing him. Several days later, Fort Grant authorities issued an arrest warrant for "Henry Antrim alias Kid."

He returned to New Mexico, where he fell in with a group of rustlers along the Ruidoso River, north of the Mescalero Apache Indian reservation. There he became obsessed with guns, horsemanship, fiddle music, whoring, and gambling. The fact that Henry was a fugitive also prompted him to change his name to Billy Bonney.

In early 1878, Bonney and his friends went to work on an immense cattle ranch owned by L. G. Murphy and J. J. Dolan. At the time, these men were in conflict with two other ranchers named Alexander McSween and John Tunstall. McSween and Tunstall were associates of the great cattle baron John Chisum. In late February, someone

(presumably a Dolan gunman) killed John Tunstall. This touched off what would come to be known as the Lincoln County War; Billy Bonney and his comrades became known as the Regulators. Bonney is known to have shared with other Regulators the slaying of five men during the Lincoln County War. On his own, he is known to have killed one other man—an obnoxious drunk from Texas named Joe Grant—whom Bonney shot in a saloon fight in 1880.

Sometime in late 1880, an owner of the Las Vegas (New Mexico) *Gazette*, W. S. Koogler, became indignant over the killing going on in Lincoln County. He wrote a complaining letter to Governor Lew Wallace and then, in December, ran a long article in the *Gazette* denouncing the "powerful gang of outlaws . . . [who were] terrorizing the people of Fort Sumner and vicinity." This army of outlaws, Koogler wrote, "is under the leadership of 'Billy the Kid' a desperate cuss, who is eligible for the post of captain of any crowd, no matter how mean and lawless (Utley, 1989, p. 237)."

Other newspapers took notice, spreading Bonney's name and stories of his alleged crimes throughout the New Mexico Territory. Then on December 27, 1880, the *New York Gazette*, drawing on Koogler's article, ran a long story about the amazing new outlaw. With this, Bonney became a celebrity. He became glamorous, the premier outlaw of the Southwest. He became "Billy the Kid."

There was, however, little truth behind the image. Although some 40 or 50 outlaws *had* imposed a reign of terror in Lincoln County, they did not operate as a single gang, nor did they accord allegiance to a single leader—certainly not to a youth of 21. Even Bonney denied the image. In a long letter to Governor Wallace, Billy wrote: "There is no such organization in existence. So the gentleman [who wrote the story] must have drawn very very heavily on his imagination." He went on to say that "Billy, 'the Kid,' is the name by which I am known in the County," but added that he was not a criminal. That was a tale, he concluded, "put out by Chisum and his tools" (Utley, 1989, p. 146). In short, Bonney's fame was a newspaper creation. Nevertheless, Pat Garrett, the Lincoln County sheriff, placed a $500 reward on his head and set out to bring him in, dead or alive.

This he eventually did on the night of July 14, 1881, when Garrett killed Bonney with one shot to the heart, delivered in a dark bedroom at the Maxwell House in Fort Sumner. However, shooting a man in the dark violated a fundamental code of the West, and public opinion quickly turned against the sheriff. And so, Pat Garrett felt compelled to tell his side of the story. Within a matter of months, Garrett collaborated with a wandering journalist named Ash Upson to publish a book extravagantly titled *The Authentic Life of Billy the Kid, the Noted Desperado of the Southwest, Whose Deeds of Daring and Blood Have Made His Name a Terror in New Mexico, Arizona & Northern Mexico.*

So began the legend. In the years to come, an astounding 30 books would be written about Billy the Kid and the Lincoln County War, along with hundreds of dime store novels and thousands of newspaper and magazine articles. He would become the subject of more than 40 Hollywood films. Such stars as Johnny Mack Brown, Buster Crabbe, Paul Newman, Marlon Brando, and Kris Kristofferson took their turn at playing the famous desperado. Billy would be celebrated in opera by the classical composer Aaron Copeland and eulogized in surrealistic folk rock ballads by Bob Dylan. Rarely in the American experience has so much been made of so little.

These cultural productions created the image of Billy the Kid as a *social bandit*. He became nothing less than the American equivalent of Robin Hood, robbing from the rich and giving to the poor. For millions of Americans, the Kid came to embody the romance and tragedy of the Old West as it was being transformed into civilized settlements of the industrial age. Billy emerged from those crossroads with his guns blazing, willing to sacrifice everything in protest against greed and injustice. Never mind the fact that this image failed to mirror reality. Billy the Kid became a symbol of American values—white American values, that is—of youth, nobility, courage, and concern for fellow citizens. White society's need to create a Billy the Kid said far more about the pathology of that society than about the pathology of Henry Antrim.

Billy the Kid was, of course, only the first in a long line of white social bandits. Whether later generations actually robbed from the rich and gave to the poor would become irrelevant. Rather, what became important was whether people *thought* they did, and thus accorded them the status of folk heroes.

The first generation of social bandits appeared in reaction to the outcome of the Civil War. Foremost among them was the former Confederate soldier and mercenary, Jesse James—who, along with his brother Frank and the Younger brothers (Cole, Bob, and Jim), were depicted in scores of dime store novels and detective magazines as modern-day Robin Hoods. Among southern loyalists, Jesse James and his gang were looked upon as heroes for carrying on the struggle against Yankee authorities who had taken over the nation's railroads and banks. "We were driven to it" would be the refrain attributed to James's 16-year spree of robbing and killing along the Missouri–Kansas border (1866–82).

A second generation of social bandits emerged from the brutally poor farm families of the Great Depression. Charles "Pretty Boy" Floyd, John Dillinger, George "Machine Gun" Kelly, and Alvin Karpis, along with Fred and "Ma" Barker and Clyde Barrow and Bonnie Parker (Bonnie and Clyde), were all depicted in the nation's press as having a sense of decency and fair play about them. In reality, they robbed gas stations, restaurants, and small-town banks. Far from being social bandits, they preyed on their fellow poor and killed them ruthlessly.

A third generation arose from such Prohibition-era gangsters as Benjamin "Bugsy" Siegel, Joe Bonanno, Meyer Lansky, Charles "Lucky" Luciano, Carlo Gambino, and "Scarface" Al Capone, perhaps the most loathsome figure of the American twentieth century. They all portrayed themselves as benevolent businessmen with an appreciation for the finer things in life: a taste for the opera, tailored clothes, expensive cars, jewels, beautiful women, and contacts in high society. Movie producers and newspaper editors found them irresistible. They were evil. By the time he was 30 years old Al Capone headed a $7 million-a-year empire in bootlegging, narcotics, loan sharking, extortion, and prostitution. On his payroll were judges, police chiefs, a reporter for the *Chicago Tribune,* and no fewer than 300 assassins. He had an estimated $50 million in the bank and a palatial estate in Miami. Capone donated to charity and was ultimately responsible for the killing of more than 1,000 victims. But he was never arrested for a single violent crime.

The image of violent white Americans as social bandits was carried well into the post–World War II era. It appealed, of course, primarily to young white males. "[A]lmost every boy in America," wrote one criminologist, "wanted to be Jesse James, the strong, fearless bandit who came to symbolize the individuality of the American West" (Nash, 1995, p. 337). This image effectively "whitewashed" the seriousness of white violence in the American consciousness through a process of turning attention away from the blood and horror of white predatory crime and refocusing it on fabricated, overly romanticized biographies. Whereas black violence was seen as dark and threatening, there was something quintessentially American about violence when it was rendered by whites. Diminished in its importance, violence then became an accepted and altogether normal rite of passage for millions of American white youths.

Conclusion: The Bully

If there is an overarching lesson to be learned here, it is this: The group that defines the law and controls public opinion is the group that will define criminal images and control the punishments for all groups, not the least of which will be their own. Throughout history, white Americans have done precisely that. Through law and culture, they have created a condition whereby white American violence has become imageless. Yet when viewed in the broad scope of history, they do have an image, a very clearly defined image. From the landing of the Vikings to the present day, white American males have used their dominant social status to exercise habitual cruelty against weaker and less powerful people. There is only one word for that. Alas, the predatory white criminal is nothing less than a bully.

Note

1. The following account is derived solely from Utley (1989). It is generally considered the most thoughtful and well-documented historical analysis of Henry Atrim published to date.

References

Boyum, David, and Kleiman, Mark A. R. (1995). "Alcohol and other drugs." In James Q. Wilson and Joan Petersilia (Eds.), *Crime*. San Francisco: Institute for Contemporary Studies, 295–326.

Brown, Richard Maxwell. (1989). "Historical patterns of violence." In Ted Robert Gurr (Ed.), *Violence in America: Protest, rebellion, reform*. Thousand Oaks, CA: Sage Publications, 23–61.

Butterfield, Fox. (1995). *All God's children: The Bosket family and the American tradition of violence*. New York: Avon.

Carter, Harvey Lewis. (1968). *"Dear old Kit": The historical Christopher Carson*. Norman: University of Oklahoma Press.

Chambliss, William J. (1994). "Why the U.S. government is not contributing to the resolution of the nation's drug problem." *International Journal of Health Services*, 24, 675–690.

Davis, William C. (Ed.) (1982). *The embattled Confederacy*. Vol. 3 of *The image of war 1861–1865*. Garden City, NY: Doubleday.

Donziger, Steven R. (Ed.). (1996). *The real war on crime: The report of the National Criminal Justice Commission*. New York: Harper Perennial.

Ezekiel, Raphael S. (1995). *The racist mind: Portraits of American Neo-Nazis and klansmen*. New York: Viking.

Fagan, Jeffrey. (1992). "Drug selling and licit income in distressed neighborhoods: The economic lives of street-level drug users and dealers." In Adele V. Harrell and George E. Peterson (Eds.), *Drugs, crime and social isolation*. Washington, DC: Urban Institute Press, 99–146.

Fogel, Robert William. (1989). *Without consent or contract: The rise and fall of American slavery*. New York: W.W. Norton and Company.

Guillemin, Jeanne. (1989). "American Indian resistance and protest." In Ted Robert Gurr (Ed.), *Violence in America: Protest, rebellion, reform*. Thousand Oaks, CA: Sage Publications, 153–172.

Gurr, Ted Robert. (1989). "Political terrorism: Historical antecedents and contemporary trends." In Ted Robert Gurr (Ed.), *Violence in America: Protest, rebellion, reform*. Thousand Oaks, CA: Sage Publications, 201–230.

Hamm, Mark S. (1997). *Apocalypse in Oklahoma: Waco and Ruby Ridge revenged*. Boston: Northeastern University Press.

——— (1996). *Terrorism, hate crime, and antigovernment violence: A review of the research*. Washington, DC: National Research Council.

Hamm, Mark S. (Ed.). (1994). *Hate crime: international perspectives on causes and control*. Cincinnati: ACJS/Anderson.

———. (1993). *American skinheads: The criminology and control of hate crime*. Westport, CT: Praeger.

Josephy, Alvin M. (Ed.). (1968). *The Indian heritage of America*. New York: Knopf.

———. (1961). *The American heritage book of Indians*. New York: Simon & Schuster.

Joyner, Charles. (1984). *Down by the riverside: A South Carolina slave community*. Urbana: University of Illinois Press.

Kennedy, John F. (1961). "Introduction." In Alvin M. Josephy (Ed.), *The American heritage book of Indians*. New York: Simon & Schuster, 8.

Litwack, Leon F. (1996) "'Blues falling down like hail': The ordeal of Black freedom." In Robert H. Abzug and Stephen E. Maizlish (Eds.), *Race and slavery in America: Essays in honor of Kenneth M. Stampp*. Lexington: University Press of Kentucky, 109–127.

Mann, Coramae R. (1993). *Unequal justice: A question of color*. Bloomington: Indiana University Press.

Miller, Jerome G. (1996). *Search and destroy: African-American males in the criminal justice system*. New York: Cambridge University Press.

Nash, Jay Robert. (1995). *Bloodletters and badmen*. New York: M. Evans.

O'Brien, Gail Williams. (1989). "Return to 'normalcy': Organized racial violence in the post-World War II South." In Ted Robert Gurr (Ed.), *Violence in America: Protest, rebellion, reform*. Thousand Oaks, CA: Sage Publications, 231–254.

Platt, Tony, and Takagi, Paul. (1979). "Biosocial criminology: A critique." *Crime and Social Justice*, 2 (Spring/Summer), 5–13.

Potter, David M. (1976). *The impending crisis: 1848–1861*. New York: Harper.

Presdee, Mike, and Carver, Gavin. (1996). *The carnival and the performing of crime: Young people, knives and other weapons.* Paper presented at the annual meeting of the American Society of Criminology. Chicago, November 21.

Sutherland, Edwin H., and Cressey, Donald R. (1978). *Criminology.* Philadelphia: Lippincott.

Toy, Eckard V. (1989). "Right-wing extremism from the Ku Klux Klan to the order, 1915 to 1988." In Ted Robert Gurr (Ed.), *Violence in America: Protest, rebellion, reform.* Thousand Oaks, CA: Sage Publications, 131–152.

Utley, Robert M. (1989). *Billy the Kid: A short and violent life.* Lincoln: University of Nebraska Press.

Wissler, Clark. (1966). *Indians of the United States.* Garden City, NY: Doubleday.

Wood, Peter H. (1974). *Black majority: Negroes in colonial South Carolina from 1670 through the Stone rebellion.* New York: Knopf.

Discussion Questions

1. Compare and contrast the five waves of white American violence described by the author.
2. How did the five waves make white violence transparent?
3. If black slaves served an economic purpose and were of value, how can their lynchings be explained?
4. What is the significance of the mutilations in the early lynchings of blacks?
5. Are there social bandits today? ♦

Conclusions

Chapter 22

Before and Beyond the Millennium: Possible Solutions

Coramae Richey Mann and Marjorie S. Zatz

In this volume we have taken you on a journey to numerous places, and into others' lives and experiences in an attempt to open your eyes to the many injustices—and their consequences—faced throughout history by people of color in the United States. These are places of poverty and despair, lives of hopelessness, and experiences of discrimination and racism. Even a few of our readers of color may be unaware of these places, lives, and experiences. The opening narratives of each section introduced events in the personal backgrounds of red, black, brown, yellow, and white Americans. Hopefully their poignant stories made what life is like for members of racial/ethnic minorities real for you while simultaneously providing a vivid contrast with the unfettered interactions experienced daily by most Euro-Americans. These accounts further demonstrate that higher socioeconomic level and elevated income offer little protection against racial stereotyping. When one is labeled a "spade," a "spick," a "squaw," or a "slant-eye," such pejora-

tives adhere and are passed on within as well as down through generations. The challenge is how to intercede in this poisonous cycle and remove the venom of racism.

Perhaps, as Derrick Bell concludes in his brilliant and insightful Foreword to this book, racism is "a permanent phenomenon" in America. But we would like to think more optimistically and feel that there is hope for change, especially through the children of the future. *Before* the millennium, we believe Bell is probably right and there is little hope for eliminating racism in America. But, *beyond* the millennium, we feel there is promise. Over time, institutional racism can be altered through policy changes at local, state, and federal levels. Similarly, when defined by ingrained personal beliefs and strongly felt emotions, the problem of individual racism in America requires long-term solutions.

You have also seen how the media exaggerate or actually distort racial characteristics and actions, especially criminal acts, and you have been made aware of the resultant harm to people of color that ensues from such practices. As Jody Miller and Peter Levin (Chapter 19) observe, "One result of this attention is that these images play into the public's fear of crime." In contrast, Miller and Levin add, the media portray Euro-American offenders either as psychologically disturbed individuals or in ways that are romanticized and lead viewers and readers to admire them. In either event, Euro-American offenders are presented in "human terms" and not, for example, in the "animalistic, aggressive, and brutal" demonic terms in which African American men are portrayed (see Fishman, Chapter nine). Clearly, the primary advantages for the media conglomerates of these racial distortions are monetary—sales of more newspapers, magazines, and tabloids, larger box-office returns at the movies, and more television advertisements and sponsors.

Yet it cannot be overlooked that there is a highly receptive media audience eager to absorb racial stereotypes that reinforce views they already embrace because this strengthens their notion of Euro-American superiority. These stereotypes make it easier to dismiss the pain felt by those who look or sound different. Michael Tonry takes this a step further, raising as a serious problem with our national character our "remarkable ability to endure suffering by others":

> We lock up our citizens at rates five to fifteen times higher than those in other Western countries. Alone among Western countries, the United States retains capital punishment, and applies it with increasing frequency. The thirty-eight prisoners executed in 1993 was the largest number since 1962. . . . That those whose suffering we so lightly endure are disproportionately black is one of the less attractive features of our national character. (1995, p. 197)

Politicians' motives for perpetuating negative racial images are more perfidious than those of the media because they are almost totally selfish. They seek to enhance their careers, with the ultimate goals of getting elected and staying elected, thereby garnering and maintaining their power, the ultimate egotistical high. The title of Tonry's thought-provoking book, *Malign Neglect*, is a condemnation of politicians' indifference to the racial effects of the policies they initiate. Tonry states, "Conservative politicians have cynically played on white Americans' fears and on racial stereotypes, exemplified by the Welfare Queen and Willie Horton" (1995, p. 209; see also Culverson, Chapter eight). The underlying motive for politicians to rely

on such racist policies is to show that they are tough on crime and thus "pander to" the fears of their constituents by appealing to their "anticrime hysteria" (Tonry, 1995, p. 180).

Whether or not politicians believe the racist stereotypes that they foster dictates the potential solution to this problem. If an individual politician embraces negative stereotypes of people of color, that is, operates on the basis of personally held racial prejudices, there is probably little that can be done to change such entrenched beliefs, even over the long term. However, if the use of racialized images is merely a political tool resulting from or in conjunction with the acceptable practices of others, often without conscious thought of its racist implications, more immediate changes can be effected.

Before the Millennium: Possible Solutions

Juvenile Justice

There are several possible short-term solutions to reduce the negative imaging of red, black, brown, and yellow American youths that often contributes to their becoming swept up by the juvenile or criminal justice system. In Chapter 13, Edwardo Portillos vividly describes the interactions of Latino youths with law enforcement personnel and other actors in the juvenile and criminal justice systems. The experiences of these young Latinos are mirrored by those of all youths of color in the United States.

Several of the contributors to this volume address the problems of gang membership and alleged gang membership (see especially Melton, Chapter five; Rodríguez, Chapter 10; Portillos, Chapter 13; Laidler, Chapter 14). In many jurisdictions, youths are assumed to belong to gangs because they fit certain criteria specified by the police or legislatures. For example, in Arizona, a criminal street gang member is defined as an individual to whom two of the following seven criteria apply: (1) self-proclamation; (2) witness testimony or official statement; (3) written or electronic correspondence; (4) paraphernalia or photographs; (5) tattoos; (6) clothing or colors; and (7) any other indicia of street gang membership (*Arizona Revised Statutes* 13-105[8]). In Arizona and many other jurisdictions, alleged membership in a street gang is a legally admissible factor in determining case processing outcomes (e.g., waiver of a juvenile to criminal court) and sanctions. The problem is that although antigang legislation is a purportedly race-neutral policy aimed at reducing violence, in reality it targets minority youths. That is, if African American and Latino teenagers and young men are routinely assumed to be gang members, and if most youths whose case files include mention of gang affiliation are African American or Latino, then policies targeting crimes by gang members end up targeting minority youths. For example, in the Phoenix, Arizona, metropolitan area, approximately 95 percent of the youths alleged in juvenile court to be gang members are Latino (Krecker and Zatz, 1999). This is particularly troubling in jurisdictions, including Arizona, where the overrepresentation of minority youths in juvenile facilities has already been recognized as a major problem.

In 1988, the *Juvenile Justice and Delinquency Prevention Act* (JJDP) was amended to reduce the disproportionate incarceration of youths of color, defined as Asians, Pacific Islanders, African Americans, Latino/as, and American Indians. Two implementation phases were described in instructions issued to the states in 1989. Phase I focused on 1990 data collection and analysis to determine if a problem ex-

isted, and Phase II called for designing programs to eliminate such racial discrimination once it was determined to exist. Five federally funded pilot studies in Arizona, Florida, Iowa, North Carolina, and Oregon documented rather conclusively that minority youths were overrepresented in the juvenile justice system. In most of the pilot states, youths of color, especially African American youngsters, experienced differential treatment at almost every stage in their processing—complaint, arrest, intake, detention, delinquency adjudication, secure confinement, and transfer to criminal court to be tried as adults. The disparity between youths of color and Euro-American youths increased at every decision point in the juvenile justice system, resulting in an "accumulated disadvantaged status" (see similarly Zatz, 1987b). By 1992, the requirement for meaningful policy change became a mandate to the states.

In addition to changes in juvenile justice processing of minority youths, other policy recommendations from the pilot states included working with the youths' families and other forms of family involvement and support; creation of individualized and alternative services such as remedial education and job training for preadjudicated and adjudicated youths; and commitments from the juvenile justice system, other agencies, and the community to train their personnel in cultural and gender sensitivity. Finally, the report stressed the importance of encouraging the media to present and accentuate positive acts by racial/ethnic minorities, instead of focusing on negative behaviors and images. Girls of color, especially African American girls and Latinas of all social classes, share the obstructions and stigmatization of sexism, racism, and biases against youths that are typical of this nation. Girls from poor families are additionally handicapped by poverty and income inequality (Chesney-Lind and Shelden, 1992).

Girls of any color in the juvenile justice system require special programs appropriate to their unique needs. However, regardless of social class, non-Euro-American girls have different experiences than do Euro-American girls. Unfortunately, very few programs exist for girls, and even fewer address the real needs of girls caught up in the juvenile justice system today. We strongly recommend that careful attention be paid to the social context in which girls of color live, especially those from inner cities, when developing programs for them.

Criminal Justice

Police contact is the crucial point that determines entry into the justice systems. There should be intensive and ongoing police training in race and community relations to improve police interactions with suspects of color. This training should make officers aware of the negative images of racial/ethnic minorities they see in the media, as well as stereotypes they hold personally, so that they can consciously strive to reduce the power of these images. Of course, this would not be as serious a problem if, as the National Criminal Justice Commission suggests:

> Police departments should as much as possible reflect the racial and ethnic composition of the communities they serve. It would be extremely difficult for an all-white police force to build trust in a primarily African-American neighborhood, or vice versa. Departments should also make efforts to assign officers to immigrant communities who are able to communicate with residents in their native language. (Donziger, 1996, p. 178)

Women of color, like their younger sisters, often face the triple jeopardy of gender, race, and class when processed by a criminal justice system that is widening its net for them, especially through increased female drug arrests. Not only is there evidence of racial prejudice toward and differential treatment by the police of women of color, there are also studies indicating that gender-based discrimination occurs throughout the criminal justice system, from detention decisions to sentencing practices (see Young, 1986; Daly and Chesney-Lind, 1988; Mann, 1989; 1995b; Daly, 1994;). Ironically, calls for fairness and gender equity in sanctioning, which were intended to improve access to job training, drug and alcohol treatment, and education for women who are incarcerated or on probation, have resulted instead in more women being locked up, and for a longer time, so as to match the sentences handed down to men.

Mothers who are arrested face additional problems, particularly if their children are present at the time of their arrest. There is frequently no provision for child care, especially if the arrest occurs at night. Police officers should be made aware of such problems and of the traumas experienced by children who observe their mother being handled roughly by the police, handcuffed, and carted away. Because many poor women of color are heads of households, the children often are sent to relatives who are not prepared to care for them or to foster care. Policies, we suggest, should reflect efforts to minimize family disruption. One way would be to release these women on their own recognizance or to assign low bail in a speedy fashion.

Edwardo Portillos (see Chapter 13) stresses that the system must recognize the diversity among Latinos and Latinas and also appreciate that no matter where they originated (e.g., Mexico, Puerto Rico, Guatemala), Latinos/as share the same language. He calls for more Spanish-speaking police officers, interpreters, and other members of the court-work group. Portillos especially emphasizes the need for bilingual attorneys to help both defendants and members of their families. Taiping Ho (Chapter 17) and Ada Pecos Melton (Chapter five) echo these problems of cultural ignorance and language barriers, which they suggest lead Asian Americans and American Indians to distrust the U.S. criminal justice system (see also Zatz, Lujan, and Snyder-Joy, 1991).

Although speaking the language of suspects and defendants would reduce some of the ambiguity often found in arrests and court decisions, the problems of gender-based and cultural ignorance could also be overcome by hiring more men and women of color and Euro-American women at every level of the juvenile and criminal justice systems. There is also a crucial need for more women of all races and minority men in our local, state, and federal judiciaries.

Unfortunately, even if Euro-American women and people of color were proportionately represented in the justice system's work force, similar to current employees with visions of equity, their hands might be tied by existing laws and established policies that are racially biased. For example, many of the contributors to this volume point out the injustice in such criminal justice policies as the War on Crime and the War on Drugs. By 1993, these wars had resulted in a six-to-one disparity in incarceration rates based on race (Mauer, 1994, p. 6). Although both "wars" are highly deleterious to Americans of color, the drug war is more obviously inherently racist (see in particular Rome, Chapter seven; Culverson, Chapter eight; and Portillos, Chapter 13).

Although crack and powder cocaine cannot be differentiated pharmacologically, offenses involving crack cocaine—

which is usually used and sold by African Americans and Latinos—invoke harsher penalties than offenses related to powder cocaine, which is the choice of Euro-American cocaine users and sellers (Tonry, 1995, p. 188; see also Bourgois, 1995). Federal sentencing guidelines treat one gram of crack as equivalent to 100 grams of powder cocaine. This one-hundred-to-one rule has been especially devastating to African Americans, because 95 percent of federal prosecutions for crack are brought against African Americans and 40 percent of powder cocaine prosecutions are brought against Euro-Americans (Tonry, 1995, p. 188). The length of federal prison sentences also reflects this racial inequity based on the type of cocaine. Tonry reports that in 1993 "on average federal prison sentences for blacks were 41 percent longer than for whites and the different penalties for crack and powder cocaine were the major reason for that difference" (1993, p. 189). These disparate rates and sentencing practices are even more alarming when it has been empirically established by the U.S. Department of Health and Human Services that the rate of drug use for African Americans and Euro-Americans is about the same (see Tonry, 1995; Donziger, 1996; Miller, 1996).

Because drug law enforcement focuses "almost exclusively on low-level dealers in minority neighborhoods" (Donziger, 1996, p. 115), such practices target and fill our jails and prisons with young African Americans and Latinos. This pattern, in effect for over a decade, contributes to the "exploding rate of incarceration of African-Americans," who, in some cities, are arrested at rates 50 times more than Euro-American rates for drug offenses (ibid., p. 117).

The criminal image of racial/ethnic minorities as "dope fiends" can only be diminished when, as the National

Criminal Justice Commission recommends, the War on Drugs is eliminated and replaced with a policy of harm reduction (ibid., pp. 200–201). Drug use and abuse should be treated as the medical problem it actually is, and thereby viewed as a "public health challenge rather than a criminal justice problem" (ibid., p. 201). As Tonry points out:

> For drug-abusing offenders, particularly, the case for increased investment in drug treatment is powerful. From the Justice Department's Drug Use Forecasting (DUF) data from urinanalyses of arrested felons, we know that one-half to three-fourths in many cities test positive for recent drug use. From both ethnographic and statistical studies of drug-using offenders, we know that high levels of drug use and high levels of offending are strongly associated. When drug use declines, offending declines. From treatment evaluation studies, we know that participation in well-run methadone maintenance programs and therapeutic communities can demonstrably reduce both later drug use and later criminality of drug-dependent offenders. Finally, also from drug treatment evaluations, we know that the best predictor of successful treatment is time in treatment, even when coerced by legal compulsion. (Tonry, 1995, pp. 202–03)

The War on Drugs has been responsible for huge increases in the number of women incarcerated in our prisons and jails. Twelve percent of the women in prisons in 1986 were convicted of drug offenses compared to 33 percent in 1991 (U.S. Department of Justice, 1994, p. 3). The increases have been especially great for women of color (Mann, 1995b). Yet as Karen Joe Laidler (Chapter 14) emphasizes, the number of treatment centers available to women is far below what is necessary, and there are almost no culturally appropriate treatment programs for Asian American women. Moreover, with all the media attention on the social and health problems posed by "crack moms," the reality is that very few treatment centers will accept pregnant women (Humphries, Dawson, Cronin, Keating, Wisniewski, and Eichfield, 1995).

The Media

Diego Castro (Chapter 11) reminds us that "we ask the media to inform and educate, be our watchdogs and monitor those in power. Moreover, we expect this to be done in a fair and neutral manner. Perhaps these are unreasonable expectations." Even if television news and other media formats want to present unbiased reports about Latinos/as and crime, they are hindered by the paucity of research that is not specific to lower-class, poorly educated Latinos/as. The plethora of studies on crime waves has demonstrated rather conclusively that the newspaper and television news media are far more reactive than they are proactive. They are especially reliant on the police for crime stories (Fishman, 1978; Hall, Critcher, Jefferson, Clarke, and Roberts, 1978; Zatz, 1987a). For this reason, we suggest that more and better research on the social problems—including crime and victimization—facing Latinos/as and other people of color must be conducted and channeled to media outlets. Only then might the reporting become less biased.

Similarly, Dennis Rome (Chapter seven) feels that crime is "over-stated" by the media. Rome, and also Jody Miller and Peter Levin (Chapter 19), call into question those who define crime and identify criminals for the larger society. As one possible solution to the racial distortion and stereotyping portrayed in the media, Rome suggests that the news media seek responses from journalists of color for an "inside perspective" on issues concerning minorities. We would add that minority media personnel should be consulted in editorial capacities before signing off on or publishing major news stories focused on people of color to ensure that stereotypes are not being fostered.

This inside perspective would also be useful for those reporters who apparently cannot distinguish between Asians and Asian Americans. As Thomas Nakayama (Chapter 15) reminds us, "This confusion does not seem to happen in the case of Africans and African Americans or Europeans and European Americans." For example, when the Democratic National Committee (DNC) and the White House faced a scandal in the spring of 1997 revolving around campaign contributions from Asians, the DNC telephoned its Asian American supporters to ask whether they were citizens. Further, "[p]hrases like *The American Spectator*'s 'Bamboo Network' or William Safire's favorite, 'The Asian Connection,' perpetuate the stereotyping that formerly brought us the 'Yellow Peril' and the 'Asiatic Hordes'" (Nash and Wu, 1997, p. 16). Taiping Ho (Chapter 17) and Nakayama (Chapter 15) suggest that this conflation of Asians and Asian Americans contributes to race-based hate crimes. In particular, Euro-American anger over perceived job losses to *Asians* must be recognized as a key factor contributing to hate crimes against Asian *Americans*.

Politicians

As Rome puts it, "The first solution is for our leaders to look racism straight in the eye and stop pretending that racism no longer exists in our society." He further observes that it is particularly crucial for African American leaders to become more active in the African American communities of this nation and thus help to stop the "continued darkening of the face of the street criminal."

Tonry (1995, p. 181) speaks of an "honest" politician as though an oxymoron exists. According to Tonry, an honest politician would carefully consider the effects of crime control policies on minority group members. If such scrutiny reveals that the policies would disproportionately impact minorities, the honest politician would reconsider them. Policies such as mandatory sentencing and other "penalty-enhancing" practices like "three strikes and you're out" reflect an initial motive "to prove that candidates and officials were tough on crime and, sometimes, to use 'anticrime' (or 'antiwelfare') as a veiled synonym for 'antiblack'" (Tonry, 1995, p. 190). However, Tonry also notes that "as long as cynical and disingenuous appeals continue to be made by politicians to the deepest fears and basest instincts of the American people, the prospects of reducing racial disparities in the justice system will remain small" (1995, p. 181).

American Indians present a special case for remedies because most of what is now the United States was originally their land. As a result of the shameful history summarized by James Riding In (Chapter two) and Suzan Harjo (Chapter three), decades of legal abuse of American Indians have accompanied their stereotyping. Similar to the reparations often demanded by African Americans but never awarded and those reparations allotted to Japanese Americans who were imprisoned in internment camps during World War II, Carol Lujan (Chapter four) calls for institutional and individual admissions of guilt for crimes and other wrongs committed against American Indians; for the federal government to honor previously established, and since ignored, laws and treaties made with American Indian governments; and for recognition by the federal government and other public and private institutions of Indian governments as sovereign nations.

The recent brouhaha over Asian and Asian American support of Democratic politicians leads Bong Hwan Kim (Chapter 16) to recommend pursuing campaign finance reform. We should begin, he suggests with the improprieties and violations by the "ultrarich multinational companies," which have the greatest influence over elected officials and public policies, rather than "singling out Asian Americans and lumping them with overseas Asians."

Finally, several contributors have commented on the dangers of defining Asian Americans as a "model minority." As a model minority, they presumably do not face social problems, such as drug dependency, that require culturally appropriate solutions. The consequence, as Karen Joe Laidler (Chapter 14) observes, is a lack of social programs for Asian Americans. Yet equally perfidious is the way in which this characterization pits one racial/ethnic minority against another. Bong Hwan Kim (Chapter 16) describes the Korean–African American antagonisms in Los Angeles and elsewhere that result from ethnic minorities being forced to compete for scarce resources. Such "divide and conquer" policies and practices must cease.

Beyond the Millennium: Possible Solutions

Changing attitudes toward and images of people of color involve long-term solutions. In order to reduce the negative stereotyping of red, black, brown, and yellow Americans, multicultural programs and studies should be incorporated in both state and privately funded educational institutions from kindergarten through college levels. Because children comprise the foundation of our future society after the millennium, they offer the only possible avenue to end racism and racial stereotyping in this nation.

Preschoolers and children at early grade levels are not racially prejudiced. This prejudice develops over time and results from the input of, and racist reinforcement by, family members, peers, and others in one's significant subgroup. As Peggy McIntosh (Chapter 18) notes, recognizing when images are racialized and eliminating racist stereotypes is a lifelong process. One means of altering these images is to vividly portray the heroic acts of American Indians, African Americans, Latinos and Latinas, and Asian Americans in history and social studies textbooks. Another is to report truthfully in school texts the history of our theft of Indian lands, patterns of genocide against Indians (e.g., giving "gifts" of blankets infected with smallpox), lynchings of African American men, internment of Japanese Americans in concentration camps during World War II, and so forth. Yet another remedy is for students to examine carefully popular culture's reliance on racialized and gendered images to market movies and TV shows and the pernicious effects of these images, and then to take political action (e.g., boycotts, lobbying against them).

Other long-term solutions necessary to erase the debilitating, harmful stereotypes that have accrued to people of color in the United States entail indepth changes to our major social institutions—housing, health, education, family, religion, economic and political—institutions that are deeply entrenched components of our social structure. Only when the racism embedded in these institutions and their practices and policies is eradicated will we be able to rid our society of its racialized images of crime and criminals.

Each of these social institutions is intimately related to the others, and each is necessary for survival. For example, without sound health and a full belly it is difficult, if not impossible, to secure a good education. Lacking a solid education, employment opportunities are severely limited. In turn, underemployment or unemployment critically restricts one's chances of ever getting ahead in life or providing a secure economic future for one's children. Thus, poverty and all of its harmful accouterments are perpetuated, and the cycle persists. Without major intervention, such cycles of poverty and hopelessness will continue to impose their debilitating effects on people of color in America. Unfortunately, as has been the case for decades, institutional racism in our social institutions is systemic.

Racial segregation in housing, for example, seriously limits educational opportunities; denies access to quality health care; hinders emergency attention from public safety agencies such as law enforcement, fire departments, and ambulance services; severely reduces employment chances; and effectively prohibits political representation. The entrenchment and perpetuation of Latino barrios, Chinatowns, and African American ghettos in our cities, as well as the forced removal of many American Indians from their original tribal lands to remote reservations, demonstrate graphically the results of imposed racial segregation. According to Shelby Steele (1990, p. 79), racial segregation is "more entrenched in American cities today than ever imagined." Unfortunately, residential segregation is not only an urban problem but is now "a national phenomenon" (Georges-Abeyie, 1990, p. 27).

Health care among poor people of color is particularly deficient. It is not unusual to find a number of factors working against the health status of im-

poverished minority Americans. The persistent conditions of poverty—poor and inadequate diet, deplorably unhealthy living conditions, and lack of money for medical care—contribute to substandard health. Further, inequality in the health care delivery system, as demonstrated by a lack of access to diagnosis and treatment and by the less skilled physicians in public clinics that most American poor are forced to use, leads to higher mortality rates throughout the entire life cycle. Poor and unsafe health care provided on Indian reservations has led to numerous complaints by American Indians. The Indian Health Service facilities are notoriously poor in terms of both quality and quantity, and only those American Indians registered with federally recognized tribes are entitled to even this minimal medical and dental care.

In addition to the obvious liabilities associated with inadequate health care, there is a possible connection between lack of emergency services and images of minority crime in urban areas. Alleged high murder rates are viewed as endemic to inner-city neighborhoods. However, it is highly possible that if not for notoriously slow emergency medical services, many homicides might have remained assaults. Recall Edwardo Portillos' (Chapter 13) example of how an emergency call for an ambulance to aid an unconscious Latino resulted instead in the appearance of a police officer. Emergency treatment of assault victims could have saved many lives had medical personnel arrived more quickly. Instead, victims die, murder statistics are updated, and the image of violence and death at the hands of people of color is strengthened.

The recent public education controversy over "ebonics," or what is known as "black English," reflects the desperate state our educational system is in and the low level to which it has sunk in providing instruction to inner-city African American children. In a country where there are more young African American males under correctional control than there are in college (Steele, 1990), it is obvious that the existing educational system is not providing the necessary incentives to deter minority youths from crime and delinquency. In fact, many teenagers, particularly African Americans and Latinos, are not dropouts but are really push-outs from the school system. The educational erosion of inner-city schools is matched in incompetence only by the American Indian educational system, "a federal system believed to be the worst in America" (Mann, 1995a, p. 264).

By the millennium, it is projected that minority students will constitute over 30 percent of the student population in the U.S. (Cole, 1991). Unless comprehensive, major reforms in the educational system are begun immediately on a national scale, another generation of youths of color will be lost—possibly to crime, drugs, prison, and the morgue. It is evident that most busing endeavors have not worked but, on the contrary, have led to and reinforced racial prejudice and racism in many jurisdictions. It is racist to assume that children of color can achieve only when they have Euro-American students as models. Before busing, before integration, many African Americans received premiere educations in segregated schools where equal equipment, equal supplies, and highly qualified teachers were available. We are not suggesting that there should never be integration; rather, we are saying that the focus must be on the *quality* of education. There should be top-notch schools and teachers in *every* community, regardless of the color of the students or the amount of money their parents earn. Inner-city schools and schools on Indian reservations must be targeted in this endeavor

if we are to have any hope of guiding minority youths in a different, more positive direction. In addition to better-trained and more minority teachers, there is a critical need for bilingual instructors to bridge the gap for non-English-speaking students and their parents.

As noted earlier, without a good education, and even for some people of color with a good education, the employment arena can be forbidding. The closing of many industrial plants, combined with the movement of substantial numbers of other industries either out of the country or to the suburbs, has reduced an already scarce job market for racial/ethnic minorities. Even if they could find employment in the suburbs, many poor people of color could not secure nearby housing, and the commute from inner-city neighborhoods can be time-consuming as well as expensive.

The economic disparity between Euro-Americans and Americans of color is sadly reflected in the latest median income, poverty, and unemployment statistics. The U.S. census reports that the median income for Euro-American households in 1993 was $32,960. Asian American and Pacific Islander households were the only ones to have a higher median income than Euro-Americans, at $38,347. The median income for African American households was $19,533, and for Latino/a households it was $22,886. (U.S. Bureau of the Census, 1996, p. 408). In 1991, 30.4 percent of African American families and 26.5 percent of Latino/a families were below the poverty level compared to 8.8 percent of Euro-American families (U.S. Bureau of the Census, 1996, p. 476). The U.S. Bureau of Labor Statistics reported that 4.9 percent of the Euro-American labor force was unemployed in 1995. In contrast, 10.4 percent of the African American labor force and 9.3 percent of the Latino/a labor force were unemployed (U.S. Bureau of the Census, 1996, p. 394).

Most people of color in America are located in the lower economic strata. The primary differentiating factor of economic inequality—race/ethnicity—was created and is perpetuated by a Euro-American power structure that wishes to maintain its economic hegemony. This dominant group makes the laws that define crime and controls the law enforcement and social control institutions that apprehend, process, and contain people of color. Yet, as Jody Miller and Peter Levin (Chapter 19) and Mark Hamm (Chapter 21) make clear, crimes committed by the dominant group are treated almost with impunity, if addressed at all.

It goes without saying that the only way to have power is to be part of the power system that makes the critical decisions about your life. People of color made up 26.3 percent of the U.S. population in 1995 (U.S. Bureau of the Census, 1996, pp. 22–23) but only 14 percent of the membership of the House of Representatives and three percent of the membership of the Senate in the 104th Congress (Congressional Research Service, 1994; Joint Center for Political and Economic Studies, 1995; National Association of Latino Elected and Appointed Officials, 1995; U.S. Bureau of the Census, 1996, p. 279). Racial gerrymandering and other dubious practices impact the political process and thus deny people of color effectual representation as lawmakers. As a result, laws, especially criminal laws, are not made by the people directly affected by them. Also, without effective representation, long-term recommendations by the National Criminal Justice Commission and others cannot be implemented. For example, political representation at the state or national levels is necessary to initiate the following Commission recommendations:

Recommendation 5: Eliminate racial and ethnic biases within the criminal justice system. Require a racial impact statement before major changes are made to crime policy. (Donziger, 1996, p. 206)

Recommendation 6: Congress should commission an independent clearinghouse to gather and report objective criminal justice information to the public. The clearinghouse should be separate from the Department of Justice. (Ibid., p. 207)

Recommendation 7: All levels of government should create crime prevention councils to develop a coordinated anti-crime strategy. (Ibid., p. 208)

Recommendation 9: In order to reduce street crime, the nation must commit itself to reducing poverty by investing in children, youth, families, and communities. (Ibid., p. 211)

Recommendation 11: Shift crime policy from an agenda of "war" to an agenda of "peace." (Ibid., p. 218)

The Commission's last recommendation leaves us much to ponder, but as Miller (1996, p. 243) correctly observes, "Without major political changes in the nation, none of this is likely to happen."

References

Bourgois, Philippe. (1995). *In search of respect: Selling crack in El Barrio.* New York: Cambridge University Press.

Chesney-Lind, Meda, and Shelden, R.G. (1992) *Girls, Delinquency, and Juvenile Justice.* Pacific Grove, CA: Brooks/Cole.

Cole, Beverly. (1991). "The school reform of the eighties and its implication for the restructuring of the nineties." *The Crisis,* 98 (8), 23–26, 46.

Congressional Research Service. (1994). *Asian Pacific Americans in the United States Congress.* Report 94-767. Washington, DC: Library of Congress.

Daly, Kathleen. (1994). *Gender, crime and punishment.* New Haven, CT: Yale University Press.

Daly, Kathleen, and Chesney-Lind, Meda. (1988). "Feminism and criminology." *Justice Quarterly, 5,* 497–538.

Donziger, Steven A. (Ed.). (1996). *The real war on crime: The report of the National Criminal Justice Commission.* New York: Harper Perennial.

Fishman, Mark. (1978). "Crime waves as ideology." *Social Problems, 25,* 531–543.

Georges-Abeyie, Daniel E. (1990). "Criminal processing of non-white minorities." In Brian D. MacLean and Dragan Milovanovic (Eds.), *Racism, empiricism and criminal justice.* Vancouver: Collective Press.

Hall, Stuart, Critcher, Chas., Jefferson, Tony, Clarke, John, and Roberts, Brian. (1978). *Policing the crisis: Mugging, the state, and law and order.* New York: Hilmes and Meier.

Humphries, Drew, Dawson, John, Cronin, Valerie, Keating, Phyllis, Wisniewski, Chris, and Eichfeld, Jennine. (1995). "Mothers and children, drugs and crack: Reactions to maternal drug dependency." In Barbara Raffel Price and Natalie J. Sokoloff (Eds.), *The criminal justice system and women: Offenders, victims and workers.* 2nd ed. New York: McGraw-Hill.

Joint Center for Political and Economic Studies. (1995). *Black elected officials: A national roster.* Washington, DC: Joint Center for Political and Economic Studies.

Krecker, Richard P., and Zatz, Marjorie S. (1999). "Anti-gang initiatives as racialized policy." In Darnell F. Hawkins, Samuel L. Myers, Jr., and Randolph N. Stone (Eds.), *Crime control and social justice: The delicate balance.* Westport, CT: Greenwood Press.

Mann, Coramae Richey. (1995a). "Women of color and the criminal justice system." In Barbara Raffel Price and Matalie J. Sokoloff (Eds.), *The criminal justice system and women offenders, victims and workers.* 2nd ed. New York: McGraw-Hill.

——. (1995b). "The contribution of institutionalized racism to minority crime." In Darnell F. Hawkins (Ed.), *Ethnicity, race, and crime: Perspectives across time and place.* Albany: State University of New York Press, pp. 259–280.

——. (1989). "Minority and female: A criminal justice double bind." *Social Justice, 16* (3), 95–114.

Mauer, Marc. (1994). *Americans behind bars: The international use of incarceration, 1992–1993.* Washington, DC: The Sentencing Project.

Miller, Jerome G. (1996). *Search and destroy: African-American males in the criminal justice system.* Cambridge: Cambridge University Press.

Nash, Phil Tajitsu, and Wu, Frank. (1997). "Asian Americans under glass." *The Nation, 264,* (12), 15–16.

National Association of Latino Elected and Appointed Officials. (1995). *National roster of Hispanic elected officials.* Washington, DC: National Association of Latino Elected and Appointed Officials.

Steele, Shelby. (1990). *The content of our character: A new vision of race in America.* New York: St. Martin's Press.

Tonry, Michael. (1995). *Malign neglect: Race, crime, and punishment in America.* New York: Oxford University Press.

U.S. Bureau of the Census. (1996). *Statistical Abstract of the United States.* Washington, DC: U.S. Department of Commerce, Economic and Statistics Administration.

U.S. Department of Justice. (1994). *Women in prison.* Bulletin. Washington, DC: U.S. Government Printing Office.

Young, Vernetta. (1986). "Gender expectations and their impact on black female offenders and victims." *Justice Quarterly, 3,* 305–327.

Zatz, Marjorie S. (1987a). "The changing forms of racial/ethnic biases in sentencing." *Journal of Research in Crime and Delinquency, 24* (1), 69–92.

——. (1987b). "Chicano youth gangs and crime: The creation of a moral panic." *Contemporary Crises, 11,* 129–158.

Zatz, Marjorie S., Lujan, Carol Chiago, and Snyder-Joy, Zoann K. (1991). "American Indians and criminal justice: Some conceptual and methodologized considerations." In Michael J. Lynch and E. Britt Patterson (Eds.), *Race and criminal justice.* New York: Harron and Hestan.

Discussion Questions

1. Why do juvenile and criminal justice programs need to be sensitive to cultural and gender differences in the populations they serve? Specify what programs should be different.

2. Name at least five social institutions that could be improved to reduce institutional racism. How would you improve them?

3. Are First Amendment (freedom of speech) issues relevant if attempts are made to curb media misrepresentations of minorities? Why or why not?

4. How would you make our politicians more responsible for eliminating racism in the justice systems?

5. Do you share our cautious optimism about the diminution of institutionalized racism beyond the millennium? ✦